ECONOMIC UNCERTAINTY, INSTABILITIES & ASSET BUBBLES

Selected Essays

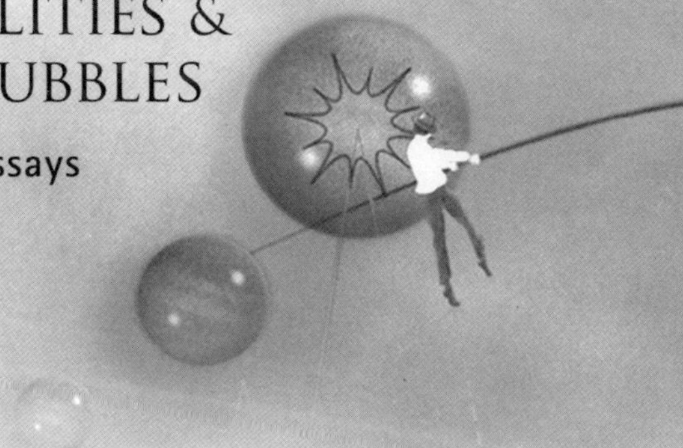

ECONOMIC UNCERTAINTY, INSTABILITIES & ASSET BUBBLES

Selected Essays

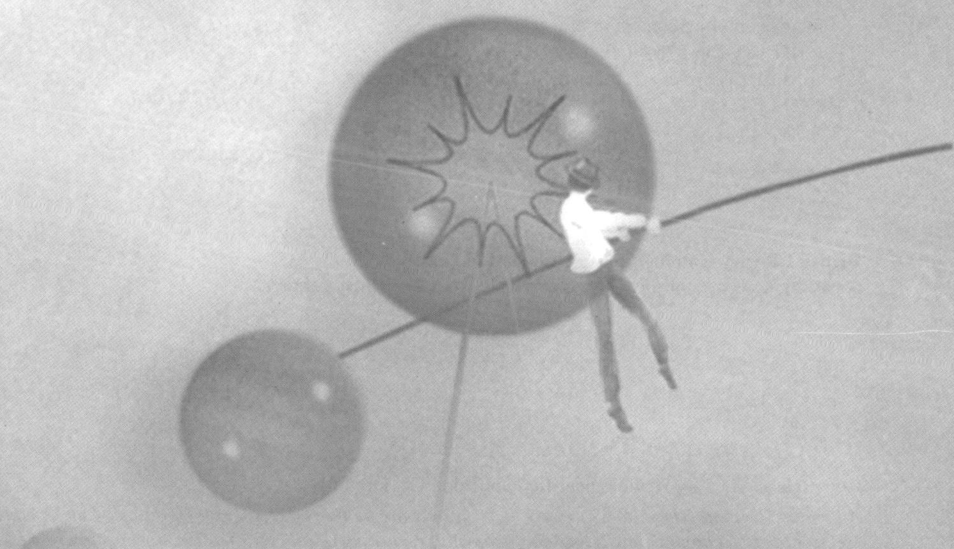

A. G. Malliaris
Loyola University Chicago, USA

World Scientific
NEW JERSEY • LONDON • SINGAPORE • BEIJING • SHANGHAI • HONG KONG • TAIPEI • CHENNAI

Published by

World Scientific Publishing Co. Pte. Ltd.
5 Toh Tuck Link, Singapore 596224
USA office: 27 Warren Street, Suite 401-402, Hackensack, NJ 07601
UK office: 57 Shelton Street, Covent Garden, London WC2H 9HE

Library of Congress Cataloging-in-Publication Data
Economic uncertainty, instabilities and asset bubbles : selected essays /
by A.G. Malliaris.
p. cm.
Includes bibliographical references.
ISBN 981-256-378-4 (alk. paper)
1. Business cycles. 2. Financial crises. I. Malliaris, A.G. II. Title.
HB3711.E428 2005
338.5'42--dc22
2005049432

British Library Cataloguing-in-Publication Data
A catalogue record for this book is available from the British Library.

Printed in Singapore by World Scientific Printers (S) Pte Ltd

Preface and Acknowledgments

Assuming that both the demand and supply for crude oil are linear and deterministic, as is taught in principles of economics, one can theorize that a unique price for oil will result. This static and simple theory can easily be challenged as we observe an almost continuous change in the price of crude oil. Our inability to predict the next change in the price of crude oil is due to the complexity of economic uncertainty that prevents us from confidently shifting supply and/or demand both in the right direction and exact magnitude.

The essays collected in this volume address several aspects of economic uncertainty. Graduate students and professional economists can benefit from this book because it both exposits some of the methodologies of addressing uncertainty in economics as well as gives numerous examples. There are three broad methodologies used in this book to model uncertainty: continuous time methodology, chaotic dynamics, and discrete econometric techniques. This book discusses these three methodologies and offers many illustrations.

My first intellectual debt is to my co-authors and my University. My co-authors are: Fwu-Ranq Chang of Indiana University, the late Jorge Urrutia of Loyola University Chicago, my beloved wife Mary E. Malliaris of Loyola University Chicago, Silvana Stefani of the University of Milano, Jerry Stein of Brown University, George Philippatos and Efi Pilarinu of the University of Tennessee, Marco Corazza of the University of Venice, Ramaprasad Bhar of Sydney University of Technology, and Marc Hayford of Loyola University Chicago. I am grateful to all for their gift to me of creative joy that was much greater than the intellectual effort needed to do the research. I am also thankful to my colleagues at Loyola University Chicago where I have worked for the past 33 years for their friendship, support and encouragement.

Secondly, I also wish to thank the following who have kindly given me permission for the use of copyrighted material.

Blackwell Publisher for the article: "Asymptotic Growth under Uncertainty: Existence and Uniqueness" in *Review of Economic Studies*, **LIV**, 1987, pp. 169–174.

Elsevier Science Ltd for the following articles: "How Big is the Random Walk in Macroeconomic Time Series: Variance Ratio Tests", *Economics*

Letters, **34**, 1990, pp. 113–116; "An Empirical Investigation Among Real, Monetary and Financial Variables", *Economics Letters*, **37**, 1991, pp. 151–158; "Interest Rates and Inflation: A Continuous-time Stochastic Approach", *Economics Letters*, **37**, 1991, pp. 351–356; "Money, Inflation and Interest Rates: Illustrations From Twelve European Economies", *European Journal of Political Economy*, **7**, 1991, pp. 275–298; "Methodological Issues in Asset Pricing: Random Walk or Chaotic Dynamics", *Journal of Banking and Finance*, **23**, 1999, pp. 1605–1635; "Is the Federal Reserve Stock Market Bubble-Neutral?", in George Kaufman, editor, *Asset Price Bubbles: Implications for Monetary and Regulatory Policies*, 2001, pp. 229–243; "How Did the Fed React to the 1990s Stock Market Bubble? Evidence From an Extended Taylor Rule", *European Journal of Operational Research*, **163**, 2005, pp. 20–29; "Global Monetary Instability: The Role of the IMF, the EU and NAFTA", *North American Journal of Economics and Finance*, **13**, 2002, pp. 72–92; "Several Illustrations of the Quantity Theory of Money: 1947–1987 and 1867–1975", *International Review of Financial Analysis*, **1**, 1992, pp. 77–93; "The Impact of the Persian Gulf Crisis on National Equity Markets", *Advances in International Banking and Finance*, **1**, 1995, pp. 43–65; "Oil and World Stock Markets' Reactions to the Gulf Crisis", *Research in International Business and Finance*, **1**, 1996, pp. 133–153; "Are There Rational Bubbles in the U.S. Stock Market? Overview and a New Test", in George Kaufman, editor, *Asset Price Bubbles: Implications for Monetary and Regulatory Policies*, 2001, pp. 125–144; "European Stock Market Fluctuations: Short and Long Term Links", *Journal of International Financial Markets, Institutions and Money*, **6**, 1996, pp. 21–33.

The Haworth Press Inc for the article: "Chaotic Behavior in Prices of European Equity Markets: A Comparative Analysis of Major Economic Regions", *Journal of Multinational Financial Management*, **3**, 1993, pp. 5–24.

Springer Science and Business Media BV for article: "Decomposition of Inflation and Its Volatility: A Stochastic Approach", *Review of Quantitative Finance and Accounting*, **5**, 1995, pp. 93–103.

Multinational Finance Society for the article: "Multi-Fractality in Foreign Currency Markets", *Multinational Finance Journal*, **6**, 2002, pp. 65–98.

Western Economic Association International for the article: "Monetary Policy and the U.S. Stock Market", *Economic Inquiry*, **42**, 2004, pp. 387–401.

University of Washington for the article: "The International Crash of October 1987: Causality Tests", *Journal of Financial and Quantitative Analysis*, **27**, 1992, pp. 353–364.

Routledge Ltd for excerpt: "Equity and Oil Markets under External Shocks", in Dilip Ghosh, editor, *The Global Structure of Financial Markets*, 1997, pp. 103–116.

Every effort has been made to trace all copyright holders in this period of rapid mergers and acquisitions. However, if any have been inadvertently overlooked, the author and the publishers will be pleased to make the necessary arrangements.

Thirdly, I would like to thank World Scientific Publishing Company for their decision to publish this book. I am grateful to Ms. Yubing Zhai, Manager and Commissioning Editor for her enthusiasm about this book and Ms. Cheong Chean Chian who, as my editor, put forth every effort to produce a handsome volume. My assistant, Ms. Fani Athanassopoulou, patiently collected all the original reprints and corresponded with copyright requests.

Finally, my very existence, marriage of 34 years, my daughter Maryanthe, and my son Steven are all illustrations of the positive components of the mystery of uncertainty. I happily dedicate this book to my wife Mary Elaine and our children Maryanthe Elizabeth and Steven Glen Malliaris.

A. G. (Tassos) Malliaris
July 1, 2005
Chicago, Illinois

[illegible]

Contents

Economic Uncertainty: An Overview

When one admits that nothing is certain one
must also admit that some things are much
more certain than others.
Bertrand Russell (1872–1970)

1. The Meaning of Uncertainty

In modeling, analyzing, evaluating and predicting aspects of economic reality, researchers currently are relying more on probabilistic rather than deterministic methods. Probabilistic methods are expected to capture the role of uncertainty arising from various complexities, measurement errors, incomplete understanding, unstable relationships, regime switching, external shocks, shifting expectations and several other random factors.

In general, uncertainty is a measure of doubt. More precisely, the term uncertainty is both a statistical and an economics concept. The statistical meaning of uncertainty attempts to describe the dispersion of outcomes for repeated occurrences of the same event. For example, a coin is tossed several times and sometimes we get a head and others we get a tail. Uncertainty means the outcome cannot be exact. This statistical meaning of uncertainty becomes more complicated in economics because we cannot repeat the same experiment precisely. For example, suppose the Fed increases its Fed funds rate by 25 basis points and we measure its impact on inflation, or unemployment or housing starts at certain time lags. If this is repeated and the Fed increases its Fed funds numerous times, the dispersion of values for inflation, or unemployment or new housing starts is an expression of uncertainty. Obviously, as social scientists we cannot hold all other variables constant as in a laboratory experiment, so economic uncertainty is more complicated.

In addition to the statistical notion of uncertainty, there is a broader methodological meaning of uncertainty in economics. In the second meaning, uncertainty cannot be measured because both the experiment and its possible outcomes have not been tried before and we have no past evidence. For example, what is the impact of the internet on the economy? We are uncertain to evaluate the outcomes because past technological discoveries were not similar to the internet.

The statistical concept of uncertainty is often called risk in economics. The broader notion of uncertainty is often called Knightian uncertainty and was introduced in Knight (1921, p. 259) who argued that "the fundamental uncertainties of economic life are the errors in predicting the future and in making present adjustments to fit future conditions".

In general, it is difficult to clearly separate the concepts of risk and uncertainty. In extreme cases like the tossing of a coin or the impact of a major terrorist attack we can clearly say that the first is an issue of two outcomes while the latter is significantly more involved. However, in every day economic life the distinction between risk and uncertainty is not straightforward. When assessing the probability of a recession, we use past data to calculate the risk but we also acknowledge that each recession is not identical to the earlier ones and thus face considerable uncertainty in our judgment.

Thus, in economics the meaning of uncertainty includes imperfect information, unstable and complex relationships among economic variables, regime changes in the macroeconomy, incompleteness of our hypotheses, measurement errors, possible shocks, changing expectations, human indeterminacy, surprising disturbances and general inability to assess rationally certain outcomes.

There are numerous methods developed to model uncertainty. In this book we motivate some key uncertainty methodologies and illustrate their use in numerous economic applications. This essay offers an overview of these methodologies as well as results obtained from their use in economic problems. Before we can present these methodologies we need a brief detour on quantitative reasoning in economics.

2. Deterministic versus Stochastic Paradigms

Economics has a long history, dating back at least to Plato and Aristotle. Schumpeter (1954) in his comprehensive history of economic analysis demonstrates that the bulk of the results of theoretical economics have been obtained without the use of advanced mathematical methods.

In his admirable book on *The Scope and Method of Political Economy*, John Neville Keynes (1891, p. 267) argues: "On the whole, we arrive at the conclusions, first, that political economy involves conceptions of a mathematical nature requiring to be analyzed in a mathematical spirit; and secondly, that there are certain departments of the science in which valuable aid may be derived from the actual employment of symbolical or diagrammatical methods."

The appropriateness of the use of mathematical methods in economics has been evaluated by Tintner (1968) who presents an exhaustive list of views by leading economists on the use of mathematics in economics and he argues convincingly on the appropriateness of employing mathematical methods in economics. If one accepts as appropriate the use of mathematical methods in economics the next logical question is this: what subset of such methods is more relevant in economic theory?

In attempting to answer such a question one may actually believe that an answer is possible. Even a casual observation of the various branches of mathematics can show long lists of mathematical methods, techniques, topics and subjects. However, Nagel (1969) successfully describes the common scientific background of most of the available mathematical methods to be rationalistic. From the classical conception of science formulated in Greek geometry and perpetuated in the powerful intellectual tradition of Newtonian physics and calculus to the current information revolution, the mathematical paradigm is primarily deterministic.

In proclaiming the ideal of science to be systematic knowledge, the rationalist approach has stimulated mathematical research of the deterministic kind. In the long history of the mathematics, the emergence of probability theory as a subject of importance is quite recent. Furthermore, probability theory is greatly influenced by the deterministic paradigm and remains a subset of mathematics rather than a genuine alternative.

Arrow (1974) has argued that the deterministic scientific emphasis is shifting towards the stochastic paradigm. The doctrine that knowledge of matters of fact is only probable rather than completely demonstrable is becoming one of the central theses of our modern scientific methodology. Arrow (1974, p. 1) goes on to say that "the uncertainties about economics are rooted in the need for a better understanding of economic uncertainty".

3. Continuous Time Modeling of Uncertainty

Merton (1982) describes the nature of economic uncertainty in some detail. He develops the intuitive ideas of economists about uncertainty in continuous time by describing some of the rules that govern it. More specifically, when we say that economic uncertainty exists some of its key properties include:

(1) Uncertainty is present at each period of time and we have a way to measure it.
(2) Uncertainty does not disappear as the time interval diminishes.
(3) Uncertainty does not cause the statistical mean and variance of the economic variable to become unbounded. Even in the presence of uncertainty, both mean and variance are finite.
(4) In an uncertain world what matters most is the present; past and future are statistically independent.

Merton (1975, 1982) claims that stochastic calculus as developed by Itô (1944, 1951, 1961) models appropriately economic uncertainty. The key notion of stochastic calculus is the random dynamic differential equation.

$$dX(t,\omega) = f(t, X(t,\omega))dt + \sigma(t, X(t,\omega))dZ(t,\omega) \tag{3.1}$$

This equation is developed in several stochastic calculus books. Here we offer an intuitive explanation. This equation says that a small change in a given economic variable can be expressed as the sum of two terms. The first term is a measure of the variable's trend and the second term is itself the product of two factors: the variable's volatility multiplied by a continuous time random shock. Put it differently, the uncertainty about the evolution of a certain economic variable described by Equation (3.1) has three components: the uncertainty of its trend, the uncertainty about its volatility and the uncertainty of some event modeled as a continuous random walk. Modeling uncertainty as a continuous random walk is the simplest and nicest way. It is the simplest because we have an equation of the form (3.1) that is not complicated and it is the nicest because the path of the variable is continuous but very kinky. If the path was continuous and smooth one could predict but by being nondifferentiable, one cannot anticipate the evolution of the variable.

The precise meaning of these mathematical ideas is given in Malliaris and Brock (1982), Karatzas and Shreve (1991) and Steele (2000). This methodology of continuous time uncertainty has found a vast number of applications, particularly in financial economics because Equation (3.1) describes well the evolution of asset prices.

4. Chaotic Dynamics

The logical way to proceed in the analysis of chaotic dynamics is to give a precise definition. The definition we give is purely mathematical and can be found in several books such as Devaney (1986). It requires, first, to explain a few terms. We do this next.

Consider a real-valued function $f: R \to R$. We are interested in the time series generated by this function starting from some arbitrary $x_o \in R$. Denote by $f^2 \equiv f[f(x)] \equiv fof(x)$ where o means composition and in general let $f^n = fofo\ldots of(x)$ mean n compositions. The time series takes the values

$$x_o, f(x_o), f^2(x_o), \ldots, f^n(x_o), \ldots, \tag{4.1}$$

for $t = 0,1,2,\ldots,n$. For (4.1) to describe a chaotic function it must satisfy three requirements.

First it must sample infinitely many values. To make this idea precise we say that $f: R \to R$ is topologically transitive if for any pair of open sets U and V in the real line R there is an integer $k > 0$ such that $f^k(U) \cap V \neq \varnothing$.

The second requirement is sensitive dependence on initial conditions. We say that the $f: R \to R$ function has sensitive dependence on initial conditions if there exists a $\delta > 0$ such that for any $x \in R$ and any neighborhood N of x, there is a $y \in N$ and an integer $n > 0$ such that

$$|f^n(x) - f^n(y)| > \delta \tag{4.2}$$

This condition says that there are time series that start very close to each other but diverge exponentially fast from each other.

The third requirement involves a property of the periodic points of the function f, namely that these periodic points are in R. We that a point $x \in R$ is periodic if for $n > 0$, $f^n(x) = x$. The least positive integer n for which $f^n(x) = x$ is called the prime period of x.

We can summarize our analysis by giving the definition of a chaotic function. We say that a function $f: R \to R$ is chaotic if it satisfies three conditions:

(1) f is topologically transitive.
(2) f has sensitive dependence on initial conditions.
(3) f has periodic points that are dense in the real numbers.

Observe that the above is a mathematical definition which is not motivated by economic price behavior. Yet, each condition can be given an economic interpretation.

The first condition requires the time series dynamics to be rich in the sense that the function takes infinitely many different values. This condition makes a chaotic map similar to a random walk because each value is different from all the previous ones. Of course, in random walks this happens because we are sampling from an infinite population. On the other hand, in chaotic dynamics we do not have sampling; instead we have a nonlinear deterministic equation that generates many different values. Note that for both random walks and for chaotic dynamics it is possible for certain values to occur more than once in the time series. What we are emphasizing is that such a repetition is very unlikely. Put differently the first condition of topological transitivity requires the time series to be rich in the sense that it takes infinitely many different values. Intuitively, such a map can move under iteration, i.e., through time, from one arbitrarily small neighborhood to any other. Since the space cannot be decomposed into two disjoint open sets which are invariant under the map (by definition) the points not only can wander anywhere (since they cannot be blocked) but actually will wander everywhere.

The second condition casts serious difficulties in forecasting. Although a chaotic map is deterministic and knowing today's value immediately allows one to compute tomorrow's price, the same exact equation can generate very dissimilar time series if we are uncertain about when the series got started and at what initial value x_o. To contrast with a random walk, recall that the past and future values are independent because we are sampling from an infinite population of values. The inability to forecast is due precisely to this statistical independence. In a chaotic function, however, we know exactly the relationship between the past and the future but we are unable to predict because we cannot be sure as to when we started and with what value. Put differently, in a chaotic function, only if we know exactly x_o can we then generate the exact sequence of values.

The third condition gives a chaotic function structure. It essentially requires that the chaotic function exhibit important regularities. However, these regularities are hidden in the sense that no researcher could explore the infinitely many patterns of the periodic points and their limits. In an analogous manner, the random walk can be said to have some structure given to it by the properties of the distribution that characterizes the population. Again, no researcher could explore the infinitely many sample paths that a random walk process can generate. This analogy between the structure of a chaotic function and a random walk should not be understood as meaning that both have exactly the same structure. Although we do not know how to compare correctly the structure of a chaotic function to that of a random walk, it suffices to remark that a chaotic function involves infinitely many iterations of a nonlinear function and therefore its structure could be viewed as being more complex compared to the structure of a random walk. More technically, one can argue that in chaotic dynamics because the set of periodic points is dense in *R*, for any point in *R*, there exists a sequence of periodic points which converges to this point. Thus, it appears intuitively that a structure exists because of the mere existence of the periodic points, but also because they are clustered around each point in the domain. Therefore, due to the fact that periodic points are dense, each point in the domain can be identified by a sequence of periodic points, which converges to it.

The essence of this brief introduction to chaotic dynamics is to highlight that in science, and perhaps also in economics, deterministic modeling remains a high goal of science. Chaotic dynamics demonstrates that exact relationships among variables can exist even when the time paths of the variables involved are highly irregular and appear to be totally random.

5. Econometric Methods

In contrast to the methods of stochastic calculus and chaotic dynamics that are both in continuous time, several econometric techniques are used in this book to address time uncertainty in discrete time. Among these techniques we mention tests of random walk, variance-ratio tests, Granger causality tests, cointegration tests, two-sided exponentially smoothing moving averages methodology, excess or abnormal return methodology, regression analysis and vector autoregressive methodology. Each of these methods is briefly discussed in the chapters where it is used so we need not explain them here.

An excellent introductory book on econometric methods is Kennedy (2003) and a standard reference for econometric methods employed in financial economics is Campbell, Lo and MacKinlay (1997).

Next, we give a brief outline of the main sections of the book and the papers they include.

6. Economic Growth and Uncertainty

The causes of economic growth are the grand object of research that gave birth to political economy. Several of the founding fathers of economics, such as Adam Smith, David Ricardo and Thomas Malthus have studied the causes of wealth and poverty of nations.

Nations prosper through the interplay of work, resources, capital, technology and institutions that encourage risk-taking and progress. Fundamentally, economic growth is about change and change is random. Using the methodology of continuous time uncertainty, Chapter 1 studies conditions imposed on the economy's production function to obtain the properties of existence and uniqueness of the stochastic economic growth equation.

Chapter 2 considers several macroeconomic variables measuring important dimensions of economic growth such as industrial production, unemployment, money supply and others, and applies the variance-ratio test to check how large is the random component in these variables. We find that most macroeconomic time series have significant random walk components with the exception of unemployment, real wages, real per capita GNP and industrial production.

Chapter 3 separates several macroeconomic variables into real and financial and uses the Granger causality methodology to discover possible relationships among these two groups. The chapter reports that money supply leads the S&P 500 Index and this index seems to lead the industrial production.

7. Stochastic Macroeconomic Models

The first two papers in this part of the book are theoretical and the other two are empirical. Both theoretical papers employ stochastic calculus techniques to extend first, Fisher's equation and second the quantity theory of money.

Recall that Fisher proposed that the nominal interest rate is the sum of the real interest rate and the expected rate of inflation. If both the real interest rate and the rate of inflation, instead of being constant or continuously deterministic, are random, then one needs to derive an extended version of Fisher's equation. This is what Chapter 4 accomplishes.

Chapter 5 begins with the famous quantity theory of money, $MV = PY$, where the variables denote money supply, velocity of circulation, the implicit price deflator and real gross domestic product respectively. Both in the static version and in the continuous deterministic version of this equation taught in a macroeconomics course, uncertainty is ignored. We know however from empirical evidence that the money supply, velocity of circulation and real GDP are random variables. Modeling this randomness as a stochastic differential equation, Chapter 5 derives a stochastic version of the quantity theory of money that gives mathematical expressions for both expected inflation and its variance.

Chapter 6 gives several graphical illustrations of the quantity theory of money. These illustrations are generated by taking time series data of money supply, velocity, real output, inflation and short-term nominal interest rates and using the two-sided exponentially weighted moving average methodology to remove noise and uncover fundamental relationships. We reconfirm that for the 1955–1979 period in the U.S., the rate of inflation and nominal interest rates were driven primarily by the rate of growth in the money supply. Over much longer periods, such as 1867–1975, these relationships do not hold because of structural economic changes.

Applying the same methodology of two-sided exponentially weighted moving averages and additional tests of cointegration to money, inflation and interest rate data from twelve European economies, Chapter 7 reports that for one half of the countries in the sample, money growth rates and inflation are cointegrated. For the other half of the countries, structural and institutional factors disturb this simple quantity theory of money relationship between money growth and inflation.

8. Randomness in Asset Markets

The first two sections present uncertainty for the macroeconomy. This uncertainty introduces deviations from fundamentals but these deviations are not very large. For example, growth in GDP is determined from growth in consumption, investments, government spending, and the foreign sector. Uncertainty plays its role in each of these components. However, data show that quarter to quarter, aggregate consumption growth does not fluctuate as much as, say, the S&P 500 Index. Other macroeconomic variables such as the rate of unemployment, the wage rate, labor productivity, growth of personal income, and others, all fluctuate from quarter to quarter, but not in substantial ways.

In contrast to most macroeconomic variables that vibrate in a disciplined fashion most of the time, asset prices fluctuate relatively much more. Quite early, Working (1934, 1958) reported that changes in futures prices were largely random, responding to random information. The efficient market hypothesis was a major advance in our thinking about asset prices because it was easy both to state and to test. The efficient market hypotheses rationalized the random behavior of asset prices by arguing that the change or flow of real world information concerning the fundamentals can be modeled as a process of random sampling from a certain probability space. Because economic agents are rational, they trade on this new information and thus prices quickly incorporate new fundamentals. In other words, assuming that traders are rational, a random flow of information produces random price fluctuations.

The randomness of asset price changes requires an explanation about the variance of such changes. If price changes are induced by changes in information, can information about the shocks in fundamental factors explain the magnitude of the observed price volatility? Or, is the variance of price changes due to other factors? Chapter 8 uses the methodology of chaotic dynamics to propose a model that explains volatility in asset pricing as the result of the degree of speculation and also the Bayesian errors made by traders.

Chapter 9 also uses the methodology of chaotic dynamics to analyze the behavior of international stock markets for indices of six European, two North American and two Far Eastern countries. Raw and de-trended weekly returns and index levels are analyzed in a non-parametric fashion and evidence is presented supporting the hypothesis of globally integrated equity markets. Chapter 10 documents statistically significant short term Granger causal relationships, as well as long-term equilibrium relationships, in the stock market indices of five European countries by using a bi-variate vector autoregressive model with an error correction term.

The final chapter in this section extends the continuous time methodology of uncertainty by replacing the continuous time random walk component. A continuous time random walk is modeled by a Brownian motion. Numerous empirical studies have challenged the appropriateness of Brownian motion to describe asset returns. Some authors have conjectured that financial returns may be independently and identically Pareto-Levy stable distributed whereas others hypothesized that asset returns may be identically but not independently fractional Brownian motion distributed. Chapter 11 offers evidence that returns follow a fractional Brownian motion or a Pareto-Levy stable distribution using data from five foreign currencies.

9. Asset Bubbles

The randomness in asset prices sometimes grows large. A sharp rise in the price of an asset over a certain period generates expectations of further increases and thus attracts new speculators. Eventually, prices increase so much that a reversal of expectations occurs, and a sharp decline in the price materializes. We call such large price increases a bubble. Economists are more precise when they say that a bubble is the deviation of an asset's price from fundamentals.

Asset price bubbles continue to be an area of both active research and major public concern because the bursting of bubbles is very costly to the economy. Thus, economists are seeking answers to questions such as:

(1) How and when can we identify a bubble?
(2) Should monetary policy attempt to target and stabilize asset prices?
(3) Can bubbles be deflated gradually?
(4) How can the economic damage after the bursting of a bubble be minimized?

Chapter 12 develops a test to identify a bubble. Applying this test to long annual U.S. stock market data spanning over a century, there is evidence of bubbles. However, this does not imply that we can use short periods of data to identify an emerging bubble. In other words, currently, economists have no certainty in recognizing a bubble soon enough and with confidence about its size.

If an asset bubble cannot be identified, should monetary policy attempt to stabilize the stock market? Chapter 13 presents evidence from the Federal Open Market Committee to show that the Fed during the 1990s was concerned with the stock market bubble. Chapter 14 estimates both static and dynamic specifications of the Taylor rule that include measures of stock market overvaluations to conclude that the Fed not only avoided neutralizing the bubble, but may, probably unintentionally, have contributed to the bubble's growth. The same conclusion is also reached in Chapter 15 that uses a forward looking Taylor rule model as well as a VAR model to address the Fed's reaction to the stock market bubble.

The basic conclusion of this section is that a bubble cannot easily be deflated, particularly if it grows past a certain point. The inability of the Fed to both identify and deflate the bubble means that the Fed follows an asymmetry in its response to the bubble: the Fed remains neutral while the bubble grows but it reduces the Fed funds rate aggressively when the bubble bursts to minimize the economic damage of such a burst.

10. Crashes and Instabilities

Financial markets exhibit a fundamental asymmetry with respect to asset bubbles. These bubbles often grow slowly, eventually become self-sustaining and when they reach very high levels, they collapse rapidly. As a bubble crashes substantial wealth is lost. However, not all crashes are due to bubbles. Major events such as a war, political instability, or major acts of terrorism have a significant impact on asset prices. This section includes five chapters on crashes and instabilities. Crashes mean substantial declines in asset prices, while instabilities mean slow recoveries or slow return to fundamentals.

Chapter 16 studies the impact of the Crash of October 1987 on other national stock markets. Using the Granger causality methodology, we conduct unidirectional and bidirectional tests and find that no lead-lag relationships existed for the pre-crash and post-crash periods. However, important feedback relationship and unidirectional causalities are found during the month of the Crash. The main conclusion of this chapter is that the U.S. stock market crash of October 1987 impacted most of the major stock markets of the world for a period of about a month. In other words, the October 1987 U.S. stock market crash took international significance for a short period.

Chapter 17 employs two event-study methodologies to analyze the response of 16 national stock markets to the Persian Gulf Crisis of 1990–1991. We find that the Persian Gulf Crisis had a negative impact on international equity prices but its impact was greater for the European, Asian, and Australian markets than for the American and Canadian markets. Chapter 18 introduces oil as the key economic resource affected by the Gulf Crisis. National stock markets of countries that are oil importing exhibit significant negative abnormal returns that are larger than those of national stock markets of countries that are oil exporting. Chapter 19 investigates separately the impact of the Gulf Crisis on equity markets and oil markets. It concludes that the Gulf Crisis had a greater impact on oil markets than on equity markets.

The last chapter is devoted to the instability of the global monetary system. In contrast to the Bretton Woods regime of 1948–1971 that supported fixed exchange rates with no volatility or uncertainty, the current system has been characterized by excessive currency volatility. The current challenge for economists and policy makers is the creation of a global monetary system that offers greater exchange rate stability without sacrificing international capital mobility. This chapter offers certain suggestions for strengthening the international financial architecture.

In conclusion, the 20 papers in this volume offer the reader instruction about numerous techniques that are used in a wide spectrum of applications for modeling economic uncertainty: from very low and continuous randomness, regular randomness in macroeconomic variables, larger random walks in asset prices, to bubbles and finally, crashes and instabilities. More importantly, these techniques are illustrated in real world economic problems, so the reader can observe the relevance of a certain method in providing an answer to a specific question.

Mark Twain once said that education is the path from ignorance to uncertainty. Bon voyage.

Bibliography

Arrow, K.J. (1974), "Limited Knowledge and Economic Analysis", *The American Economic Review*, 64, 1–10.

Campbell, J., A.W. Lo and A. Craig MacKinlay (1997), *The Econometrics of Financial Markets*, Princeton, NJ: Princeton University Press.

Devaney, R. (1986), *An Introduction to Chaotic Dynamical Systems*, Menlo Park, California: Benjamin/Cummings Publishing.

Itô, K. (1944), "Stochastic Integral", *Proceedings of the Imperial Academy*, 20, 519–524.

Itô, K. (1951), "On a Formula Concerning Stochastic Differentials", *Nagoya Mathematics Journal*, 3, 55–66.

Itô, K. (1961), *Lectures on Stochastic Processes*, Tata Institute of Fundamental Research, India.

Karatzas, I. and S. Shreve (1991), *Brownian Motion and Stochastic Calculus*, Second Edition, New York: Springer.

Kennedy, P. (2003), *A Guide to Econometrics*, Fifth Edition, Cambridge: MIT Press.

Keynes, J.N. (1891), *The Scope and the Method of Political Economy*, London: Macmillan & Company.

Knight, F.H. (1921), *Risk, Uncertainty and Profit*, New York: Houghton Mifflin.

Malliaris, A.G. and W. Brock (1982), *Stochastic Methods in Economics and Finance*, Amsterdam: North-Holland Publishing Company.

Merton, R.C. (1975), "Theory of Finance From the Perspective of Continuous Time", *Journal of Financial and Quantitative Analysis*, 10, 659–674.

Merton, R.C. (1982), "On the Mathematics and Economic Assumptions of Continuous-Time Models", Sharpe, W.F. and C.M. Cootner, editors, *Financial Economics: Essays in Honor of Paul Cootner*, Englewood Cliffs, New Jersey: Prentice Hall, 19–51.

Nagel, E. (1969), *Principles of the Theory of Probability*, 12th printing, Chicago: The University of Chicago Press.

Schumpeter, J. (1954), *History of Economic Analysis*, New York: Oxford.

Steele, M. (2000), *Stochastic Calculus and Financial Applications*, New York: Springer.

Tintner, G. (1968), *Methodology of Mathematical Economics and Econometrics*, Chicago: The University of Chicago Press.

Working, H. (1934), "A Random-Difference series for the Use in the Analysis of Time Series", *Journal of the American Statistical Association*, 29, 11–24.

Working, H. (1958), "A Theory of Anticipatory Prices", *American Economic Review*, 48, 188–199.

Economic Growth and Uncertainty

Review of Economic Studies (1987) LIV, 169-174
0034-6527/87/00110169$02.00

Asymptotic Growth under Uncertainty: Existence and Uniqueness

FWU-RANQ CHANG
Indiana University

and

A. G. MALLIARIS
Loyola University of Chicago

First version received July 1985; *final version accepted June* 1986 (*eds.*)

This paper demonstrates, using the Reflection Principle, the existence and uniqueness of the solution to the classic Solow equation under continuous time uncertainty for the class of strictly concave production functions which are continuously differentiable on the nonnegative real numbers. This class contains all CES functions with elasticity of substitution less than unity. A steady state distribution also exists for this class of production functions which have a bounded slope at the origin. A condition on the drift-variance ratio of the stochastic differential equation alone, independent of technology and the savings ratio, is found to be *necessary* for the existence of a steady state.

1. INTRODUCTION

Stochastic calculus techniques have been used to study continuous time economic growth under uncertainty. For example, Bourguignon (1974) and Merton (1975) have extended the neoclassical model of economic growth developed by Solow (1956) to incorporate uncertainty in a continuous time framework by extensive use of Ito's lemma. However, the existence and uniqueness of the solution to the stochastic equation of evolution in the proposed models have been assumed without proof. In addition, Merton proves the existence of a steady state distribution for the class of production functions satisfying the Inada conditions. While it is important to include Cobb-Douglas production functions in the analysis, the Inada conditions unfortunately rule out all other CES production functions (Wan (1971, p. 39)).

This paper fills the gap in the literature by proving the existence and uniqueness of the solution to the stochastic Solow equation for the class of strictly concave production functions which are continuously differentiable on the semi-closed interval of non-negative real numbers. This class of functions contains all CES production functions with elasticity of substitution less than unity. A steady state distribution also exists for this class of production functions which have a bounded slope at the origin. This result complements Merton's theorem on the existence of a steady state with Inada-type production functions.

The existence and uniqueness gap in the literature is partly attributed to the fact that Ito's theorem on the existence and uniqueness of the solution to a given stochastic differential equation cannot be directly applied because the stochastic Solow equation has a non-negativity constraint on the capital-labour ratio. The theorem only applies to stochastic processes with state space the whole real line. The technique presented in this paper is to extend the original equation from the non-negative real numbers to the whole real line by "reflection". Such an extension is akin to the Reflection Principle in complex analysis, see, for example, Ahlfors (1966). The production function is extended to a new function which is defined on the whole real line by assigning the value of the mirror image as the mirror image of the value, where the mirror is the y-axis.

The advantage of this reflection is that both the drift and the variance are *odd* functions of the capital-labour ratio. Then, the differentiability of the original function is extended if the production function is continuously differentiable at the origin. Hence, the existence and uniqueness theorems for equations with continuously differentiable coefficients can be applied. Note that the condition $f'(0) < \infty$ is needed for reflection. Then we proceed to verify that this solution is the desired one by showing that capital-labour ratios never change signs. Specifically, if the initial condition is positive, then the solution to the equation is always positive.

The conditions we impose on the production function $f(k)$ are rather standard: f is strictly concave, continuously differentiable on the nonnegative real line, $f(0) = 0$ and $f'(\infty) = 0$. It is known that the solution is uniquely defined up to a Brownian stopping time (i.e. explosion time). Based on the nature of the derived equation, we show that, with probability one, the explosion time is $+\infty$. The solution technique employed in this paper rules out the possibility of $k_t = 0$ as an accessible barrier. In the proof of our main theorem, a condition on the drift-variance ratio of the stochastic differential equation alone, independent of technology and the savings ratio, is found to be *necessary* for the existence of a steady state distribution. This result further complements Merton's finding.

This paper is organized as follows. We summarize mathematical results needed for this analysis in Section 2. Then we restate Merton's derived stochastic Solow equation, describe our reflection technique and state and prove our main theorem in Section 3. Concluding remarks are given in Section 4.

2. MATHEMATICAL PRELIMINARIES

For convenience, we shall list the basic definitions and theorems from stochastic calculus employed in this paper.

Given a probability space $(\Omega, \mathbf{F}, \mathbf{P})$, let $\{z_t\}$ be a Wiener process and let $\{\mathbf{F}_t\}$ be the filtration generated by the Wiener process $\{z_t\}$. That is, $\mathbf{F}_t$ is the smallest σ-field with respect to which z_t is measurable, $\{\mathbf{F}_t\}$ is an increasing family, and $\mathbf{F}_t$ is independent of the σ-field generated by the process $z(t+s) - z(t)$, $s \geqq 0$. Assume f and g are measurable in (t, ω). Consider a stochastic differential equation of the form

$$\begin{gathered} dX_t = f(t, X_t)dt + g(t, X_t)dz_t \\ X_0 = c \end{gathered} \tag{1}$$

defined on $t \in [0, T]$. In integral form this equation is written as

$$X_t = c + \int_0^t f(s, X_s)ds + \int_0^t g(s, X_s)dz_s. \tag{2}$$

Definition. An equation of the form of (1) is called an *Ito stochastic differential equation.* A stochastic process X_t is called a *solution* of an Ito stochastic differential equation in $[0, T]$ if it satisfies the following properties:

(a) X_t is $\mathbf{F}_t$-measurable,

(b) the functions $f(t, X_t(\omega))$ and $g(t, X_t(\omega))$ are such that, with probability 1, $\int_0^T |f(s, X_s(\omega))|ds < \infty$ and $\int_0^T |g(s, X_s(\omega))|^2 ds < \infty$,
(c) for all $t \in [0, T]$, with probability 1, equation (2) holds.

A well-known sufficient condition on the existence and uniqueness of solutions to stochastic differential equation (1) is

Ito's Theorem. *Suppose that the stochastic differential equation* (1) *is given, where* X_t, X_0, f, g *and* z_t *satisfy the following two properties: there exists a constant* M *such that*

(a) *for every* $t \in [0, T]$, *every* $x \in R$ *and every* $y \in R$,

$$|f(t, x) - f(t, y)| + |g(t, x) - g(t, y)| \leqq M|x - y|,$$

(b) *for every* $t \in [0, T]$ *and every* $x \in R$

$$|f(t, x)|^2 + |g(t, x)|^2 \leqq M^2(1 + |x|^2).$$

Then, the stochastic differential equation (1) *has in* $[0, T]$ *a unique solution* X_t *which is continuous with probability* 1 *and which satisfies the initial random variable condition* $X_0 = c$.

For a proof of this theorem see Arnold (1974, p. 106).

Remark. Conditions (a) and (b) in Ito's Theorem are called Lipschitz condition and Restriction on Growth condition, respectively.

For $f, g \in C^1(R)$, the following two theorems will be useful when the drift and the variance are autonomous and continuously differentiable as in the case of the stochastic Solow equation. The first one is the

Bounded Slope Theorem. *If* f *and* g *are of bounded slope, i.e.* $\|f'\|_\infty$ *and* $\|g'\|_\infty$ *are finite, then* (1) *has a unique solution for* $t \geqq 0$.

See McKean (1969, Section 3.2).

Let $\tau_n = \min\{t: |X_t| = n\}$ be a stopping time. Let $\tau = \lim_{n\to\infty} \tau_n$ be the *explosion time* of X_t. Then the second theorem is the

Nonexplosive Theorem. *If there exists a constant* B *such that*

$$f^2 + g^2 \leqq B(1 + X^2), \tag{3}$$

then (1) *has a unique solution* for $t \geqq 0$.

This theorem follows from the theorem in McKean (1969, Section 3.3), which states that (1) has a unique solution up to the explosion time τ, and Problem 1 of that section, which states that (3) implies $\tau = +\infty$ with probability one.

3. STOCHASTIC SOLOW EQUATION

Merton (1975) derived the stochastic Solow equation when the population size is characterized by a diffusion process, i.e.

$$dL = nLdt + \sigma Ldz, \tag{4}$$

where n is the expected growth rate of population per unit of time and σ is the instantaneous variance. Both n and σ are exogenously given and assumed constant. By Ito's lemma, the stochastic Solow equation is given by

$$dk_t = [s(k_t)f(k_t) - (n - \sigma^2)k_t]dt - \sigma k_t dz_t, \quad k_0 = c > 0. \tag{5}$$

Notice that equation (5) is defined on $k_t \geqq 0$. Therefore, the theorems stated in the previous section cannot be directly applied. Merton (1975) assumes that a unique solution of (5) exists without further elaboration.

The technique presented in this paper is to extend the original equation from the non-negative real numbers to the whole real line by "reflection". We first extend the production function $f(k_t)$ to a new function defined on the whole real line as

$$\tilde{f}(k_t) = \begin{cases} f(k_t) & \text{if } k_t \geqq 0, \\ -f(-k_t) & \text{if } k_t < 0. \end{cases}$$

Thus, $\tilde{f}$ is an *odd* function defined on R. Next, we extend the saving function $s(k)$ to the whole real line by setting $\tilde{s}(k) = s(-k)$, for $k < 0$, and $\tilde{s}(k) = s(k)$ for $k \geqq 0$. In other words, $\tilde{s}(k)$ is an *even* function. Let $F(k_t) = \tilde{s}(k_t)\tilde{f}(k_t) - (n - \sigma^2)k_t$ and $G(k_t) = -\sigma k_t$. Clearly F and G are odd functions on R. The following stochastic differential equation

$$dk_t = F(k_t)dt + G(k_t)dz_t, \quad k_0 = c > 0, \tag{6}$$

is an *extension* of equation (5) in the sense that any solution to (6) with $k_t \geqq 0$ is a solution to equation (5) and that any solution to (5) solves (6).

In what follows we shall first demonstrate the existence and uniqueness of the solution to equation (6). Then we show that the solution thus found is everywhere positive if the initial condition is positive, $k_0 = c > 0$. Therefore, equation (5) has a unique solution.

Now we state and prove the Existence and Uniqueness Theorem of the Stochastic Solow Equation.

Theorem. *If the production function f is strictly concave, continuously differentiable on* $[0, \infty)$, $f(0) = 0$, *and* $\lim_{k\to\infty} f'(k) = 0$, *then there is a unique solution to* (5).

Proof. First, we extend (5) to (6). By assumption, $f(k)$ is strictly concave and $f(0) = 0$. The boundedness of savings ratio, $0 < s(k) \leqq 1$, implies that there exists a constant $B_0 > 0$ such that

$$|\tilde{s}(k)\tilde{f}(k)| \leqq B_0 \quad \text{for } |k| \leqq k^*, \tag{7}$$

where $k^* \neq 0$ is the solution to $f(k) = k$, and

$$|\tilde{s}(k)\tilde{f}(k)| \leqq |k| \quad \text{for } |k| > k^* \tag{8}$$

Notice that, if k^* does not exist, then (8) is automatically satisfied.

Choose $B = \text{Max}\,\{6B_0^2, 6(n - \sigma^2)^2, 3\sigma^2\}$. Clearly,

$$\begin{aligned} F^2 + G^2 &= [\tilde{s}(k_t)\tilde{f}(k_t) - (n - \sigma^2)k_t]^2 + \sigma^2 k_t^2 \\ &\leqq 2[(\tilde{s}(k_t)\tilde{f}(k_t))^2 + (n - \sigma^2)^2 k_t^2] + \sigma^2 k_t^2 \leqq B(1 + k_t^2). \end{aligned}$$

Thus, the solution exists and is unique by the Nonexplosive Theorem.

Next, notice that the stochastic process that satisfies the following equation

$$dk_t = -(n-\sigma^2)k_t dt - \sigma k_t dz_t \quad \text{with } k_0 > 0, \tag{9}$$

is lognormal whose solution is given by

$$k_t = k_0 \exp\left\{\int_0^t -(n-\sigma^2/2)ds - \int_0^t \sigma dz_s\right\} > 0. \tag{10}$$

The addition of $\tilde{s}(k_t)\tilde{f}(k_t)dt$, when $k_t > 0$, to (9) will simply shift the stochastic process (10) upward. Consequently, a zero capital-labour ratio is an inaccessible boundary, hence, the solution to (6) is everywhere positive provided $k_0 = c > 0$. ||

Corollary. *There is a unique solution to* (5) *for all CES production functions with elasticity of substitution less than unity.*

Remark. If $k_0 = c < 0$, the k_t of (10) is everywhere negative. The addition of $\tilde{s}(k_t)\tilde{f}(k_t)$ to (10) will forever lower the value of k_t. Note that we can also obtain this by looking at $-k$, since both the drift and the variance are odd functions.

An advantage of our approach is that the solution is decomposed into two parts $\tilde{s}(k)\tilde{f}(k)dt$ and a lognormal equation (10). To show the existence and uniqueness of the solution to equation (5), *no* restrictions on parameters n and σ are required as we can see from the proof. Since the explosion time is $+\infty$, we know that $k_t = \infty$ is an inaccessible boundary. From the proof of the theorem, we see $k_t = 0$ is also inaccessible. Thus, the theorem demonstrates that the solution to (5) will neither explode nor degenerate to zero in finite time, a useful result in studying growth paths.

Equation (10) also helps us see that

$$n - \sigma^2/2 \geqq 0, \tag{11}$$

is *necessary* for the existence of a steady state distribution; otherwise, the drift grows exponentially with time. In fact, condition (11) without equality, is one of a set of sufficient conditions for the existence of a steady state as pointed out by Merton (1975, footnote 1, p. 379). This observation is particularly useful because it is a restriction only on the source of uncertainty, population size in this case. It states that the drift-variance ratio cannot be less than one-half. Note especially that the necessity part is independent of conditions on the production function and the savings ratio, as long as they are not negative.

Finally, it can be shown that a steady state distribution exists for this class of production functions if the following bounded slope condition

$$s(0)f'(0) > n - \sigma^2/2, \tag{12}$$

is satisfied. This is because we assume $f'(0) < \infty$ instead of $f'(0) = \infty$. The rest of the proof follows Merton's argument. Thus, in addition to Cobb-Douglas production functions, a steady state distribution also exists for some CES production functions.

4. REMARKS AND CONCLUSION

The method of reflection presented in this paper is fairly general. The key is to make sure that both the drift and the variance have a finite slope at the origin so that the extended functions after reflection maintain nice properties of the original functions on the entire real line. In this regard, the method applies to sources of uncertainty other than population growth as well. For example, technical change is often argued as a more important cause of changes in the aggregate behaviour of the economy. As long as technical progress can be shown to follow a diffusion process, the above argument for the existence and uniqueness of the corresponding stochastic differential equation is still valid.

In summary, the demonstration of the existence and uniqueness of the solution to the stochastic Solow equation places the stochastic Solow model of economic growth under uncertainty on firm mathematical foundations. It also opens the possibility that the corresponding optimal stochastic control problem has a non-empty set of admissible feedback controls. It is hoped that the reflection technique introduced in this paper would have applications in the development of existence theorems for various stochastic control problems.

Acknowledgement. The authors are grateful to William Brock for suggesting this problem, and to Robert Becker, John Boyd, Michael Magill and two anonymous referees for their valuable comments. None of the above are responsible for errors that remain. An earlier version of this paper, entitled "Properties of Continuous Time Stochastic Economic Growth," was presented at the 1981 Winter Meeting of the Econometric Society.

REFERENCES

ARNOLD, L. (1974) *Stochastic Differential Equations: Theory and Applications* (New York: John Wiley and Sons).

AHLFORS, L. (1966) *Complex Analysis* 2nd ed. (New York: McGraw-Hill).

BOURGUIGNON, F. (1974), "A Particular Class of Continuous Time Stochastic Growth Models", *Journal of Economic Theory*, **9**, 141–158.

MCKEAN, H. P., JR. (1969) *Stochastic Integrals* (New York: Academic Press).

MERTON, R. (1975), "An Asymptotic Theory of Growth Under Uncertainty", *Review of Economic Studies*, **42**, 375–393.

SOLOW, R. (1956), "A Contribution to the Theory of Economic Growth", *Quaterly Journal of Economics*, **70**, 65–94.

WAN, H. Y., JR. (1971) *Economic Growth* (New York: Harcourt Brace Jovanovich, Inc).

Economics Letters 34 (1990) 113–116
North-Holland

How big is the random walk in macroeconomic time series *

Variance ratio tests

A.G. Malliaris and Jorge L. Urrutia
Loyola University of Chicago, Chicago, IL 60611, USA

Received 28 December 1989
Accepted 9 March 1990

The paper applies the Lo and MacKinlay (1988) and Cochrane (1988) variance-ratio test to the data sample used by Nelson and Plosser (1982), who studies the stationarity properties of 14 macroeconomic variables. The results of our empirical tests indicate that the macroeconomic time series have significant random walk components, with the exception of unemployment, real wages, real per capita GNP and industrial production. These results generally agree with those reported earlier by Nelson and Plosser who found that 13 out of 14 macroeconomic variables followed random walk and with Cochrane who, more recently, found that GNP had a small random walk component. The contribution of this paper lies in its use of a very recent methodology to estimate the magnitude of the random walk component of certain macroeconomic time series.

1. Introduction

In their seminal paper, Nelson and Plosser (1982) investigated whether macroeconomic time series are better characterized as stationary fluctuations around a deterministic trend, or as non-stationary processes that have no tendency to return to a deterministic path. Using long annual time series for 14 measures of U.S. output, spending, money, prices and inflation, with starting dates from 1860 to 1909 and ending in 1970, they were unable to reject the hypothesis that these time series are non-stationary processes with no tendency to return to a trend line.

The Nelson and Plosser (1982) paper generated important research in at least two directions. First, numerous studies explored the time-series properties of economic data using the Dickey and Fuller (1981) methodology. For a recent survey of this literature see West (1988) or Quah (1987). Second, the business cycle research was greatly influenced with real theories receiving more emphasis. For a recent survey of this literature see Dotsey and King (1987).

In view of their significance, the results of the Nelson and Plosser (1982) paper have been challenged. Sims (1988) expresses Bayesian skepticism on unit roots econometrics, while DeJong and Whiteman (1988) use the likelihood principle approach to discover that for many of the series considered by Nelson and Plosser the required prior is excessively sharp. When this prior is relaxed

* We are thankful to Professors Charles R. Nelson and Charles I. Plosser for supplying us with their data. We thank Hang Chang and Wichai Saenghirunwattana for their computational assistance.

by DeJong and Whiteman (1989), the data tend to support the trend-stationary property of the time series. On the other hand, Perron (1988) suggests a nonparametric transformation of a certain critical value which when compared with Fuller's critical value gives results similar to those of Nelson and Plosser.

Cochrane (1988) used the variance of k-differences to estimate the random walk component of GNP. He found that the random walk component of GNP was rather small, that is about one-third the variance of yearly GNP growth rates. However, Monte Carlo simulation results allowed him to conclude that the random walk component of GNP is even smaller than one-third. Cochrane also found large standard error indicating that the random walk component could not be measured accurately.

The purpose of this paper is to determine estimates of the measure of the random walk components in the U.S. economic data used by Nelson and Plosser by employing the new methodology of variance tests introduced into the finance literature by Lo and MacKinlay (1988). In section 2 we briefly summarize the methodology of the variance ratio test and in section 3 we present our results and conclusion.

2. The variance-ratio test

Cochrane's results differ from those reported by other researchers. He explains the difference by arguing that conventional criteria for time series model identification and estimation can produce misleading estimates of the random walk component of a series like GNP. He suggests that in the absence of credible identifying restrictions, it is best to leave the short run dynamics out altogether, as the variance of k-differences does.

In this paper we use the variance ratio test developed by Lo and MacKinlay (1988) to estimate the random walk component of the macroeconomic variables of Nelson and Plosser's study. This test is robust with respect to heteroscedasticity and non-normal random disturbances. Following Cochrane, the intuition behind this approach is the following: If the natural logarithm of a time series, denoted y_t, is a pure random walk of the form

$$y_t = \mu + y_{t-1} + \epsilon_t$$

then, the variance of its k-differences grows linearly with the difference k; that is, $\text{var}(y_t - y_{t-k}) = k\sigma\epsilon^2$. On the other hand, if y_t is stationary about a trend

$$y_t = bt + \sum_{j=0}^{\infty} a_j \epsilon_{t-j}$$

the variance of its k-differences approaches a constant, twice the unconditional variance of the series $\text{var}(y_t - y_{t-k}) = 2\sigma_y^2$.

Now, if we suppose that fluctuations in y_t are partly permanent and partly temporary they can be modeled as a combination of a stationary series and a random walk. In this case the $(1/k)\ \text{var}(y_t - y_{t-k})$ should settle down to the variance of the shock to the random walk or permanent component, and $(1/k)\ \text{var}(y_t - y_{t-k})$ divided by the variance of the first difference $\text{var}(y_t - y_{t-1})$, that is, the variance ratio, should correspond to the estimate of the measure of the random walk component of the series.

3. Results and conclusions

In our empirical test we use the same data sample of Nelson and Plosser (1982) supplied to us by the authors. They are annual observations for 14 measures of U.S. output, spending, money, prices and inflation, with starting dates from 1860 to 1909 and ending in 1970. All series were transformed to natural logarithms.

Table 1 presents the results of the variance-ratio test, for several k's. The large variance-ratios reported in the table indicate that most of the macroeconomic variables contain a large permanent or random walk component and a small temporary component. In effect, the random walk component is 40 percent or more of the variance for most of the series. Umemployment rate, real wages, real per capita GNP, and industrial production, on the other hand, exhibit large temporary components. In

Table 1
$1/k$ times the variance of k-differences of the natural logs of annual data k (years). [a]

Series	1	2	3	4	5	10	15	20	25	30
Real GNP	1.00	1.36	1.53	1.54	1.46	1.10	0.70	0.70	0.50	0.40
	(0.15)	(0.29)	(0.40)	(0.47)	(0.50)	(0.60)	(0.40)	(0.60)	(0.50)	(0.40)
Nominal GNP	1.00	1.46	1.70	1.77	1.72	1.80	1.60	1.30	0.80	0.60
	(0.15)	(0.31)	(0.44)	(0.54)	(0.59)	(0.90)	(1.10)	(1.00)	(0.80)	(0.70)
Real per capita GNP	1.00	1.35	1.51	1.52	1.45	1.11	0.68	0.68	0.43	0.27
	(0.15)	(0.28)	(0.39)	(0.46)	(0.49)	(0.56)	(0.45)	(0.54)	(0.41)	(0.30)
Industrial production	1.00	1.04	0.98	0.96	0.90	0.57	0.45	0.41	0.33	0.32
	(0.11)	(0.16)	(0.19)	(0.21)	(0.23)	(0.21)	(0.20)	(0.22)	(0.21)	(0.23)
Employment	1.00	1.33	1.42	1.43	1.35	1.12	0.81	0.67	0.49	0.39
	(0.13)	(0.25)	(0.32)	(0.38)	(0.40)	(0.48)	(0.45)	(0.44)	(0.38)	(0.35)
Unemployment rate	1.00	1.10	0.94	0.86	0.79	0.52	0.37	0.24	0.19	0.20
	(0.13)	(0.20)	(0.21)	(0.23)	(0.23)	(0.23)	(0.20)	(0.16)	(0.14)	(0.18)
GNP deflator	1.00	1.44	1.73	1.91	2.00	2.17	2.14	1.62	1.03	0.53
	(0.13)	(0.26)	(0.39)	(0.50)	(0.59)	(0.93)	(1.17)	(1.06)	(0.79)	(0.47)
Consumer price index	1.00	1.59	1.90	2.02	1.98	2.22	2.36	2.22	2.03	1.84
	(0.11)	(0.25)	(0.37)	(0.45)	(0.50)	(0.81)	(1.08)	(1.20)	(1.27)	(1.29)
Wages	1.00	1.49	1.73	1.86	1.91	2.16	1.87	1.27	0.82	0.76
	(0.14)	(0.29)	(0.42)	(0.53)	(0.61)	(1.01)	(1.12)	(0.92)	(0.70)	(0.75)
Real wages	1.00	0.61	0.28	0.25	0.23	0.15	0.11	0.10	0.09	0.10
	(0.14)	(0.12)	(0.07)	(0.07)	(0.07)	(0.07)	(0.07)	(0.07)	(0.08)	(0.10)
Money stock	1.00	1.64	2.08	2.39	2.58	2.83	2.27	1.39	0.89	0.83
	(0.13)	(0.30)	(0.47)	(0.62)	(0.76)	(1.22)	(1.24)	(0.91)	(0.68)	(0.73)
Velocity	1.00	1.12	1.12	1.06	0.96	0.79	0.77	0.81	0.68	0.66
	(0.12)	(0.18)	(0.23)	(0.25)	(0.25)	(0.30)	(0.37)	(0.46)	(0.45)	(0.49)
Bond yield	1.00	1.11	1.27	1.35	1.43	1.77	2.28	2.29	1.79	1.20
	(0.14)	(0.22)	(0.31)	(0.38)	(0.45)	(0.83)	(1.36)	(1.65)	(1.52)	(1.18)
Common stock prices	1.00	1.22	1.22	1.19	1.10	0.77	0.83	0.71	0.58	0.44
	(0.12)	(0.20)	(0.25)	(0.28)	(0.29)	(0.30)	(0.40)	(0.41)	(0.39)	(0.33)

[a] Standard errors (in parentheses) are the Bartlett standard error computed as $(4k/3T)^{0.5}((\sigma_k^2/k)/\sigma_1^2)$.

effect, the variance ratios for these four series at $k = 30$ indicate that the random walk component is small. As Cochrane, we have also found that $1/k$ times the variance of k differences for the log of the real per capita GNP settles down to about one-third of the variance of first differences.

The standard error reported in table 1 are large for $k = 15$ or larger. Large standard errors seem to imply that it is not possible to estimate the measure of the random walk component precisely. Cochrane pointed out this fact for the real per capita GNP and his observation is confirmed in our case also.

Finally, we want to emphasize one important theoretical point. This paper does not use the variance ratio to test the null of unit root, that is to test if the macroeconomic variables follow random walks, as Lo and MacKinlay do to test if stock prices follow a random walk process. Instead, we use the variance ratio as Cochrane does; that is, we estimate the measure of the random walk component of the series. In fact, testing for random walk with the variance ratio test, requires a special assumption: The time series is assumed to be a random walk with no temporary component. In other words, the variance ratio test requires that the first difference of the series studied not to have autocorrelations. The assumption of pure random walk does not apply to most of the series in our data because no acceptable economic theories exist that claim that GNP, employment, wages, or money stock, should be random walks without any temporal component. However, if the series has permanent and temporary components, the variance ratio can be considered to be an estimate of the measure of the random walk component.

References

Cochrane, John H., 1988, How big is the random walk in GNP?, Journal of Political Economy 96, no. 5, 833–920.

DeJong, David and Charles Whiteman, 1989, Trends and random walks in macroeconomic time series: A reconsideration based on the likelihood principle, Working paper no. 89-04 (University of Iowa, Iowa City, IA).

Dickey, D.A. and W.A. Fuller, 1979, Distribution of the estimators of the autoregressive time series with a unit root, Journal of the American Statistical Association 74.

Dickey, D.A. and W.A. Fuller, 1981, Likelihood ratio statistics for autoregressive time series with a root, Econometrica 49, 1057–1072.

Dotsey, Michael and Robert King, 1987, Business cycles in: The new palgrave: A dictionary of economics, Vol. 1 (The Macmillan Press Limited, London) 302–310.

Lo, A. and A.C. MacKinlay, 1988, Stock market prices do not follow random walks: Evidence from a simple specification test, Review of Financial Studies 1, 41–66.

Nelson, Charles and Charles Plosser, 1982, Trends and random walks in macroeconomic time series: Some evidence and implications, Journal of Monetary Economics 10, 139–162.

Perron, Pierre, 1988, Trends and random walks in macroeconomic time series: Further evidence from a new approach, Journal of Economic Dynamics and Control 12, 297–332.

Quah, Danny, 1987, What do we learn from unit roots in macroeconomic time series?, Working paper no. 2450 (NBER, Cambridge, MA).

Sims, C.A., 1988, Bayesian skepticism on unit root econometrics, Journal of Economic Dynamics and Control 12, 463–474.

West, Kenneth, 1988, On the interpretation of near random-walk behavior in GNP, The American Economic Review 78, 202–209.

Economics Letters 37 (1991) 151–158
North-Holland

An empirical investigation among real, monetary and financial variables *

A.G. Malliaris and Jorge L. Urrutia
Loyola University of Chicago, Chicago, IL 6011, USA

Received 22 May 1991
Accepted 22 July 1991

This paper attempts to make an empirical contribution to the literature on the relationships among real, monetary and financial variables of the economy. Using the methodology of Granger's causality tests, our results indicate that: (i) Money Supply and S&P 500 exhibit contemporaneous causality; (ii) Money Supply seems to lead the S&P 500 Index and, (iii) the S&P 500 Index seems to lead the Industrial Production Index. Our findings tend to confirm the important role played by Money Supply in the economy and the popular hypothesis that stock return fluctuations are a leading indicator of future real economic activity. However, our results also show that the causal relationships among these three economic variables are not as statistically significant as the economic and financial literature suggests.

1. Introduction

The relationships among real economic variables, monetary variables and financial variables have been topics of active research for economists for a long time. Harberler (1937) has skillfully summarized a wealth of economic theories attempting to explain the nature and causes of economic fluctuations. The great depression of 1930's and the remarkable intellectual impact of the Keynes' *General Theory*, interrupted the rich multidimensional research agenda of the pre-Keynesian economists and during the 1950s to the late 1960s, the Keynesian doctrine of aggregate demand and activist fiscal policy caused intellectual atrophy in the areas of monetary and financial fluctuations. Friedman and Schwartz (1963a, 1982), among other economists, redirected the attention of researchers on the role of money, while financial economists, such as Sharpe (1964), focused on financial assets.

More recently, numerous studies have focused on specialized issues. Rozeff (1974) has studied the relationship between money and stock prices, and Barro (1977) has analyzed the potential relationship between monetary factors and real output. Although Barro's work indicates that money surprises are much more important that actual money, recent work by Mishkin (1982) suggests that actual money is also a factor in explaining departures of actual GNP from potential GNP. Fama (1981) investigates the relationships among stock returns, real economic activity, inflation, and money. Plosser (1989) reviews an extensive literature on real business cycles and

* We are thankful to several colleagues for constructive comments, and to Avinash Bhandari and Wichai Saenghirunwattana for computational assistance.

emphasizes the significant role of technological shocks on the production function and the economy's real output. Mankiw (1989) criticizes Plosser's ideas and cites the significant role of tight monetary policies.

While a grand theory of the relationships among real, monetary and financial fluctuations is currently unavailable, Kydland and Prescott (1990) offer an in-depth methodological procedure into the measurement of fluctuations for various variables and conclude that M1 moves contemporaneously with the cycle while the much larger M2 leads the cycle, suggesting that credit considerations could play an important role in future business cycle theory.

Furthermore, during the past decade a large number of papers investigate the excessive volatility in stock market returns and question the validity of the efficient financial markets hypothesis. Shiller (1989) summarizes the bulk of these studies and argues that volatilities in speculative asset prices are excessive relative to the volatilities in real or monetary variables. This evidence increases the challenge to business cycle theorists who must now explain, not only potential relations among changes in levels of real, monetary, and financial variables, but also relations among their volatilities. Actually, this is not a new idea; Friedman and Schwartz (1963b) had shown that changes in the volatility of money generated changes in the volatility of output.

The purpose of this paper is to make an empirical contribution to the literature on the relationships among real, monetary and financial dimensions of the economy both in terms of fluctuations in rates of change and in terms of volatilities. We have chosen to study these relationships using monthly data. This is the shortest possible period for which data is available for all three dimensions: real, monetary, and financial. In choosing monthly data we wish to investigate potential relationships that might not be present on an annual basis, say because of data averaging.

On a monthly basis, the most representative variable measuring real economic activity is the Index of Industrial Production. Monetary factors are represented by M1, and the financial activity is appropriately represented by returns on the S&P 500 Index. We investigate lead-lag relationships among these three macroeconomic variables using Granger's causality tests for both rates of change and volatilities. In using this causality methodology, we wish not only to empirically investigate the relationships among these three variables but to also test the popular hypothesis in the financial press which claims that stock market returns are a leading indicator of future real economic activity.

2. Data

The sample data correspond to monthly average figures for the Standard and Poor 500 Index, and M1 (Money Supply, not seasonally adjusted), and to the monthly Industrial Production Index (seasonally adjusted), all three for the time period January 1970 through June 1989. The S&P 500 and Money Supply data were obtained from the *Federal Reserve Bulletin*. The Industrial Production data were collected from the *Business Conditions Digest*.

3. Methodology

The causal tests of Granger (1969) are essentially tests of the predictive ability of time series models and there are several ways of implementing them. A description of several testable forms of Granger's causality can be found in Pierce and Haugh (1977), Geweke, Meese and Dent (1983), and Guilkey and Salemi (1982).

The simple causal model of the Granger test (1969) is

$$X_t = \alpha_0 + \sum_{j=1}^{m} a_j Y_{t-j} + \sum_{j=1}^{m} b_j X_{t-j} + e_t \tag{3.1}$$

$$Y_t = \beta_0 + \sum_{j=1}^{m} c_j X_{t-j} + \sum_{j=1}^{m} d_j Y_{t-j} + \mu_t \tag{3.2}$$

The definition of causality given above implies that Y is causing X provided some a_j is not zero in eq. (3.1). Similarly, X is causing Y if some c_j is not zero in eq. (3.2). If both of these events occur, there is a feedback. The F-statistic, which corresponds to a Wald test, is calculated by estimating the above expression in both unconstrained and constrained forms (full and reduced models) and follows and χ^2/m distribution [see, i.e., Guilkey and Salemi (1982), and Geweke, Meese, and Dent (1983)].

A more general model with contemporaneous causality can be constructed by including the current values of X and Y in eqs. (3.1) and (3.2), respectively. The contemporaneous equations imply that X and Y may affect each other contemporaneously through a_0 and c_0. However, the null hypotheses with contemporaneous causality differ from those that test Granger causality because they allow the coefficient at lag zero to enter the models. The null hypothesis with contemporaneous causality are tested with an F-statistic. Indeed, the possibility of 'instantaneous causality' is ruled out in tests of Granger's causality [see i.e. Granger (1969), Geweke (1978), and Kawaller, P. Koch and I. Koch (1987)].

Engle and Granger (1987) show that if two nonstationary variables are cointegrated a vector autoregression in the first differences is mispecified. For example, if Money Supply and Industrial Production are both nonstationary in levels, but the first differences of each variable are stationary, it is said that the two variables are integrated of order one. Now, if the difference between the Money Supply and the Industrial Production (or any linear combination of the two variables) is stationary, the two variables are said to be cointegrated. Because the presence of cointegration can cause the Granger's causality tests to be mispecified, it is necessary to test for integration before running the causality tests. If cointegration is found, an error-correcting model must be constructed.

We conduct Augmented Dickey and Fuller tests and find that Money Supply, Industrial Production, and The S&P 500 Index are integrated of order one or stationary in the first difference. Following we test for the presence of cointegration using the Durbin–Watson statistic and the Augmented Dickey and Fuller test. We find that the three variables are not cointegrated. Therefore, we conclude that Granger's Causality tests are well-specified and no error-correcting model is needed [1].

4. Granger causality Tests

This section presents and analyzes the empirical findings of the Granger's causality tests. The results of the standard Granger causality tests for the natural logarithm of the variables are presented in table 1. As the χ^2 statistics indicate, the null hypothesis of no-causality cannot be

[1] The empirical results of the tests of integration and cointegration are not presented here for the sake of space but they are available from the authors upon request.

Table 1
Granger causality tests for the first difference of natural logarithm of variables. [a]

Models (I) $X_t = \alpha_0 + \sum_{j=1}^{6} a_j Y_{t-j} + \sum_{j=1}^{6} b_j X_{t-j}$ $(Y \Rightarrow X)$

(II) $Y_t = \beta_0 + \sum_{j=1}^{6} c_j X_{t-j} + \sum_{j=1}^{6} d_j Y_{t-j}$ $(X \Rightarrow Y)$

Direction of causality	a_j, c_j Regression coefficients, std. errors and t-statistics in parentheses $j=1$	$j=2$	$j=3$	$j=4$	$j=5$	$j=6$	χ^2 $H_0: \sum_{j=1}^{6} \alpha_j = 0$, $\sum_{j=1}^{6} c_j = 0$
Money supply ⇒ S&P 500	−0.0716	0.2524	−0.0563	0.2784	−0.1022	0.1748	
	(0.1613)	(0.1649)	(0.1813)	(0.1825)	(0.1653)	(0.1641)	0.69
	(−0.44)	(1.53)	(−0.31)	(1.53)	(0.62)	(1.07)	
S&P 500 ⇒ Money supply	−0.0037	0.0155	0.0308	−0.0161	0.0334	−0.0001	
	(0.0018)	(0.0290)	(0.0306)	(0.0301)	(0.0302)	(0.0297)	0.49
	(−0.13)	(0.51)	(1.02)	(−0.53)	(1.12)	(−0.01)	
Money supply ⇒ Industrial production	0.0661	0.0291	0.0641	0.0061	0.0189	0.0072	
	(0.0363)	(0.0374)	(0.0408)	(0.0414)	(0.0375)	(0.0370)	0.71
	(1.82)	(0.78)	(1.57)	(0.15)	(0.51)	(0.20)	
Industrial production ⇒ money supply	0.0614	0.0417	−0.0546	0.0314	−0.0787	−0.0757	
	(0.0018)	(0.1272)	(0.1374)	(0.1379)	(0.1373)	(0.1372)	0.29
	(0.48)	(0.30)	(−0.40)	(0.23)	(−0.57)	(−0.60)	
S&P 500 ⇒ industrial production	0.0055	0.0305	0.0157	0.0505	−0.0240	0.0360	
	(0.0149)	(0.0156)	(0.0154)	(0.0154)	(0.0156)	(0.0149)	4.28
	(0.37)	(1.96) *	(1.02)	(3.27) *	(−1.54)	(2.40) *	
Industrial production ⇒ S&P 500	−0.0827	−0.2711	0.0201	−0.2773	−0.1720	−0.1771	
	(0.3081)	(0.3288)	(0.3237)	(0.3232)	(0.3231)	(0.3005)	1.01
	(−0.27)	(−0.83)	(0.06)	(−0.86)	(−0.53)	(−0.59)	

[a] χ^2_{crit} at 5% = 12.59, at 10% = 10.64.
* Significantly different from zero at the 5% significance level.

rejected. Practically no lead-lag relationship is detected, except for some individual coefficients that are statistically significant implying that the S&P 500 Index may lead Industrial Production. We have repeated the standard Granger's causality test using as input data in eqs. (3.1) and (3.2) the standard deviation of the first difference of the natural logarithm of the variables [2]. The results shown in table 2 are not different from those presented in table 1. That is the null hypothesis of no-causality cannot be rejected.

The results of the tests of contemporaneous causality are presented in Table 3 for the first differences of the natural logarithm of the variables, and in table 4 for the standard deviations. As it was indicated earlier, the tests generated in tables 3 and 4 are not exactly Granger's tests, because the regressions include also the current values of the variables. An F-statistic is used to

[2] The standard deviation is computed using a moving window procedure: First we take twelve monthly data and estimate the standard deviation. Then we reestimate the standard deviation by deleting the three oldest monthly data and by adding three most recent monthly data (always keeping twelve monthly observations in our sample).

Table 2
Granger causality tests for the standard deviation of the first difference of natural logarithm of variables

Models (I) $X_t = \alpha_0 + \sum_{j=1}^{6} a_j Y_{t-j} + \sum_{j=1}^{6} b_j X_{t-j}$ $(Y \Rightarrow X)$

(II) $Y_t = \beta_0 + \sum_{j=1}^{6} c_j X_{t-j} + \sum_{j=1}^{6} d_j Y_{t-j}$ $(X \Rightarrow Y)$

Direction of causality	a_j, c_j Regression coefficients, std. errors and t-statistics in parentheses $j=1$	$j=2$	$j=3$	$j=4$	$j=5$	$j=6$	χ^2 $H_0: \sum_{j=1}^{6} \alpha_j = 0, \sum_{j=1}^{6} c_j = 0$
Money supply ⇒ S&P 500	−0.3957 (0.7424) (−0.53)	0.6229 (1.0163) (0.61)	0.2647 (0.9618) (0.28)	1.7793 (0.9564) (1.86) [b]	−2.5100 (1.0215) (−2.46) [a]	0.2283 (0.7557) (0.30)	2.10
S&P 500 ⇒ Money Supply	−0.0184 (0.0230) (−0.80)	0.0207 (0.0284) (0.73)	−0.0076 (0.0285) (−0.27)	−0.0156 (0.0286) (−0.54)	0.0317 (0.0294) (1.08)	−0.0320 (0.0224) (−1.43)	0.72
Money supply ⇒ Industrial production	−0.2087 (0.2170) (−0.96)	0.3941 (0.2888) (1.37)	0.1373 (0.2706) (−0.51)	0.0244 (0.2719) (0.09)	−0.0199 (0.2873) (−0.07)	0.0201 (0.2001) (0.10)	0.43
Industrial production ⇒ Money supply	−0.0621) (0.0791) (−0.79)	0.1028 (0.1090) (0.94)	−0.0477 (0.1037) (−0.46)	0.1644 (0.1030) (1.60)	−0.2155 (0.1056) (−2.04) [a]	0.0298 (0.0799) (0.37)	1.21
S&P 500 ⇒ Industrial production	0.0711 (0.0336) (2.12) [a]	−0.0158 (0.0458) (−0.35)	−0.0619 (0.0464) (−1.33)	−0.0159 (0.0448) (−0.36)	0.0516 (0.0437) (1.13)	0.0082 (0.0390) (0.21)	1.45
Industrial Production ⇒ S&P 500	−0.0194 (0.5071) (−0.04)	1.0131 (0.6794) (1.49)	−1.5008 0.6576) (−2.28) [a]	1.1324 (0.6589) (1.72) [b]	−0.5339 (0.6694) (−0.80)	0.2903 (0.4897) (0.59)	1.13

χ^2_{crit} at 5% = 12.59, at 10% = 10.64.
[a] Significantly different from zero at the 5% significance level.
[b] Significantly different from zero at the 10% significance level.

test the null hypothesis of no-causality. Results in table 3 indicate that the S&P 500 and Money Supply exhibit contemporaneous causality and that the S&P 500 Index leads Industrial Production. Also, several statistically significant individual regression coefficients seem to indicate that Money Supply tends to lead the S&P 500 Index. This later result is confirmed in table 4 where we can observe that the null hypothesis of no-causality is rejected at the 5% significance level.

5. Summary and conclusion

This paper attempts to make an empirical contribution to the literature on the relationships among real, monetary and financial sectors. The three sectors are represented by the Industrial Production Index, Money Supply, and S&P 500 Index, respectively. We use Granger's causality tests to investigate lead-lag relationships among the three indicators and have found that: (i) S&P

Table 3
Tests of contemporaneous causality for the first difference of natural logarithm of variables.

Models (I) $X_t = \alpha_0 + \sum_{j=0}^{6} a_j Y_{t-j} + \sum_{j=1}^{6} b_j X_{t-j} \quad (Y \Rightarrow X)$

(II) $Y_t = \beta_0 + \sum_{j=1}^{6} c_j X_{t-j} + \sum_{j=1}^{6} d_j Y_{t-j} \quad (X \Rightarrow Y)$

Direction of causality	a_j, c_j Regression coefficients, std.errors and t-statistics in parentheses $j=0$	$j=1$	$j=2$	$j=3$	$j=4$	$j=5$	$j=6$	F H_0: $\sum_{j=0}^{6} a_j = 0$, $\sum_{j=0}^{6} c_j = 0$
Money supply ⇒ S&P 500								
	0.2846	−0.0337	0.3916	0.0616	0.3259	−0.0893	0.1358	
	(0.1607)	(0.1619)	(0.1820)	(0.1804)	(0.1836)	(0.1647)	(0.1648)	1.04
	(1.77) [b]	(−0.21)	(2.15) [a]	(−0.34)	(1.78) [b]	(−0.54)	(0.82)	
S&P 500 ⇒ Money supply								
	0.0510	−0.0213	0.0232	0.0284	−0.0149	0.0296	0.0043	
	(0.0288)	(0.0305)	(0.0308)	(0.0300)	(0.0300)	(0.0296)	(0.0282)	0.87
	(1.77) [b]	(−0.70)	(0.75)	(0.95)	(−0.50)	(1.00)	(0.15)	
Money supply ⇒ Industrial production								
	0.0298	0.0701	0.0436	0.0633	0.0109	0.0199	0.0029	
	(0.0368)	(0.0367)	(0.0415)	(0.0409)	(0.0419)	(0.0376)	(0.0374)	0.70
	(0.81)	(1.91) [b]	(1.05)	(1.55)	(0.26)	(0.53)	(0.08)	
Industrial production ⇒ Money supply								
	0.1028	0.0192	0.0351	−0.0615	0.0277	−0.0757	−0.0756	
	(0.1272)	(0.1376)	(0.1378)	(0.1383)	(0.1375)	(0.1373)	(0.1266)	0.34
	(0.81)	(0.14)	(0.26)	(−0.45)	(0.20)	(−0.55)	(−0.60)	
S&P 500 ⇒ Industrial production								
	0.0093	0.0026	0.0318	0.0155	0.0504	−0.0247	0.0364	
	(0.0149)	(0.0157)	(0.0157)	(0.0154)	(0.0155)	(0.0156)	(0.0150)	3.70 *
	(0.62)	(0.17)	(2.02) [a]	(1.01)	(3.26) [a]	(−1.58)	(2.43) [a]	
Industrial production ⇒ S&P 500								
	0.1941	−0.1580	−0.2754	0.0071	−0.2844	−0.1710	−0.1845	
	(0.3129)	(0.3316)	(0.3294)	(0.3248)	(0.3239)	(0.3235)	(0.3012)	0.92
	(0.62)	(−0.48)	(−0.84)	(0.02)	(−0.88)	−0.53)	(−0.61)	

$F^{crit}_{7,213}$ at 5% = 2.01, at10% = 1.72.
[a] Significantly different from zero to the 5% significance level.
[b] Significantly different from zero to the 10% significance level.
* Null is rejected at the 5% significance level.

500 and Money Supply exhibit contemporaneous causality; (ii) Money Supply tends to lead the S&P 500 Index; and, (iii) the S&P Index tends to lead the Industrial Production Index.

Our results agree with Barro (1977), Friedman and Schwartz (1963a, 1963b, 1982), Mishkin (1982) and Kydland and Prescott (1990) about the important role played by Money Supply in the economy. Our findings also seem to confirm the popular hypothesis that fluctuations in stock market returns are a leading indicator of future real economic activity. However, our empirical results also indicate that the causal relationships among the rates of change and their volatilities for

Table 4
Tests of contemporaneous causality for the standard deviation of the first difference of natural logarithm of variables.

Models (I) $X_t = \alpha_0 + \sum_{j=0}^{6} a_j Y_{t-j} + \sum_{j=1}^{6} b_j X_{t-j} \quad (Y \Rightarrow X)$

(II) $Y_t = \beta_0 + \sum_{j=0}^{6} c_j X_{t-j} + \sum_{j=1}^{6} d_j Y_{t-j} \quad (X \Rightarrow Y)$

Direction of causality	a_j, c_j Regression coefficients, std. errors and t-statistics in parentheses $j=0$	$j=1$	$j=2$	$j=3$	$j=4$	$j=5$	$j=6$	F H_0: $\sum_{j=0}^{6} a_j = 0$, $\sum_{j=0}^{6} c_j = 0$
Money supply ⇒ S&P 500								
	−1.07979	0.6863	0.4556	0.4518	1.2850	−2.1832	0.1740	
	(0.7483)	(1.0503)	(1.0132)	(0.9614)	(1.0073)	(1.0368)	(0.7494)	2.13 *
	(−1.44)	(0.65)	(0.45)	(0.47)	(1.28)	(−2.11) [a]	(0.23)	
S&P 500 ⇒ Money supply								
	−0.0338	0.0115	0.0193	−0.0065	−0.0284	0.0441	−0.0402	
	(0.0234)	(0.0308)	(0.0282)	(0.0282)	(0.0297)	(0.0304)	(0.0229)	0.92
	(−1.44)	(0.37)	(0.69)	(−0.23)	(−0.96)	(1.46)	(−1.76) [b]	
Money Supply ⇒ Industrial production								
	−0.0437	−0.1656	0.3890	−0.1287	0.0032	−0.0083	0.0192	
	(0.2222)	(0.3097)	(0.2925)	(0.2765)	(0.2946)	(0.2958)	(0.2019)	0.36
	(−0.20)	(−0.54)	(1.33)	(−0.47)	(0.01)	(−0.03)	(0.10)	
Industrial production ⇒ Money supply								
	−0.0161	−0.0452	0.0978	−0.0448	0.1585	−0.2093	0.0265	
	(0.0818)	(0.1176)	(0.1129)	(0.1057)	(0.1083)	(0.1111)	(0.0823)	1.03
	(−0.20)	(−0.38)	(0.87)	(−0.42)	(1.46)	(−1.88) [b]	(0.32)	
S&P 500 ⇒ Industrial production								
	0.0246	0.0465	−0.0115	−0.0605	−0.0070	0.0403	0.0152	
	(0.0348)	(0.0485)	(0.0465)	(0.0467)	(0.0467)	(0.0486)	(0.0405)	1.30
	(0.71)	(0.96)	(−0.25)	(−1.30)	(0.15)	(0.83)	(0.38)	
Industrial production ⇒ S&P 500								
	0.3658	−0.3794	1.0855	−1.5439	1.2583	−0.6531	0.3583	
	(0.5180)	(0.7208)	(0.6902)	(0.6634)	(0.6855)	(0.6933)	(0.5012)	1.03
	(0.71)	(−0.53)	(1.57)	(−2.33) [a]	(1.84) [b]	(−0.84)	(0.72)	

$F^{crit}_{7,55}$ at 5% = 2.17, at 10% = 1.82.
[a] Significantly different from zero to the 5% significance level.
[b] Significantly different from zero to the 10% significance level.
* Null is rejected at te 10% significance level.

the three variables are not as statistically significant as the economic and financial literature suggests.

References

Barro, Robert J., 1977, Unanticipated money, output and the price level in the United States, Journal of Political Economy 86, 549–580.

Engle, R. and C.W.J. Granger, 1987, Co-integration and error-correction: Representation, estimation, and testing, Econometrica 55, 251–276.
Fama, Eugene, 1981, Stock returns, real activity, inflation and money, American Economic Review 71, 545–564.
Friedman, Milton and Anna Schwartz, 1963a, A monetary history of the United States, 1867–1960 (Princeton University Press, Princeton, NJ).
Friedman, Milton and Anna J. Schwartz, 1963b, Money and business cycles, Review of Economics and Statistics 45, 32–64.
Friedman, Milton and Anna Schwartz, 1982, Monetary trends in the United States and the United Kingdom (University of Chicago Press, Chicago, IL).
Geweke, John, 1978, Testing the exogeneity specification in the complete dynamic simultaneous equations model, Journal of Econometrics 6, 163–185.
geweke, John, Richard Meese and Warren Dent, 1983, Comparing alternative tests of causality in temporal systems, Journal of Econometrics 21, 161–194.
Granger, C.W.J., 1969, Investigating causal relations by econometric models and cross spectral methods, Econometrica 37, 428–438.
Guilkey, David K., and Michael K. Salemi, 1982, Small sample properties of three tests for Granger causal ordering in a bivariate stochastic system, The Review of Economics and Statistics 64, 668–680.
Haberler, Gottfried, 1937, Prosperity and depression: A theoretical Analysis of cyclical movements (George Allen and Unwin Ltd., London).
Kawaller, Ira, Paul Koch and Timothy Koch 1987, The temporal price relationship between S&P 500 futures and the S&P 500 index, *The Journal of Finance* 42, 1309–1329.
Kydland, Finn E., and Edward C. Prescott, 1990, Business cycles: Real facts and a monetary myth, Quarterly Review of the Federal Reserve Bank of Minneapolis 14, 3–18.
Mankiw, Gregory N., 1989, Real business cycles: A new Keynesian perspective, The Journal of Economic Perspectives 3, 79–90.
Mishkin, Frederick, 1982, Does unanticipated money matter? An econometric investigation, Journal of Political Economy 91, 22–51.
Pierce, David A., and Larry D. Haugh 1977, Causality in temporal systems: Characterizations and a survey, Journal of Econometrics 5, 265–293.
Plosser, Charles I., 1989, Understanding real business cycles, The Journal of Economic Perspectives 3, 51–71.
Rozeff, Michael, 1974, Money and stock prices; Market efficiency and the lag in effect of monetary policy, Journal of Financial Economics 2, 245–302.
Sharpe, William 1964, Capital asset prices: A theory of capital market equilibrium under conditions of risk, Journal of Finance 19, 425–442.
Shiller, Robert, 1989, Market volatility (MIT Press, Cambridge, MA).

Stochastic Macroeconomic Models

Economics Letters 37 (1991) 351–356
North-Holland

Interest rates and inflation *

A continuous time stochastic approach

A.G. Malliaris, Walter F. Mullady Sr. Professor
Loyola University of Chicago, Chicago, IL 60611, USA

M.E. Malliaris
Loyola University of Chicago, Chicago, IL 60611, USA

Received 27 August 1991
Accepted 21 October 1991

This paper investigates the theoretical foundations of Fisher's equation which expresses the nominal interest rate as the sum of the real interest rate and the expected rate of inflation. To emphasize Fisher's (1930) original formulation and Sargent's (1973) recent suggestion that nominal interest rates and inflation are simultaneously determined rather than having the causation go from inflation to interest rates, we develop a two-equation continuous time stochastic model to build a more solid theoretical foundation of Fisher's equation. Assuming that the nominal interest rate and the rate of inflation follow Itô processes we derive an Itô equation that allows us to express and compute the expected real interest rate and its volatility. These two equations generalize the traditional Fisher equation and an illustration using US long data from 1865–1972 shows the usefulness of our results.

1. Introduction

Keynes (1930, pp. 198–210) observed that A.H. Gibson, a businessman, had written several articles during the 1920's about the fact that interest rates exhibited a high correlation with inflation. Keynes called this empirical relationship between interest rates and inflation the 'Gibson paradox' because it appeared contradictory to the classical monetary theory prediction that the interest rate is independent of the price level. Fisher (1930) proposed his, by now famous, hypothesis to explain the Gibson paradox. Fisher suggested that the nominal interest rate, R, is the sum of the real rate of return on assets, r, with such return fixed in real terms and the expected rate of inflation denoted as $\mathrm{E}(\mathrm{d}P/\mathrm{d}t)(1/P)$, that is,

$$R = r + \mathrm{E}\left(\frac{\mathrm{d}P}{\mathrm{d}t}\frac{1}{P}\right), \tag{1}$$

* Earlier versions of this paper were presented at the Winter Meetings of the Econometric Society and at seminars at Northwestern University and the University of Oklahoma. We are thankful to numerous colleagues and seminar participants for useful comments. Any remaining errors are our responsibility.

where P denotes some index of the economy's price level, such as the consumer price index, or the GNP implicit price deflator. Tanzi (1980) reviews the earlier literature and Tobin (1987) overviews Fisher's ideas on this topic, and clarifies three, often overlooked, important issues about (1).

First, in its simplest form, Fisher's equation connects the nominal interest rate to the real interest rate and the actual inflation i.e. $R = r + (\mathrm{d}P/\mathrm{d}t)\ (1/P)$ and as such it is first of all an identity relating the unobservable value of real interest rate r to two observable variables, the nominal interest rate and the rate of actual price inflation.

Second, Fisher viewed (1) as an equilibrium condition in the financial markets and for this purpose he replaced the actual inflation $(\mathrm{d}P/\mathrm{d}t)(1/P)$ by the expected inflation $\mathrm{E}((\mathrm{d}P/\mathrm{d}t)\ (1/P))$. In such a formulation, (1) relates one observable variable, i.e. the nominal interest rate R, to two unobservable ones, which makes (1) impossible to test empirically.

Third, Fisher recognized that in the longer run, steady-state equilibrium would also be characterized by equality of actual and expected inflation, $(\mathrm{d}P/\mathrm{d}t)\ (1/P) = \mathrm{E}((\mathrm{d}P/\mathrm{d}t)\ (1/P))$. Assuming such an equilibrium condition allows one to use data for the two observables, nominal interest rates and inflation, to compute the real rate of interest.

Sargent (1973) in his comprehensive article on this topic concludes that Fisher's explanation of the paradox is inadequate it posits an unidirectional influence flowing from inflation to interest rates. He suggests that an adequate theory claiming to explain the Gibson paradox must account for the fact that in a rational expectations environment interest rates and inflation are being mutually determined.

Tobin (1987) claims that it was not actually Fisher but some of his followers who frequently cited (1) in support of a complete and prompt transmission of inflation into nominal interest rates. Such view usually assumes the constancy of the real interest rate and empirically tests for market efficiency articulated by Fama (1975, p. 269): 'If the inflation rate is to some extent predictable, and if the one-period equilibrium expected real return does not change in such a way as to exactly offset changes in the expected rate of inflation, then in an efficient market there will be a relationship between the one-period nominal interest rate observed at a point in time and the one-period rate of inflation subsequently observed'.

Tobin (1987, p. 375) writes that 'Fisher's view throughout his career was quite different. For one thing, neither Fisher's theory of interest nor his reading of historical experience suggested to him that equilibrium real rates of interest should be constant. Fisher's original views as well as Sargent's (1973) suggestions. In section 3 we use long term data from Friedman and Schwartz (1982) to illustrate the theoretical results. A brief summary and the main conclusions are summarized in the last section.

2. A continuous time stochastic approach

To follow up on Tobin's claims about Fisher's actual view of (1) and also Sargent's obvious suggestion of the mutual interdependence inflation and interest rates and simultaneously to do it in a way that the market methodology is preserved we propose the following model. Assume that nominal interest rates and inflation follow Itô's stochastic differential equations given by

$$\frac{\mathrm{d}Q}{Q} = \mu_R(t, R)\,\mathrm{d}t + \sigma_R(t, R)\,\mathrm{d}Z_R, \tag{2}$$

$$\frac{\mathrm{d}P}{P} = \mu_P(t, P)\,\mathrm{d}t + \sigma_P(t, P)\,\mathrm{d}Z_P, \tag{3}$$

with

$$dZ_R\, dZ_P = \rho_{RP}\, dt. \tag{4}$$

Note that (2) describes the nominal return of an asset per unit of time as an Itô process. For example, (2) may describe the nominal return of a bond valued at $\$Q$ at time t. Therefore, μ_R denotes the instantaneous nominal interest rate, that is, $\mu_R \equiv R$, and σ_R denotes its instantaneous volatility. In (3), inflation is expressed again as an Itô process with μ_P denoting the instantaneous rate of expected inflation, that is, $E(dP/dt)\,(1/P) \equiv \mu_P$, and σ_P denoting inflation volatility. Observe that both nominal interest rates in (2) and inflation in (3) are shocked by random forces denoted by dZ_R and dZ_P respectively. These variable denote standardized Wiener processes and in order to implement Fisher's views and Sargent's suggestion of the mutual interdependence of inflation and interest rates we postulate in (4) that these Wiener processes are correlated, with $\rho_{RP} \neq 0$. The methodological and mathematical foundations of continuous time stochastic modelling are presented in Malliaris and Brock (1982) and Merton (1975, 1982).

Next we define the real value of an asset, denoted by q, as in Fischer (1975)

$$q = Q/P, \tag{5}$$

and ask the question: what is the behavior of q in view of the two processes in (2) and (3)? Itô's lemma and calculations yield the answer to this question, namely,

$$dq/q = d\left(\frac{Q}{P}\right)\Big/\left(\frac{Q}{P}\right) = \left[\mu_R - \mu_P - \sigma_R\sigma_P\rho_{RP} + \sigma_P^2\right] dt + \sigma_R\, dZ_R - \sigma_P\, dZ_P. \tag{6}$$

Equation (6) describes the proportional change in the real rate of interest as an Itô process and is consistent with Fisher's view of the nonconstancy of the real rate of interest. Taking the expectation and variance of (6) we get

$$E\left(\frac{dq}{q}\right) = \mu_R - \mu_P - \sigma_R\sigma_P\rho_{RP} + \sigma_P^2, \tag{7}$$

$$\mathrm{Var}\left(\frac{dq}{q}\right) = \sigma_R^2 - 2\sigma_R\sigma_P\rho_{RP} + \sigma_P^2. \tag{8}$$

The pair of eqs. in (7) and (8) generalize in a mathematically precise and an economically important way Fisher's equation in (1). Mathematically, $E(dq/q)$ measures the real return and therefore (7) generalizes Fisher's equation (1). Since $E(dq/q) \equiv r$ then (7) can be written as

$$r = \mu_R - \mu_P - \sigma_R\sigma_P\rho_{RP} + \sigma_P^2, \tag{9}$$

which reduces to Fisher's equation if we assume that $\sigma_R = \sigma_P = 0$, i.e., if we assume that both the volatilities of nominal interest rates and inflation are zero. In other words, our modelling has enabled us to generalize Fisher's equation. More specifically, since we have already observed that $\mu_R = R$ and $E(dP/dt)\,(1/P) \equiv \mu_P$, making these two substitutions and rearranging terms, (9) can be written as

$$R = r + E\left(\frac{dP}{dt}\frac{1}{P}\right) + \sigma_R\sigma_P\rho_{RP} - \sigma_P^2. \tag{10}$$

This last equation illustrates that Fisher's eq. (1) is a special case of (10) obtained when volatilities are ignored. It is worth recalling at this point that Fisher (1930, 1963) and numerous researchers of this topic realize that a more accurate relation for (1) can be obtained from

$$1+R=(1+r)\left[1+\mathrm{E}\left(\frac{\mathrm{d}P}{\mathrm{d}t}\frac{1}{P}\right)\right], \tag{11}$$

where $(1+R)$ denotes the nominal increase of a \$1 debt, $(1+r)$ measures the real productivity increase and $1+\mathrm{E}(\mathrm{d}P/\mathrm{d}t)(1/P)$ denotes the increase in value due to expected inflation. From (11) we conclude that

$$R=r+\mathrm{E}\left(\frac{\mathrm{d}P}{\mathrm{d}t}\frac{1}{P}\right)+r\mathrm{E}\left(\frac{\mathrm{d}P}{\mathrm{d}t}\frac{1}{P}\right), \tag{12}$$

which is a more accurate discrete time version of (1). The reason that (1) is stated as Fisher's equation instead of (12) is because the term $r\mathrm{E}(\mathrm{d}P/\mathrm{d}t)(1/P)$ is arithmetically insignificantly small. Our term $\sigma_R\sigma_P\rho_{RP}$ in (10) actually captures the impact of $r\mathrm{E}(\mathrm{d}P/\mathrm{d}t)(1/P)$ (12). But even if the more accurate version of Fisher's equation in (12) is used, still the continuous time modelling yields a generalization because of the extra term σ_P^2 in (9) and, more importantly, because it yields one whole additional equation (8) describing the variance of the real interest rate. In other words, we need not assume as fisher's followers claim that the real interest rate is constant and by allowing it to vary, the square root of equation (8) describes the time path of its volatility. There is no a priori reason why the variance of the real rate of return should be zero in (8). If (8) is not zero, then the real rate of interest is not constant and equation (8) describes the volatility of the real rate of interest as the sum of the volatility of the nominal interest rate and inflation, less two times their covariance.

3. U.S. data 1865–1972

Friedman and Schwartz (1982) have collected and analyzed extensively annual US data for the period 1865–1972. We use their data for our two variables: short-term nominal interest rates on commercial paper and inflation. Simple calculations show that the average nominal interest rate and its volatility (standard deviation) are $\mu_R=0.042183$ and $\sigma_R=0.020949$, while the average rate of inflation and its volatility are $\mu_P=0.013084$ and $\sigma_P=0.05269$. Assuming that expected inflation was correctly anticipated and therefore that expected inflation was equal to actual inflation, Fisher's equation (1) yields an average real interest rate for the US during 1865–1972 given by

$$r=R-\mathrm{E}\left(\frac{\mathrm{d}P}{\mathrm{d}t}\frac{1}{P}\right)=R-\frac{\mathrm{d}P}{\mathrm{d}t}\frac{1}{P}=0.042183-0.013084=0.029099. \tag{13}$$

Next, we wish to show the numerical results obtained from eqs. (7) and (8) derived using stochastic calculus techniques. Observe that we need to compute ρ_{RP} from (4). To accomplish this, first use the values of $\mu_R=0.042183$, $\sigma_R=0.020949$, $\mu_P=0.013084$, and $\sigma_P=0.05269$ to write (2) and (3) as

$$\frac{\mathrm{d}Q}{Q}=0.042183\ \mathrm{d}t+0.020949\ \mathrm{d}Z_R, \tag{14}$$

$$\frac{\mathrm{d}P}{P}=0.013084\ \mathrm{d}t+0.05269\ \mathrm{d}Z_P. \tag{15}$$

Next, use the actual time series of nominal interest rates and (14) to solve for dZ_R. Similarly, obtain a time series for errors dZ_P from (15), using the actual annual inflation or deflation. For purposes of diagnostics we checked and confirmed that $E(dZ_R) = E(dZ_P) = 0$ and $Var(dZ_R) = Var(dZ_P) = 1$. From these two time series dZ_R and dZ_P, obtained as just described, we can readily compute their correlation coefficient ρ_{RP}. It is found to be $\rho_{RP} = -0.19681$. The negative sign indicates that the various shocks that have affected prices positively had an average negative impact on nominal interest rates. This finding cannot be supported by the efficient market hypothesis but is nevertheless an empirical phenomenon of this period during which inflation was highly volatile while nominal interest rate were much more stable and responded to such inflation volatility with lags.

With these calculations completed, (9) yields

$$
\begin{aligned}
r &= \mu_R - \mu_P - \sigma_R\sigma_P\rho_{RP} + \sigma_P^2, \\
&= (0.042183) - (0.013084) - (0.020949)(0.05269)(-0.19681) + (0.05269)^2, \\
&= 0.032092476, \qquad (16)
\end{aligned}
$$

while the variance of the real interest rate is given by

$$
\begin{aligned}
\text{Var}\ r &= \sigma_R^2 - 2\sigma_R\sigma_P\rho_{RP} + \sigma_P^2, \\
&= (0.20949)^2 - 2(0.020949)(0.05269)(-0.19681) + (0.5269)^2, \\
&= 0.003649576. \qquad (17)
\end{aligned}
$$

Note that (16) slightly overestimates the real interest rate obtained from the simple, traditional Fisher equation in (13). The reason is that inflation's volatility during this period was very high and therefore the term σ_P^2 is not negligible. Also, although the term $\sigma_R\sigma_P\sigma_{RP}$ is very small, the fact that ρ_{RP} is negative also ends up contributing to the real interest rate. On the basis of one application of the generalized Fisher equation one could not claim that (13) underestimates the real interest rate. However, it is illustrative that (16) gives a much more accurate estimation of the real interest rate since it contains four terms instead of just two for the simple Fisher equation. In other words, the generalization of Fisher's equation having four terms in (16) instead of only two terms in (13) is not trivial. It would have been arithmetically trivial, although still interesting analytically, if the two extra terms in (16) were numerically always negligible.

Finally, observe that taking the square root of (17) we obtain that the volatility of the real interest rate during 1865–1972 was 0.060411721. This implies that the real interest rate was not a constant during this period. Thus equation (17) supplies us with useful information which is not available from Fisher's elementary theory.

4. Conclusions

This paper investigates the theoretical foundations of Fisher's equation which expresses the nominal interest rate as the sum of the real interest rate and the expected rate of inflation. Following Fisher, we assume that an equilibrium condition in financial markets implies that expected inflation equals actual inflation and therefore one can study the impact of inflation (expected and actual) on nominal interest rates).

To emphasize Fisher's (1930) original formulation and Sargent's (1973) recent suggestion that nominal interest rates and inflation and simultaneously determined rather than having the causation go from inflation to interest rates, we develop a two-equation continuous time stochastic model to build a more solid theoretical foundation of Fisher's equation. Assuming that the nominal interest rate and the rate of inflation follow Itô processes we derive an Itô equation that allows us to express and compute the expected real interest rate and its volatility. These two equations generalize the traditional Fisher equation and an illustration using US long data from 1865–1972 shows the usefulness of our results.

References

Fama, E.F., 1975, Short-term interest rates as predictors of inflation, The American Economic Review 65, 269–282.

Fischer, S., 1975, The demand for index bonds, Journal of Political Economy 83, 509–534.

Fisher, I., 1930, The theory of interest (MacMillan and Company, New York).

Fisher, I., 1963, The purchasing power of money (Kelley, Publisher).

Friedman, M. and A.J. Schwartz, 1982, Monetary trends in the United States and the United Kingdom (University of Chicago Press, Chicago, IL).

Keynes, J.M., 1930, A treatise on money (MacMillan, London).

Malliaris, A.G. and W.A. Brock, 1982, Stochastic methods in economics and finance (North-Holland, Amsterdam).

Merton, R.C., 1975, Theory of finance from the perspective of continuous time, Journal of Financial and Quantitative Analysis 10, 659–674.

Merton, R.C., 1982, On the mathematics and economic assumptions of continuous time models, in: W.F. Sharpe and C.M. Cootner, eds., Financial economics: Essays in honor of Paul Cootner (Prentice-Hall, Englewood Cliffs, NJ) 19–51.

Sargent, T.J., 1973, Interest rates and prices in the long run: A study of the Gibson paradox, Journal of Money, Credit and Banking 5, 385–449.

Tanzi, V., 1980, Inflationary expectations, economic activity, taxes, and interest rates, American Economic Review 70, 12–21.

Tobin, J., 1987, Irving Fisher (1867–1947), in: The new Palgrave: A dictionary of economics, Vol. 2, 369–376.

Review of Quantitative Finance and Accounting, 5 (1995): 93–103

Decomposition of Inflation and its Volatility: A Stochastic Approach

A.G. MALLIARIS AND MARY E. MALLIARIS
Department of Economics and Department of Management Science, Loyola University of Chicago, 820 N. Michigan Avenue, Chicago, Illinois 60611

Abstract. This paper presents a decomposition of inflation and its volatility. According to the traditional quantity theory of money, the rate of inflation is decomposed into three components: the rate of change in the money supply, plus the rate of change in the velocity of circulation, minus the rate of change in real output. We derive a generalization of this decomposition by postulating that the rate of change of money supply, velocity, and output follow diffusion equations. Using stochastic calculus techniques, two expressions are obtained decomposing inflation and its volatility as a sum of several economically important terms. We also use two sets of U.S. data to illustrate these decompositions with actual numbers.

Key words: inflation, volatility, quantity theory variables, stochastic modeling

1. Introduction

Inflation has played a significant role in economic history for as long as money has been used as a means of exchange. The importance of inflation as a topic of economic research is evidenced by the existing large literature surveyed earlier by Bronfenbrenner and Holzman (1963) and more recently by Parkin (1987).

This is a paper on inflation using a quantity theory of money framework. Friedman and Schwartz (1982) state that the quantity theory of money is "a theory that has taken many different forms and traces back to the very beginning of systematic thinking about economic matters." We do not wish here to review this theory in detail. Recently, Friedman (1987) has surveyed this theory very skillfully. In section 2, the quantity theory variables are introduced and the deterministic decomposition of inflation is obtained in equation (3). The extension of the quantity theory of money in the continuous time stochastic case is presented in section 3, and section 4 derives the stochastic decomposition of inflation and its volatility using the celebrated Itô's lemma. Section 5 offers a discussion of the generalization, and section 6 presents two numerical illustrations from two different data sets. The last section summarizes the paper and offers a conclusion about the contribution of this research.

2. Nonstochastic quantity theory of money

Let M, V, P, and Y denote the money stock, velocity of circulation, the implicit price deflator, and real gross national product respectively. The identity

$$MV \equiv PY \quad \text{or} \quad P \equiv MV/Y \tag{1}$$

has received great attention by economists. Fisher (1963) notes that: "This theory, though often crudely formulated, has been accepted by Locke, Hume, Adam Smith, Ricardo, Mill, Walker, Marshall, Fetter, Kemmerer, and most writers on the subject. The Roman, Julius Paulus, about 200 A.D., states his belief that the value of money depends upon its quantity."

We observe that economists have considered the variables M, V, P, and Y to be functions of time and by taking time derivatives they have obtained from (1)

$$\dot{P} = \frac{(\dot{M}V + \dot{V}M)Y - \dot{Y}MV}{Y^2} = \frac{\dot{M}V}{Y} + \frac{\dot{V}M}{Y} - \frac{\dot{Y}}{Y}\frac{MV}{Y} \tag{2}$$

where a dot above a variable denotes time derivative. From (2) we conclude that

$$\frac{\dot{P}}{P} = \frac{\dot{M}}{M} + \frac{\dot{V}}{V} - \frac{\dot{Y}}{Y} \tag{3}$$

which simply tells us that the proportional change in the price level is equal to the sum of the proportional change in the money stock, plus the proportional change in the velocity of money, minus the proportional change in real output. Note that in decomposing the rate of inflation into three terms, equation (3) relates sample averages during the estimation period.

3. Stochastic quantity theory of money

A casual observation of actual data for $\dot{M}/M$, $\dot{V}/V$, and $\dot{Y}/Y$ shows that these are not smooth deterministic variables. For example, figure 1 plots annual rates of change for money growth, real output, and velocity for 1947–1988, and suggests that these rates follow Itô processes. Following Merton (1975, 1982), we postulate that the behavior of the proportional rate

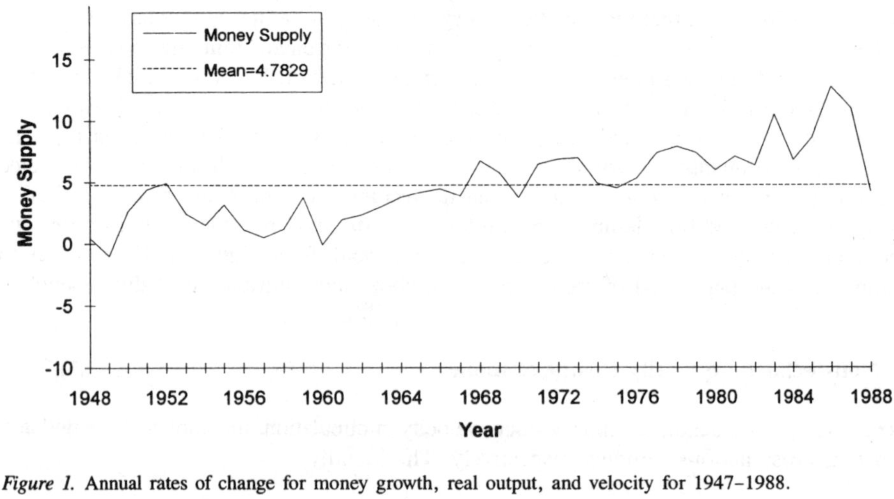

Figure 1. Annual rates of change for money growth, real output, and velocity for 1947–1988.

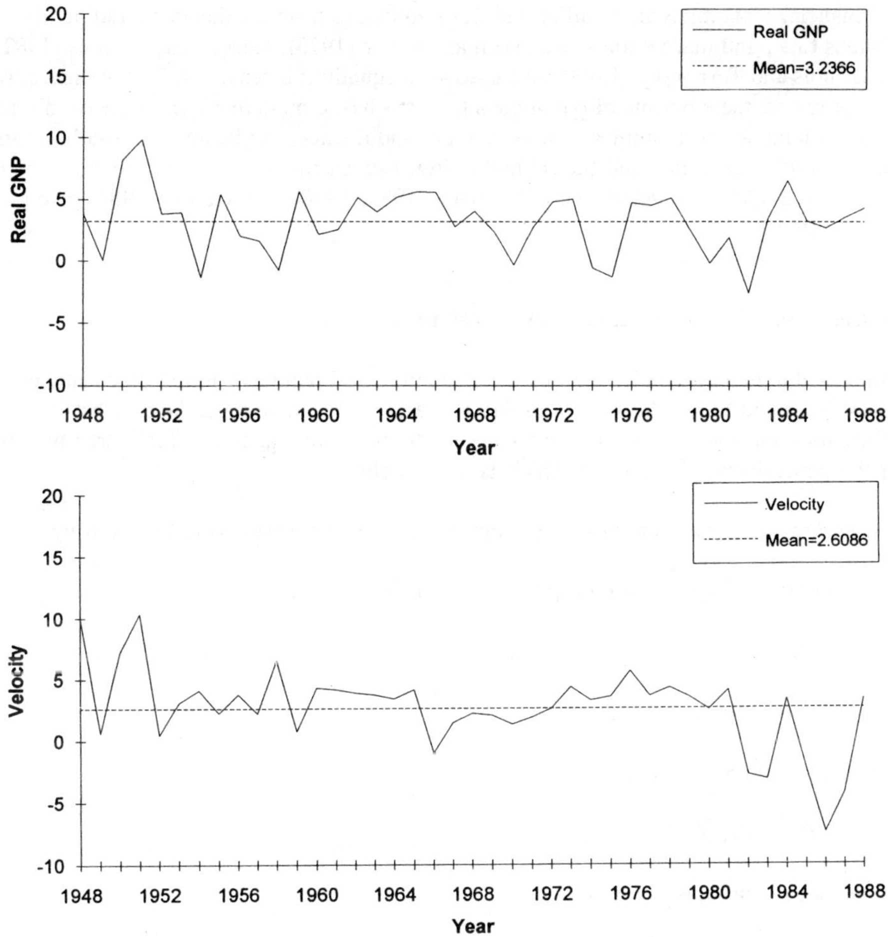

Figure 1. Continued.

of growth of money, velocity, and output are described by the Itô equations given in (4), (5), and (6).

$$\frac{dM(t)}{M(t)} = \mu_M(t, M)dt + \sigma_M(t, M)dZ_M(t) \tag{4}$$

$$\frac{dV(t)}{V(t)} = \mu_V(t, V)dt + \sigma_V(t, V)dZ_V(t) \tag{5}$$

$$\frac{dY(t)}{Y(t)} = \mu_Y(t, Y)dt + \sigma_Y(t, Y)dZ_Y(t). \tag{6}$$

Financial economists are familiar with Itô's equations from the theory of trading in continuous time, and macroeconomists, such as Fischer (1975), Gertler and Grinols (1982), or Grinols and Turnovsky (1993) have used such equations extensively. To save space, we do not review the elements of continuous time stochastic modeling. An extensive discussion, with numerous examples from economics and finance, can be found in Malliaris and Brock (1982). Gikhman and Skorokhod (1969) exposit the mathematical foundations of stochastic modeling in detail, while Malliaris (1983, 1990) and Merton (1982) give general overviews.

4. Decomposition of inflation and its volatility

Suppose that money supply, velocity of circulation, and real GNP follow stochastic processes described by the Itô equations (4)–(6). Heuristically, one may argue that the rate of inflation must also follow a process described by an Itô equation. This is true because of the generalized Itô's lemma which is stated below.

Generalized Itô's Lemma. Let n one-dimensional Itô processes $X_i(t)$ be given by

$$dX_i(t) = f_i(t)dt + \sigma_i(t)dZ_i(t), \qquad i = 1, 2, \ldots, n$$

Suppose that $u = u(t, x_1, x_2, \ldots, x_n)$: $[0, T] \times R^n \to R$ has partial derivatives

$$u_t, \quad u_{x_i}, \quad u_{x_i x_j}, \quad i, j \leq n$$

which are continuous. Then, the process

$$Y(t) = u[t, X_1(t), \ldots, X_n(t)]$$

is also an Itô process given by

$$dY(t) = u_t dt + \sum_{i=1}^{n} u_{x_i} dX_i + \frac{1}{2} \sum_{i=1}^{n} \sum_{j=1}^{n} u_{x_i x_j} dX_i dX_j$$

where the product $dX_i dX_j$ can be calculated using the following multiplication rules:

$$dZ_i dZ_j = \rho_{ij} dt \qquad \text{for } i \neq j, \quad i, j \leq n;$$

$$dZ_i dZ_j = dt \qquad \text{for } i = j, \quad i, j, \leq n;$$

$$dt dZ_i = 0, \qquad \text{for } i = 1, 2, \ldots, n.$$

$$dt dt = 0.$$

Using Itô 's lemma, equations (4)–(6) and the identity (1), several calculations yield that inflation follows at Itô process given by

$$\frac{dP}{P} = [\mu_M + \mu_V - \mu_Y + \sigma_M\sigma_V\rho_{MV} - \sigma_M\sigma_Y\rho_{MY} - \sigma_V\sigma_Y\rho_{VY} + \sigma_Y^2]dt$$
$$+ [\sigma_M dZ_M + \sigma_V dZ_V - \sigma_Y dZ_Y]. \quad (7)$$

Recall that all terms in (7) are random variables. When we write μ_M we actually denote a random variable $\mu_M(t, \omega)$: $[0, T] \times \Omega \to R$. This means that dP/P is a random variable and one can compute its expectation and variance. These are given by

$$E\left(\frac{dP}{P}\right) = E(\mu_M + \mu_V - \mu_Y + \sigma_M\sigma_V\rho_{MV} - \sigma_M\sigma_Y\rho_{MY} - \sigma_V\sigma_Y\rho_{VY} + \sigma_Y^2)dt; \quad (8)$$

$$\mathrm{Var}\left(\frac{dP}{P}\right) = (\sigma_M^2 + \sigma_V^2 + \sigma_Y^2 + 2\sigma_M\sigma_V\rho_{MV} - 2\sigma_M\sigma_Y\rho_{MY} - 2\sigma_V\sigma_Y\rho_{VY})dt \quad (9)$$

Equations (8) and (9) are both informative and intuitively clear. Equation (8) says that expected inflation is the sum of the expected growth in money supply and velocity minus the expected growth in output as well as the result of four more terms which we discuss in the next section. Equation (9) relates the variance of inflation to the three variances σ_M^2, σ_V^2, σ_Y^2 and also to three other terms.

5. Discussion

Several remarks can be made about (7). First, this equation generalizes the deterministic quantity theory equation (3). To obtain (3) from (7) simply assume that the three diffusion coefficients are zero; that is, let $\sigma_M = \sigma_V = \sigma_Y = 0$. This tells us that the deterministic quantity theory of money ignores the existence of nonzero variances in the data concerning money supply, velocity of money, and real output.

Second, equation (7) identifies several terms which are important. These terms are $\sigma_M\sigma_V\rho_{MV}$, $\sigma_M\sigma_Y\rho_{MY}$, $\sigma_V\sigma_Y\rho_{VY}$ and σ_Y^2. The economic meaning of these terms is straightforward. Note that $\sigma_M\sigma_V\rho_{MV}$ denotes the covariance between the proportional rates of change of money supply and velocity; $\sigma_M\sigma_Y\rho_{MY}$ denotes the covariance between the proportional rates of change of money supply and real output; finally, $\sigma_V\sigma_Y\rho_{VY}$ denotes the covariance between the proportional rates of change of velocty and real output; σ_Y^2 denotes the variance of the proportional rate of change of real output. The three terms in the second bracket in (7) are the three sources of noise, dZ_M, dZ_V, dZ_Y, each multiplied by the standard deviations of the proportional rate of change of the money supply, velocity, and real output, respectively.

Third, equation (7), not only identifies several terms described above, but also specifies the exact relationship among these terms. Although economists recognize the importance of covariances between rates of growth of money supply and real output, no equation has appeared in the economic or econometric literature that has a specification such as (7). Some insights are occasionally obtained about the various covariances in (7) from simple single-equation econometric models, but such models are not as complete as (7). For example, one can regress linearly dP/P on dM/M and dY/Y and obtain some estimates of covariances, but such a model would be a special case of (7).

Fourth, because of the tautological nature of the quantity theory of money, (7) gives a rather exhaustive list of factors that can affect dP/P. Such a list of factors can be of great importance both theoretically and empirically. Theoretically, the interest in (4)–(6) is motivated by the goal of obtaining general results. Empirically, the computation of $E(dP/P)$ and $\mathrm{Var}(dP/P)$ can be expected to be more interesting in a general model than in a specialized one.

Fifth, equations (7)–(9) remain tautological. Lucas (1980) has suggested that some theoretical models, such as Sidrauski (1967a, 1967b) or Tobin (1965), have been developed to illustrate the dependence of inflation on the growth of money supply. Therefore, the deterministic quantity theory of money and its implications have some theoretical coherence. Aspects of the present stochastic version of the quantity theory of money could be supported by Gertler and Grinols (1982) and more recently Den Haan (1990) and Grinols and Turnovsky (1993). More specifically, Grinols and Turnovsky (1993) develop a three-agent model with continuous time stochastic variables, uncertain private production, uncertain government expenditures, and forward-looking rational agents. Although Grinols and Turnovsky (1993) wish to study the role of risk in a stochastic macroeconomic model with a financial sector, they confirm that an increase in the growth rate of money supply increases inflation and also that increased uncertainty in monetary growth rates also affects the variablity of inflation. Thus their results support our equations (8) and (9).

6. Examples

We now use two annual U.S. data sets to numerically decompose inflation and its volatility. The first data set, obtained from Gordon (1990), uses annual rates of growth of real GNP, the implicit price deflator Ml, and velocity for the post-WWII period 1947–1988. To compute the expectation of U.S. inflation and its variance from (8) and (9), we need numerical expressions for the three Itô processes describing money supply, velocity, and real GNP changes. In other words, we need estimates for the six functions μ_M, σ_M, μ_V, σ_V, μ_Y, and σ_Y in (4)–(6). From equations (8) and (9) we also observe that we need estimates for the three correlation functions ρ_{MV}, ρ_{MY}, and ρ_{VY}. The simplest and most important case is when these six random functions are approximated by their sample annual means and standard deviations for the data used during the sample period 1947–1988. Straightforward calculations allow us to write

$$\frac{dM(t)}{M(t)} = .0478\,dt + .0303\,dZ_M(t) \tag{10}$$

$$\frac{dV(t)}{V(t)} = .0261\,dt + .0336\,dZ_V(t) \tag{11}$$

$$\frac{dY(t)}{Y(t)} = .0324\,dt + .0262\,dZ_Y(t) \tag{12}$$

as numerical expressions for (4)–(6). This is the most important case because we wish to contrast the traditional deterministic quantity theory of money, which uses constant sample means as explained in section 2, with the generalized stochastic version. This can be done when we compare the one deterministic equation (3) with the two stochastic equations (8) and (9). Note that (3) relates sample means which suggests that we also use sample means in (8).

The implication of (10)–(12) is that the level variables $M(t)$, $V(t)$, and $Y(t)$ follow stochastic processes of the form

$$M(t) = M(0)\exp\{[.0478 - 0.5(.0303)^2]t + .0303Z_M(t)\}$$

$$V(t) = V(0)\exp\{[.0216 - 0.5(.0336)^2]t + .0336Z_V(t)\}$$

$$Y(t) = Y(0)\exp\{[.0324 - 0.5(.0262)^2]t + .0262Z_Y(t)\}$$

where $M(0)$, $V(0)$, $Y(0)$ denote money supply, velocity, and real GNP for the initial year of 1947; t denotes time measured in years since 1947; and $Z_M(t)$, $Z_V(t)$, and $Z_Y(t)$ are standardized Wiener processes. These three last equations are generalizations of the simple deterministic equations that describe the usual exponential rate of growth of $M(t)$, $V(t)$, and $Y(t)$. Furthermore, when taking the natural logarithms of each of these last three equations we may conclude that such a natural logarithm is a random variable distributed normally with a certain mean and variance. For example

$$\ln\frac{M(t)}{M(0)} = \left[.0478 - \frac{1}{2}(.0303)^2\right]t + .0303Z_M(t)$$

has mean $[.0478 - 0.5(.0303)^2]t$ and variance $(.0303)^2t$. Since the logarithm of $M(t)/M(0)$ is a normally distributed random variable we say that the money supply, velocity, and real output are lognormally distributed. For a detailed analysis of these issues, see Cox and Rubinstein (1985).

The next question to be addressed is the computation of the three correlation functions. Again, the instantaneous random correlations are approximated by their sample averages during 1947–1988 as follows: we work backward by computing the annual errors $dZ_M(t)$, $dZ_V(t)$, and $dZ_Y(t)$ from (10)–(12) and the actual corresponding rates. In other words, for each period t in our sample 1947–1988, given the actual rates $dM(t)/M(t)$, $dV(t)/V(t)$, $dY(t)/Y(t)$, and the approximations in (10)–(12), we solve for $dZ_M(t)$, $dZ_V(t)$, and $dZ_Y(t)$. Afterward we use the error sets $\{dZ_M(t), dZ_V(t), dZ_Y(t), t = 1948\text{–}1988\}$ to compute $\rho_{MV} = -.5770$, $\rho_{MY} = .1321$, and $\rho_{VY} = .2757$. Parenthetically, we also report that the error sets $\{dZ_M(t), dZ_V(t), dZ_Y(t)\}$ satisfy the required properties of a standardized Wiener process that $E(dZ_M) = E(dZ_V) = E(dZ_Y) = 0$ with all three variances being equal to 1.

With the above preliminaries completed, the U.S. rate of inflation and its variance during 1947–1988 can be decomposed as:

$$\begin{aligned}\frac{dP}{P} &= \mu_M + \mu_V - \mu_Y + \sigma_M\sigma_V\rho_{MV} - \sigma_M\sigma_Y\rho_{MY} - \sigma_V\sigma_Y\rho_{VY} + \sigma_Y^2 \\ &= (0.0478) + (0.0261) - (0.0324) + (0.0303)(0.0336)(-0.5770) \\ &\quad - (0.0303)(0.0262)(0.1321) - (0.0336)(0.0262)(0.2757) + (0.0262)^2 \\ &= 0.0413 \end{aligned} \tag{13}$$

$$\begin{aligned}\text{Var}\,\frac{dP}{P} &= \sigma_M^2 + \sigma_V^2 + \sigma_Y^2 + 2\sigma_M\sigma_V\rho_{MV} - 2\sigma_M\sigma_Y\rho_{MY} - 2\sigma_V\sigma_Y\rho_{VY} \\ &= (.0303)^2 + (.0336)^2 + (.0262)^2 + 2(.0303)(.0336)(-.5770) \\ &\quad - 2(.0303)(.0262)(.1321) - 2(.0336)(.0262)(.2757) \\ &= 0.00087 \end{aligned} \tag{14}$$

Note from (14) that inflation's standard deviation is given by $\{\text{Var}\, dP/P\}^{1/2} = .0295$, that is, inflation's annualized volatility during 1947–1988 is 2.95%.

If, instead of using (13) and (14) to decompose inflation and its variance we compute, from inflation data during 1947–1988, its average and standard deviation we obtain 4.15% and 2.52%, respectively. Obviously, the tautological nature of the quantity theory of money forces these numbers to be equal to (13) and (14), except for rounding off errors. However, analysis of (13) and (14) gives a much richer insight into inflation and its variance than do the two numbers 4.15% and 2.52%, because we have an explicit numerical expression of these numbers as sums and differences of specific terms.

To contrast the above results with another period we use next the long-run U.S. data collected and reported in Friedman and Schwartz (1982) for the period 1869–1947. In this sample M, Y, and P denote M2, national income, and the implicit price deflator.[1] Using the same procedure, the approximations of (4)–(6) are now given by

$$\frac{dM(t)}{M(t)} = .0607\,dt + .0681\,dZ_M(t) \tag{15}$$

$$\frac{dV(t)}{V(t)} = -.0196\,dt + .0725\,dZ_V(t) \tag{16}$$

$$\frac{dY(t)}{Y(t)} = .0330\,dt + .0727\,dZ_Y(t) \tag{17}$$

while $\rho_{MV} = .1304$, $\rho_{MY} = .5129$, $\rho_{VY} = .7531$.

In contrast to (13) and (14), inflation and its variance for the almost century-long data sample are decomposed below:

$$
\begin{aligned}
\frac{dP}{P} &= \mu_M + \mu_V - \mu_Y + \sigma_M\sigma_V\rho_{MV} - \sigma_M\sigma_Y\rho_{MY} - \sigma_V\sigma_Y\rho_{VY} + \sigma_Y^2 \\
&= (.0607) + (-.0196) - (.0330) + (.0681)(.0725)(.7531) \\
&\quad - (.0681)(.0727)(.5129) - (.0725)(.0727)(.7531) + (.0727)^2 \\
&= 0.001 \qquad (18)
\end{aligned}
$$

$$
\begin{aligned}
\text{Var}\,\frac{dP}{P} &= \sigma_M^2 + \sigma_V^2 + \sigma_Y^2 + 2\sigma_M\sigma_V\rho_{MV} - 2\sigma_M\sigma_Y\rho_{MY} - 2\sigma_V\sigma_Y\rho_{VY} \\
&= (.0681)^2 + (.0725)^2 + (.0727)^2 + 2(.0681)(.0725)(.1304) \\
&\quad - 2(.0681)(.0727)(.5129) - 2(.0725)(.0727)(.7531) \\
&= 0.003449 \qquad (19)
\end{aligned}
$$

From (19) we compute an annual inflation volatility of 5.87%. The actual numbers for inflation and its volatility obtained directly from annual inflation data during 1869–1947 are identically the same, i.e., 0.1% and 5.87%, respectively.

What insights can the decompositions of these two sample periods offer? First, actual inflation during 1947–1988 was much higher than actual inflation during 1869–1947; the respective numbers are 4.15% and 0.1%. Equations (12) and (17) tell us that real output during these two periods grew at a similar rate, i.e., 3.24% for 1947–1988 and 3.3% for 1869–1947. What then explains the substantial difference in inflation rates? Looking at money growth rates complicates the picture: Money grew at a slower rate during 1947–1988 than it did during 1869–1947, i.e., 4.78% in contrast to 6.07%. Intuitively, one would expect faster money growth to contribute to higher inflation when real output grows at the same rate. The decomposition shows that the velocity of money solves partially the puzzle: During 1869–1947, the velocity of money declined by 1.96% per year while it grew by 2.61% during 1947–1988.

The second and final insight concerns the volatility of inflation. Observe that it is much higher during 1869–1947 than during the post-WWII period, i.e., 5.87% compared to 2.52%, respectively. The deterministic quantity theory of money offers no explanations for such differences. An economist's intuition would suggest that higher inflation volatility may be generated by higher volatility of money growth and/or higher volatility of real output. Such an intuition is supported by the data. During 1869–1947, the volatilities of money growth and real output were 6.81% and 6.42%, compared to 3.03% and 2.62% respectively for 1947–1988. But without a specific model these volatilities cannot be put into an algebraic expression. Equations (14) and (19) show the exact decomposition of inflation volatilities as a sum of the volatilities of money growth, output growth, and velocity change with also, their three covariances.

7. Summary and conclusions

This paper addresses the important question of how inflation and its volatility can be decomposed into several terms to offer insights into the economic sources that generate inflation.

Such a decomposition requires an acceptable inflation model and this paper uses the quantity theory to extend its deterministic dynamic version into a continuous time dynamic stochastic version. This generalization is justified both by the actual behavior of the quantity theoretic variables and by the underlying methodological background of diffusion modeling. The generalization obtained yields two expressions that decompose both inflation and its variance into several, economically meaningful terms. Finally two examples illustrate the numerical decomposition and contrast the factors that explain U.S. inflation and its volatility.

Acknowledgments

We wish especially to thank Professors Stanley Pliska, George Catsiapis, F.R. Chang, and William Margrabe for useful comments and suggestions on earlier drafts. Two anonymous referees have helped us substantially in improving the current version and we are grateful to them. An earlier version was presented at the North American Economics and Finance Association Meetings.

Notes

1. Those familiar with the Friedman and Schwartz (1982) book will recall that their data cover the period 1869–1977. We thank two anonymous referees who suggested that we only use 1869–1947 to avoid an overlap with our first example and thus to sharpen the contrast between the two illustrations.

References

Bronfenbrenner, M. and F. Holzman, "A Survey of Inflation Theory." *American Economic Review* 53, 593–611, (1963).

Cox, John C. and Mark Rubinstein, *Options Markets*. Englewood Cliffs, NJ: Prentice-Hall, Inc., 1985.

Den Haan, Wouter J., "The Optimal Inflation Path in a Sidrauski-Type Model with Uncertainty." *Journal of Monetary Economics* 25, 389–409, (1990).

Fischer, S., "The Demand for Index Bonds." *Journal of Political Economy* 83, 509–534, (1975).

Fisher, I., *The Purchasing Power of Money*. Augustus M. Kelley, 1963.

Friedman, Milton, "Quantity Theory of Money." *The New Palgrave: A Dictionary of Economics*, vol 4. New York: The Stockton Press, 1987.

Friedman, Milton and Anna J. Schwartz, *Monetary Trends in the United States and the United Kingdom*. Chicago: University of Chicago Press, 1982.

Gertler, M. and E. Grinols, "Monetary Randomness and Investment." *Journal of Monetary Economics* 10, 239–258, (1982).

Gikhman, I. and A.V. Skorokhod, *Introduction to the Theory of Random Processes*. Philadelphia: Saunders, 1969.

Gordon, Robert J., *Macroeconomics*, 5th Ed. Boston: Little, Brown and Company, Inc., 1990.

Grinols, Earl L. and Stephen J. Turnovsky, "Risk, the Financial Market, and Macroeconomic Equilibrium." *Journal of Economic Dynamics and Control* 17, 1–36, (1993).

Lucas, Jr., Robert E., "Two Illustrations of the Quantity Theory of Money." *The American Economic Review* 70, 1005–1014, (1980).

Malliaris, A.G., "Itô's Calculus in Financial Decision Making." *Society for Industrial and Applied Mathematics* 25, 481–496, (1983).

Malliaris, A.G., "Itô's Calculus: Derivation of the Black-Scholes Option-Pricing Model." In C.F. Lee, J.E. Finnerty, and D.H. Wort, *Security Analysis and Portfolio Management*. Glenview, IL: Scott, Foresman and Company, 1990.

Malliaris, A.G. and W.A. Brock, *Stochastic Methods in Economics and Finance*. Amsterdam: North Holland Publishing Company, 1982.

Merton, R.C., "Theory of Finance from the Perspective of Continuous Time." *Journal of Financial and Quantitative Analysis* 10, 659–674, (1975).

Merton, R.C., "On the Mathematics and Economic Assumptions of Continuous Time Models." In W.F. Sharpe and C.M. Cootner, eds., *Financial Economics: Essays in Honor of Paul Cootner*. Englewood Cliffs, NJ: Prentice-Hall, 1982.

Parkin, M., "Inflation." *The New Palgrave Dictionary of Economics*, vol. 2. New York: The Stockton Press, 1987.

Sidrauski, M., "Inflation and Economic Growth." *Journal of Political Economy* 796–810, (1967a).

Sidrauski, M., "Rational Choice and Patterns of Growth in a Monetary Economy." *American Economic Review: Papers and Proceedings* 57, 534–544, (1967b).

Tobin, J., "Money and Economic Growth." *Econometrica* 33, 671–684, (1965).

Several Illustrations of the Quantity Theory of Money: 1947–1987 and 1867–1975

A.G. MALLIARIS

This paper explores empirical relationships that involve the five quantity theoretic variables: rates of change in money supply, velocity, real output, inflation and also short-term nominal interest rate. Unlike, earlier studies that employ, primarily, regression methods to identify statistical relationships, this study uses the two-side exponentially weighted moving average methodology. This method smooths the original data to various degrees depending on the values of a given weight parameter to exclude as much noise as possible and, thus identifies probable trends. Using intermediate-term and long-term data sets, some much analyzed quantity theoretic relationships are reconfirmed, some new ones are proposed and finally, some less known, are reemphasized.

I. INTRODUCTION

Milton Friedman and Anna Schwartz (1982, p. 17) state that the quantity theory of money is

> a theory that has taken many different forms and traces back to the very beginning of systematic thinking about economic matters. It has probably been tested with quantitative data more extensively than any other set of propositions in formal economics—unless it be the negatively sloping demand curve. Nonetheless, the quantity theory has been a continual bone of contention.

We are reminded of Bertrand Russell who said, "My sad conviction is that people can only agree about what they are not really interested in."

This is one more paper about the quantity theory of money. It is motivated by the work of Friedman and Schwartz (1963a, 1982), who have exhaustively investigated the economic role of money in general and specifically its impact on inflation, nominal interest rates and real output. The primary tool of the Friedman and Schwartz methodology is regression analysis. However, our paper is patterned after Lucas (1980), who presented empirical illustrations of two central implications of the quantity theory of money by using a two-sided exponentially weighted moving average methodology applied to data for the period 1955–1975. The two central implications of the quantity theory of money studied by Lucas refer to the notion that a given change in the rate of change in the quantity of money induces, first, an

A.G. Malliaris • The Walter F. Mullady Sr. Professor of Business Administration, Department of Economics, Loyola University of Chicago, 820 North Michigan Avenue, Chicago, IL 60611.

International Review of Financial Analysis, Volume 1, Number 1, 1992, pages 77–93. **ISSN: 1057-5219**

equal change in the rate of price inflation and, second, an equal change in nominal interest rates.

This paper has three goals. Its first goal is to reexamine the two illustrations by Lucas (1980) using the same methodology of the two-sided exponentially weighted moving average with more extensive data covering the period 1947 to 1987. Observe that Lucas's data of 1955–1975 are a subset of our set of quarterly data for the 1947–1987 period. It is shown that the 1947–1987 data verify Lucas's results.

The second goal is to use the same two-sided exponentially weighted moving average method and the 1947–1987 data to extract further illustrations of the quantity theory of money. These illustrations were not studied by Lucas, but some have been extensively researched by Friedman and Schwartz (1982, especially chapters 9 and 12), who used, however, regression techniques. More specifically, two additional illustrations of the quantity theory of money are exposited in this paper:

(1) For quarterly data for 1947–1987, we illustrate that, as the rate of change in the quantity of money increases, the rate of change of real GNP increases up to a certain maximum rate; then, further increases in the rate of change in the quantity of money are associated with lower rates of real GNP.
(2) In view of the existing relationship between rate of change in the quantity of money and nominal interest rates, we also illustrate that low nominal interest rates are associated with low rates of change of real GNP, with real GNP reaching a maximum rate of growth for some critical level of nominal interest rate and dropping for interest rates higher than this critical level.

The third goal, motivated by Friedman and Schwartz (1963b, 1982), is to use their annual 1867–1975 data and the two-sided exponentially weighted moving average methodology to investigate whether the several illustrations of the quantity theory of money obtained from the 40-year period after World War II also hold for the longer 1867–1975 period. Furthermore, companion research in Malliaris (1987), using the methods of stochastic calculus presented in Malliaris and Brock (1982) has connected analytically the behavior of the variances of rates of change of the quantity theoretic variables. Illustrations of such volatility behavior for these variables during 1867–1975 are also reported here.

The paper is organized as follows. In Section II, we make a few comments about the quantity theory of money. In Section III, we review the two-sided exponentially weighted moving average method and describe the sets of data used. Sections IV, V and VI give graphical presentations of key illustrations. The major findings are summarized in Section VII.

II. THEORETICAL REMARKS

The illustrations involve rates of change of four variables: money supply, velocity, price level and real GNP, denoted by M, V, P and Y, respectively. They also involve one other variable—namely, nominal interest rate—denoted by r. The variables M, V, P, and Y are related by the well-known equation,

$$MV = PY \tag{1}$$

which, following Friedman and Schwartz (1982, pp. 16–72), results by equating the demand for money, M^d, and a given supply M^s. Recall that

$$M^d = kPY \tag{2}$$

describes the Cambridge cash-balances approach to the demand for money with $k = 1/V$. Using the equilibrium condition $M^d = M^s$, Equation (1) is obtained from Equation (2) and $M^s = M$.

Taking natural logarithms of Equation (1) and then differentiating with respect to time, we write

$$\frac{\dot{P}}{P} = \frac{\dot{M}}{M} + \frac{\dot{V}}{V} - \frac{\dot{Y}}{Y} \tag{3}$$

where a dot denotes the time derivative (d/dt).

At this elementary level, the introduction of nominal interest rates can be achieved using the Fisher equation, where the nominal interest rate is the sum of the real rate of return on assets plus the anticipated rate of inflation, with the latter being expressed by the actual inflation $\dot{P}/P$ obtained from Equation (3). Thus, the quantity theoretic background of this study involves Equation (3) and its connection to nominal interest rates via Fisher's equation.

Beyond the elementary quantity theory of money, the monetary growth models of Sidrauski (1967a, 1967b) and others can be used to justify changes in the rate of change in the quantity of money to rates of change in inflation and to changes in nominal rates of interest. Actually, in the Sidrauski neoclassical monetary growth model, a given change in monetary expansion and its consequences on inflation and interest rates are treated explicitly in the steady-state solution of the system of differential equations.

The Sidrauski monetary model does not treat the Mundell-Tobin effect. According to Mundell (1963) the nominal rate of interest rises by less than the rate of inflation; therefore, the real rate of interest falls during periods of inflation. This result is based on the fact that inflation reduces real money balances and that the resulting decline in wealth stimulates increased saving. Whiteman (1984) develops a model that isolates the Mundell-Tobin effect and claims that the Lucas (1980) results are not necessarily evidence against the Mundell-Tobin effect. In this paper, we do not make any claims about the Mundell-Tobin effect.

Assuming, as in Malliaris (1987), that the variables in Equation (3) are stochastic, we can compute the variance of inflation as follows:

$$\begin{aligned}\operatorname{Var}\left(\frac{\dot{P}}{P}\right) &= \operatorname{Var}\left(\frac{\dot{M}}{M}\right) + \operatorname{Var}\left(\frac{\dot{V}}{V}\right) + \operatorname{Var}\left(\frac{\dot{Y}}{Y}\right) + 2\operatorname{Cov}\left(\frac{\dot{M}}{M}, \frac{\dot{V}}{V}\right) \\ &\quad - 2\operatorname{Cov}\left(\frac{\dot{M}}{M}, \frac{\dot{Y}}{Y}\right) - 2\operatorname{Cov}\left(\frac{\dot{V}}{V}, \frac{\dot{Y}}{Y}\right)\end{aligned} \tag{4}$$

Equation (4) links the variance of inflation to the variances and covariances of the other three quantity theoretic variables. In Section VI, we illustrate relationships among

$$\mathrm{Var}\left(\frac{\dot{P}}{P}\right), \ \mathrm{Var}\left(\frac{\dot{M}}{M}\right), \ \mathrm{Var}\left(\frac{\dot{V}}{V}\right) \text{ and } \mathrm{Var}\left(\frac{\dot{Y}}{Y}\right)$$

following Friedman and Schwartz (1963b) and, more recently, Friedman (1984).

To sum up, the analytical background of this study involves the traditional notions of the quantity theory of money and its connection to nominal interest rates via Fisher's equation. Such a background may be found in Friedman (1987). At an advanced analytical level, the quantity theory of money remains a controversial area of research. LeRoy and Raymon (1987) survey numerous papers on money and inflation and also develop a monetarist model to conclude that the theoretical foundations of the quantity theory of money are currently nonexistent. On the other hand, Grandmont (1983) reconsiders the classical and neoclassical monetary theories using a general equilibrium approach to clarify the foundations of the neutrality of money. Therefore, readers may find our illustrations as examples of the quantity theoretic relationships that are obtained from the smoothing methodology described next.

III. DATA AND METHODOLOGY

Two sets of time series data are used in this study. Data set I is quarterly data for the period 1947–1987; data set II is annual data for the period 1867–1975. Data set I is obtained from Gordon (1990) and various issues of the Federal Reserve Bulletin, and data set II is obtained from Friedman and Schwartz (1982).

For each set of data, we have money supply ($M1$ for data set I and $M2$ for data set II), implicit price deflator (P_t), real output Y (GNP for data set I and national income for data set II) and short-term nominal interest rate (90-day Treasury bill rate for data set I and a short-period commercial paper rate for data set II). Although we follow Friedman and Schwartz (1982) in using their estimates of $M2$ in data set II, we have selected $M1$, in data set I, in order to compare our results with Lucas's (1980). For M_t, P_t and Y_t, we work with rate of change, such as

$$m_t \equiv \left(\frac{\dot{M}}{M}\right)_t = [\ln (M_t) - \ln (M_{t-1})]100$$

$$p_t \equiv \left(\frac{\dot{P}}{P}\right)_t = [\ln (P_t) - \ln (P_{t-1})]100$$

$$y_t \equiv \left(\frac{\dot{Y}}{Y}\right)_t = [\ln (Y_t) - \ln (Y_{t-1})]100 \quad (5)$$

For a given time series X_t, the two-sided exponentially weighted moving average is given by

$$X_t(\beta) = \frac{1-\beta}{1+\beta} \sum_{k=-\infty}^{\infty} \beta^{|k|} X_{t+k} \tag{6}$$

for $0 \leq \beta < 1$. When $\beta = 0$, we obtain the original scatter diagram, and, when $\beta = 1$, everything collapses to the origin. The actual effect of Equation (6) is to smooth the original series, and, after extensive calculations, we report results that correspond to $\beta = 0.95$. This is similar to Lucas, who shows that the illustrations improve as β increases to 0.95. This means that the $X_t(0.95)$ of Equation (6) are very close to the sample average values of the original series, which captures the long-term character of the quantity theory relationships. Note that Equation (6) is applied to each of m_t, p_t, y_t and r_t. Figures 1 and 2 present actual and smoothed time series data for money growth and inflation.

After two original time series, say m_t and p_t, are smoothed, the pair $m_t(0.95)$ and $p_t(0.95)$ of the two-sided exponentially weighted moving average is plotted to yield an illustration of the quantity theory of money. Some of the various plots of filtered paired observations are also expressed statistically using regression analysis. The only purpose these regressions serve is to give numerical expressions of the long-run relationships between smoothed quantity theoretic variables.

Whittle (1963), Lucas (1980), Mills (1982), McCallum (1984) and Whiteman (1984) develop in detail the statistical properties of the two-sided exponentially weighted moving average methodology with agreement that such a methodology is a reasonable technique for capturing long-run behavior, where the long run is modeled by the signal, low-frequency characteristics of a given series. As Friedman and Schwartz (1982, p. 8) have concluded, it takes a considerable time, measured in phases, not months or quarters, before a change in the rate of monetary growth is fully reflected in prices. Of course, reduced form correlations described in our illustrations are complicated functions of both the real economy and the laws of the relevant time series, neither of which is explicitly modeled. This is precisely the reason

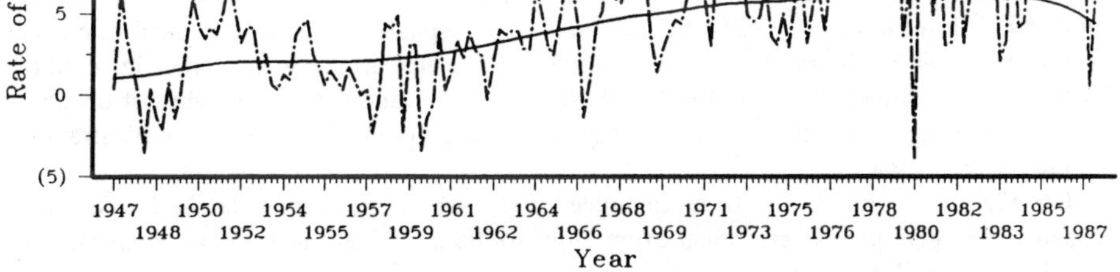

FIGURE 1. Money supply. Unsmoothed and smoothed annual rate of change. Quarterly data (1947–1987).

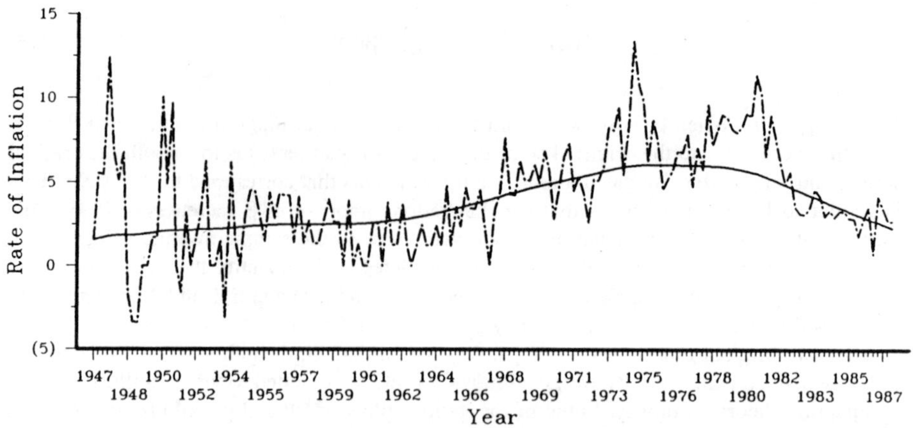

FIGURE 2. Inflation. Unsmoothed and smoothed annual rate of change. Quarterly data (1947–1987).

we use the characterization of quantity theoretic illustrations instead of evidence. Recently, Lucas (1986) returned to these quantity theoretic illustrations to exposit the use of rationality and adaptation in economic theory.

IV. QUARTERLY ILLUSTRATIONS, 1947–1987

When one uses quarterly data for 1947–1987, the two-sided exponentially weighted moving average yields several useful illustrations. Figure 3, which follows, plots the relationship between smoothed rates of money growth and inflation, whereas Figure 4 plots the relationship between smoothed rates of money growth and interest rates. Note that, although data set I contains 164 quarterly observations (that is, four observations for each of the 41 years from 1947 to 1987), we use a minimum of 32 observations from each of the two ends of the time series of this data set to guarantee that the two-sided exponentially weighted smoothing is sufficiently balanced. Note that, as Equation (6) is applied to the 164 observations, initially the smoothed value is influenced more by the future data and less by the past data. On the other hand, toward the end, it is influenced more by the past data and less by the future data. The selection of 32 observations from each side is somewhat arbitrary, but can be justified by both the low value of the weight $\beta^{32} = 0.95^{32} = 0.1937$ and the total number of observations. Increasing the number from 32 to say 50 (a weight of 0.077) changes the illustrations in only a minor way.

For Figures 3 and 4, we have calculated the linear regressions, standard errors and R-squared to give precise statistical expressions to the graphical illustrations. Respectively, for Figures 3 and 4, we have

$$\text{Inflation} = \underset{(0.0914)}{0.1406} + \underset{(0.0201)}{0.9359}\,(\text{Money}); \qquad R^2 = 0.9567;$$

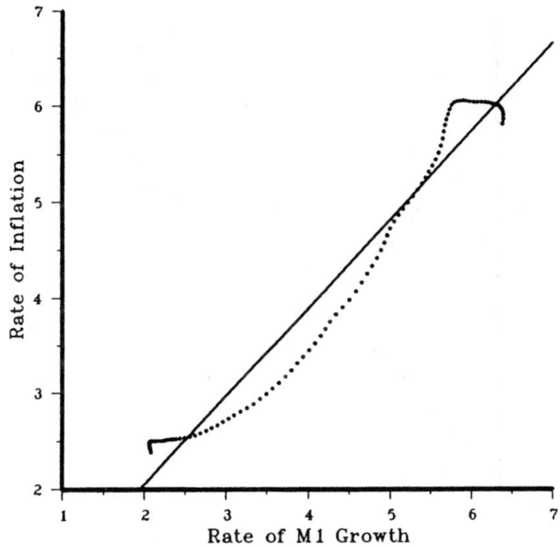

FIGURE 3. Inflation and money. Smoothed annual rate of change. Quarterly data (1955–1979). β = .95.

$$\text{Interest Rate} = \underset{(0.682)}{0.1128} + \underset{(0.0150)}{1.0557}\ \text{Money}; \qquad R^2 = 0.9806.$$

Figures 3 and 4 are very similar to the analogous ones in Lucas (1980) and illustrate that, for the period 1955–1979, long-run average smoothed changes in the rate of monetary growth generated almost equal longrun average smoothed changes in inflation and also in nominal interest rates. Similar results are presented in Malliaris (1988) using annual data for 1947–1987. Thus, the first goal of this paper is established by confirming the robustness of the earlier results of Lucas (1980) for a much longer period. In other words, we have given evidence, presented in Figures 3 and 4, in support of the quantity theory of money during the post-World War II period.

Next, we move on to our second goal. Analytically, using the same quarterly data and the same two-sided smoothing methodology, we now search for additional illustrations between monetary growth and real GNP growth. From a narrow, technical point of view, such illustrations cannot be labeled quantity theoretic. In its narrow tautological expression, the quantity theory of money assumes full employment, with money being unable to induce changes in real output. However, there is an enormous literature that focuses on the effects of nominal money changes on real output, and, because quantity theorists such as Friedman and Schwartz (1963, 1982) have studied this problem, we choose to analyze it under the quantity theoretic paradigm.

Blanchard (1987) gives a comprehensive survey on the evolution of ideas on the issue of money and output. According to him, the study of why money affects output can be separated historically in two periods: from Keynes to the early 1970s and the reconstruction effort from

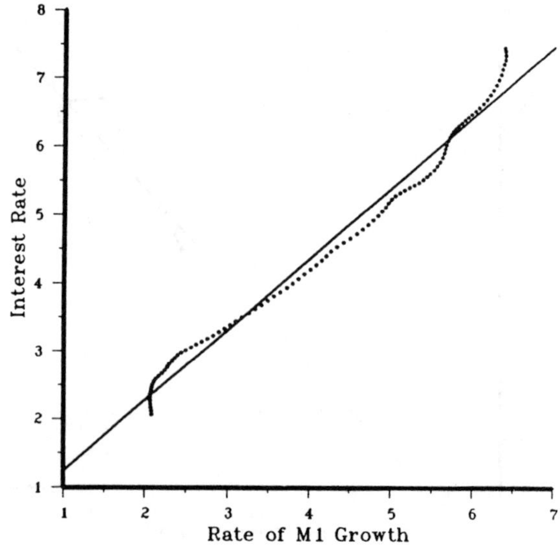

FIGURE 4. Interest rate and money. Smoothed annual rate of change. Quarterly data (1955–1979). $\beta = .95$.

the mid-1970s to present. His main conclusion is that substantial progress has been made in our understanding of the money-output relationship, but no grand synthesis is currently available. Our illustrations are quite interesting to encourage continued theoretical investigations toward such a synthesis.

As before, allowing for sufficient balance on both sides—that is, allowing for 32 observations on each side—Figure 5 is obtained. The relationship is given by the quadratic equation

$$\underset{(0.1261)}{\text{GNP} = 0.9298} + \underset{(0.0673)}{1.3665\,(\text{Money})} - \underset{(0.0081)}{0.1828\,(\text{Money})^2}; \qquad R^2 = 0.8947,$$

which implies that, during the period 1955–1979, real GNP growth was maximized at 3.48% when monetary growth was targeted at 3.74%. This gives an empirical illustration of Friedman's (1959) *k*% monetary growth rule. Actually whereas Friedman's *k*% money growth rate was motivated by the need for sufficient liquidity to support economic growth without inflation, Figure 5 unveils that such a rule, if chosen appropriately, could actually be associated with maximum output growth. Our results in Figure 5 are relevant to legislation recently introduced by U.S. Rep. Stephen Neal (House Joint Resolution 409) to direct the Federal Reserve to strive for price stability gradually over a five-year period, and maintain price stability thereafter for the purpose of achieving maximum sustainable growth, exactly as shown in Figure 5.

Obviously, the results in Figure 5 need to be appropriately qualified: they are derived from a period during which inflation was predominantly accelerating. Monetary growth, inflation and real growth are complicated dynamic processes which, during this period, had not reached long-run steady-state values. These actual dynamic processes of the post-World War

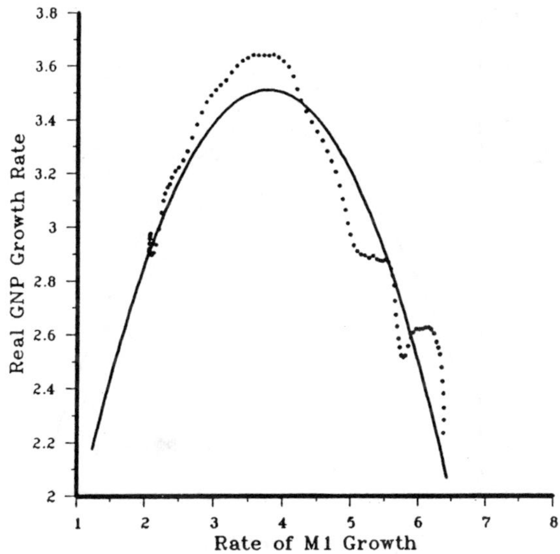

FIGURE 5. Real GNP and money. Smoothed annual rate of change. Quarterly data (1955–1979). β = .95.

II U.S. economic history do not tell us what would be the case if the corresponding rates of monetary growth were experienced as a steady state. Friedman (1988) suggests that the particular peak in Figure 5 may simply be a reflection of the point at which expectations adjusted sufficiently to the rates of monetary growth so as to produce an overshooting of price inflation relative to monetary growth. Readers may offer alternative interpretations of Figure 5.

Figure 6 plots smoothed rates of real GNP growth and nominal interest rates for the balanced subset 1955–1979. In view of the earlier, almost 45° line, illustrations between M and P and also between M and r in Figures 3 and 4, the pattern in Figure 6 is similar to the pattern in Figure 5.

Since inflation and nominal interest rates follow the behavior of the nominal money supply, their relation to real GNP growth is similar. As already noted, Friedman (1959) has detected this pattern and has advocated a rule of a constant rate of money growth around 4%. This rule seems to have two corollaries: real GNP growth is maximized when inflation is kept at $p\%$; and real GNP growth is maximized when interest rates are at $r\%$. Our illustrations give a precise reduced form relationship and identify the rate of money growth, and interest rates that are associated with maximum real growth. Obviously, the specific numbers are influenced by the specific sample period.

In summary, the quarterly data confirm the two illustrations of Lucas (1980) and also identify two additional illustrations, which are presented in Figures 5 and 6. In particular, the illustrations of these figures are interesting empirical evidence concerning the statistical and economic trade-offs that seem to exist between growth of real GNP on the one hand and either monetary growth or nominal short-term interest rates on the other. Although Friedman (1968) has argued in favor of the stabilizing role of monetary policy, Figures 5 and 6 provide

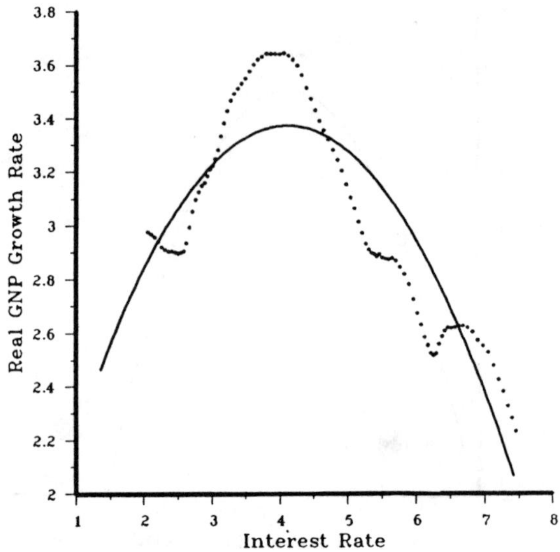

FIGURE 6. Real GNP and interest rate. Smoothed annual rate of change. Quarterly data (1955–1979). $\beta = .95$.

us with quantitative illustrations of his arguments. These illustrations of the quantity theory of money are both new and interesting.

V. ANNUAL ILLUSTRATIONS, 1867–1975

The annual data for 1867–1975 provide a comprehensive record of U.S. economic history. Numerous scholars such as Burns and Mitchell (1946), Abramovitz (1956), Friedman and Schwartz (1963a, 1982) and Moore (1950) have studied both qualitatively and quantitatively this period of the U.S. economy, which was characterized by dramatic population growth, technological advances, business and financial innovations, major labor movements and business cycles, a major economic depression and several wars.

Having reviewed several illustrations of the quantity theory of money in earlier sections, one wonders what kind of illustrations the long-time series 1867–1975 might reveal. This section presents the major results of various statistical calculations based on a smoothing β coefficient of 0.95 which is exactly the same as the one used for the annualized quarterly data in the previous section.

Figure 7 illustrates the relationship between the two-sided exponentially weighted moving averages of rates of monetary growth and price inflation. The methodology that yielded an approximate 45° line relation earlier now produces an irregular nonlinear pattern. Noting that smoothed data are plotted counter clockwise in Figure 7 we can interpret the relationship as having at least two major characteristics. First, the smoothed rate of change in monetary growth and inflation move in the same direction (they either both increase or both decrease),

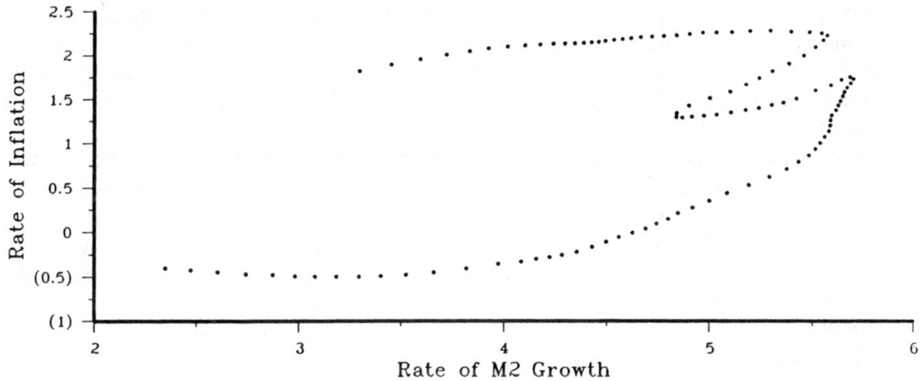

FIGURE 7. Inflation and money. Smoothed rate of change. Annual data (1867–1975). β = .95.

and, second, on the average, as time increases, a given rate of monetary growth becomes associated with a higher rate of inflation. In other words, Figure 7 shows a gradual structural change in the relationship between changes in the rate of change of money and of changes in price inflation. Although such a structural change is not predicted by the quantity theory of money, one could not use Figure 7 to refute the theory because the co-movements in these two variables still prevail.

Figure 8 shows the quantitative relationship between smoothed rates of change in the quantity of money to smoothed nominal interest rates. Again, the relationship depicted in Figure 8 has a shape similar to that of Figure 7. Notice, however, that the smoothed data are plotted clockwise (i.e., in the opposite direction to that shown in Figure 7). Although interest rates increase or decline as rates of change in the quantity of money increase or decline, respectively, it is an empirical phenomenon of the period 1867–1975 that a given change in the quantity of money is associated with a lower interest rate. This historical observation puts the economic experiences of the last decade in an appropriate long-term perspective.

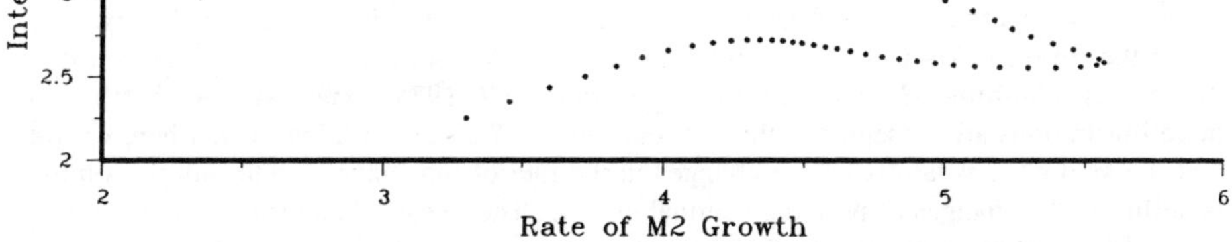

FIGURE 8. Interest rate and money. Smoothed rate of change. Annual data (1867–1975). β = .95.

Both Figures 7 and 8 plot all smoothed data. No matter how many observations are used from each end to give a better balance, the smoothing process does not uncover a linear path. Therefore, we chose to plot all smoothed data for the reader to show that, independent of how many points (from the beginning and the end of the plot) are removed, the final pattern remains complex.

There are two immediate explanations for such a complex pattern. First, the long-time data for the period 1867 to 1975 cover the years of the Great Depression and World War II. Second, the long 1867–1975 period can be divided into three subperiods: 1867 to 1879, the Greenback period; 1880 to 1940, the intermediate gold standard period; and 1940 to 1975, the most recent period, essentially studied in earlier sections. Extensive experimentation with these subperiods has failed to yield straightforward relationships.

Figures 7 and 8 demonstrate that the quantity theory of money holds only partially in predicting co-movements between certain variables. However, the remarkable changes that occurred in the economic structure over a century distort the linear relationship exhibited in Figures 3 and 4 for shorter periods. Can one conclude that the quantity theory of money holds for the long-run, say 20 to 40 years, but not for the very long-run, say 100 years? Dewald (1988) offers some suggestions on this important question by distinguishing between monetarism and the quantity theory of money. He argues that simplistic monetarism was widely interpreted as providing an alternative to short-run Keynesian economics and, as such, monetarism is not very useful. On the other hand, the quantity theory of money continues to play an important role by emphasizing useful long-run relationships among major economic variables. We agree with Dewald on the importance of the quantity theory of money and wish to qualify that some distinction should be made between the long-run (20 to 40 years) and the very long-run (100 years).

VI. BEHAVIOR OF VOLATILITIES

With the exception of Friedman and Schwartz (1963b) and Friedman (1984), the quantity theory of money—both in its historical development and in its various empirical studies—has little to say about the behavior of the volatility of its variables as measured by standard deviations. Since actual data show that the rates of change of money, real national income, velocity and inflation and also nominal interest rates exhibit variability, it is instructive to attempt to identify the behavior of such volatility.

In this section, we show some patterns of smoothed standard deviations. We follow Friedman and Schwartz (1963b) to compute standard deviations using four observations, and these standard deviations are smoothed using the two-sided exponentially weighted moving average method that has been our main statistical tool. Evans (1984) analyzes the effects on output of monetary growth and interest rate variability using a different methodology.

For the period 1947–1987, using quarterly data, we do not obtain any regular behavior of the various volatilities. However, for the long period 1867–1975, some results are better, and these illustrations are presented in the last four figures. We start with Figure 9, where we see that the smoothed volatility of the changes in the rate of monetary growth induces similar volatility in the changes of nominal national income. The linear relationship is good enough to satisfy the intuition of the quantity theorist and to reconfirm the findings of Friedman and Schwartz (1963b) and, more recently, of Friedman (1984). Figure 10 demonstrates that

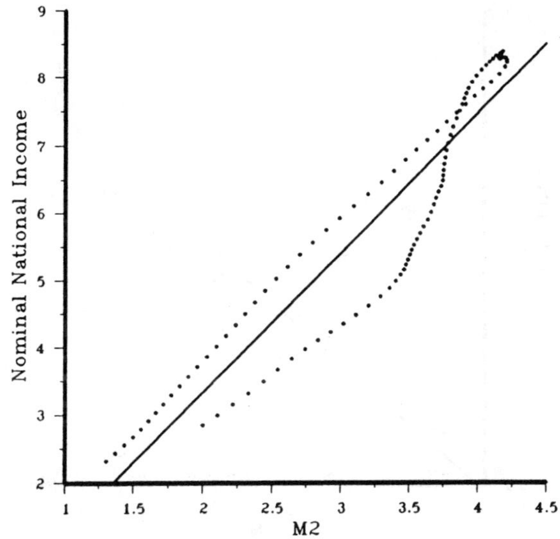

FIGURE 9. Nominal national income and money. Smoothed moving four-year standard deviations. Annual rate of change (1867–1975). $\beta = .95$.

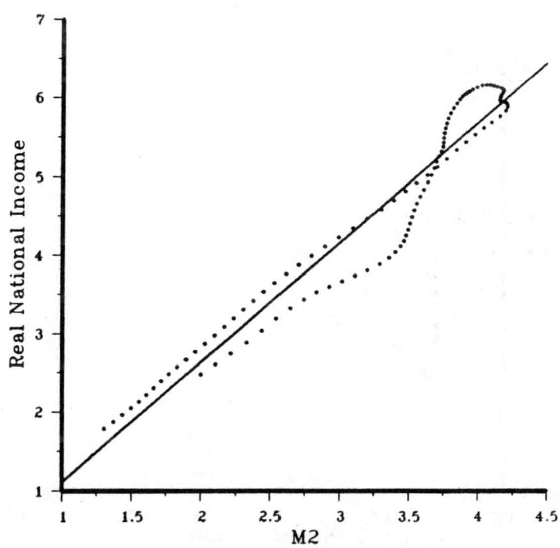

FIGURE 10. Real national income and money. Smoothed moving four-year standard deviations. Annual rate of change (1867–1975). $\beta = .95$.

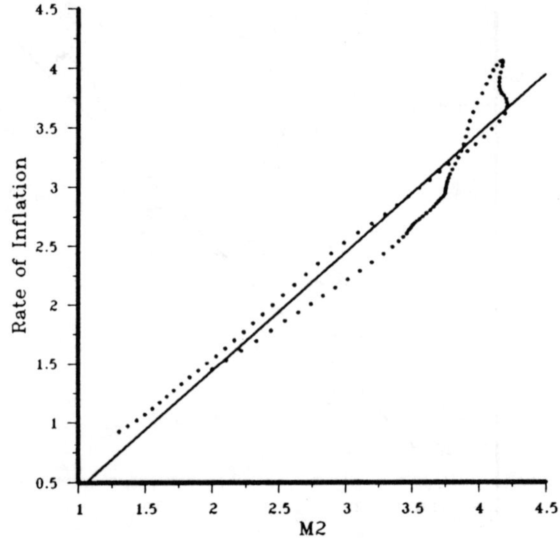

FIGURE 11. Inflation and money. Smoothed moving four-year standard deviations. Annual rate of change (1867–1975). β = .95.

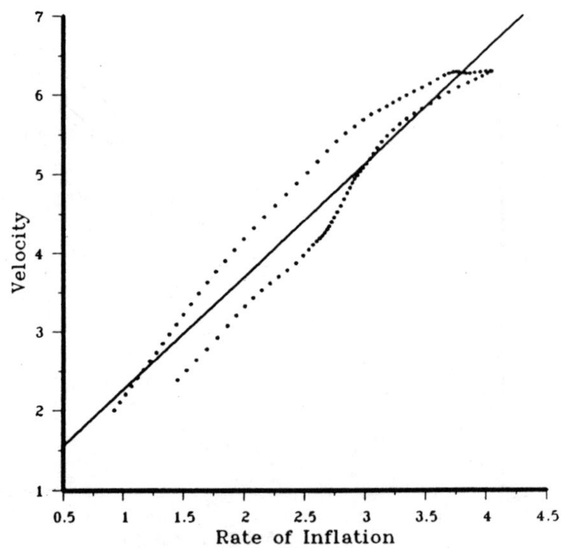

FIGURE 12. Velocity and inflation. Smoothed moving four-year standard deviations. Annual rate of change (1867–1975). β = .95.

volatilities in the rate of growth of money are associated with volatilities in the rate of growth of real national income. Finally, in Figures 11 and 12, we show two relationships: first, volatility in money growth translates to similar volatility in inflation; and, second, volatility in inflation is associated with volatility in the velocity of money.

VII. SUMMARY AND CONCLUSIONS

This paper presents several figures that involve the five quantity theoretic variables: rates of change in money supply, velocity, real output, inflation and also short-term nominal interest rates. Unlike earlier studies that employ primarily regression methods to identify statistical relationships, this paper uses the two-sided exponentially weighted moving average method. This method smooths the original data to various degrees depending on the values of a weight parameter β to identify trends and to exclude as much noise as possible. Two U.S. sets of data are used: intermediate-term quarterly data for 1947–1987, and long-term data for 1867–1975. These are four main findings:

First, the quarterly intermediate-term data confirm Lucas's (1980) findings that a given change in the rate of change in the quantity of money induces both an equal change in the rate of inflation and an equal change in short-run nominal interest rates.

Second, the intermediate-term data also show that a given change in the rate of change in the quantity of money or in nominal interest rates induces increases or decreases in the rate of change of real GNP depending on the initial level of these changes. These illustrations demonstrate that, during the post-World War II period, maximum real GNP growth is associated with a given level of monetary growth and with a given level of nominal interest rates.

Third, the long-term annual data identify nonlinear, complex relationships that do not confirm the earlier results. They show that quantity theoretic relationships do not prevail in their analytical forms over a century and that structural economic changes exert important influences. These empirical results require theoretical attention and should encourage economic theorists to supply analytical explanations.

Fourth, the volatility in the variables described by the long-term data has motivated an investigation into potential patterns. The illustrations demonstrate that some analytical patterns exist and are empirically quite specific. Even over a century, with changing patterns for the influence of monetary growth changes on inflation and nominal interest rates, the smoothed volatilities of monetary growth, nominal income, real income, inflation and velocity are highly correlated.

In conclusion, this study has investigated and confirmed several relationships among quantity theoretic variables using the technique of two-sided exponentially weighted smoothing. Two suggestions arise for future research. First, the results of the smoothing methodology must be evaluated by using various cointegration tests. Second, the deterministic dynamic quantity theory of money must be extended to the continuous time stochastic case.

ACKNOWLEDGMENTS

I happily acknowledge my intellectual debt to Professor Milton Friedman who helped me greatly with detailed written comments and suggestions on two earlier drafts. I am also thankful to William A. Brock, George Constantinides, George Kaufman, and Donald Meyer for stimulating discussions and encouragement and to Jack Potthast, Alexander Valvassori, Hang Chang and Wichai Saenghirunwattana for computational assistance. I also wish to thank an anonymous referee and the editors of this Journal for a detailed review that shaped the final version of this study. Earlier versions of this paper were presented at the Econometric Society Meetings, the Midwest Finance Association Meetings and seminars at Northwestern University, the Research Department of the Federal Reserve Bank of Chicago, The University of Oklahoma, The London School of Economics and the Third Symposium on Money, Banking and Insurance at the University of Karlsruhe, West Germany. I am grateful to several participants for helpful comments and I accept responsibility for any remaining errors. Finally, I am pleased to dedicate this study to Professor Milton Friedman on the occasion of his 79th birthday.

References

Abramovitz, Moses. 1956. "Resource and Output Trends in the United States Since 1870." *American Economic Review: Papers and Proceedings* 46: 5–23.

Blanchard, O.J. 1987. "Why Does Money Affect Output? A Survey." NBER Working Paper No. 2285. Cambridge, MA.

Burns, Arthur F., and Mitchell, W.C. 1946. *Measuring Business Cycles*. New York: NBER.

Dewald, William G. 1988. "Monetarism is Dead; Long Live the Quantity Theory." *Federal Reserve Bank of St. Louis Review* 70: 3–18.

Evans, Paul. 1984. "The Effects on Output of Money Growth and Interest Rate Volatility in the United States." *Journal of Political Economy* 92: 204–222.

Friedman, Milton. 1959. *A Program For Monetary Stability*. New York: Fordham University Press.

Friedman, Milton. 1968. "The Role of Monetary Policy." *American Economic Review* 58: 1–17.

Friedman, Milton. 1984. "Monetary Policy for the 1980s." Pp. 23–60 in *To Promote Prosperity*, edited by John H. Moore. California: Hoover Institute Press.

Friedman, Milton. 1987. "Quantity Theory of Money." *The New Palgrave: A Dictionary of Economics* 4: 3–20. New York: The Stockton Press.

Friedman, Milton. 1988. Private communication.

Friedman, Milton and Schwartz, Anna J. 1963a. *A Monetary History of the United States, 1867–1960*. Princeton, NJ: Princeton University Press.

Friedman, Milton and Schwartz, Anna J. 1963b. "Money and Business Cycles." *Review of Economics and Statistics* 45: 32–64.

Friedman, Milton and Schwartz, Anna J. 1982. *Monetary Trends in The United States and the United Kingdom*. Chicago: University of Chicago Press.

Gordon, Robert J. 1990. *Macroeconomics*. 5th Edition. Boston: Little, Brown.

Grandmont, Jean-Michel. 1983. *Money and Value*. New York: Cambridge University Press.

LeRoy, Stephen and Raymon, Neil. 1987. "A Monetarist Model of Inflation." *Journal of Economic Theory* 42: 275–310.

Lucas, Jr., Robert E. 1980. "Two Illustrations of the Quantity Theory of Money." *The American Economic Review* 70: 1005–1014.

Lucas, Jr., Robert E. 1986. "Adaptive Behavior and Economic Theory." *Journal of Business* 59: S401–S426.

Malliaris, A. G., and Brock, W. A. 1982. *Stochastic Methods in Economics and Finance*. New York: North-Holland.

Malliaris, A. G. 1987. "Economic Uncertainty: Its Continuous Modeling and Methodology." Pp. 107–

121 in *Economic Essays in Honor of Professor P. Christodoulopoulos*, edited by G. Bitros and C. Davos. Athens, Greece.

Malliaris, A. G. 1988. "Illustrations of the Quantity Theory of Money: Annual Data 1947–1987." Pp. 453–468 in *Symposium on Money, Banking and Insurance*, edited by W.R. Heilmann. Karlsruhe, West Germany.

McCallum, Bennett T. 1984. "On Low-Frequency Estimates of Long-Run Relationships in Macroeconomics." *Journal of Monetary Economics* 14: 3–14.

Mills, Terrence C. 1982. "Signal Extraction and Two Illustrations of the Quantity Theory." *American Economic Review* 72: 1162–1168.

Moore, Geoffrey H. 1980. *Business Cycles, Inflation, and Forecasting*. Cambridge, MA: Ballinger.

Mundell, Robert A. 1963. "Inflation and Real Interest." *Journal of Political Economy* 71: 280–283.

Sidrauski, M. 1967a. "Rational Choice and Patterns of Growth in a Monetary Economy." *American Economic Review: Papers and Proceedings* 57: 534–544.

Sidrauski, M. 1967b. "Inflation and Economic Growth." *Journal of Political Economy* 75: 796–810.

Whiteman, Charles H. 1984. "Lucas on Quantity Theory: Hypothesis Testing Without Theory." *American Economic Review* 74: 742–749.

Whittle. Peter. 1963. *Prediction and Regulation by Linear Least-Square Methods*. London, England: Van Nostrand-Reinhold.

European Journal of Political Economy 7 (1991) 275–298. North-Holland

Money, inflation and interest rates: Illustrations from twelve European economies*

A.G. Malliaris

Department of Economics, Loyola University of Chicago, 820 North Michigan Avenue, Chicago, IL 60611, USA

Silvana Stefani

Department of Mathematics, Faculty of Economics and Business, University of Brescia, Corso Mameli 27, 25122 Brescia, Italy

Accepted for publication March 1991

1. Introduction

Milton Friedman and Anna Schwartz (1963, 1982) have extensively studied the economic role of money in general, and more specifically, its impact on inflation, nominal GNP and nominal interest rates. Their first investigation concentrated on the United States economy, while Friedman and Schwartz (1982) studied both the U.S. and the United Kingdom economies.

Our paper is motivated by the work of Friedman and Schwartz (1963, 1982) and attempts to study the economic role of money in several European economies during the past four decades. More specifically, we investigate the impact of monetary growth on inflation and nominal interest rates for the following twelve European economies: Belgium, Denmark, Finland, France,

*We are grateful to Professor Milton Friedman for his numerous writings on similar topics and for his detailed comments on companion research. We also wish to acknowledge the competent research assistance of Wichai Saenghirunwattana and Magali Zuanon who helped with the data collection. This work has been partially supported by MPI 40% grant 'Teoria del Controllo e dei Sistemi in Economia' to Silvana Stefani. Finally, we thank an anonymous referee of this journal who suggested to consider certain critical econometric issues, not covered in an earlier version. All remaining errors are our responsibility.

0176-2680/91/$03.50

Greece, Italy, the Netherlands, Norway, Spain, Sweden, West Germany and the United Kingdom.

In contrast to Friedman and Schwartz who use regression analysis to study the role of money on inflation and nominal interest rates, in this paper we make use of the two-sided exponentially weighted moving average methodology discussed in Whittle (1963) and used recently by Lucas (1980, 1986) and also by Malliaris (1987, 1991) to illustrate the empirical content of the quantity theory of money. In particular we wish to explore if the results obtained by Lucas (1980) for the U.S. economy also hold for the twelve European countries in our sample.

The paper is organized in seven sections. Section 2 and 3 review the fundamental ideas of the quantity theory of money that are relevant in our study and outline the two-sided exponentially weighted moving average methodology. The data are described in section 4 and the graphical illustrations are presented and interpreted in section 5. Section 6 comments on issues of econometric cointegration to contrast our smoothing methodology to cointegration. A summary, further remarks and conclusions are collected in the last section.

2. Money, inflation, and interest rates

In this paper we study the empirical behavior of three macroeconomic variables: money supply, price level and nominal short term interest rates denoted by M, P and r. The first two variables are related by the well known quantity theory of money equation

$$MV = PY \tag{2.1}$$

where, V and Y denote velocity of money and real total output for a given time respectively. Following Friedman and Schwartz (1982, p. 16–72) eq. (2.1) results by equating the demand for money, M^d and a given supply M^s. Recall that

$$M^d = kPY \tag{2.2}$$

describes the Cambridge cash-balances approach to the demand of money with $k = 1/V$. Using the equilibrium condition $M^d = M^s$, eq. (2.2) and $M^s = M$ then yield (2.1).

Taking natural logarithms of (2.1) and then differentiating with respect to time we write

$$\dot{P}/P = (\dot{M}/M) + (\dot{V}/V) - (\dot{Y}/Y) \tag{2.3}$$

where a dot denotes the time derivative (d/dt).

At this elementary level, the introduction of nominal interest rates could be achieved by making use of the Fisher equation, where the nominal interest rate is the sum of the real rate of interest plus the anticipated rate of inflation with the latter being expressed by the actual inflation $\dot{P}/P$ obtained from (2.3). The implicit assumptions are that the economy is at full employment with a constant real rate of interest, and also that expected inflation is obtained from the smoothing technique described in the next section.

Thus, the quantity theoretic background of this study involves eq. (2.3) and its connection to nominal interest rates via Fisher's equation. More specifically we are interested in investigating the two central implications of the quantity theory of money studied by Lucas (1980) to determine whether these implications hold for the twelve European economies. These two central implications refer to the notion that a given change in the rate of monetary growth induces, first, an equal change in the rate of price inflation and, second, an equal change in nominal interest rates.

Beyond the elementary quantity theory of money, the monetary growth models of Sidrauski (1967a, b) and others can be used to justify associating rates of change of the quantity of money to rates of change in inflation and to changes in nominal rates of interest. Actually, in the Sidrauski neoclassical monetary growth model, a given change in monetary expansion and its consequences on inflation and interest rates is treated explicitly in the steady state solution of the system of differential equations.

The Sidrauski monetary model does not treat the Mundell–Tobin effect. According to Mundell (1963) the nominal rate of interest rises by less than the rate of inflation and therefore the real rate of interest falls during periods of inflation. The result is based on the fact that inflation reduces real money balances and the resulting decline in wealth stimulates increased saving. Whiteman (1984) develops a model that isolates the Mundell–Tobin effect and claims that the Lucas (1980) results are not necessarily evidence against the Mundel–Tobin effect. In this paper we do not make any claims about the Mundell–Tobin effect.

To sum up, the analytical background of this study involves the traditional notions of the quantity theory of money and its connection to nominal interest rates via Fisher's equation. Such a background may be found in Friedman (1987) or Dewald (1988). At an advanced analytical level, the quantity theory of money remains a controversial area of research. LeRoy and Raymon (1987) survey numerous papers on money and inflation and also develop a monetarist model to conclude that the theoretical foundations of the quantity theory of money are presently nonexistent.

On the other hand, Grandmont (1983) reconsiders classical and neoclassical monetary theories using a general equilibrium approach to clarify the foundations of the neutrality of money. Therefore, readers may find these illustrations as examples of the quantity theoretic relationships, that are obtained from statistical methods. We emphasize, following Lucas (1980), that our graphs are only illustrations, as opposed to statistical tests of theoretically derived null hypotheses with specified alternative hypotheses.

3. Methodology

Suppose that for a given country we have annual time series for money supply M_t, price level P_t and nominal short term interest rates r_t. For two of these time series we work with rates of change as follows:

$$m_t \equiv [\ln(M_t) - \ln(M_{t-1})] \times 100,$$

$$p_t \equiv [\ln(P_t) - \ln(P_{t-1})] \times 100.$$

For a given time series X_t, the two-sided exponentially weighted moving average is defined as

$$X_t(\beta) = \frac{1-\beta}{1+\beta} \sum_{k=-\infty}^{\infty} \beta^{|k|} X_{t+k} \tag{3.1}$$

for $0 \leqq \beta \leqq 1$. When $\beta = 0$ we obtain the original scatter diagram and when $\beta = 1$ everything collapses to the origin. The actual effect of (3.1) is to smooth the original series and after extensive calculations we report results that correspond to $\beta = 0.95$. This is similar to Lucas (1980) who shows that the illustrations improve as β increases to 0.95. This means that the $X_t(0.95)$ of (3.1) are very close to the sample average values of the original series which capture the long-term character of the quantity theory relationships. Note that (3.1) is applied to m_t, p_t and r_t respectively.

After the original time series are smoothed, the pairs $[m_t(0.95), p_t(0.95)]$ and $[m_t(0.95), r_t(0.95)]$ of the two-sided exponentially weighted moving averages are plotted to yield an illustration of the quantity theory of money. The various plots of filtered paired observations are also expressed statistically using regression analysis. The only purpose these regressions serve is to give numerical expressions of the long run relationships between quantity theoretic variables.

Whittle (1963), Lucas (1980), Mills (1982) and Whiteman (1984) develop in detail the statistical properties of the two-sided exponentially weighted moving average methodology with agreement that such methodology is a reasonable technique for capturing *long run behavior*, where the long run is modeled by the signal, low-frequency characteristics of a given series. As

Friedman and Schwartz (1982, p. 8) have concluded 'it takes a considerable time, measured in phases, not months or quarters, before a change in the rate of monetary growth is fully reflected in prices'. Of course, reduced form correlations described in our illustrations are complicated functions of both the real economy and the laws of the relevant time series, neither of which is explicitly modeled.

This is precisely the reason why we use the characterization of quantity theoretic illustrations instead of evidence. McCallum (1984) emphasizes that one could not use long periodicity aspects of the time series to prove long run economic relationships. We agree with McCallum (1984, p. 13) that low-frequency measures are not designed to reflect the distinction between anticipated and unanticipated fluctuations. In this paper we do not argue that our results will prove well specified dynamic models, but more modestly we only contribute through graphical illustrations to the ongoing quantity theoretic research. Recently, Lucas (1986) returned to these quantity theoretic illustrations to exposit the use of rationality and adaptation in economic theory.

To further illustrate the mechanics of (3.1) and to substantiate the comments in the next section suppose that we have two time series generated by

$$x_t = \rho x_{t-1} + e_t, \tag{3.2}$$

$$y_t = x_t + \varepsilon_t, \tag{3.3}$$

with $0 \leqq \rho \leqq 1$ and both e_t and ε_t being normally distributed with mean zero and variances σ_e^2 and σ_ε^2.

The system (3.2)–(3.3) may be interpreted as follows. First, assume that both x_t and y_t denote rates of change. Second, (3.3) denotes that y_t depends on x_t. Third, for the purpose of clarification let x_t denote money growth and let y_t denote inflation or deflation. The system (3.2)–(3.3) says that monetary authorities try to control the current rate of money supply growth at ρx_{t-1} but the actual rate x_t is also affected by shocks e_t. Agents anticipate the money supply growth x_t to directly influence current inflation but the actual inflation y_t is also affected by random shocks ε_t.

If the variance of the noise ε_t is small relative to the variance of the noise e_t, this means that the current observation of inflation measured by y_t is a good estimate of the signal x_t. Therefore, in this case, the current quantity theoretic forces, x_t, dominate the other real forces denoted by ε_t and very little smoothing is necessary to uncover the relationship between x_t and y_t. On the other hand, if the noise variance ε_t is high, the smoothing parameter β will be near one and the best estimate of the true signal x_t will be a very long moving average of y_r.

4. The data

The main source of our data has been the *International Financial Statistics*, various issues. This is obviously a secondary source because it compiles its data from numerous national business publications. However it is considered highly reliable. For twelve European countries we have collected, if available, yearly data on money supply, rate of inflation and short term nominal interest rates. Money supply figures are in local currency. We were unable to collect short term nominal interest rates for Denmark, Finland, and Greece. The period studied is 1950 to 1986 with shorter periods for some countries due to data nonavailability.

5. Illustrations

In this section we present two sets of graphical illustrations of the quantity theory of money. Using the two-sided exponentially weighted moving average methodology we have experimented with various beta coefficients. The illustrations presented were obtained using $\beta=0.95$. The economic meaning of such a high beta is that the data are noisy and only the average of a long series captures long term trends. It is interesting to note that Lucas (1980) and Malliaris (1987) also concuded that $\beta=0.95$ is most appropriate in smoothing out U.S. data.

To contrast the unsmoothed and the smoothed data we show in fig. 1 unsmoothed data for rates of growth of money supply and inflation for the United Kingdom 1950–1986. As expected there is no clear pattern in this scatter diagram. On the other hand, the subsequent 12 diagrams illustrate an emerging pattern for smoothed rates of money growth and inflation. Although the pattern for these twelve European countries is not identically the same, it nevertheless exhibits a general behavior: namely a linear and positive relationship between smoothed rates of money supply growth and smoothed rates of inflation. For economies at or near full employment, the quantity theorist would expect a permanent 1% increase in the growth of money supply to result in a 1% increase in inflation. Our empirical results for the twelve European countries do not conform to this pure version of the quantity theory of money because none of these countries were at or near full employment during the period 1950–1986. However, both the graphical illustrations and the summary regressions in table 1 show two important results.

First, for all countries a positive relationship exists between smoothed rates of money supply growth and smoothed inflation. Second, with the exception of two countries, France and West Germany, the remaining ten countries demonstrate at least a 0.63% increase in long run average inflation resulting from a 1% permanent increase in the country's money supply.

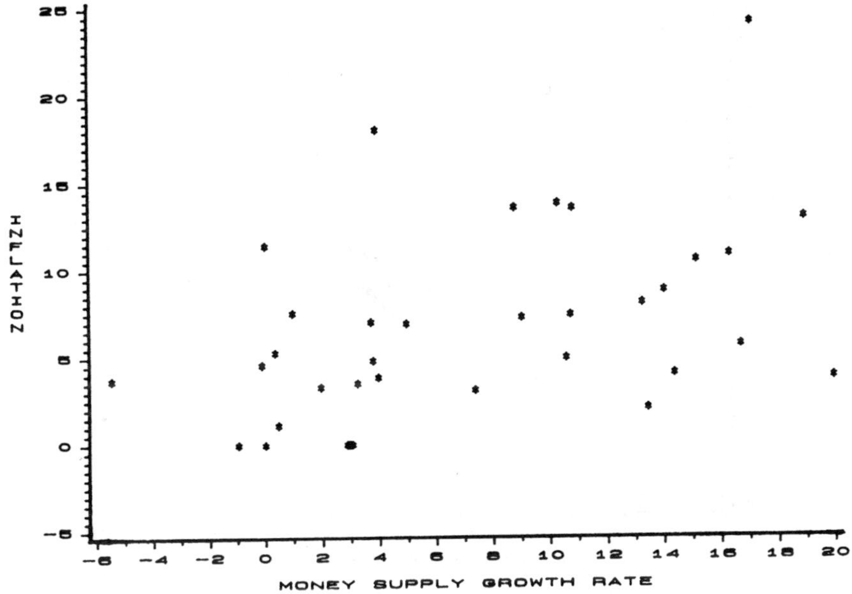

Fig. 1. Unsmoothed rate of change of annual data (1950–1986); $\beta = 0.00$; United Kingdom.

These two observations give support to the claim that inflation and money supply growth are positively correlated, as was found by Lucas (1980) for the U.S. Note that table 1 contains standard errors, if the reader is interested in the significance of the coefficients reported.

Figs. 14–22 and table 2 refer to the relationships between smoothed rates of money supply growth and smoothed nominal interest rates for the nine European countries. As already mentioned, data were not available for Denmark, Finland and Greece. Standard errors are in parentheses.

Although scatter diagrams for the unsmoothed variables are not presented, it is easy to visualize that no evident pattern could be identified. The smoothing process allows the emergence of a pattern which as in the case of money-inflation, is positive. Again, despite many structural and regulatory differences among these nine countries, it is important to note that the quantity theoretic prediction of increases in money growth eventually generating increases in nominal interest rates, holds true. For all nine countries, the coefficient of the slope between smoothed money growth and smoothed nominal interest rates is positive and at least 0.33, with the exception of Spain which has a coefficient of 0.1982. Note however from the graphs and also from the R-squared of these regressions that linear relationships are not the most appropriate, certainly in the case of Spain, West Germany, France and Italy. A nice linear pattern, however, holds for

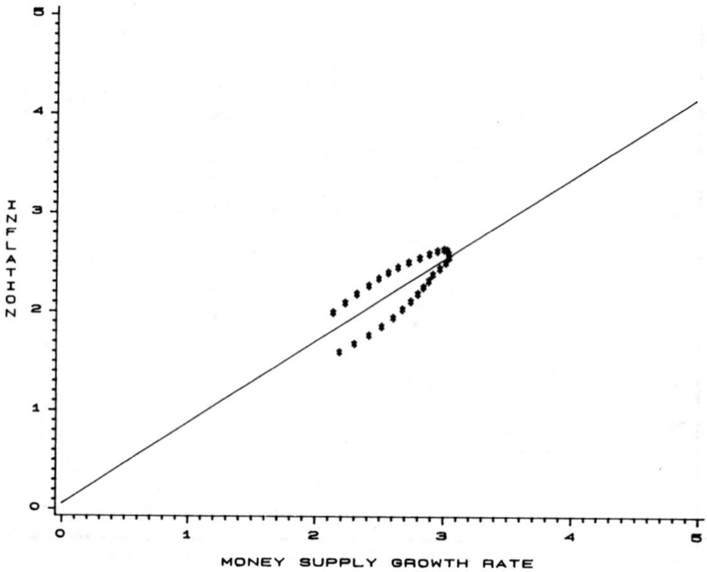

INFLATION = .0570 + .8252(MONEY GROWTH)
R-SQUARE = .6018

Fig. 2. Smoothed rate of change of annual data (1959–1986); $\beta=0.95$; Belgium.

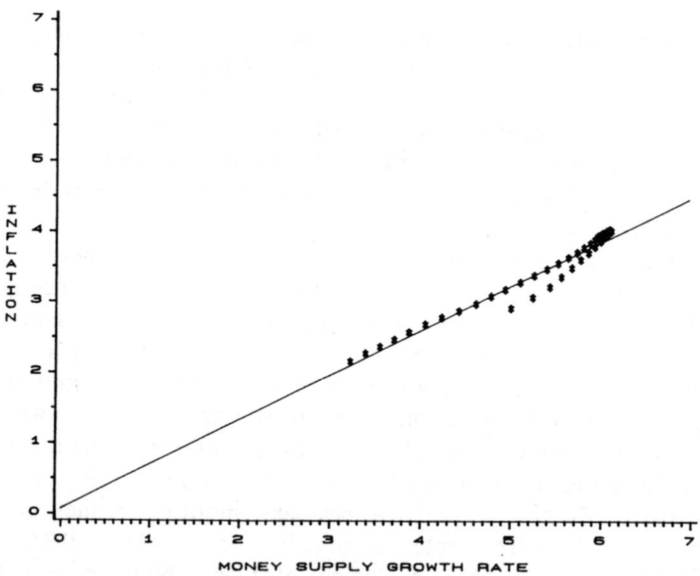

INFLATION = .0744 + .6325(MONEY GROWTH)
R-SQUARE = .9577

Fig. 3. Smoothed rate of change of annual data (1950–1986); $\beta=0.95$; Denmark.

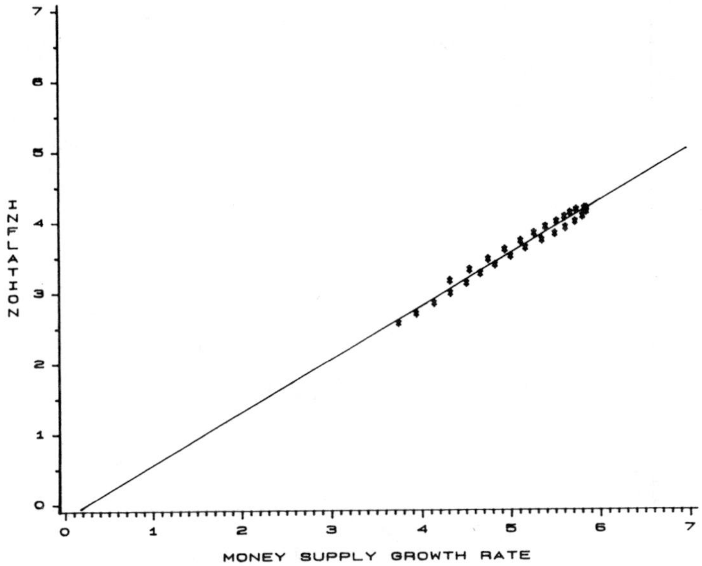

INFLATION = −0.1806 + .7456(MONEY GROWTH)
R-SQUARE = .9751

Fig. 4. Smoothed rate of change of annual data (1959–1986); $\beta = 0.95$; Finland.

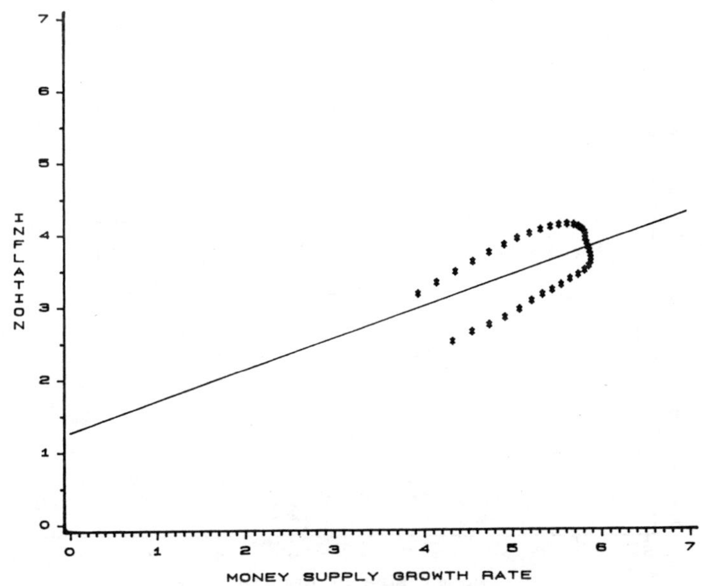

INFLATION = 1.2782 + .4316(MONEY GROWTH)
R-SQUARE = .2924

Fig. 5. Smoothed rate of change of annual data (1950–1986); $\beta = 0.95$; France.

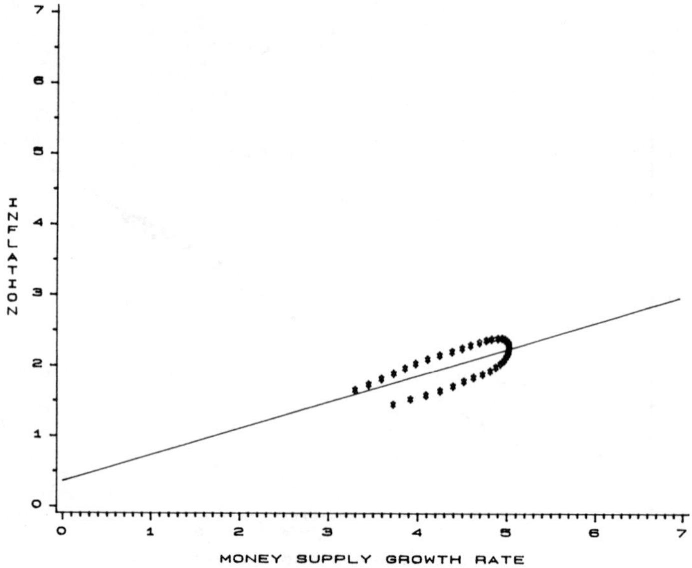

INFLATION = .3625 + .3741(MONEY GROWTH)
R-SQUARE = .4949

Fig. 6. Smoothed rate of change of annual data (1950–1986); $\beta = 0.95$; Germany.

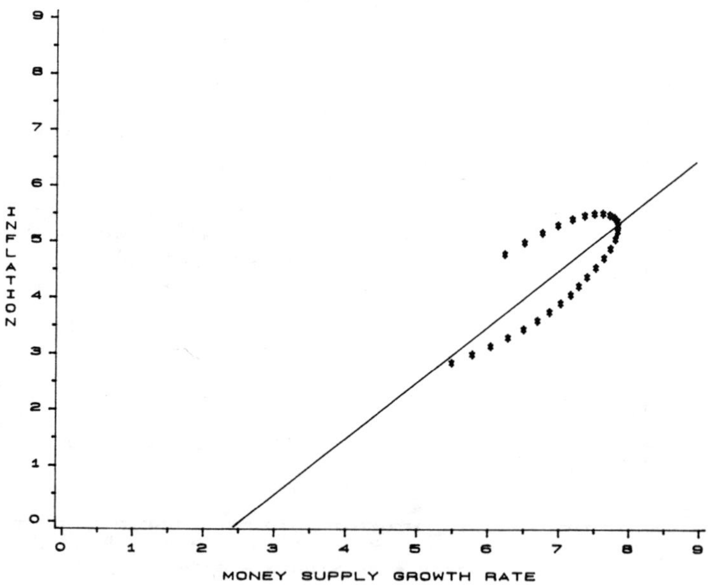

INFLATION = −2.5143 + 1.0014(MONEY GROWTH)
R-SQUARE = .5939

Fig. 7. Smoothed rate of change of annual data (1959–1986); $\beta = 0.95$; Greece.

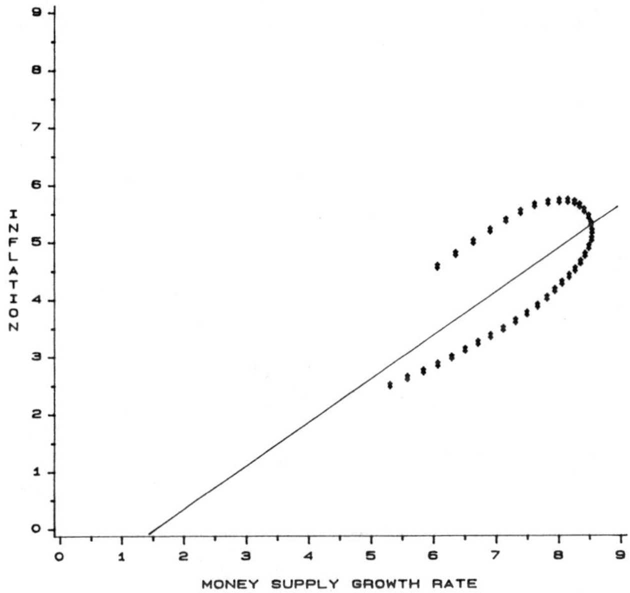

INFLATION = −1.1636 + .7561(MONEY GROWTH)
R-SQUARE = .4949

Fig. 8. Smoothed rate of change of annual data (1950–1986); $\beta = 0.95$; Italy.

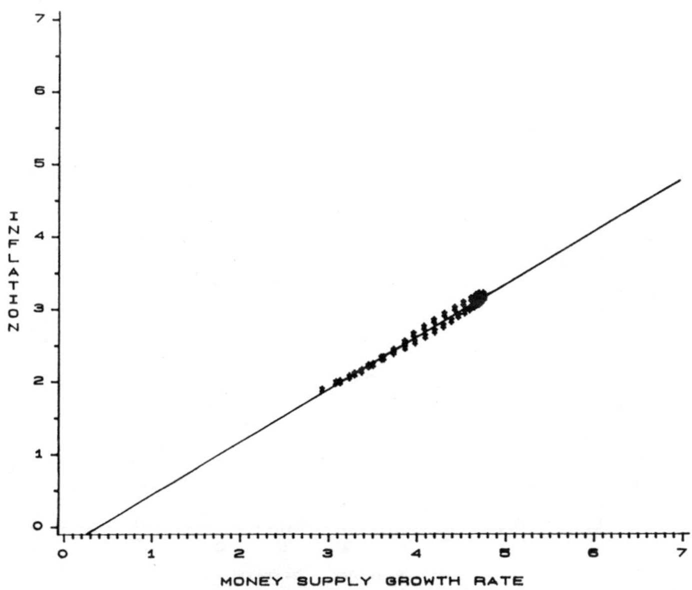

INFLATION = −0.2745 + .7256(MONEY GROWTH)
R-SQUARE = .9837

Fig. 9. Smoothed rate of change of annual data (1950–1986); $\beta = 0.95$; Netherlands.

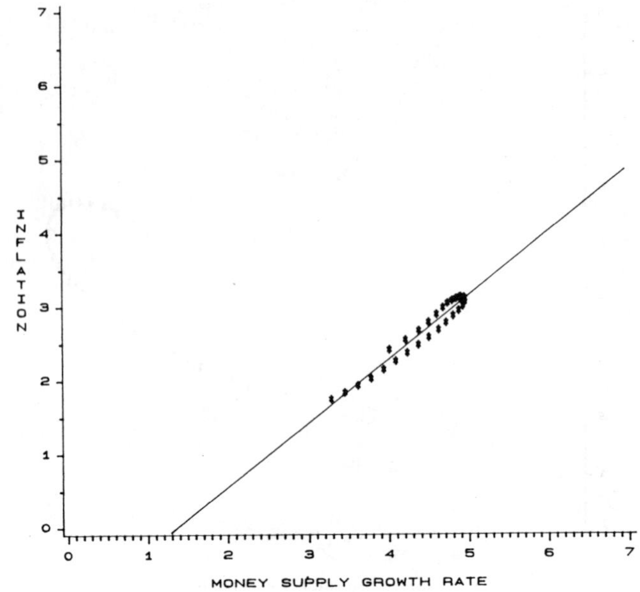

INFLATION = −1.1743 + .8644(MONEY GROWTH)
R-SQUARE = .9521

Fig. 10. Smoothed rate of change of annual data (1959–1986); $\beta = 0.95$; Norway.

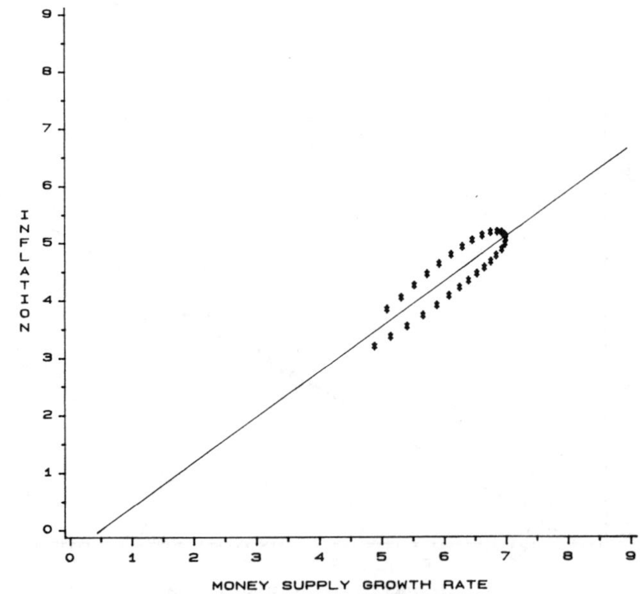

INFLATION = −0.3838 + .7849(MONEY GROWTH)
R-SQUARE = .7711

Fig. 11. Smoothed rate of change of annual data (1959–1986); $\beta = 0.95$; Spain.

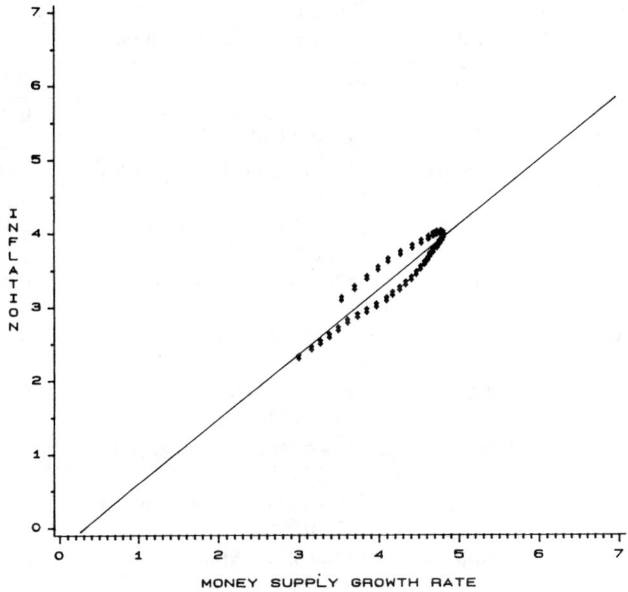

INFLATION = -0.2732 + .8763(MONEY GROWTH)
R-SQUARE = .8774

Fig. 12. Smoothed rate of change of annual data (1950–1986); $\beta=0.95$; Sweden.

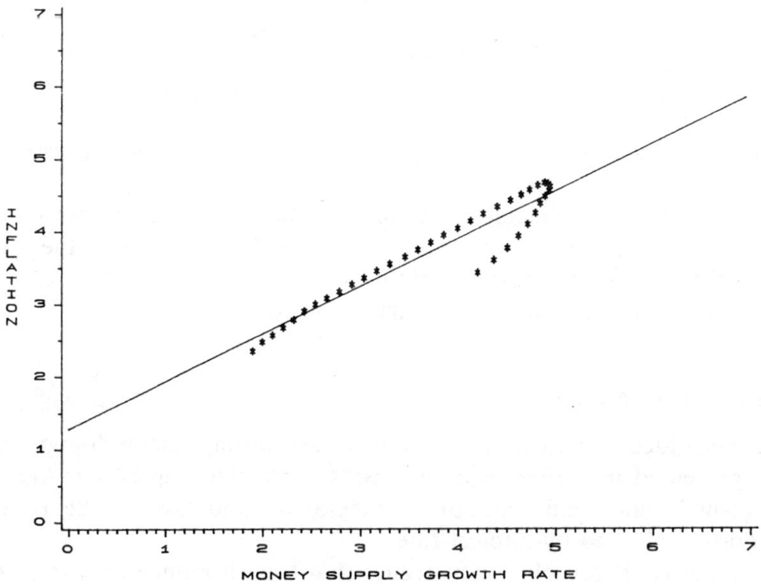

INFLATION = 1.2832 + .6537(MONEY GROWTH)
R-SQUARE = .9094

Fig. 13. Smoothed rate of change of annual data (1950–1986); $\beta=0.95$; United Kingdom.

Table 1
Smoothed rates of money growth and inflation.

Country	Regression equation	R-Squared
Belgium	Inflation = 0.0570 + 0.8252 (Money growth) (0.3547) (0.1316)	0.6018
Denmark	Inflation = 0.0744 + 0.6325 (Money growth) (0.1191) (0.0225)	0.9577
Finland	Inflation = −0.1806 + 0.7456 (Money growth) (0.1198) (0.0234)	0.9751
France	Inflation = 1.2782 + 0.4317 (Money growth) (0.6070) (0.1135)	0.2924
Germany (West)	Inflation = 0.3625 + 0.3741 (Money growth) (0.2894) (0.0639)	0.4949
Greece	Inflation = −2.5143 + 1.0014 (Money growth) (1.1540) (0.1624)	0.5939
Italy	Inflation = −1.1636 + 0.7561 (Money growth) (0.9680) (0.1291)	0.4949
Netherlands	Inflation = −0.2745 + 0.7256 (Money growth) (0.0647) (0.0158)	0.9837
Norway	Inflation = −1.1743 + 0.8644 (Money growth) (0.1700) (0.0380)	0.9521
Spain	Inflation = −0.3838 + 0.7849 (Money growth) (0.3234) (0.0839)	0.7711
Sweden	Inflation = −0.2732 + 0.8763 (Money growth) (0.2340) (0.0554)	0.8774
United Kingdom	Inflation = 1.2832 + 0.6537 (Money growth) (0.1366) (0.0349)	0.9094

the United Kingdom which is similar to that found by Lucas (1980) for the U.S.

One reasonable conclusion of the investigation between smoothed rates of growth of money supply and nominal interest rates is that the quantity theoretic prediction of a positive relationship holds, albeit such a relationship is not necessarily linear for the countries studied.

6. Tests of cointegration

The two-sided exponentially weighted smoothing methodology and its results presented in earlier sections raise an interesting question. Are money stock growth rates and inflation cointegrated[1] and how is the process of cointegration affected by interest rates?

The quantity theory of money argues that even if money growth rates and

[1]We are grateful to an anonymous referee for encouraging us to investigate aspects of cointegration between our variables.

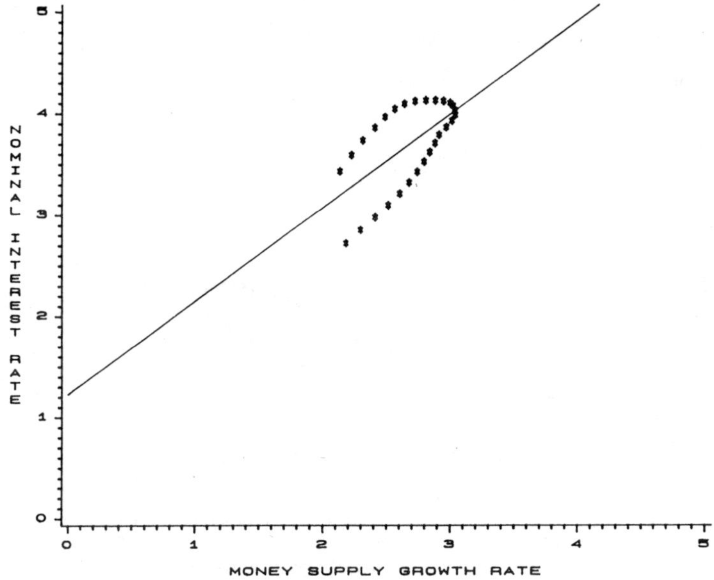

INTEREST RATE = 1.2289 + .9174(MONEY GROWTH)
R-SQUARE = .3871

Fig. 14. Smoothed rate of change of annual data (1959–1986); $\beta = 0.95$; Belgium.

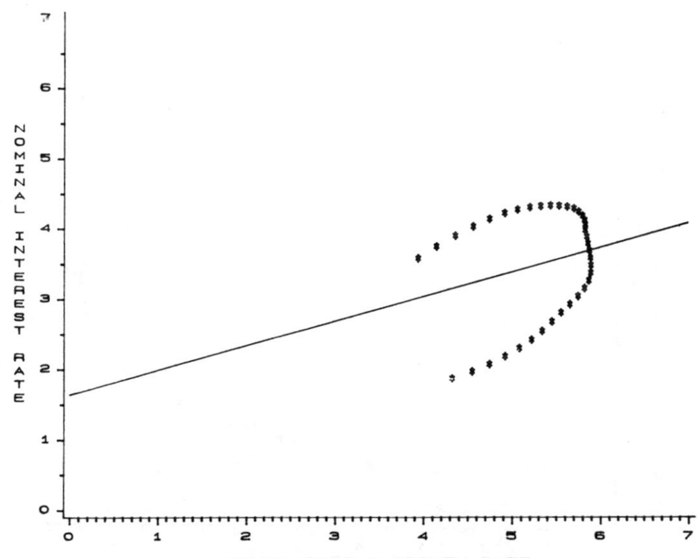

INTEREST RATE = 1.6440 + .3475(MONEY GROWTH)
R-SQUARE = .0637

Fig. 15. Smoothed rate of change of annual data (1950–1986); $\beta = 0.95$; France.

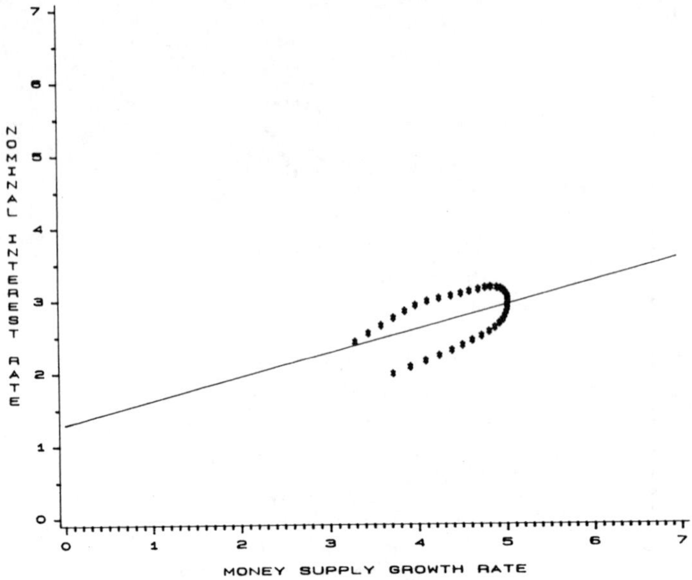

INTEREST RATE = 1.2979 + .3261(MONEY GROWTH)
R-SQUARE = .2459

Fig. 16. Smoothed rate of change of annual data (1950–1986); $\beta = 0.95$; Germany.

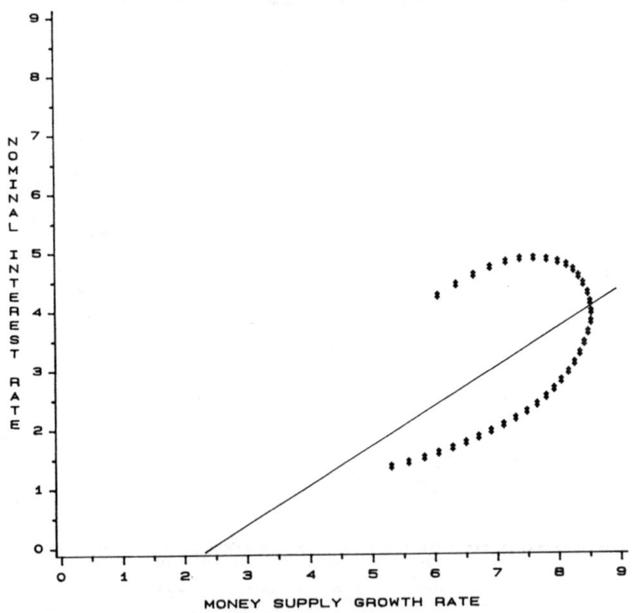

INTEREST RATE = −1.6011 + .6631(MONEY GROWTH)
R-SQUARE = .2596

Fig. 17. Smoothed rate of change of annual data (1950–1986); $\beta = 0.95$; Italy.

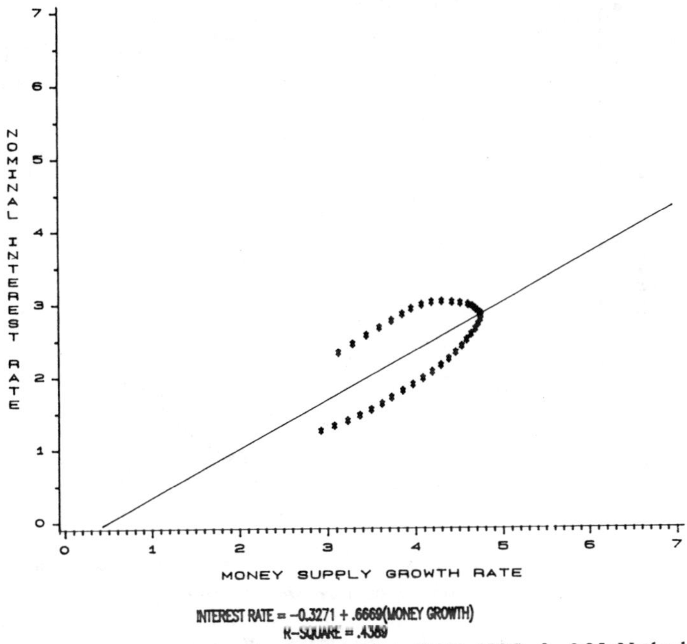

Fig. 18. Smoothed rate of change of annual data (1950–1986); $\beta = 0.95$; Netherlands.

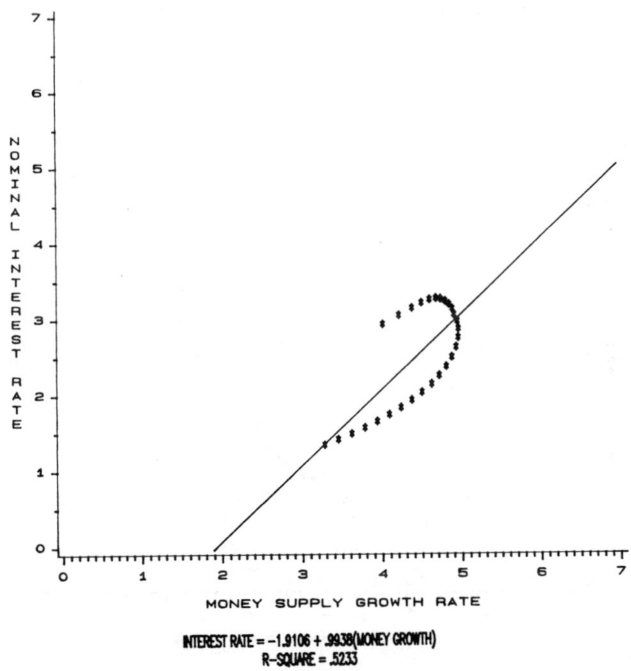

Fig. 19. Smoothed rate of change of annual data (1959–1986); $\beta = 0.95$; Norway.

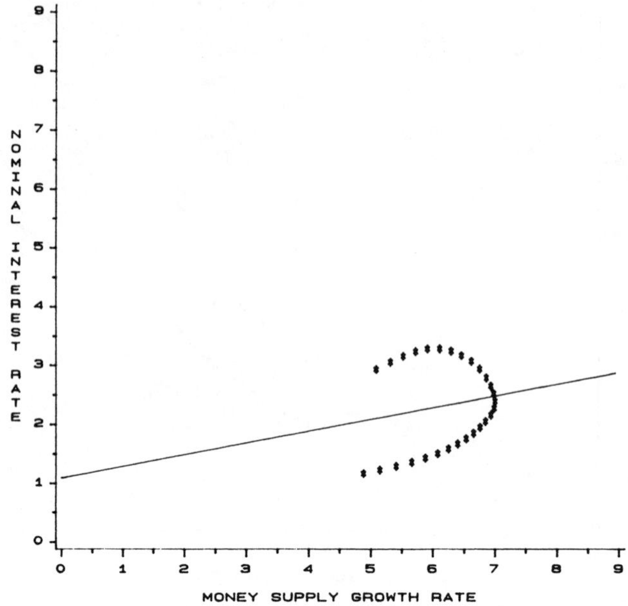

INTEREST RATE = 1.0944 + .1962(MONEY GROWTH)
R-SQUARE = .0308

Fig. 20. Smoothed rate of change of annual data (1959–1986); $\beta = 0.95$; Spain.

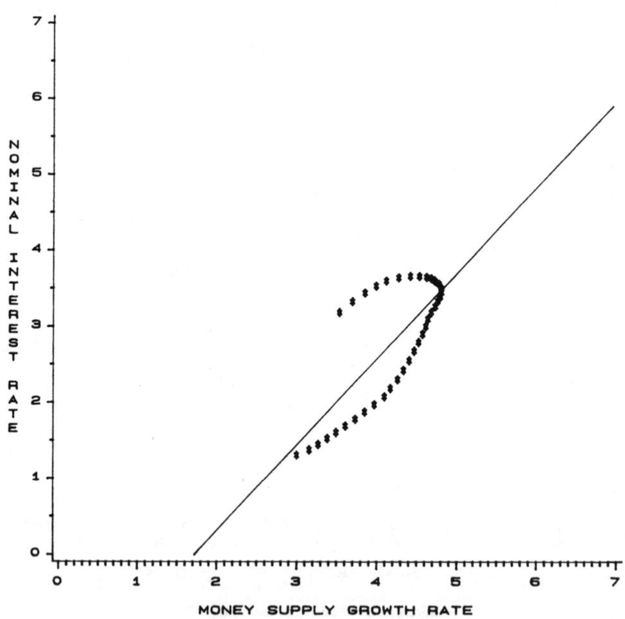

INTEREST RATE = −1.9358 + 1.1264(MONEY GROWTH)
R-SQUARE = .5512

Fig. 21. Smoothed rate of change of annual data (1959–1986); $\beta = 0.95$; Sweden.

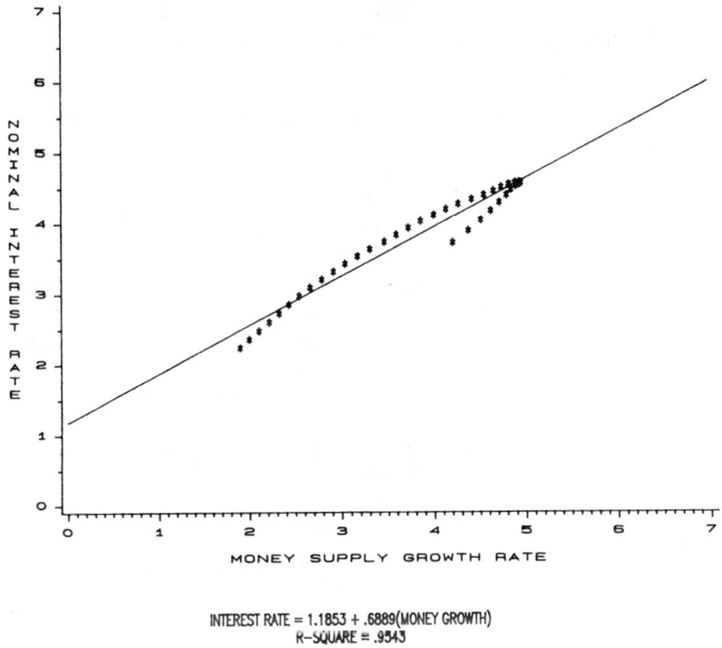

Fig. 22. Smoothed rate of change of annual data (1950–1986); $\beta=0.95$; United Kingdom.

inflation wander extensively as independent time series, they are expected not to drift too far apart. The smoothing methodology of section 3 is one way to capture the tendency for money growth rates and inflation or for money growth rate and nominal interest rates to move together. Another methodology that tests whether two random walk processes actually are influenced by economic forces that keep them together is cointegration.

In this section we test for cointegration between money growth rates and inflation and also between rates of monetary growth and nominal interest rates. Because our primary purpose as stated in the introduction is to extend Lucas's (1980) methodology and results to the twelve European economies, our analysis on cointegration is brief.

Engle and Granger (1987) propose several test statistics for testing the null hypothesis of no-cointegration. In this paper we use the Dickey–Fuller test which is more powerful than other simpler tests, such as the Durbin–Watson test.[2]

[2]In companion research we use both the Durbin–Watson test on the Dickey–Fuller test with sufficient evidence that the latter is more powerful. For details see Malliaris and Urrutia (1991).

Table 2
Smoothed rates of money growth and interest rates.

Country	Regression equation	R-Squared
Belgium	Interest rate = 1.2289 + 0.9174 (Money growth) (0.6100) (0.2264)	0.3871
France	Interest rate = 1.6440 + 0.3475 (Money growth) (1.2038) (0.2251)	0.0637
Germany (West)	Interest rate = 1.2979 + 0.3261 (Money growth) (0.4373) (0.0965)	0.2459
Italy	Interest rate = − 1.6011 + 0.6631 (Money growth) (1.4191) (0.1893)	0.2596
Netherlands	Interest rate = −0.3271 + 0.6669 (Money growth) (0.5231) (0.1275)	0.4389
Norway	Interest rate = − 1.9106 + 0.9938 (Money growth) (0.8318) (0.1850)	0.5233
Spain	Interest rate = 1.0944 + 0.1982 (Money growth) (1.3618) (0.2182)	0.0308
Sweden	Interest rate = − 1.9358 + 1.1264 (Money growth) (0.7263) (0.1718)	0.5512
United Kingdom	Interest rate = 1.1853 + 0,6889 (Money growth) (0.0998) (0.0255)	0.9543

The Dickey and Fuller test of cointegration consists of first running the two cointegration equations

$$p_t = a_0 + a_1 m_t + \varepsilon_t, \tag{6.1}$$

$$r_t = b_0 + b_1 m_t + \theta_t, \tag{6.2}$$

and then also running the following auxiliary Dickey and Fuller regressions on the residuals:

$$\varepsilon_t - \varepsilon_{t-1} = -\alpha\varepsilon_{t-1} + u_t, \tag{6.3}$$

$$\theta_t - \theta_{t-1} = -\beta\theta_{t-1} + v_t. \tag{6.4}$$

The null hypothesis is H_0: $\alpha = 0$, that is, money growth rates and inflation are not cointegrated, and also H_0: $\beta = 0$, that is, money growth rates and interest rates are not cointegrated.

Table 3 exhibits the results of the Dickey–Fuller test of cointegration. Observe that the results are mixed for the case of money growth and inflation. For six countries, namely Belgium, Greece, Italy, Norway, Spain and the United Kingdom the null hypothesis of no cointegration cannot be rejected. On the other hand, for Denmark, Finland, France, Germany, the

Table 3
Dickey–Fuller tests of cointegration.
Cointegration equations: $p_t = a_0 + a_1 m_t + \varepsilon_t$, $r_t = b_0 + b_1 m_t + \theta_t$

Dickey and Fuller regression: $\varepsilon_t - \varepsilon_{t-1} = -\alpha\varepsilon_{t-1} + u_t$, $\theta_t - \theta_{t-1} = -\beta\theta_{t-1} + v_t$

Country	α	β
Belgium	0.392872 (0.160483)(2.448)	0.23014 (0.117104)(1.965)
Denmark	0.569448 (0.157838)(3.608)*	n/a
Finland	0.644337 (0.169539)(3.801)*	n/a
France	0.75278 (0.159498)(4.72)*	0.178555 (0.110304)(1.619)
Germany	0.767646 (0.158149)(4.854)*	0.44989 (0.14140)(3.182)
Greece	0.386437 (0.15788)(2.448)	n/a
Italy	0.365858 (0.134468)(2.721)	0.422989 (0.174749)(2.421)
Netherlands	0.653346 (0.161347)(4.049)*	0.197766 (0.113177)(1.747)
Norway	0.533657 (0.184897)(2.886)	0.1976594 (0.140384)(1.408)
Spain	0.302278 (0.145232)(2.081)	1.075812 (0.354282)(3.037)
Sweden	0.703911 (0.154154)(4.566)*	0.2571778 (0.137043)(1.877)
United Kingdom	0.510267 (0.15941)(3.201)	0.517448 (0.151682)(3.411)*

The Dickey–Fuller critical value at 5% is 3.37 obtained from Engle and Granger (1987, p. 269). This table reports the Dickey and Fuller regression coefficient with standard errors below (in parentheses) and *t*-statistics next to standard errors (also in parentheses). Stars by *t*-statistics indicate that the null hypothesis is rejected.

Netherlands and Sweden we can conclude that money gowth rates and inflation are cointegrated.

The results are more uniform for the case of money growth rates and interest rates. From table 3, we conclude that the null of no-cointegration is rejected for only one country, i.e. the United Kingdom. Thus we conclude that monetary growth rates and nominal interest rates are not cointegrated for the other eight countries, namely, Belgium, France, Germany, Italy, the Netherlands, Norway, Spain and Sweden.

In conclusion, with some exceptions, the recent methodology of cointegration verifies that some cointegration exists between our variables. An open and very difficult question, which is beyond the scope of this paper, arises: what is the relationship between the methodologies of cointegration and the two-sided weighting moving averaging? The reader can observe that cointegration implies better graphical results after the process of smoothing. But it is very difficult to conclude from our graphs if the variables are necessarily cointegrated. Obviously, these two methodologies supplement one another nicely. For example, the graphical relationship between smoothed money growth rates and inflation is closer to being linear than the one between smoothed money growth rates and nominal interest rates. This observation is justified by the fact that money growth rates and inflation are cointegrated for more countries than money growth rates and interest rates.

7. Conclusions

This paper investigates the economic relationships between monetary growth and its impact on inflation and nominal interest rates for twelve European economies during the period 1950–1986.

Unlike earlier studies that employ primarily regression methods to identify statistical relationships, this paper uses the two-sided exponentially weighted average method. This method smooths the original data to various degrees depending on the values of a weight parameter β to identify trends and to exclude as much noise as possible.

Three sets of annual data were collected from the *International Financial Statistics*: nominal money supply, rate of inflation and nominal short term interst rates. Data were collected for twelve European economies: Belgium, Denmark, Finland, France, Greece, Italy, the Netherlands, Norway, Spain, Sweden, West Germany, and the United Kingdom.

Using the available data and performing the two-sided exponentially weighted moving average methodology we generated two sets of illustrations and two summary tables. Our results give support to the two quantity theoretic implications which refer to the notion that a given change in the rate of monetary growth induces, first, an equal change in the rate of price inflation and, second, an equal change in nominal interest rates. We find that for ten European countries, except France and West Germany, a given 1% change in the rate of monetary growth induces a positive change in the rate of inflation ranging between 0.63% for Denmark to 1% for Greece. In other words we do not observe exactly what the quantity theory predicts in terms of equal changes but we do find that these changes on average across countries are such that 1% change in money growth induces an average 0.78% change in inflation.

The support for the second implication is also evident but, again, it does not exhibit the theoretical prediction of equal changes between monetary growth and changes in nominal interest rates. We find that the relationship is positive and proportional but the slope of this relationship is less than 1. Actually, we find that a linear relationship between smoothed money growth and smoothed nominal short run interest rates for most countries is not an appropriate fit. Structural and regulatory conditions suggest a nonlinear relationship between money growth and nominal interest rates.

To substantiate our findings we also test for cointegration using the recent econometric research of Engle and Granger (1987). Our tests for cointegration confirm the graphical illustrations. We find that for one half of the countries in our sample, money growth rates and inflation are cointegrated. However, we find that money growth and interest rates are cointegrated only in the United Kingdom.

In conclusion, both the two-sided exponentially weighted moving average methodology and the recent econometric technique of cointegration give sufficient evidence that, for several European countries, increases in monetary growth eventually generate increases in inflation and nominal interest rates.

References

Dewald, W.G., 1988, Monetarism is dead; long live the quantity theory, Federal Reserve Bank of St. Louis Review 70, July/Aug., 3–18.

Engle, R. and C.W.J. Granger, 1987, Co-integration and error correction: Representation, estimation and testing, Econometrica 55, 251–276.

Friedman, M., 1987, Quantity theory of money, The new Palgrave: A dictionary of economics, Vol. 4 (The Stockton Press, New York), 3–20.

Friedman, M. and A.J. Schwartz, 1963, A monetary history of the United States, 1867–1960 (Princeton University Press for NBER).

Friedman, M. and A.J. Schwartz, 1982, Monetary trends in the United States and the United Kingdom (University of Chicago Press, Chicago, IL).

Grandmont, J.-M., 1983, Money and value (Cambridge University Press, New York).

LeRoy, S. and N. Raymon, 1987, A monetarist model of inflation, Journal of Economic Theory 42, 275–310.

Lucas, Jr., R.E., 1980, Two illustrations of the quantity theory of money, The American Economic Review 70, 1005–1014.

Lucas, Jr., R.E., 1986, Adaptive behavior and economic theory, Journal of Business 59, S401–S426.

Malliaris, A.G., 1987, Illustrations of the quantity theory of money: Annual U.S. Data 1947–1987, in: W.R. Heilmann, ed., Symposium on Money, Banking and Insurance (University of Karlsruhe), 453–468.

Malliaris, A.G., 1991, Several illustrations of the quantity theory of money: 1947–1987 and 1867–1975, The International Journal of Financial Analysis, forthcoming.

Malliaris, A.G. and J. Urrutia, 1990, Linkages of national stock markets: Statistical evidence before, during and after the October 1987 crash, Recent Advances in International Banking and Finance, Vols. IV and V, 341–385.

McCallum, B.T., 1984, On low-frequency estimates of long-run relationships in macroeconomics, Journal of Monetary Economics 14, 3–14.

Mills, T.C., 1982, Signal extraction and two illustrations of the quantity theory, American Economic Review 72, 1162–1168.

Mundell, R.A., 1963, Inflation and real interest, Journal of Political Economy 71, 280–283.
Sidrauski, M., 1967a, Rational choice and patterns of growth in a monetary economy, American Economic Review Proceedings 57, 534–544.
Sidrauski, M., 1967b, Inflation and economic growth, Journal of Political Economy 75, 796–810.
Whiteman, C.H., 1984, Lucas on quantity theory: Hypothesis testing without theory, American Economic Review 74, 742–749.
Whittle, P., 1963, Prediction and regulation by linear least-square methods (Van Nostrand–Reinhold, London, England).

Randomness in Asset Markets

ELSEVIER

Journal of Banking & Finance 23 (1999) 1605–1635

Journal of BANKING & FINANCE

www.elsevier.com/locate/econbase

Methodological issues in asset pricing: Random walk or chaotic dynamics

A.G. Malliaris [a,1], Jerome L. Stein [b,*]

[a] *Department of Economics, Loyola University, 820 N. Michigan Avenue, Chicago, IL 60611, USA*

[b] *Division of Applied Mathematics, Brown University, Box F, Providence, RI 02912, USA*

Received 27 September 1997; accepted 5 January 1999

Abstract

We analyze the theoretical foundations of the efficient market hypothesis by stressing the efficient use of information and its effect upon price volatility. The "random walk" hypothesis assumes that price volatility is exogenous and unexplained. Randomness means that a knowledge of the past cannot help to predict the future. We accept the view that randomness appears because information is incomplete. The larger the subset of information available and known, the less emphasis one must place upon the generic term randomness. We construct a general and well accepted intertemporal price determination model, and show that price volatility reflects the output of a higher order dynamic system with an underlying stochastic foundation. Our analysis is used to explain the learning process and the efficient use of information in our archetype model. We estimate a general unrestricted system for financial and agricultural markets to see which specifications we can reject. What emerges is that a system very close to our archetype model is consistent with the evidence. We obtain an equation for price volatility which looks a lot like the GARCH equation. The price variability is a serially correlated variable which is affected by the Bayesian error, and the Bayesian error is a serially correlated variable which is affected by the noisiness of the system. In this manner we have explained some of the determinants of what has been called the "randomness" of price changes.

* Corresponding author. Tel.: 1-401-863-2143; fax: 1-401-863-1355.

E-mail addresses: tmallia@luc.edu (A.G. Malliaris), jerome-stein@brown.edu (J.L. Stein)

[1] Tel.: 312-915-6063.

0378-4266/99/$ - see front matter

PII: S0378-4266(99)00017-5

JEL classification: D82; D83; D84; G12; G14

Keywords: Efficient market hypothesis; Chaos; Price volatility; Speculation; Asymmetric information

---

1. Aims of the paper

The efficient market hypothesis (EMH) was a major advance in our thinking about asset markets. The current state of the art can be described as follows. A.W. Lo wrote: "The EMH is disarmingly simple to state, has far reaching consequences for academic pursuits and business practice and yet is surprisingly resilient to empirical proof or refutation. Even after three decades of research and literally thousands of journal articles, economists have not yet reached a consensus about whether markets – particularly financial markets – are efficient or not" (Lo, 1997, p. 239).

The source of the problem is that "efficiency is an implication of the rational use of information in a competitive market... There are binding limitations in our knowledge of what price behavior to expect in an "efficient" market, so in turn there is limited reliable evidence on 'efficiency'... the wide range of anomalous evidence that has been uncovered highlights the limitations of 'efficiency' as a construct and our knowledge of asset pricing"(Ball, 1994, pp. 35–36).

It is agreed that the EMH per se is not a well-defined and empirically refutable hypothesis. To make it operational, one must specify additional structure, in particular – the information set (Lo, 1997, p. 239). The aim of this paper is to analyze the theoretical foundations of the EMH by stressing the structure, in particular the role of the efficient use of information and its implications for price volatility. We suggest that price volatility processes reflect the output of a higher order dynamic system with an underlying stochastic foundation. We analyze the economic scenarios which may generate seemingly chaotic processes with a strange attractor, which can be interpreted statistically. We do not accept the deterministic chaos model but show how a higher order stochastic dynamic system may clarify the relation between price variability and the information set or learning process. This will show what we think is an economically relevant way of looking at both the random walk and the chaos literature.

Section 2 is a brief evaluation of the literature which motivates our paper. In Section 3, we start with a simple and generally accepted model of asset markets to define, describe and analyze three key variables: price volatility, speculation and Bayesian errors made by agents. The Bayesian error is the difference between the true or full information expectation of the fundamentals and the subjective expectation. The latter results from the optimum use of information, taking into account the costs and benefits of sampling from the information set. Market efficiency is intimately linked to the Bayesian error.

In Section 4 we propose a model of three differential equations that relate these three variables. We explain how, by changing the parameters continuously, the system changes from unexplained randomness to asymptotic stability to a Lorenz chaotic one. In the latter, the motion converges to a narrow region – very complicated kind of strip – called a strange attractor (SA). With the SA, a statistical model can be adapted to describe motion. Thereby we come full circle: from unexplained randomness to the seeming randomness within the SA. Our first contribution lies in offering an economic adaptation of the Lorenz equations. Section 5 uses data from the agricultural and financial futures markets to estimate a general model in two versions. Our results show that our dynamic model in price volatility and Bayesian error has significant cogency.

2. Evaluation of the literature

The early observation by Working (1934, 1949), that changes in futures prices tend to be largely random, eventually directed researchers to seek theories for such a statistical phenomenon. Samuelson (1965) developed the EMH to rationalize the random walk behavior in the following way: (1) The current price $p(t)$ of an asset fully reflects all relevant information. This comes about by speculation based upon rational expectations, where the anticipations of the market participants are based upon the distribution of relevant information. (2) The change or flow of the real world information concerning the fundamentals, denoted $e(t)$, was then modeled as a process of random sampling from an arbitrary space. (3) Since sampling is random, the EMH claims that asset price changes are also random. In this manner, statistical notion of a random sample of information is connected by the EMH to the economic notion of unpredictable price changes. Samuelson's 1965 analysis is completely general.

During the past 20 years, the theory of market efficiency has been refined analytically, mathematically and statistically. A major advance has been the use of the stochastic calculus to explain the pricing of derivatives (Merton, 1990).

The randomness of asset price changes hypothesized by the EMH requires an explanation about the variance of such changes. If price changes are induced by changes in information, can information concerning the shocks in fundamental factors explain the magnitude of the observed price volatility? Or, is the variance of price changes due to other factors? No economic theory was adduced to explain volatility. The literature following Shiller (1989) documents that prices are "too volatile". This evidence raises the crucial question: what factors other than rationally expected future fundamental shocks could explain such evidence of high volatility? Among several such factors, speculation not based upon rational expectations – noise traders – has received special attention.

The topic of speculation and price volatility has been studied at both the theoretical and the empirical level. In an efficient market, since futures price changes are unpredictable, speculation should not be profitable. Friedman (1953) argued that profitable speculation reduces the price variance. This insight has generated many empirical papers which examined the profitability of speculation. However, it was shown in many theoretical articles that his conclusion only follows under special conditions, and that plausible models can be developed explaining excess volatility by the speculative behavior of noise traders.

Moreover, a very large literature developed concerning the statistical distribution of the changes in spot or futures prices. Are they normal, or are they leptokurtic and if leptokurtic, how fat are the tails? The theoretical foundations underlying these studies are not always clear. It was not surprising to find that along with numerous studies confirming market efficiency, there were many rejecting it, and that there is no agreement concerning the statistical distribution functions of price changes. The major problem with this type of research is that it is incapable of understanding the underlying structure of the model whereby we are able to evaluate market efficiency.

This state of events has led some researchers to take a different approach: Is there a non-linear methodology, deterministic chaos, as an alternative to the stochastic approach of the EMH, which generates a time series sequence of price changes that appear random when in fact such a sequence is non-random? Numerous expository articles such as Baumol and Benhabib (1989), the collection of articles edited by Benhabib (1992), and the book by De Grauwe et al. (1993) have appeared that use various single variable chaotic maps to illustrate the intellectual possibilities of the deterministic approach. [2]

There is a serious critique of the chaos literature by Granger (1994), and of the De Grauwe et al. book by Allen (1995). Granger argues that: "If the purpose of this research effort is to show that it is possible to produce economic theory that has chaos as an outcome then this certainty has been achieved, but it is unclear why more than one paper is required that shows this. The recent papers produce more general models but are still not realistic and are not in a form that is empirically testable in any specific fashion" (Granger, 1994, p. 142). Granger continues saying "...as an econometrician I would want...evidence that...[the chaos model] reproduced many features of an actual economy, not just a couple, and that it suggested and correctly predicted features that have not been previously tested" (p. 144).

---

[2] See also the work of Brock et al. (1986, 1988, 1991) and Brock and Malliaris (1989).

The empirical evidence for deterministic chaos is extremely weak. For example, De Grauwe et al. (1993) examined several exchange rates. In no case could they find a strange attractor. When they used other tests concerning the correlation dimension, they found that for a few currencies in some subperiods, there was some visual evidence for chaos. They concluded that: "The empirical analysis presented in this book can certainly not be considered as conclusive evidence of chaos in the foreign exchange market" (p. 257).

We do not find that the deterministic chaos models in economics have cogency, for the following reason. If a model is chaotic, then short run forecasting is quite feasible, but longer run forecasting is impossible. The evidence is just the opposite. Several examples can be given: (a) Short period, for example monthly or quarterly, rates of inflation cannot be predicted, but in the long run the quantity theory of money is valid. [3] (b) Short run movements in the exchange rate are unpredictable and none of the short run theoretical relationships is better than the martingale hypothesis. However, in the longer run, the real exchange rate can be explained quite well by the fundamentals of productivity and thrift at home and abroad, [4] and conditional upon that real rate, PPP explains the nominal exchange rate in the long run.

3. An archetype model

We address ourselves to the issues raised at the beginning of this paper by specifying a linear, two period, well-accepted optimizing model that explains actual and expected prices in cash and futures markets of a storable commodity, the change in the price and price variance. We explain the learning process where all available information is used optimally by agents by introducing the notion of a Bayesian error. The latter is defined as the difference between the subjective and objective expectations of stochastic variables. We then obtain an expression for price volatility as the sum of two factors: the exogenous variance of the fundamentals and the endogenous variance of the Bayesian errors. We generalize the archetype or basic model to a continuous time differential equation system explaining price volatility. Our system contains the essential contributions of both stochastic models and chaotic

[3] See Figs. 1 and 2(a)–(e) in Stein (1994). Fig. 1 shows a very close relation between the GDP deflator and M2/real GDP. Fig. 2(a)–(e) shows no significant relation between inflation and either current or lagged money growth. Long range forecasting is feasible, but short range forecasting is less successful. To explain the relation between inflation and unemployment, Stein uses a second order dynamic model. Again, one must understand the underlying structure in order to formulate a significant statistical test.

[4] This is the theme of the book by Stein et al. (1995).

dynamics. It is capable of yielding as special cases the results implicit in the theory of efficient markets and the chaos models.

Eqs. (1a) and (1b) are inverse demand curves for a commodity, which relate price $p(t)$ and consumption $C(t)$. The intercept of demand is $U(t)$ and the slope is $b(t)$.

$$p(1) = U(1) - b(1)C(1), \tag{1a}$$

$$p(0) = U(0) - b(0)C(0). \tag{1b}$$

Consumption in period $t = 0$ is production $Z(0)$ less the quantity S of inventory investment: Eq. (2a). Consumption in period $t = 1$ is production $Z(1)$ plus the inventory disinvestment: Eq. (2b). There are no stocks left over at the end of period $t = 1$, and the transversatility condition is used to avoid Ponzi processes.

$$C(0) = Z(0) - S, \tag{2a}$$

$$C(1) = Z(1) + S. \tag{2b}$$

The exogenous fundamental in our model is $Pn(t) = U(t) - b(t)Z(t)$, $t = 0, 1$, in Eq. (2c). It is the price in period t that would have occurred if there were no carryover, i.e., if $S = 0$, and $e(t) = \Delta Pn$ in Eq. (3c) is the change in the exogenous fundamental.

$$Pn(t) = U(t) - b(t)Z(t), \; t = 0, 1. \tag{2c}$$

Eqs. (3a) and (3b) result when Eqs. (2a)–(2c) are substituted into Eqs. (1a) and (1b).

$$p(0) = Pn(0) + b(0)S, \tag{3a}$$

$$p(1) = Pn(1) - b(1)S, \tag{3b}$$

$$e = Pn(1) - Pn(0), \quad e \sim (m, \operatorname{var} e), \tag{3c}$$

$$\begin{aligned} \operatorname{var} e &= \operatorname{var}[Pn(1) - Pn(0)] \\ &= \operatorname{var}\{[U(1) - b(1)Z(1)] - [U(0) - b(0)Z(0)]\}. \end{aligned} \tag{3d}$$

Eq. (4) is the relation between the price differential $dp = p(1) - p(0)$ and the quantity of storage S. Samuelson calls this relation the net price curve. Others call it the demand for storage. The average of the slopes $b(0)$ and $b(1)$ is denoted as b. The difference of the intercepts $Pn(1) - Pn(0)$ is e. This is the price differential that would exist if there were no storage, and results from changes in U and Z, which are the fundamental exogenous stochastic elements. Let e be distributed with a mean of m and variance of $\operatorname{var} e$.

$$dp = p(1) - p(0) = e - 2bS \quad \text{(Net Price Curve)}. \tag{4}$$

Take the objective expectation of Eq. (4) over the distribution of stochastic variable e and derive Eq. (5). The term $m = E(e)$ is the objective (true) expectation of stochastic variable e.

$$Ep(1) - p(0) = m - 2bS \quad \text{(Expected Net Price Curve)}. \tag{5}$$

The objectively Expected Net Price Curve E(NPC) is graphed in Fig. 1. The variance of the net price curve resulting from var e is the first of two sources of price volatility var (dp). We have given an economic meaning to the concept of "the fundamentals" $Pn(t)$ and to $e = \Delta Pn(t)$.

Refer to the agent who carries inventories (storage) as the dealer. He has three options. He can sell the commodity at time $t = 0$ at the spot price $p(0)$. He can hold the inventory unhedged, and sell it at uncertain price $p(1)$. If there is a futures market, he can hedge his inventory s by selling a quantity of futures at price $q(1;0)$. The notation $q(T;t)$ is the futures price at time t for a contract maturing at $T > t$. The futures price at maturity $q(1;1)$ is the prevailing spot price $p(1)$, so that $q(1;1) = p(1)$ is the boundary condition. When the dealer optimizes, he will hold the quantity of stock s such that the differential between the futures price $q(1;0)$ and the spot price $p(0)$ is equal to the marginal carrying costs $\text{MC} = c\sum s = cS$. Assume that there are many competitive dealers, whose total number is normalized at unity. Then the supply of storage in Eq. (6) relates the total supply of storage S to the difference between the futures price and the current spot price.

$$q(1;0) - p(0) = cS, \quad \sum s = S > 0. \tag{6}$$

The futures market consists of many participants with different subjective expectations of the price that will prevail at $t = 1$. There are commercial firms,

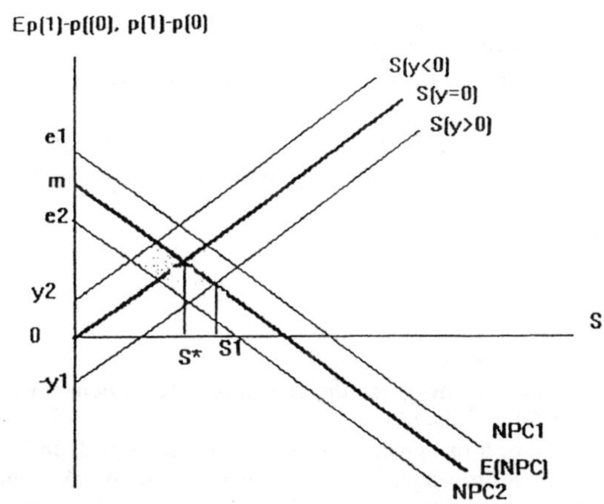

Fig. 1. Determinants of expected price change $Ep(1) - p(0)$, and storage S.

professional speculators and amateur speculators in the futures market. Some participants are more knowledgeable than others, for reasons explained below. The futures price equates the supply of futures with the demand. Futures are supplied by short hedgers, and by those who think that $p(1)$ will be less than $q(1;0)$. Futures are demanded by long hedgers, and by those who think that $p(1)$ will exceed $q(1;0)$. Speculation is done by commercials themselves who also hedge. The storage, production, hedging and speculation decisions of the commercials are the results of an optimization process. [5] Some speculation is generated by the non-commercials, who are pure speculators. Questions usually asked are whether there is too much speculation, and whether the speculation is rational or based upon noise trading.

The market equilibrium futures price is a weighted average of the prices subjectively expected by the market participants [6] to prevail at $t = 1$. The weight of the ith group is w_i, and its subjective expectation [7] is $E_i p(1;0)$. Denote the weighted average of subjectively expected prices by $Ep(1;0) = \sum w_i E_i p(1;0)$. The subjective expectation is taken at time $t = 0$.

$$q(1;0) = Ep(1;0) = \sum w_i E_i p(1;0), \quad \sum w_i = 1. \tag{7}$$

Define the Bayesian error, denoted by y in Eq. (8) as the difference between the subjective expectation held by the market $Ep(1;0)$ and the objective (rational) expectation $Ep(1)$. The characteristics of the Bayesian error are discussed below. The Bayesian error refers to the situation where the market participants do not know the objective mean $Ep(1)$. When the market has Muth Rational Expectations (MRE), then by definition $y = 0$ there is no Bayesian error. The subjective and objective expectations are the same. The convergence to MRE is the situation where both the mean and the variance of the Bayesian error converge to zero.

$$\begin{aligned} y &= Ep(1;0) - Ep(1) = \text{Bayesian error} \\ &= \text{subjective anticipation} - \text{objective expectation}. \end{aligned} \tag{8}$$

The futures price $q(1;0) = Ep(1;0)$ is the sum of the objectively expected price $Ep(1)$ and the market Bayesian error y, using Eqs. (7) and (8).

$$q(1;0) = Ep(1) + y. \tag{9}$$

[5] See Stein (1986, Chapters 2 and 3) for the derivation of equations used here. See also Peck (1985) for an analysis of futures markets.

[6] There may or may not be a risk premium between the futures price and the expected price by the market. See Peck (1985). For simplicity, assume that there is no risk premium.

[7] $E_i p(1;0)$ is the subjective expectation of the ith agent at time $t = 0$ of the spot price which will prevail at time $t = 1$.

Using Eq. (9) in Eq. (6), the supply of storage is Eq. (10). The objective MRE expectation is $Ep(1)$ and the Bayesian error is y,

$$Ep(1) - p(0) = -y + cS. \quad \text{Supply of Storage} \tag{10}$$

In Fig. 1 supply of storage equation (10) is graphed as curve SS, and the expected net price curve – Eq. (5) – is graphed as *E*(NPC). The variance of the supply of storage function results from the variance of the Bayesian error var y. This is the second source of variation in price volatility.

A general optimizing model is described by Eqs. (10), (5) and (3a) for *endogenous* variables $Ep(1) - p(0)$, S, $p(0)$, in terms of the endogenous Bayesian error y (discussed below) and the *fundamental exogenous* variables $Pn(t)$. The solution of the model is described by Eqs. (11)–(15). Fig. 1 describes the determination of the quantity of storage S and the expected price differential $Ep(1) - p(0)$, Eqs. (11) and (12). The expectations are taken over the space of (e, y).

The price $p(0)$ at $t=0$ is Eq. (15) based upon the demand curve at time $t=0$, Eq. (3a), and the quantity of storage equation (11). Given the quantity stored, the actual price change [8] will be given by the realized net price curve, NPC1 or NPC2, depending upon the realized value of stochastic variable e.

If the market has MRE such that there is no Bayesian error ($y=0$), the quantity stored will be S^* in Fig. 1. If the market has a positive Bayesian error $y > 0$, the quantity stored will be $S1 > S^*$, Eq. (11).

Solution of archetype model

$$S = (m + y)/(2b + c), \tag{11}$$

$$Ep(1) - p(0) = [cm - 2bE(y)]/(2b + c), \tag{12}$$

$$dp = p(1) - p(0) = e - v(m + y), \tag{13}$$

$$p(1) - Ep(1) = (e - m) - v(y - E(y)), \tag{14}$$

$$p(0) = Pn(0) + b(0)(m + y)/(2b + c). \tag{15}$$

Rational expectations: $y=0$; Fundamentals $e = Pn(1) - Pn(0) \sim (m, \text{var}\, e)$; $v = 2b/(2b + c)$.

We now have equations which describe the sources of price volatility within the context of the two period optimizing model, in terms of objective fundamentals. When there are rational expectations, there is no Bayesian error,

[8] Eq. (17) for the change in price $dp = p(1) - p(0) = [p(1) - Ep(1)] + [Ep(1) - p(0)]$ equals Eqs. (14) + (12).

$y = 0$: the subjective expectation is equal to the objective expectation of the fundamentals.

3.1. Price volatility

The issue of where price variance comes from involves the concept of randomness. The concept of randomness is profound. [9] By randomness one means that knowing all past events is no help in predicting the future. The rolling of dice or tossing of a coin are taken as the prime examples. But the world is determined by physical laws. If we knew the velocity and spin of the thrown dice or coin, we would be able to predict the outcome of a toss. Randomness appears because the available information is either inaccurate or incomplete. A deterministic system may exhibit random behavior if part of the information is unknown. Our strategy has been to try to complete the information.

The price change implied by the model – Eq. (13) – above has a mean and variance given by Eqs. (16a)–(16c), defined over the sample space (e, y). The mean is a linear combination of the expected change in the fundamentals $E(e)$ and the expected Bayesian error $E(y)$. The fundamental $e = \Delta Pn = \Delta[U(t) - B(t)Z(t)]$ is the change in price that would have occurred if there were no storage. It is the intercept of the expected net price curve E(NPC) in Fig. 1, based upon Eq. (5). The variance of dp is based upon the variance of the fundamentals var (e) – resulting from the variance of the net price curve – and the variance of the supply of storage curve produced by the variance of the Bayesian error var y and their covariance.

The variance of the price change and the stock of the commodity can be seen in Fig. 1. If the fundamental e varied between e_1 and e_2 (with a mean of m), and the Bayesian error varied between y_1 and y_2 (with a mean of zero), the var (dp) and var (S) would lie within the shaded area.

$$E(dp) = (1 - v)m - vE(y), \tag{16a}$$

$$\text{var}\,(dp) = \text{var}\,e + v^2\,\text{var}\,y - 2v\,\text{cov}(y, e), \tag{16b}$$

$$v = 2b/(2b + c). \tag{16c}$$

In Eq. (16b), the variance of dp has two parts. The variance of the fundamentals var e is exogenous, but we must also consider the variance of the Bayesian error and covariance. In the case where there are MRE, the Bayesian error $y = 0$. Storage would be S^* in Fig. 1. The actual price differential would be where the realized net price curve NPC intersects the vertical line at $S = S^*$.

[9] Two excellent books on this subject, which have profoundly influenced our presentation and are a delight to read, are by Ekeland (1988, 1993).

The price variance stems solely from the exogenous fundamentals var e. The MRE hypothesis ignores the Bayesian learning process.

So far, we have added the concept of the Bayesian error, which involves the learning process. It is our concept of rational expectations, when all information is used *optimally*. In the next section we derive the mean and variance of the Bayesian error. In Section 4 we explain the interaction among the price variance, the Bayesian error and composition of market participants. Thereby we provide an economic explanation of some of the information that is unknown. It is the unknown information which produces the randomness of price changes.

3.2. Bayesian error [10]

Efficiency is an implication of the rational use of information in a competitive market. We now discuss a rational learning process which uses all available information optimally. The MRE hypothesis is an arbitrary assumption that all systematic information is known. At all times, the subjective expectation of the market is the same as the objective expectation. The MRE hypothesis contains no theory to explain the speed of convergence of the subjective to the objective expectation. Our focus here is upon the process of convergence, which is called Asymptotically Rational Expectations (ARE). The Bayesian error $y(t)$ is defined the difference between the subjective and the objective expectation taken at time t of the price which will prevail at time $T > t$. There are two efficient methods of learning: (i) the use of OLS estimation based upon publicly available information and (ii) Bayesian learning which utilizes current private information. It has been proved in the references above that OLS learning tends to produce cobweb like behavior and a slow convergence to MRE, and Bayesian learning produces a more rapid convergence.

The market participants attempt to predict the expected change in price $Ep(1) - p(0)$ in Eq. (12). The first part $cm/(2b + c)$, where $m = E(Pn(1) - Pn(0))$ is the effect of the expected value of the fundamentals m. We use the terms "estimates of the fundamentals" and "estimate of the market price" interchangeably.

The market participants may be able to act in a Bayesian manner, and use all available information in the most efficient manner. They start with a prior concept of what will be the expected price. This may be what is based upon

[10] The analysis of the Bayesian errors, the learning process, and Eqs. (17)–(19c) are derived from Stein (1986, pp. 92–93, 1991, ch. 5, 1992a). The Asymptotically Rational Expectation (ARE) process is contrasted with OLS learning in Stein (1992b). The analysis here of the process of ARE is based upon these references.

public information. They invest resources to "take a sample" to from the subset of the current information set which becomes private information concerning $Pn(t)$. On that basis they have a private estimate of the expected price. The posterior expectation of the price is a weighted average of the prior and the sample. In each period prior to the maturity date T of the contract, the participants take a sample from the information set and form a new prior estimate of the fundamentals or population mean. A sequence is generated of subjective estimates of the population mean. Corresponding to each subjective estimate, there is a Bayesian error between the unknown population mean and the subjective estimate. It has been proved [11] that: (i) the Bayesian errors are serially correlated; (ii) when the distributions of the fundamental exogenous economic variables Pn are constant, the expectation and variance of the Bayesian error decline asymptotically to zero as the cumulative number of samples grows steadily.

The expectations of the Bayesian error that will be made at time t, conditional upon information known at time $t=0$, is $Ey(t)$ as described by Eq. (17). The precision (reciprocal of the variance) of the initial prior is $f(0)$, n is the sample size that is taken at time t from the information set and nt is the cumulative items sampled up through time t. The precision (reciprocal of the variance) of the underlying distribution is k. Thus $1/k$ represents the noisiness of the underlying system.

$$Ey(t) = [f(0)/(f(0) + nkt)]y(0). \tag{17}$$

If an initial Bayesian error $y(0)$ were made, then the expectation of that Bayesian error converges monotonically to zero with time, if the distribution of the stochastic variables is stationary. The variance of the Bayesian error is given by Eq. (18). It is positively related to the variance of the underlying distribution of the fundamentals ($\text{var}\, e = 1/k$) and inversely to nt, the sum of the items sampled.

$$\text{var}\, y(t) = \text{var}\,[Ep(T;t) - Ep(T)] = 1/knt = \text{var}\, dp/nt. \tag{18}$$

The number of items sampled is an endogenous variable, determined by an optimizing process. There is a cost $G(n)$ of sampling to obtain information, as well as a loss of profits from not knowing the objective expectation. This will determine the optimal sample size n. The convexity of the cost of sampling is $g = G''(n)$ and c is again the slope of the marginal cost function $\text{MC} = cS$. The optimal sample size n is Eq. (19a). When the optimal sample size is taken, the variance of the Bayesian error is Eq. (19b) and the expected Bayesian error is Eq. (19c). Eqs. (19b) and (19c) describe the Bayesian error.

---

[11] See the references above.

Asymptotically rational expectations

$$n = 1/(2gckt)^{1/3}, \tag{19a}$$

$$\operatorname{var} y(t) = (2gc/k^2t^2)^{1/3}, \tag{19b}$$

$$Ey(t) = f(0)y(0)/[f(0) + (kt)^{2/3}/(2gc)^{1/3}]. \tag{19c}$$

$y(t)$ = Bayesian error = $Ep(T;t) - Ep(T)$ = subjective less objective expectation; var $dp = 1/k$ = noisiness of the system; $f(0)$ = precision of the initial prior; g = second derivative of costs of sampling.

Fig. 2 describes how the absolute value of the mean (Eq. 19c) and variance (Eq. 19b) of the Bayesian error converge asymptotically to zero. Curve H (high), is based upon parameters such that the underlying noise (var $dp = 1/k$) is great, or that there are highly convex costs of sampling (g is high), relative to curve L (low). The convergence rates whereby var y goes to zero are faster along curve L. That is why this process is called ARE.

3.3. *The diversity of agents*

The MRE hypothesis ignores the diversity of agents and assumes that the subjective anticiptions are always equal to the objective expectations of the unknown fundamentals. There is considerable evidence that agents have different expectations. An excellent example is provided by Kandel and Pearson

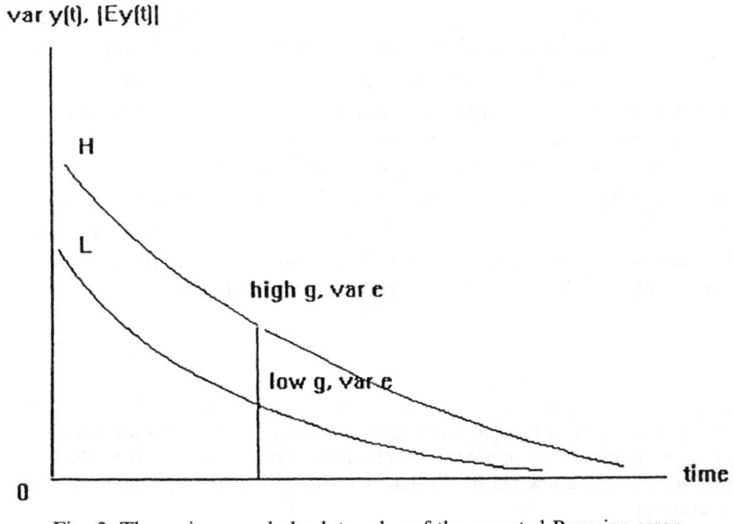

Fig. 2. The variance and absolute value of the expected Bayesian error.

(1995). They had data on changes in expectations, held by financial analysts employed by major US brokerage firms, of annual earnings around public information releases of quarterly earnings. They show that these financial analysts had very different models and they interpret the public information differently.

Many papers assume that there are several types of agents, with different expectations functions. [12] Some have rational expectations, others are noise traders, others are chartists. The resulting dynamics depend crucially upon the weights assigned to the different groups. Our approach in analyzing how an "efficient" market functions is based upon the optimal use of information, and is consistent with many scenarios. An unlikely possibility is that all traders have the same costs of sampling. A more likely situation is that there are intergroup differences. The major commercials have less convex costs of sampling than do the large speculators or small commercials. Hence, the variance of the Bayesian errors (as well as their expectations) are lower. The expected profits of a group is negatively related to the variance of their Bayesian errors. [13] These variables will be of considerable importance in the subsequent analysis.

At any time, the market has a positive variance of the Bayesian error: $\text{var}\, y > 0$. Each group, whether it be commercial firms, professional speculators or amateur speculators has a variance of its Bayesian error. A noise trader is defined as one whose costs of information are highly convex (g is large). He takes a small sample and is on curve H in Fig. 2. The large commercial traders and professional speculators have lower marginal costs of sampling (g), take larger samples (n) and hence are on curve L in Fig. 2. As the weight of the noise traders rises or declines it will raise or lower the variance of the market Bayesian error. Insofar as a rise in the quantity of speculation is due to the entrance of more small traders, the price variance will rise. If the rise in speculation is due to the entrance of more large commercial and non-commercial traders, price variance will decline. The Bayesian error $y = Ep(1;0) - Ep(1)$ affects the futures price and hence the SS curve.

We have explained that there are two sources of the variance of price change in Eq. (16b): the variance of the fundamentals $\text{var}\, e$ and $\text{var}\, y$, the variance of the Bayesian error. The efficient use of information is the process called ARE as described above. The MRE is a limit point of ARE.

[12] Stein (1986, Chapter 3) has rational traders and noise traders. See Cartapanis (1996) for a discussion of the heterogeneity of expectations in the foreign exchange market. De Grauwe et al. (1993) have traders who know the steady state and chartists whose expectations are based upon moving average processes.

[13] Stein (1986, Chapter 5).

4. Generalization of the archetype model

We are now ready to focus upon our main problem: What will be the characteristics of price variability? Our strategy is to use the logic or economic intuition of the archetype model above, but not be strictly constrained to the simplified two period or linear form. The general model can yield a rich variety of non-linear dynamics which has elements of both non-random and random behavior. The time series characteristics of the price variability are very sensitive to seemingly slight changes in the specifications of the structural equations, even though speculation always seems to be stabilizing.

4.1. The logical structure

The archetype model above can be summarized in the flow chart. The price variability depends upon the variability of the fundamentals and the variability of the Bayesian errors – Eq. (16b). The variability of the Bayesian errors depends upon the noisiness of the system and the diversity of agents – Eq. (19b). The diversity of agents is affected by the noisiness of the system and heterogenity of views, in the manner discussed below.

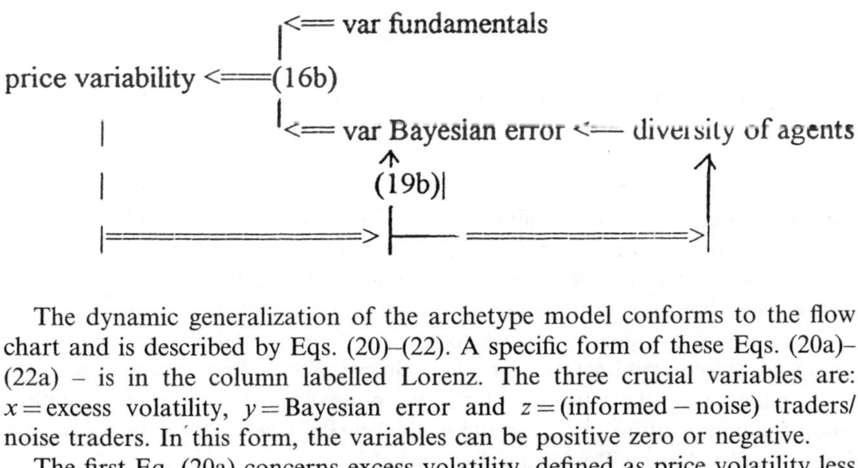

The dynamic generalization of the archetype model conforms to the flow chart and is described by Eqs. (20)–(22). A specific form of these Eqs. (20a)–(22a) – is in the column labelled Lorenz. The three crucial variables are: x = excess volatility, y = Bayesian error and z = (informed – noise) traders/noise traders. In this form, the variables can be positive zero or negative.

The first Eq. (20a) concerns excess volatility, defined as price volatility less the volatility of the fundamentals. It states that if the Bayesian error were constant, then excess volatility would converge to the Bayesian error at speed s.

The second Eq. (21a) states that the Bayesian error is not constant, but has a dynamics. As is seen in the flow chart, it is affected by the noisiness of the system and the composition of agents. We measure the composition of agents as z = (informed – noise) traders/noise traders. The marginal costs of information determines how informed the trader will be, as shown in Eq. (19a) for the optimal sample size. It is convenient to refer to z as the "composition variable".

Dynamic generalization of archetype model

Generalization.

$$dX(t) = \Phi[X(t)],$$

$$dx/dt = F(x,y), \tag{20}$$

$$dy/dt = G(x,y,z), \tag{21}$$

$$dz/dt = H(x,y,z). \tag{22}$$

Lorenz specification.

$$dx/dt = -sx + sy, \tag{20a}$$

$$dy/dt = x(r-z) - y, \tag{21a}$$

$$dz/dt = xy - bz, \tag{22a}$$

x = excess volatility; y = Bayesian error; z = (informed – noise) traders/noise traders.

$$X = (x,y,z); \quad \Phi = (F,G,H).$$

If the system were not noisy, then the Bayesian error would converge to zero. However, the noisiness of the system affects the dynamics of the Bayesian errors.

The composition effect upon the Bayesian errors is of the form [14] $x(r-z)$. Parameter r represents the minimum information needed for stability in a given market. In other words, r reflects a critical fraction of informed traders. A "noise trader" in our model is one whose marginal cost of sampling is high and hence bases his expectation upon a "small amount" of information. A large commercial or professional has a low marginal cost of information and his views are based upon a large sample of information. As the noisiness of the system increases, the variance of the Bayesian error will change depending upon the composition of the agents in the market z relative to the value of r. The critical value r will vary among markets.

If $z > r$, the market is dominated by informed traders in excess of the critical value. When the market is dominated by informed traders, then the greater the variation in the fundamentals the easier it is to separate signal from noise. Then a rise in the noisiness of the system decreases the Bayesian error. If $z < r$, the

[14] This is the argument in Stein (1986, pp. 129–140, 1992a).

market is thin, the market is dominated by noise traders. These agents cannot differentiate signal from noise and a rise in the noisiness of the system increases the Bayesian error.

Eq. (22a) describes the composition of traders. If a system were not noisy, there would be no diversity of beliefs and no incentive for informed speculative activity. The composition of informed traders would converge to zero $(\mathrm{d}z/\mathrm{d}t|xy = 0) = -bz$. A noisy system leads to a diversity of beliefs. If beliefs were uniform such that the market is described by a "representative agent", there would not be any trading activity. The amount of informed speculation done by the large commercials and professional speculators is positively related to the expected profits from speculation. It has been proved [15] that these profits depend upon the difference of Bayesian errors between the informed and uniformed and the relative weight of the two groups. Hence the first term in Eq. (22) xy the product of noisiness of the system and the Bayesian error, which reflect the difference in beliefs, induces more informed speculators to enter the market. The second term reflects the decrease in profits from investment in information resulting from an increase in the fraction of informed traders.

4.2. Stochastic type non-linear dynamics: Asymptotic stability or a strange attracting set [16]

Eqs. (20a)–(22a) constitute an extremely rich system in its implications for the time series of price changes. Our model is a mixture of non-linearities ultimately driven by stochastic elements. If there were no exogenous variability of the fundamentals, there would be no Bayesian error. Without a variance to the Bayesian error, we would not have the dynamical system above.

There are some important mathematical points which are necessary to understand the system above. Suppose that we have a system of ordinary differential equations $\mathrm{d}X/\mathrm{d}t = F(X)$, $X = (x, y, z)$ such as Eqs. (20)–(22) in the general model above, with a fixed point $F(0) = 0$. If the linearization of the origin $X = 0$ has no purely imaginary eigenvalue then the Hartman–Grobman theorem states that the number of eigenvalues with positive and negative real parts determine the topological equivalence of the flow around the origin. If however there are eigenvalues with zero real parts, then the flow near the origin can be complicated. This is the situation in the column labelled Lorenz specification.

In system (20a)–(22a), there are three fixed points $X = (x, y, z)$: the first is the origin $X(1) = (0, 0, 0)$. The other two are denoted $X(2)$ and $X(3)$. The stability or instability of these points is indicated in the table below. The rows refer to

[15] Stein (1986, p. 139).

[16] See Guckenheimer and Holmes (1983) and Sparrow (1982).

the fixed points or equilibria. The crucial variable is the critical parameter r. The columns refer to the value of r. The larger the value of r relative to 1 and to r^* defined below, the less stable is the system.

The study of qualitative changes in the number and stability of equilibria of dynamical systems as parameters are varied is called *bifurcation* theory. For given parameter values, a system is called structurally stable if small changes in the parameters do not change the qualtitative properties of the phase portrait or solution curves. Any other values of the parameters is called a bifurcation value. In our economic interpretation we focused upon term $x(r - z)$ in Eq. (21a). If $z = $ (informed/noise traders $- 1) > r$, then a rise in the noisiness of the system decreases the Bayesian error. Hence, a low value of r is a force for stability. There is a value of $r = r^*$ at which a Hopf bifurcation occurs.

When the value r is less than unity, (the first column) then the origin is the only fixed point; and it is a *sink*: an asymptotically stable point. [17] When $r^* > r > 1$, (column two) then there are three fixed points. The origin is now a saddle, but the other two fixed points are sinks (symptotically stable). When $r > r^* > 1$, in the third column, then all three fixed points are saddles.

Let $s > (1 + b)$, the speed of convergence of the excess volatility in Eq. (20a) is greater than the sum of the speeds of convergence in the other two equations. This is a sensible requirement because if there were no Bayesian error, we would expect: (a) an extremely rapid convergence of the excess volatility to zero, and (b) a rapid convergence to a rational expectations equilibrium. When $(s - b - 1) > 0$, then r^* is positive.

The Lorenz model – bifurcations

Fixed point	$1 > r > 0$	$r^* > r > 1$	$r > r^* > 1$
$X(1)$	Sink	Saddle	Saddle
$X(2)$	–	Sink	Saddle
$X(3)$	–	Sink	Saddle

$$X(1) = (0, 0, 0);$$

$$X(2) = (\sqrt{b(r-1)},\ \sqrt{b(r-1)},\ r-1);$$

$$X(3) = (-\sqrt{b(r-1)},\ -\sqrt{b(r-1)},\ r-1)r^* = s(s+b+3)/(s-b-1) > 0.$$

At $r = r^*$, a Hopf bifurcation occurs at the fixed points $X(2)$ and $X(3)$, since the eigenvalues of the matrix are $\lambda = -(s+b+1)$ and $\lambda = \pm i\sqrt{2s(s+1)/(s-b-1)}$. Two eigenvalues have zero real parts. As indicated

[17] At $r = 1$, one of the eigenvalues is is zero, and the other two are negative.

in column three, for all $r > r^*$, all three fixed points are saddles. However, there is an attracting set: a strange attractor.

When $r > r^* > 1$, column three, the system has a strange attractor. A set that attracts nearby solutions in forward time, but is more complicated than an equilibrium or periodic orbit is called a strange attractor. If the system started in the neighborhood of the origin $X(1)$, it would start off like a saddle point and diverge from the origin. It will loop around $X(2)$, move on to $X(3)$, then return to the $X(2)$ and then on to $X(3)$ and indefinitely. It seems that the system is moving randomly in a narrow region, called a *strange attractor* (SA), which contains $X(1)$ and $X(2)$.

4.3. Economic implications

There are several reasons (a)–(f) why the system equation (20a), (21a), (22a) with strange attractors may be more attractive an explanation than simply assuming that excess price volatility is a random variable with a zero expectation. The crucial parameter r reflects the type of market and composition of agents. In markets where public information is insufficient to know the underlying parameters, private information is valuable; however, there are costs of sampling. The greater these marginal costs, the greater must be the number of people engaged in this activity if the market is to learn the fundamentals. In this case, we say that r is large. If the costs of information are low, a small number of speculators may be sufficient to learn the fundamentals and model; and we say that r is small. When $r < 1$, there is a unique equilibrium and it is a sink. When $r > r^*$, then there is a strange attractor.

(a) The dynamics are derived from an explicit optimizing model involving interactions among agents: the Archetype model. Of necessity, there is an underlying uncertainty, the variance of the fundamentals produces the Bayesian errors.

(b) The system does not wander aimlessly. Either it converges to one of the three steady states or it is drawn into an equilibrium region: the SA.

(c) Within the SA, the movement is unpredictable. It has been shown, by Sinai, Ruelle and Bowen, that there exists an ergodic measure, such that it is legitimate to explain the observations within the SA in probabilistic terms. From a statistical point of view, we may consider that the series of observations taken from SA as the results of independent draws. The "randomness" of the observations is to be interpreted as the inability to predict the value of the next observation, given its past history. That is why we refer to the situation where the system converges to the invariant set SA as "stochastic chaos".

(d) This non-linear dynamic specification may explain why empirical researchers do not find structural stability, and results from time series analyses are ambiguous and inconclusive. The mean and variance of the distribution of variable $X(t)$ implied by the SA are highly variable and differ by the time interval and initial conditions. The search to determine the statistical distribution function of price changes (normal, leptokurtic, ARCH and GARCH processes) are ad hoc specifications, which reflect economic ignorance of the underlying system. The bifurcation and strange attractor specification of the general model may possibly provide an explanation for the inconclusive results from the time series analysis.[18]

(e) The non-linear dynamics provides economic structure for the question: do speculative prices fluctuate randomly.

(f) The model sheds light upon the relations between price variability and speculation (by non-commercials), since price variability, speculation and learning are interrelated in a non-linear manner. Policy implications are easily drawn from each model concerning the effects of encouraging or discouraging speculation by non-commercials. Thus non-linear dynamics are much richer economics than is the random walk. The question is whether this type of chaos models is a demonstrably better explanation than the EMH, or a wider model along the lines formulated in the theoretical section above.

5. Which hypothesis is consistent with the evidence?

5.1. Research design

Randomness is a situation where the future appears to be independent of the past and is unpredictable, whereas determinism is a situation where the future is predictable once we know the initial conditions and the dynamic equations. The Lorenz model shows how subsystems may exhibit randomness, even though the total system is deterministic. Ekeland (1988, [19] p. 62), drawing upon the brilliant work of Poincaré, put the matter lucidly:

[18] An excellent evaluation of the chaos and more general dynamics of biological populations is in May (1987). The biological cases are closer to economics than are the examples from physics. May explains how simple and natural models of various kinds of biologic populations exhibit cyclic and chaotic dynamics. It is the interaction with other species that imply that natural populations are usually governed by higher order systems. The object is to understand how parameters characterizing the dynamics of a population derive from the behavior of individuals. He then asks whether population parameters will typically have values leading to interesting dynamics. He concludes that: "In the natural world, the role of non-linear phenomena (including possibly chaos) in the dynamics of many infectious diseases of humans and animals is being understood in an increasingly explicit way. But for most natural populations, I believe environmental noise and other complications make it difficult to find examples of time series that show period doubling, intermittancy, transitions to chaos, and other dynamical features that are clearly exhibited in some physiological and biochemical systems".

[19] His books, "Calcul, l'imprévu" and "Au hasard", were translated in the references cited below, and are thought provoking and delights to read.

"Randomness appears because the available information, though accurate, is incomplete. If determinism means that the past determines the future, it can only be a property of reality as a whole, of the total cosmos. As soon as one isolates, from this global reality, a sequence of observations to be described and analyzed, one runs the risk of finding only randomness in that particular projection of the deterministic whole."

Our major question is where does "randomness" come from? What missing elements in the global model produce what is called "randomness" in the micro-model, the particular projection of the global model.

We formulated a general model, Eqs. (20)–(22), involving price variability, Bayesian errors and composition of agents in the market. We then explained how quantitative changes of the parameters of a general higher order theoretical model can change the qualitative nature of the solution. This part of the paper is concerned with the question: which set of parameters is consistent with the evidence.

There is a phenomenological approach to the analysis of data developed for physical sciences. This approach attempts to infer the multidimensional attractor underlying the observed time series without any understanding of the underlying mechanism. Although this approach has its merits, it requires extremely long runs of data which limit its usefulness to economists. Our approach is hypothesis testing, rather than the phenomonological time series analysis, because we want to understand the economic interrelationships which generate price volatility.

Price volatility, Bayesian errors and the composition of agents are dynamically interrelated in the general system, Eqs. (20)–(22) denoted $\mathrm{d}X(t)/\mathrm{d}t = \Phi[X(t)]$, where $X = (x, y, z)$, and $\Phi = (F, G, H)$. We cannot test the Lorenz specification specifically because $x(t)$ is price variability less the variability of the fundamentals and we do have a good measure of the variability of the fundamentals. In the Lorenz system, the values of x and y can be positive and negative. By just using price volatility as a measure of x, the value of $x > 0$ does not conform to the Lorenz model. Hence, we consider general non-linear and linear systems $\mathrm{d}X(t)/\mathrm{d}t = \Phi[X(t)]$ to see if we can explain what produces price variability and Bayesian errors. The Rational Expectations Hypothesis of Muth (MRE) assumes that Bayesian errors are random variables with no structure or predictability. In terms of Eq. (21), the MRE hypothesis is that $\delta G/\delta X = 0$, $X = (x, y, z)$. Similarly the EMH hypothesis assumes that price variability is a purely random variable: in Eq. (20), $\delta F/\delta X = 0$, $X = (x, y, z)$.

We consider (a) several markets and commodities: the S&P 500 futures contracts and agricultural commodities corn and soybeans; (b) several functional forms for $\Phi = (F, G, H)$, and (c) several periods. Our aim is to see if we can explain price variability and Bayesian errors in terms of the generalization Eqs. (20)–(22) of the Archetype model. Our conclusions documented below support the generalization of the Archetype model.

Conclusions:

- The pure random walk hypothesis of price changes is rejected.
- The Bayesian errors influence price variability.
- There is a structure to the Bayesian errors.
- The MRE hypothesis is rejected.

The composition of agents is independent of the other variables.

Tables 1–4 and summary Table 5 refer to the financial markets. Tables 6 and 7 refer to the agricultural markets.

5.2. Financial markets

All the data refer to S&P 500 futures contracts covering a period from September 1992 until December 1996. Price volatility, denoted x_t, is the annualized standard deviation of a sample of 10 daily returns. The 10 days standard deviation of the difference between the futures price at t and the price at expiration ($t = T$) is denoted as y_t and represents the Bayesian errors. In other words, for every contract, we subtract the daily settlement price from the last known settlement price for the nearest contract and then calculate the 10 days rolling standard deviation. We have also experimented with another measure of the variance of the errors i.e. the absolute value of the difference between today's price of the index and its value at expiration of the contract. Both measures give similar results. From the Commoditity Futures Trading Commission we take the weekly Traders Commitment Report (published every Friday), which describes the positions of large speculators and hedgers as well as small speculators and hedgers. We define the composition of agents, denoted z_t, as the ratio of large speculators who are long divided by open interest. Since z_t represents weekly data, we match the daily volatility x_t and error y_t with the composition of agents variable based on the report dates of the Traders Commitment.

In Tables 1 and 2 we examine Eqs. (20b)–(22b) of a less restrictive system than the Lorenz model to investigate whether volatility and Bayesian errors follow random walks. This is a non-linear specification of the generalized model in Eqs. (20)–(22), (20a)–(22a). Table 1 presents regression coefficients and t-statistics. Table 2 concerns Wald tests of linear combinations of parameter values.

$$x_t = [1 - c_1]x_{t-1} + c_2 y_{t-1} + \varepsilon_{1t}, \tag{20b}$$

$$y_t = c_3 y_{t-1} + x_{t-1}[c_4 - z_{t-1}] + \varepsilon_{2t}, \tag{21b}$$

$$z_t = [1 - c_5]z_{t-1} + c_6 x_{t-1} y_{t-1} + \varepsilon_{3t}. \tag{22b}$$

Consider now the linear system (20c)–(22c), based on Eqs. (20)–(22). We wish to investigate if the pure random walk paradigm holds for all the variables x_t, y_t, z_t, and if there is a structure to the Bayesian errors.

Table 1
Non-linear system estimation-values of coefficients

Financial markets								
Period	N		$c(1)$	$c(2)$	$c(3)$	$c(4)$	$c(5)$	$c(6)$
1995	52		0.147683	0.003347	0.477307	21.87112	0.021231	0.002997
		t-statistics	1.919417	1.958609	3.760994**	3.826966**	0.582718	0.437006
1996	51		0.168032	0.002381	0.258976	38.72963	0.074515	0.002164
		t-statistics	1.599364	1.31123	1.67514	4.331704**	1.712146	1.172743
1995–1996	103		1.175264	0.002899	0.41528	28.30789	0.015451	0.0002
		t-statistics	2.609179*	2.3343*	3.997327**	5.03766**	0.780082	0.14391
September 1992–	217		0.247893	0.004831	0.554586	17.06722	0.019644	0.000084
December 1996		t-statistics	5.243159**	4.755081**	7.509463**	4.968178**	1.151635	0.065996

* Denotes significance at the 5% confidence level.
** Denotes significance at the 1% confidence level.

Table 2
Hypothesis testing – Wald coefficients; non-linear system

Financial markets						
Period	N		Null hypotheses			
			$c(1)=0$ $c(2)=0$	$c(2)=0$	$c(1)=0$ $c(3)=0$ $c(5)=0$	$c(2)=0$ $c(6)=0$
1995	52	χ^2	3.941546	3.836151	15.64022	4.100573
		Probability	0.139349	0.050159	0.001344	0.128698
1996	51	χ^2	2.756151	1.719324	6.304722	2.959558
		Probability	0.252063	0.18978	0.09769	0.227688
1995–1996	103	χ^2	6.835365	5.448955	17.28646	5.454953
		Probability	0.032788	0.01958	0.000617	0.065384
September 1992–December 1996	217	χ^2	27.49642	22.61079	61.1752	22.6121
		Probability	0.000001	0.000002	0	0.000012

$$x_t = c_1 x_{t-1} + c_2 y_{t-1} + c_3 z_{t-1} + \varepsilon_{1t}, \tag{20c}$$

$$y_t = c_4 x_{t-1} + c_5 y_{t-1} + c_6 z_{t-1} + \varepsilon_{2t}, \tag{21c}$$

$$z_t = c_7 x_{t-1} + c_8 y_{t-1} + c_9 z_{t-1} + \varepsilon_{3t}. \tag{22c}$$

We summarize the results of Tables 1–4 of the non-linear and linear systems in Table 5. It is seen that the data are consistent with the archetype model with one exception. The composition of agents is a random walk.

5.3. Agricultural commodities

We now examine the generalized non-linear system for agricultural variables: corn and soybeans: Tables 6 and 7. Our estimates of the variables (x, y, z) are as follows. We have weekly data for corn and soybean futures contracts traded at the Chicago Board of Trade from January 1993 to December 1994. Price volatility, denoted by x_t, is implied by the Black–Scholes option pricing model and computed by the Chicago Board of Trade. The variance of errors, denoted by y_t is the absolute values of the difference between the futures price at time t and the futures price at the expiration of the nearby contract. [20] The composition of agents, denoted by z_t is the ratio of the number of contracts bought by large speculators divided by the open interest, that is, divided by all outstanding futures contracts.

[20] The absolute value of the expectation and variance of the Bayesian errors are similar in shape, see Fig. 2.

Table 3
Linear system estimation-values of coefficients – financial markets

Period	*N*		*c*(1)	*c*(2)	*c*(3)	*c*(4)	*c*(5)	*c*(6)	*c*(7)	*c*(8)	*c*(9)
1995	52		0.697047	0.002528	0.269524	15.66926	0.31926	18.80474	0.114872	−0.001144	0.909123
		t-statistics	6.979095**	1.374053	[illegible].908716	2.093513*	2.315194*	1.777056	2.765443**	−1.495307	15.48038**
1996	51		0.665845	0.001777	0.63071	20.80853	0.237151	60.53896	−0.031798	0.001009	0.907134
		t-statistics	5.548372**	0.924383	2.033158*	1.965357	1.398574	2.211993*	−1.193884	2.36613*	13.176**
1995–1996	103		0.712765	0.002769	0.277488	25.00252	0.420329	7.388377	0.001846	0.000145	0.971158
		t-statistics	9.162927**	2.293458**	2.614672**	3.630301**	3.932716**	0.78631	0.081816	0.41526	31.54657**
September 1992–	217		0.611958	0.004099	0.436693	9.57186	0.512353	23.88324	0.014529	−0.000012	0.954730
December 1996		*t*-statistics	11.42511**	4.194483**	4.818344**	2.382893**	6.990185**	3.513854**	0.921832	−0.039903	35.8003**

* Denotes significance at the 5% confidence level.
** Denotes significance at the 1% confidence level.

Table 4
Hypothesis testing – Wald coefficients: Linear system; financial markets

Period	N		Null hypothesis			
			$c(1)=0$ $c(5)=0$ $c(9)=0$	$c(1)=1$ $c(5)=1$ $c(9)=1$	$c(2)=c(3)=0$ $c(4)=c(6)=0$ $c(7)=c(8)=0$	$c(2)=0$ $c(3)=0$
1995	52	χ^2	288.4116	288.4116	37.1677	9.344199
		Probability	0	0	0	0.009353
1996	51	χ^2	271.7912	48.12123	51.97235	7.30625
		Probability	0	0	0	0.025912
1995–1996	103	χ^2	1190.138	66.4536	58.1939	12.7536
		Probability	0	0	0	0.001701
September 1992–	217	χ^2	1587.6	146.1495	117.306	48.21681
December 1996		Probability	0	0	0	0

Table 5
Summary of Tables 1–4: Financial markets, longer periods

Hypothesis	Non-linear model	Conclusion	Linear model	Conclusion
Price variability is a random walk	$C(1)=0$	Reject	$C(2)=0$	Reject
	$C(2)=0$		$C(3)=0$	
Bayesian error random	$C(3)=0$	Reject	$C(4)=0$	Reject
	$C(4)=0$		$C(5)=0$	
			$C(6)=0$	
Price variability independent of Bayesian errors	$C(2)=0$	Reject		
Composition of agents random walk	$C(5)=0$	Accept	$C(8)=0$	Accept
	$C(6)=0$		$C(9)=0$	
All variables are random walks			$C(1)=1$	Reject
			$C(5)=1$	
			$C(9)=1$	
			Others	
			$C(i)=0$	

The conclusions are seen clearly in Table 7, the Wald tests. For the entire period, the results are the same as those found for financial markets. The price variability is neither random nor a random walk. It is influenced by the Bayesian errors. The Bayesian errors are neither random (as assumed in the MRE hypothesis) nor random walks. The composition of agents, however, is a random walk.

6. Conclusions

The aim of our paper is to analyze the theoretical foundations of the efficient market hypothesis by stressing the efficient use of information and its effect

Table 6

Values of coefficients from system estimation: $x_t = c(1)x_{t-1} + c(2)y_{t-1}$; $y_t = c(3)x_{t-1} - c(4)x_{t-1}z_{t-1} + c(5)y_{t-1}$; $z_t = c(6)z_{t-1} + c(7)x_{t-1}y_{t-1}$[a]

Commodity	Period	$C(1)$	$C(2)$	$C(3)$	$C(4)$	$C(5)$	$C(6)$	$C(7)$
Corn	January 1993–December 1994	0.871886**	0.086754*	−0.105118	−0.027477*	0.692318**	0.996669**	−0.0000889
		(18.32261)	(2.029803)	(−0.509720)	(−1.768015)	(10.17364)	(68.19037)	(−0.224902)
Corn	January–December 1993	0.932341**	0.031155	0.434205	0.007542	0.707621**	0.991582**	0.000889
		(17.21280)	(0.700313)	(1.210064)	(0.334792)	(7.756978)	(39.86482)	(0.3556)
Corn	January–December 1994	0.825401**	0.135264*	−0.628648*	−0.073650**	0.632155**	0.984880**	−0.000307
		(11.01738)	(1.872283)	(2.084178)	(−2.736716)	(6.333528)	(65.20979)	(−0.972821)
Soybeans	January 1993–December 1994	0.852024**	0.429578*	−0.002310	−0.001493	0.775010**	1.001594**	−0.005547*
		(17.28032)	(2.163062)	(−0.047218)	(−0.752885)	(11.84851)	(71.45370)	(−1.775370)
Soybeans	January–December 1993	0.862833**	0.475209**	0.046012	0.001228	0.842916**	1.014184**	−0.004281
		(16.30281)	(2.598100)	(0.401926)	(0.256321)	(10.35966)	(52.42731)	(−0.775628)
Soybeans	January–December 1994	0.864158**	0.267357	0.012756	−0.002701	0.535107**	0.994622**	−0.006958*
		(8.862383)	(0.573671)	(0.285637)	(−1.516465)	(4.887126)	(50.84558)	(−1.885839)

[a] *Note*: An (**) and (*) indicate that the coefficient is significant at the 1% and 10% confidence levels, respectively. The *t*-statistics is given in parenthesis.

Table 7

Wald coefficient tests: $x_t = c(1)x_{t-1} + c(2)y_{t-1};\ y_t = c(3)x_{t-1} - c(4)x_{t-1}z_{t-1} + c(5)y_{t-1};\ z_t = c(6)z_{t-1} + c(7)x_{t-1}y_{t-1}$[a]

Parameter restriction Null hypotheses	Commodity	January 1993–December 1994		January 1993–December 1993		January 1994–December 1994	
		χ^2	Probability	χ^2	Probability	χ^2	Probability
Restriction 1. Price variance is a random walk: $C(1)=1;\ C(2)=0$	Corn	7.317363	0.025766	1.590846	0.451390	5.557753	0.062108
Reject	Soybeans	9.069919	0.010727	8.684261	0.013009	2.733767	0.254900
Restriction 2. Bayesian errors random: $C(3)=0;\ C(4)=0;\ C(5)=0$	Corn	354.0297	0.000000	185.9297	0.000000	193.8882	0.000000
Reject	Soybeans	325.1237	0.000000	167.3906	0.000000	181.1952	0.000000
Restriction 3. Bayesian errors random walk: $C(3)=0;\ C(4)=0;\ C(5)=1$	Corn	20.92695	0.000109	11.54009	0.009137	14.66806	0.002123
Reject	Soybeans	11.96054	0.007520	4.067382	0.254279	18.24999	0.000391
Restriction 4. Composition of agents random: $C(6)=0;\ C(7)=0$	Corn	7172.763	0.000000	3112.694	0.000000	5947.188	0.000000
Reject	Soybeans	7436.462	0.000000	4214.733	0.000000	3531.458	0.000000
Restriction 5. Composition of agents random walk: $C(6)=1;\ C(7)=0$	Corn	0.253217	0.881078	1.028678	0.597896	4.276984	0.117832
Accept	Soybeans	4.393699	0.111153	0.713924	0.699799	5.965239	0.050660
Restriction 6. All variables random walks: $C(1)=1;\ C(2)=0;\ C(3)=0;\ C(4)=0;\ C(5)=1;\ C(6)=1;\ C(7)=0$	Corn	26.37768	0.000431	13.75545	0.055706	23.78946	0.001241
Reject	Soybeans	25.21629	0.000695	12.40919	0.087880	26.74112	0.000371

[a] *Note*: An (**) and (*) indicate that the null hypothesis is rejected at the 1% and 10% confidence levels, respectively. The acceptance or rejection noted refers to the longer period.

upon price volatility. The "random walk" hypothesis assumes that price volatility is exogenous and unexplained. Randomness means that a knowledge of the past cannot help to predict the future. We accept the view that randomness appears because information is incomplete. An analogy with the classic examples of randomness: a coin tossing or dice rolling experiment is pertinent. If we knew the spin and velocity of a coin or a die, we could predict the outcome. They are deterministic processes. However, that information is unavailable. The global reality is deterministic, but human beings can only know a minute subset. The larger the subset of information available and known, the less emphasis one must place upon the generic term randomness.

We constructed a general and well accepted intertemporal price determination model. Our analysis was used to explain the learning process and the efficient use of information in our archetype model. The Bayesian error is the difference between the objective and subjective expectations of the specified fundamentals. The objective expectation is not known because it depends upon information that is not available to the observer. It is generated by a global deterministic system. The subjective estimate is arrived at via Bayesian learning, taking into account the costs and benefits of further sampling from a multidimensional space. We derived the determinants of the dynamics of the Bayesian error. Thus we expanded the information set or further specified a component of what was attributed to "randomness".

We showed that the resulting system is of third order in price variability, Bayesian error and composition of agents. One very specific possibility is that the system is chaotic, and moves into a strange attractor, wherein the resulting movements of price variability can be described statistically as random. In that case, randomness is chaotic randomness.

We estimated a general unrestricted system for financial and agricultural markets to see which specifications we can reject. What emerges is that a system very close to our archetype model is consistent with the evidence. Price variability is a serially correlated variable which is affected by the Bayesian error. The Bayesian error is a serially correlated variable which is affected by the noisiness of the system. It has the dynamics graphed in Fig. 2. Putting the two together, we obtain an equation for price volatility which looks a lot like the GARCH equation.[21] The price variability is a serially correlated variable which is affected by the Bayesian error, and the latter is a serially correlated variable which is affected by the noisiness of the system. In this manner we have explained some of the determinants of what has been called the "randomness" of price changes.

[21] For example, see Taylor (1994).

Acknowledgements

We are grateful to Dimitrios Bouroudzoglou and Caglar Alkan for extensive computations.

References

Allen, P.R., 1995. Review of De Grauwe et al.. Journal of Economic Literature 33, 224–225.

Ball, R. (1994). The development, accomplishments and limitations of the theory of stock market efficiency, Managerial Finance 20, Special issue on. The Predictability of Stock Market Prices, edited by Nuno Crato.

Baumol, W., Benhabib, J., 1989. Chaos: Significance, mechanism and economic applications. Journal of Economic Perspectives 3, 77–105.

Benhabib, J. (Ed.), 1992. Cycles and Chaos in Economic Equilibrium. Princeton University Press, Princeton, NJ.

Brock, W.A., 1988. Nonlinearity and complex dynamics in economics and finance. In: The Economy as an Evolving Complex System, SFI Studies in the Sciences of Complexity. Addison-Wesley, Reading, MA.

Brock, W.A., Dechert, W., Scheinkman, J., 1986. A test for independence based on the correlation dimension. Working paper, Department of Economics, University of Wisconsin, University of Chicago and University of Houston.

Brock, W.A., Hsieh, D.A, Le Baron, B., 1991. Nonlinear Dynamics, Chaos and Instability: Statistical Theory and Economic Evidence. MIT Press, Cambridge, MA.

Brock, W.A., Malliaris, A.G., 1989. Differential Equations, Stability and Chaos in Dynamic Economics. North-Holland, Amsterdam.

Cartapanis, A., 1996. L'héterogénéité des anticipations dans les modèles de change. Economie Appliquée XLIX (3), Les taux de change dans les années 1990.

De Grauwe, P., Dewachter, H., Embrechts, M., 1993. Exchange Rate Theory: Chaotic Models and Foreign Exchange. Basil Blackwell, Oxford.

Ekeland, I., 1988. Mathematics and the Unexpected. University of Chicago Press, Chicago.

Ekeland, I., 1993. The Broken Dice. University of Chicago Press, Chicago.

Friedman, M., 1953. The case for flexible exchange rates. In: Essays in Positive Economics. University of Chicago Press, Chicago.

Granger, C., 1994. Is chaotic economic theory relevant for economics? Journal of International and Comparative Economics 3, 139–145.

Guckenheimer, J., Holmes, P., 1983. Nonlinear Oscillations, Dynamical Systems and Bifurcation of Vector Fields. Springer, New York.

Kandel, E., Pearson, N., 1995. Differential interpretation of public signals and trade in speculative markets. Journal of Political Economy 103, 831–872.

Lo, A.W., 1997. Fat tails, long memory, and the stock market since the 1960s. Economic Notes 2, 213–246.

May, R.M., 1987. Chaos and the dynamics of biological populations. Proceedings of the Royal Society London A 413, 27–44.

Merton, R., 1990. Continuous Time Finance. Basil Blackwell, Oxford.

Peck, A., 1985. The economic role of traditional commodity futures markets. In: Peck, A.E. (Ed.), Futures Markets, Their Economic Role. American Enterprise Institute, Washington, DC.

Samuelson, P., 1965. Proof that properly anticipated prices fluctuate randomly. Industrial Management Review 6, 41–49.

Shiller, R., 1989. Market Volatility. MIT Press, Cambridge, MA.
Sparrow, C., 1982. The Lorenz Equations: Bifurcations, Chaos and Strange Attractors. Springer, New York.
Stein, J.L., 1986. The Economics of Futures Markets. Basil Blackwell, Oxford.
Stein, J.L., 1991. International Financial Markets. Basil Blackwell, Oxford.
Stein, J.L., 1992a. Cobwebs, rational expectations and futures markets. Review of Economics and Statistics 74, 127–133.
Stein, J.L., 1992b. Price discovery processes. Supplement to the Economic Record.
Stein, J.L., 1994. Can a central bank achieve price stability? Review, Federal Reserve Bank of St. Louis, April/May.
Stein, J.L., Allen, P.R. et al., 1995. Fundamental Determinants of Exchange Rates. Oxford University Press, Oxford.
Taylor, S.J., 1994. Predicting the volatility of stock prices using ARCH models, with UK examples. In: The Predictability of Stock Market Prices. University Press,Nancy.
Working, H., 1934. A random-difference series for use in the analysis of time series. Journal of the American Statistical Association 29, 11–24.
Working, H., 1949. Investigation of economic expectations. American Economic Review 39.

Chaotic Behavior in Prices of European Equity Markets: A Comparative Analysis of Major Economic Regions

George C. Philippatos
Efi Pilarinu
A. G. Malliaris

SUMMARY. Brock's Residual Test Theorem and the BDS statistical test are the dynamic tools employed in this paper for analyzing international stock market data. Raw and detrended weekly returns and index levels for eleven International Indices (European, North-American, and from the Far East and Pacific region) are analyzed in a non-parametric fashion. By utilizing non-linearity tests adapted from chaos theory evidence is presented supporting integrated equity markets.

I. INTRODUCTION

The primary purpose of this paper is to apply techniques adapted from chaos theory to analyze the behavior of international stock

---

George C. Philippatos is affiliated with the University of Tennessee, Knoxville, TN. Efi Pilarinu is associated with Salomon Brothers, New York, NY. A. G. Malliaris is affiliated with Loyola University of Chicago, Chicago, IL.

The authors thank J. Doukas, P. Theodossiou, G. Koutmos, and A. Shafie for constructive comments that helped to improve the contents of this paper.

[Haworth co-indexing entry note]: "Chaotic Behavior in Prices of European Equity Markets: A Comparative Analysis of Major Economic Regions." Philippatos, George C., Efi Pilarinu, and A. G. Malliaris. Co-published simultaneously in *Journal of Multinational Financial Management* (The Haworth Press, Inc.) Vol. 3, No. 3/4, 1993, pp. 5-24; and: *European Equity Markets and Corporate Financial Decisions* (ed: John Doukas, and Ike Mathur) The Haworth Press, Inc., 1993, pp. 5-24. Multiple copies of this article/chapter may be purchased from The Haworth Document Delivery Center [1-800-3-HAWORTH; 9:00 a.m. - 5:00 p.m. (EST)].

markets. The stochastic approach to modeling the complexity and the apparent randomness of financial markets constitutes at present the most popular methodology. However, there exist many stylized facts that have recently led the profession to reevaluate the use of the random walk framework and its companions (EMH). An informative collection of some of these disturbing phenomena can be found in Brock (1992). These puzzles have contributed to consideration of a new research methodology based on techniques adapted from complex systems theory, which includes chaotic processes.

Pathways that may lead to chaotic and erratic dynamics have been investigated by several authors. Benhabib and Day (1981) and Gaertner (1988), analyze consumer choice. Day (1983) and Dana and Montrucchio (1986), analyze a classical economic growth model and a dynamic oligopoly setting, respectively. Baumol and Benhabib (1989) and Shaffer (1991), consider models of firm behavior. Lorenz (1992) proves the existence of a strange attractor for a Kaldor type business cycle model. The Santa Fe Institute Volume (1988), presents collectively the work of scientists from various disciplines in discussing the issue of the *Economy as an Evolving Complex System.* Examples include households that heavily discount the future, incomplete markets, abandonment of the equilibrium assumption in favor of learning dynamics, complex and chaotic dynamics in tastes and technology, and other settings shown to lead to complex and random appearing behavior produced by deterministic mechanisms.

Recently, researchers have been investigating for the presence of non-linear dependencies hidden in the assumed IID residuals of various stochastic models. The key idea is that although standard statistical techniques may support a specific statistical specification, there may exist additional non-linear structure which these techniques cannot detect. Empirical research in Finance employing tools from chaos theory (correlation dimension estimates) examines whether there exists additional structure above and beyond that captured by fitting stochastic models to log transformed, detrended/deseasonalized stock return series. For example, Scheinkman and LeBaron (1989), have examined U.S. daily and weekly returns from the value weighted (VW) CRSP index but the dependencies detected do not seem to be captured from an ARCH type specification. Brock (1987) has examined subsets of the same data and also monthly returns of the value weighted (VW) and equally weighted (EW) NYSE index. Genotte and Marsh (1986), have examined subsets of the same monthly data and also adjusted for the January effect. Hsieh (1991), has examined weekly returns of various portfolios and indices, daily returns and 15-minute returns of the S&P500. Willey (1992), has tested for non-linear dependencies in the daily prices of the Standard & Poor's 100 Stock Index and the NASDAQ 100 Stock Index. Finally, Philippatos and Pilarinu (1994) have analyzed weekly stock prices from various International Indices.

All these studies have examined whether there exists predictability over and above stochastic financial stock return models (e.g., random walk, martingale, ARCH, GARCH).[1] Since it has been shown empirically by Fischer and Palasvirta (1990) and others that the various national markets are somewhat integrated and move more or less in tandem with the U.S. market, it is interesting to hypothesize that some of the major financial markets of the world exhibit similar chaotic dynamics. Hence, we test empirically for the presence of deterministic non-linearities in the markets of the following six European countries: United Kingdom, Belgium, Switzerland, France, Germany, and Italy. The results in the European Region are then compared empirically to the respective results from the North-American Region (Canada and U.S.), and from the Far Eastern and Pacific Rim Region (Australia and Japan), as well as the results from the World Index. It is found that the non-linear dependencies, quantified using techniques adapted from chaos theory, are similar across both the European indices and the non-European International Indices.

Specifically, in this paper some new techniques adapted from chaos theory are employed, since they appear more promising in revealing non-linear dependencies. These dependencies may lead to the re-evaluation of the asset price paradigm postulating that tomorrow's expected value is equal to today's actual price and thus readily admitting that no short run prediction can be accomplished. In fact, we examine indices of ten industrialized countries from Europe, North America, the Far East, and the Pacific region and the World index and investigate whether the spatial correlations are different across countries. More importantly we wish to address the issue of the appropriate choice of the single observable examined, when quantifying static or dynamic properties of a multidimensional complex system. Section II presents an informal and intuitive view of chaos theory. Section III discusses the methodology used. In Section IV, the results are presented and compared to previous research in the local Capital Markets. Section V deals with the implications of this work and future directions of research.

II. CHAOS AND RANDOMNESS

Illustrations of simple non-linear equations that exhibit rich behavioral variety have been presented across various disciplines (May (1974)). The interesting feature of such systems stems from the fact that the time series generated from a range of parameter values (the chaotic region) is virtually indistinguishable from a random series. Not only standard statistical tests but even frequency domain analysis cannot identify the underlying dependencies (Bunov and Weiss (1979)).

Malliaris and Philippatos (1991) have studied the discrete logistic map (a one-dimensional non-linear map) as a model for changes in prices and contrasted the time sequence with that produced from a random number generator. The two series not only appear indistinguishable, but standard statistical tests fail to detect the underlying differences. In the random case no dependencies exist and in the chaotic case each price is exactly determined from the previous price. It is thus important to understand the source of complex and random appearing behavior in a system. Time series generated from chaotic systems are capable of deceiving certain statistical tests. Randomness with a deterministic origin arises from the three properties that define chaotic behavior: (a) sensitivity to initial conditions, (b) transitivity, and (c) a dense set of periodic points. An intuitive and non-mathematical view of these properties reveals the difference of random and complex behavior with a deterministic origin versus a stochastic one.[2]

(a) *Sensitivity to initial conditions.* Since a chaotic map is a deterministic system it may be fully predictable. However, this is only true if one knows the initial value with complete accuracy. An inaccuracy of an infinitely small order in measuring the initial condition of the system, may grow exponentially as the system evolves in time. Indeed this property renders the system practically unpredictable even if the law of motion is known. The difference between a chaotic and a purely random process (which is also unpredictable) lies in what causes randomness. In the latter case it is due to statistical independence, but for chaotic systems it is due to the lack of infinitely accurate information coupled with sensitivity to initial conditions. In practical terms, this property allows for major effects to be caused by small imperceptible changes. It is a manifestation of the accumulated effect of the feedback (feed forward) non-linear mechanisms at work, since sensitivity to initial conditions cannot be present in a linear world.

(b) *Transitivity.* Chaotic prices may wander anywhere. They can sore up and plunge to zero.

(c) *The periodic chaotic prices are dense in the real numbers.* Chaotic maps may well resemble random and complex appearing processes, but structure is present. Each sequence of periodic points converges.

A very important property of certain chaotic maps is the existence of a "strange attractor." This is a compact set towards which trajectories from almost all initial conditions converge. In simple terms, it is a region that may contain more points than other regions. This set can be detected by examining a time series in increasing d-dimensional spaces, simply by coupling delayed values. For a random process all space is filled in any d-dimensional reconstruction. However, for a chaotic process not all space is filled and moreover, it may be the case that the attractor in d-dimensions has a non-integer dimension (fractal). In practice, it is possible to distinguish complexity and randomness due to random sampling from that resulting from simple causes (chaos). This is accomplished by observing the correlation behavior of a time series in higher dimensional spaces.[3] Our empirical interest is in discovering low dimensional chaos because as the dimension increases the chaotic process becomes indistinguishable from a purely random process.

III. METHODOLOGY

Correlation Dimension Invariant

The correlation dimension is a measure of the average local spatial correlation of the series. It can be used to distinguish random from deterministic-chaotic series, simply because pure randomness has a completely different average local spatial correlation behavior than that of a random appearing, but truly chaotic system. The basis of this difference is the existence of strange attractors in chaotic systems. In simple terms, in a system that has a strange attractor as time evolves the system converges to a set (strange attractor). The importance of this property can be readily visualized if one embeds the scalar time series into higher dimensional spaces. The idea is as follows: Examine phase plots (i.e., plots of delayed values) at various dimensions. A completely random series will fill the space in all cases. In essence, any two, three, or higher dimensional plots of delayed values of a random series will not show any structure, by assumption. But a chaotic series reveals a completely different hidden structure, although a simple inspection of a chaotic time series makes it look indistinguishable from a random one.[4] The structure unfolds as one increases the dimensions of the delayed value vectors (plotted in the phase plots) and observes that less space is filled and essentially everything lies within a set that has a small dimension. Looked at from another point of view, the idea is that if one observes the near neighborhood behavior of the two series at increasing scales (resolution parameters), these neighborhoods will include more points at an increasing rate. However, for the chaotic series this increase moves at a decreasing rate that in fact saturates at some point.

The correlation dimension D quantifies the average spatial correlation. It is the average information gained by increased resolution, by taking into account conditional probabilities:[5]

$$D = \lim_{\varepsilon \to 0} \lim_{N \to \infty} \frac{\log C(\varepsilon)}{\log \varepsilon}$$

$$C(\varepsilon) = \frac{\{\# (x_i, x_j) : \|x_i - x_j\| < \varepsilon\}}{N^2}$$

Since the true law of motion governing the system under examination is unknown and the only available information is a single observable of the system, we employ the time delay method for reconstructing the phase space (Takens (1983)). Assume that the only available measurement is a single variable x_i, $i = 1, 2, \ldots, N$. There exists a diffeomorphism between the n-dimensional true generating process and the reconstructed d-histories, if $d < 2n + 1$. Thus, by "transforming" the single time series into vector series of various dimensions, we embed the reconstructed phase space into the true one:

$$x_i^d = (x_i, x_{i+\tau}, x_{i+2\tau}, \ldots, x_{i+(d-1)\tau}),\ i = 1,2,\ldots N - (d-1)\tau$$

Having created the d-histories by coupling τ delayed values, we then calculate the correlation integral $C^d(\varepsilon)$:

$$C(\varepsilon) = \frac{\{\#\,(x_i^d, x_j^d) : \left\| x_i^d - x_j^d \right\| < \varepsilon\}}{N_n^2}$$

As ε changes the number of points included in the correlation integral also change. If structure exists and not all the degrees of freedom are exploited by the system, then proportionally fewer new neighborhoods will be included as ε increases. For example, consider a three dimensional object embedded in a four dimensional space. For any increase in the resolution parameter, the increase in the points included in the correlation integral is only due to three out of four available directions. Grassberger and Procaccia (1983) have shown that there exists a scaling relationship between the correlation integral $C^d(\varepsilon)$ and the correlation dimension D as the resolution ε shrinks:

$$C^d(\varepsilon) \approx \varepsilon^D$$

In practice, since the true dimension (N) is unknown we study the behavior of the correlation integral $C^d(\varepsilon)$ for increasing embedding dimensions d. We estimate D^d for each embedding dimension value d:

$$D^d = \lim_{\varepsilon \to 0} \frac{\log C^d(\varepsilon)}{\log \varepsilon}$$

If as d increases so does D^d, then the system is viewed as being high dimensional. If D^d converges or saturates to some level D, then

D is the estimated correlation dimension. In practice, one can detect structure by inspecting the logarithmic plots of the correlation integral versus the resolution parameter at various embedding dimensions. If structure exists, these plots (known as Grassberger-Procaccia plots (GP), (1983)) will appear like parallel lines. If the series are completely random, the slopes will be equal to each embedding dimension.

Brock's Residual Test Theorem

Brock's Residual Test Theorem exploits an important property of chaotic dynamical systems. It is a direct application of the invariance to coordinate transformations of these systems. In other words, the two invariant measures, namely the correlation dimension and the Lyapunov exponents, of a time series should be the same as those of the residuals of the original series constructed from a linear time series model with a finite number of lags (Brock and Dechert (1986)). This theorem has been used in most financial applications, in order to detect additional structure above and beyond particular stochastic specifications. In fact, it is a clever way of distinguishing low dimension estimates that are due to the presence of near unit root processes from chaos.

In practice, by comparing the correlation dimension estimates of the original series and of the filtered series, one should reject a linear generating process if these values are the same. However, caution is required in such comparisons for two important reasons: (a) There does not exist a statistical test that enables us to distinguish between two correlation dimension estimates, and (b) There exists a considerable bias in the correlation dimension estimates of relatively small sample sizes as those typically employed in economic and financial studies[6] (Ramsey and Yuan (1989), Ramsey et al. (1990)).

BDS Statistical Test

The BDS statistic is a non-parametric test of non-linearity (Brock, Hsieh, and LeBaron (1991)). It tests the null hypothesis that a time series is Independently and Identically distributed (IID) against an unspecified alternative using a non-parametric technique.

Under the null hypothesis of an independently and identically distributed process, the correlation integral $C_m(\varepsilon,T)$ at any fixed embedding dimension m and resolution parameter ε and for a finite sample size T, converges with probability one to $(C_1(\varepsilon)^m)$. This limiting quantity is the correlation integral of a completely random series. For a random series, as the embedding dimension increases, so do the points included in an ε-sphere by a power law whose exponent is equal to the embedding dimension. This property leads to a statistical test for randomness. It is shown that the standardized difference of the correlation integral of a series from a completely random series $(D_m(\varepsilon,T))$, has a normal limiting distribution with mean zero and variance $b^2m(\varepsilon)$:

$$W_m(\varepsilon,T) = T^{1/2} * \frac{D_m(\varepsilon,T)}{b_m(\varepsilon,T)}$$

where $$D_m(\varepsilon,T) = C_m(\varepsilon,T) - [C_1(\varepsilon,T)]^m$$

$$b_m(\varepsilon,T) =$$

$$4 * \left[K^m + 2\sum_{j=1}^{m-1} K^{m-j} * C^{2j} + (m-1)^2 * C^{2m} - m^2 * K * C^{2m-2}\right]$$

where $C = C_1(\varepsilon,T)$ and

$$K = \frac{6}{T(T-1)(T-2)} * \sum_{t<s<r} I_\varepsilon(x_t,x_s) * I_\varepsilon(x_s,x_r)$$

$I_\varepsilon(x_t, x_s)$ is the indicator function that equals 1 if $\|x_t - x_s\| < \varepsilon$ and zero otherwise, where $\|.\|$ is the sup-norm.

The BDS statistic is the mathematical analog of comparing the GP plots of the original data with those of a scrambled counterpart. It essentially quantifies the difference of the correlation integral values at each embedding dimension m of the original series $(C_m(\varepsilon))$ with those of a completely random part, which scales as a power of the embedding dimension $(C_1(\varepsilon)^m)$.

IV. EMPIRICAL FINDINGS

The database (Table 1) consists of the 833 percentage weekly logarithmic price relatives[7] of ten International Indices from Europe, North America and the Far East of Industrialized Countries and of the World Index (Barrons National Business and Financial Weekly). The sample period is from January 16, 1976 to December 27, 1991. All indices are based on local currencies and are value weighted (i.e., weights proportional to their market capitalizations). The World Index is constructed from the ten International Indices as a value weighted portfolio based on the dollar value of GNP for each country.

Recall that the implementation of Brock's Residual test theorem requires a comparison of the correlation dimension behavior of the raw series and a detrended counterpart. Furthermore, although there exists no statistical test that quantifies the difference between the correlation dimension estimates of two series, the behavior of the actual observable of the system (i.e., prices) is compared to that of a transformed one (i.e., returns). In effect, the correlation dimension estimates and the BDS statistic are obtained for the following four different time series for each country:

TABLE 1. Stock Indices

Region	***Country***	***Index***
North America	Canada	TSE 300
	United States	S&P 500
Europe	United Kingdom	Financial Times Stock Exchange 100
	Belgium	Stock Index
	Switzerland	Swiss Bank Corporation
	France	Agefi
	Germany	Commerzbank
	Italy	M.I.N.
Far East and Pacific Region	Australia	All Ordinaries
	Japan	Topix

The original return series

Residuals of an OLS regression on the return series

Transformed index level series

Residuals of an OLS regression on the index level series.

Tables 2-6 show the results (i.e., correlation integral values, BDS statistic values) for embedding dimension values 2, 4, 6, 8 and for five resolution parameter values ranging from 0.50 to 1.50 multiples of the standard deviation of the data.[8]

BDS Statistic

The BDS statistic is high for all four series of each country (critical value of 1.96 with a 5% significance). Thus, the BDS test of price and return series of raw and filtered series seem to reject the IID hypothesis. However, if one compares the results between raw and filtered data it is evident that only price series and not returns exhibit a dramatic drop of the BDS test. For example, the analysis of the weekly data from the United Kingdom at an embedding dimension equal to 8 and a resolution parameter equal to 1.5 standard deviations shows:

BDS	Index levels	Returns
Raw	400.88	6.20
Filtered	18.71	6.32

Previous studies that analyze domestic stock markets have examined daily and weekly return series. These BDS values found in the present study for national markets are very different from those reported by Willey (1992) for two U.S. stock indices, the S&P100 and the NASDAQ100. Willey finds values significantly lower than the critical value of the BDS statistic for both raw and detrended series of the logged first difference values used. Thus the null of an IID process is retained. By comparing our results of the return series we can infer that the difference stems from the aggregation level examined (daily versus weekly).[9] However, the present results

TABLE 2. Correlation Integral Values and BDS Statistic for (a) United Kingdom and (b) Belgium

M	ε	Index Levels	BDS	Residuals of index levels	BDS	Returns	BDS	Residuals of Returns	BDS
(a)									
2	0.5	**0.34953**	142.2895	**0.1515**	8.6529	**0.09127**	1.8703	**0.0912**	1.8944
4	0.5	**0.33745**	412.4978	**0.03311**	14.6336	**0.00925**	3.7858	**0.00921**	3.7049
6	0.5	**0.32804**	1569.4685	**0.00898**	22.6495	**0.001**	4.6302	**0.00099**	4.4655
8	0.5	**0.32013**	7148.0919	**0.00261**	34.6994	**0.00011**	5.5262	**0.0001**	4.2967
2	0.75	**0.44337**	177.7483	**0.29628**	9.3958	**0.1919**	1.5494	**0.19223**	1.6851
4	0.75	**0.43303**	372.2178	**0.11818**	14.9177	**0.04063**	3.8577	**0.04063**	3.8118
6	0.75	**0.42484**	954.9433	**0.05611**	21.4314	**0.00967**	5.9761	**0.00972**	6.0286
8	0.75	**0.41799**	2857.8244	**0.0285**	30.3534	**0.00251**	8.0806	**0.00253**	8.1564
2	1	**0.52414**	196.2778	**0.442**	10.0061	**0.31244**	1.5705	**0.31271**	1.8149
4	1	**0.51633**	330.6326	**0.24763**	15.3706	**0.10566**	3.8061	**0.10582**	3.9326
6	1	**0.50994**	650.9538	**0.15994**	20.9269	**0.03909**	5.6740	**0.03927**	5.8307
8	1	**0.50486**	1458.8323	**0.10969**	27.7354	**0.01538**	7.2973	**0.01543**	7.4010
2	1.25	**0.57581**	186.5996	**0.56643**	9.7522	**0.4398**	1.7178	**0.4405**	2.0550
4	1.25	**0.56881**	278.3061	**0.38051**	14.4858	**0.20533**	3.8051	**0.20596**	3.9833
6	1.25	**0.56368**	472.9702	**0.28405**	18.5905	**0.10201**	5.3554	**0.10258**	5.5248
8	1.25	**0.55966**	899.6118	**0.22337**	23.0083	**0.05258**	6.4537	**0.05295**	6.6056
2	1.5	**0.63623**	133.7091	**0.66538**	8.8703	**0.56094**	1.9272	**0.56118**	2.2257
4	1.5	**0.62733**	174.6506	**0.49801**	13.0765	**0.32879**	3.8927	**0.32903**	4.0428
6	1.5	**0.61994**	252.5437	**0.40141**	16.0624	**0.20133**	5.2662	**0.20171**	5.4146
8	1.5	**0.61369**	400.8883	**0.33597**	18.7171	**0.12674**	6.2044	**0.12698**	6.3247
(b)									
2	0.5	**0.36061**	134.7723	**0.28609**	12.8682	**0.11869**	3.36917	**0.1162**	3.03201
4	0.5	**0.35096**	377.6721	**0.14797**	24.4488	**0.01652**	4.79822	**0.01507**	3.74476
6	0.5	**0.34304**	1378.9667	**0.10013**	46.2411	**0.00257**	6.00099	**0.00225**	5.20077
8	0.5	**0.33624**	6008.7512	**0.07711**	98.1732	**0.00047**	8.46797	**0.0004**	7.76859
2	0.75	**0.46455**	146.9046	**0.42731**	11.7609	**0.23887**	4.26843	**0.23424**	3.1294
4	0.75	**0.45654**	289.8383	**0.26609**	18.9247	**0.0651**	5.50278	**0.06133**	4.41659
6	0.75	**0.44976**	691.9357	**0.19976**	28.4753	**0.01941**	6.62904	**0.01755**	5.52131
8	0.75	**0.44398**	1914.7565	**0.16654**	45.3559	**0.0064**	8.44749	**0.00549**	7.0007
2	1	**0.53113**	170.9854	**0.54445**	11.6768	**0.36689**	4.84653	**0.36439**	3.21979
4	1	**0.52582**	284.4413	**0.3776**	16.0232	**0.1499**	6.02782	**0.1466**	4.89638
6	1	**0.52106**	551.7202	**0.29899**	21.1171	**0.06619**	7.19384	**0.0638**	6.17877
8	1	**0.517**	1215.5457	**0.25559**	28.4425	**0.0313**	8.70322	**0.02979**	7.66073
2	1.25	**0.57853**	168.8451	**0.64022**	12.4459	**0.48923**	5.20063	**0.48756**	3.23046
4	1.25	**0.57289**	250.8035	**0.48473**	15.1312	**0.26062**	6.38723	**0.25642**	4.93468
5	1.25	**0.57042**	320.8271	**0.43621**	16.4444	**0.19385**	6.77102	**0.18988**	5.47583
7	1.25	**0.56614**	576.4005	**0.37358**	19.9613	**0.11223**	7.87811	**0.10804**	6.50813
9	1.25	**0.56237**	1138.5051	**0.33357**	24.5258	**0.06801**	9.20531	**0.06423**	7.64901
2	1.5	**0.63958**	126.3754	**0.7097**	12.1855	**0.59879**	5.80872	**0.59705**	3.14201
4	1.5	**0.6325**	164.4213	**0.57005**	14.1781	**0.38437**	7.08995	**0.37852**	5.11376
6	1.5	**0.62658**	237.0304	**0.48481**	15.8367	**0.25663**	7.85322	**0.25028**	6.18198
8	1.5	**0.62194**	375.2754	**0.43134**	18.1190	**0.17742**	8.73775	**0.17072**	7.04836

TABLE 3. Correlation Integral Values and BDS Statistic for (a) Switzerland and (b) France

M	ε	Index Levels	BDS	Residuals of index levels	BDS	Returns	BDS	Residuals of Returns	BDS
(a)									
2	0.5	0.37689	102.8531	0.19721	12.1732	0.12495	6.4649	0.12342	5.6085
4	0.5	0.36233	261.5042	0.06306	20.0498	0.01965	8.5359	0.01927	8.0066
6	0.5	0.35066	849.7740	0.02538	33.5070	0.00368	11.6886	0.00345	10.4271
8	0.5	0.34094	3276.9096	0.01051	55.9121	0.00068	13.8755	0.00062	12.3827
2	0.75	0.44897	139.8323	0.34468	11.9078	0.24391	6.0594	0.24198	5.7029
4	0.75	0.43731	285.2078	0.16929	18.2292	0.07183	8.3823	0.07103	8.2155
6	0.75	0.42773	709.2088	0.10142	27.4958	0.02501	11.7184	0.02452	11.4260
8	0.75	0.41954	2052.0855	0.06374	40.8463	0.00915	15.0581	0.00904	14.9613
2	1	0.50297	178.1099	0.47933	11.4853	0.37019	6.0992	0.36819	5.7316
4	1	0.49065	312.3603	0.29881	17.0162	0.15791	8.1885	0.15672	8.0116
6	1	0.48222	647.5016	0.21775	23.6212	0.07672	10.9865	0.0754	10.6173
8	1	0.4751	1534.3571	0.16731	31.9279	0.03922	13.6081	0.03817	13.0687
2	1.25	0.5662	165.8033	0.59258	11.2747	0.49894	6.9297	0.4949	6.4575
4	1.25	0.55303	248.6523	0.42518	16.0527	0.27715	8.7295	0.27394	8.5651
6	1.25	0.54288	425.2325	0.34126	20.6249	0.16776	10.7963	0.16486	10.5839
8	1.25	0.53414	814.3343	0.28698	25.6368	0.10537	12.5334	0.10308	12.3089
2	1.5	0.63391	126.3799	0.68356	11.0910	0.60983	7.4664	0.60697	6.9911
4	1.5	0.61984	164.0890	0.53635	15.1697	0.40185	8.9122	0.39887	8.6475
6	1.5	0.60893	235.6737	0.45817	18.6455	0.28067	10.4614	0.27767	10.1778
8	1.5	0.6002	371.5333	0.40652	21.9402	0.20231	11.7561	0.19901	11.3751
(b)									
2	0.5	0.35132	125.0025	0.26428	15.6075	0.10314	4.4993	0.12249	3.57013
4	0.5	0.34121	361.6413	0.12285	26.0531	0.01187	4.65315	0.01631	3.34355
6	0.5	0.33333	1372.5552	0.0707	45.9314	0.00166	6.93042	0.00253	459255
8	0.5	0.32664	6227.9195	0.04312	86.7570	0.00025	9.16101	0.00042	5.694
2	0.75	0.46079	132.3467	0.41206	15.3329	0.21208	4.81668	0.2503	4.97629
4	0.75	0.45072	261.6756	0.26409	24.0203	0.04945	4.9905	0.06967	5.19951
6	0.75	0.44274	627.4124	0.20044	36.7662	0.01307	6.52775	0.02102	5.95041
8	0.75	0.43584	1744.1363	0.16135	58.8341	0.00379	8.44404	0.00698	7.37185
2	1	0.53231	149.5863	0.51829	14.2514	0.33406	4.90744	0.37667	5.47758
4	1	0.52523	246.3632	0.36968	20.5499	0.12101	5.23734	0.15638	6.01763
6	1	0.51968	472.5046	0.30437	28.3530	0.04789	6.47687	0.06973	6.92587
8	1	0.51468	1027.4024	0.26596	39.9308	0.01996	7.66447	0.03285	8.05027
2	1.25	0.58196	151.5834	0.59684	12.6662	0.45524	4.99207	0.50098	5.94916
4	1.25	0.57303	221.4746	0.4479	17.3006	0.22136	5.44429	0.26999	6.24946
6	1.25	0.5665	367.3392	0.37838	22.2826	0.11483	6.51418	0.15449	7.14527
8	1.25	0.56104	679.8461	0.33755	28.6581	0.06176	7.40653	0.09205	8.08106
2	1.5	0.64708	119.7243	0.65929	10.9830	0.56601	4.88432	0.60605	5.72204
4	1.5	0.63725	152.6766	0.51329	14.7652	0.33686	5.4188	0.38844	6.17596
6	1.5	0.62928	215.0439	0.44046	18.3343	0.20959	6.28565	0.26137	7.11767
8	1.5	0.62252	331.5061	0.39231	21.9002	0.13378	6.93408	0.18106	7.90053

TABLE 4. Correlation Integral Values and BDS Statistic for (a) Germany and (b) Italy

M	ε	Index Levels	BDS	Residuals of index levels	BDS	Returns	BDS	Residuals of Returns	BDS
(a)									
2	0.5	0.34608	135.8093	0.20378	15.2037	0.10344	6.54479	0.10231	6.51315
4	0.5	0.328	386.8586	0.07682	27.3901	0.01317	8.62825	0.01286	8.65672
6	0.5	0.31369	1441.6557	0.03703	51.9035	0.00191	10.9958	0.0018	10.6230
8	0.5	0.30187	6436.8829	0.01938	107.8070	0.00031	14.5980	0.00028	13.9469
2	0.75	0.44268	173.6088	0.35071	16.1395	0.21325	6.55167	0.21077	6.74641
4	0.75	0.4295	360.6907	0.19639	25.6049	0.05441	8.73911	0.05336	9.04262
6	0.75	0.41861	916.3282	0.13596	42.1102	0.01532	10.6561	0.01496	11.1073
8	0.75	0.40896	2711.9430	0.10235	74.1047	0.00478	13.8592	0.00456	14.1043
2	1	0.50684	227.0280	0.472	15.8958	0.33746	6.80058	0.33413	6.85221
4	1	0.49419	395.1699	0.31634	23.1559	0.13259	9.15899	0.13034	9.30803
6	1	0.48437	810.0234	0.24788	33.0805	0.05662	10.9718	0.0556	11.3175
8	1	0.47621	1897.6321	0.20903	49.3219	0.02593	13.4260	0.02536	13.8734
2	1.25	0.57072	189.1624	0.56707	15.2087	0.46172	7.2351	0.45796	7.0026
4	1.25	0.55784	281.5219	0.41908	21.1389	0.24315	10.0183	0.23897	9.82732
6	1.25	0.54663	476.3601	0.34973	27.6920	0.13842	12.0896	0.13446	11.8147
8	1.25	0.53685	902.0133	0.30901	36.7861	0.08297	14.3591	0.07936	13.9043
2	1.5	0.63208	134.9655	0.64731	14.4060	0.57533	7.54599	0.57205	7.17835
4	1.5	0.62043	176.7728	0.50652	18.9364	0.36562	10.1687	0.36167	9.96753
6	1.5	0.61038	256.3069	0.43473	23.1748	0.24591	11.8251	0.2427	11.7559
8	1.5	0.60133	407.9381	0.39142	28.3488	0.17204	13.4995	0.16883	13.3831
(b)									
2	0.5	0.38967	118.1428	0.24792	10.6870	0.12252	3.48499	0.12249	3.5701
4	0.5	0.37436	287.2782	0.10121	18.5261	0.0163	3.26786	0.01631	3.3436
6	0.5	0.36131	882.4280	0.05572	33.8001	0.00251	4.44437	0.00253	4.5926
8	0.5	0.3498	3202.6313	0.03381	64.7369	0.00039	4.90919	0.00042	5.6940
2	0.75	0.4701	153.9017	0.3983	11.3608	0.25119	5.10709	0.2503	4.9763
4	0.75	0.45976	296.7052	0.22403	16.9764	0.06985	5.16534	0.06967	5.1995
6	0.75	0.4511	688.4484	0.15697	26.1501	0.02115	5.9506	0.02102	5.9504
8	0.75	0.44314	1845.0238	0.12014	41.1349	0.00701	7.34163	0.00698	7.3719
2	1	0.51955	211.6555	0.5193	11.6045	0.37737	5.4544	0.37667	5.4776
4	1	0.51185	361.2259	0.34171	15.3764	0.15634	5.87251	0.15638	6.0176
6	1	0.50528	722.2126	0.25826	20.3277	0.06974	6.80499	0.06973	6.9259
8	1	0.49927	1643.8643	0.2117	27.5877	0.0329	7.94232	0.03285	8.0503
2	1.25	0.55823	210.6335	0.612	12.0955	0.5013	5.9273	0.50098	5.9492
4	1.25	0.54999	326.4808	0.44693	14.8595	0.26965	6.12587	0.26999	6.2495
6	1.25	0.54344	581.0165	0.35609	17.7246	0.15443	7.07501	0.15449	7.1453
8	1.25	0.53804	1163.4267	0.30261	21.8432	0.09214	8.03869	0.09205	8.0811
2	1.5	0.61252	158.6913	0.68717	12.9052	0.60695	5.7892	0.60605	5.7220
4	1.5	0.60137	216.6015	0.54045	14.9002	0.38892	6.12017	0.38844	6.1760
6	1.5	0.59238	330.3036	0.45059	16.6208	0.2622	7.11656	0.26137	7.1177
8	1.5	0.58464	556.4121	0.39156	18.9379	0.18198	7.92148	0.18106	7.9005

TABLE 5. Correlation Integral Values and BDS Statistic for (a) Canada and (b) United States

M	ε	Index Levels	BDS	Residuals of index levels	BDS	Returns	BDS	Residuals of Returns	BDS
(a)									
2	0.5	**0.26508**	715.6151	**0.16668**	6.66878	**0.13776**	3.83404	**0.13545**	3.48695
4	0.5	**0.24747**	3142.4688	**0.04337**	12.97701	**0.02336**	5.73899	**0.02246**	5.57991
6	0.5	**0.23374**	19580.1077	**0.01583**	24.11166	**0.00439**	6.98643	**0.00406**	6.65665
8	0.5	**0.22191**	149209.474	**0.00776**	54.61056	**0.0008**	7.29379	**0.0007**	6.6353
2	0.75	**0.36961**	523.0852	**0.29378**	5.93158	**0.26308**	4.32287	**0.25982**	3.66782
4	0.75	**0.35484**	1418.5990	**0.11607**	10.86721	**0.08048**	5.88999	**0.07825**	5.48027
6	0.75	**0.34276**	4980.3077	**0.05678**	16.7128	**0.02695**	7.09106	**0.02576**	6.69278
8	0.75	**0.33223**	20849.6570	**0.03359**	27.99887	**0.00952**	8.3551	**0.00881**	7.70136
2	1	**0.46339**	267.1342	**0.41729**	5.42344	**0.39567**	5.2861	**0.39579**	4.51817
4	1	**0.44841**	521.7622	**0.2089**	8.84756	**0.17645**	6.67909	**0.17514**	5.99576
6	1	**0.4368**	1231.3830	**0.11737**	11.5749	**0.08308**	7.41748	**0.08212**	6.81576
8	1	**0.42684**	3365.3171	**0.07389**	15.74827	**0.04114**	8.43521	**0.04039**	7.77709
2	1.25	**0.56465**	185.8130	**0.53298**	4.46016	**0.52163**	5.74554	**0.52245**	5.24036
4	1.25	**0.54817**	277.8109	**0.31639**	6.98849	**0.29677**	6.81803	**0.2972**	6.48276
6	1.25	**0.53563**	473.3419	**0.20118**	8.54516	**0.17582**	7.36006	**0.17617**	7.08292
0	1.25	**0.52492**	902.7569	**0.13624**	10.38453	**0.10931**	8.31368	**0.10899**	7.93881
2	1.5	**0.68596**	137.2288	**0.63306**	3.64354	**0.62303**	5.81457	**0.02204**	5.41831
4	1.5	**0.67056**	162.1309	**0.42673**	5.53165	**0.41604**	7.03802	**0.41548**	6.76417
6	1.5	**0.65878**	208.5907	**0.29813**	6.35569	**0.28641**	7.48901	**0.28569**	7.25104
8	1.5	**0.64805**	200.1335	**0.21643**	7.29735	**0.20384**	8.18779	**0.20269**	7.90941
(b)									
2	0.5	**0.32621**	146.5547	**0.14155**	11.4517	**0.09275**	4.4184	**0.09255**	4.3234
4	0.5	**0.31517**	471.5580	**0.03269**	20.7714	**0.00911**	3.9348	**0.00903**	3.7789
6	0.5	**0.30691**	2029.8368	**0.0103**	38.5680	**0.00099**	5.1241	**0.00099**	5.0967
8	0.5	**0.29986**	10510.1263	**0.00392**	81.6125	**0.00013**	7.8990	**0.00013**	8.0493
2	0.75	**0.44414**	139.2251	**0.27607**	11.5941	**0.1934**	4.5197	**0.19289**	4.3292
4	0.75	**0.43333**	288.5192	**0.11314**	19.7586	**0.03993**	4.5503	**0.03967**	4.4029
6	0.75	**0.42504**	730.7389	**0.05739**	31.1663	**0.00858**	4.7924	**0.00851**	4.7149
8	0.75	**0.41818**	2156.6149	**0.03351**	53.5035	**0.00186**	4.8466	**0.00184**	4.7361
2	1	**0.52808**	147.1702	**0.41156**	11.2753	**0.3146**	4.6781	**0.3138**	4.4448
4	1	**0.51994**	244.1053	**0.22838**	18.2189	**0.10605**	5.2029	**0.10526**	4.9868
6	1	**0.51358**	471.6673	**0.14829**	25.7391	**0.03716**	5.5943	**0.03667**	5.3746
8	1	**0.50818**	1034.6057	**0.10704**	37.9552	**0.01327**	5.8442	**0.01302**	5.6232
2	1.25	**0.58744**	150.4926	**0.53064**	10.9034	**0.44038**	4.6600	**0.43939**	4.3486
4	1.25	**0.57999**	217.9729	**0.34804**	16.4096	**0.20485**	5.1574	**0.20355**	4.8973
6	1.25	**0.5741**	356.7665	**0.25434**	21.0320	**0.09786**	5.3791	**0.09695**	5.1789
8	1.25	**0.56922**	650.5895	**0.2022**	27.7203	**0.04784**	5.6719	**0.04729**	5.5070
2	1.5	**0.65156**	123.1837	**0.62978**	10.3601	**0.56059**	5.0031	**0.55951**	4.6074
4	1.5	**0.64071**	155.7479	**0.45826**	14.6127	**0.3288**	5.5576	**0.32701**	5.2393
6	1.5	**0.63312**	216.6186	**0.35766**	17.3297	**0.19684**	5.7273	**0.19514**	5.4553
8	1.5	**0.62746**	329.1723	**0.29691**	20.9563	**0.11979**	5.9219	**0.11838**	5.6707

TABLE 6. Correlation Integral Values and BDS Statistic for (a) Australia and (b) Japan

M	ε	Index Levels	BDS	Residuals of index levels	BDS	Returns	BDS	Residuals of Returns	BDS
(a)									
2	0.5	0.32441	221.98045	0.26387	12.37628	0.11424	3.80586	0.1087	3.58537
4	0.5	0.3091	716.00974	0.1144	23.10215	0.01416	4.21288	0.01267	3.74322
6	0.5	0.29659	3092.5926	0.06768	43.37883	0.00203	6.17336	0.00163	4.85917
8	0.5	0.28574	16099.6106	0.04671	89.5645	0.00021	3.02381	0.00016	2.57096
2	0.75	0.44087	201.45878	0.43998	11.30787	0.23788	4.20812	0.22539	3.64904
4	0.75	0.42888	424.36987	0.2581	17.85313	0.06091	4.6619	0.05348	3.54664
6	0.75	0.419	1097.7116	0.18382	26.57669	0.01705	5.96649	0.01392	4.77177
8	0.75	0.41042	3314.12114	0.1428	39.3433	0.00491	6.76271	0.00358	4.9126
2	1	0.51837	196.48457	0.59271	9.99028	0.37943	4.59286	0.36167	4.0842
4	1	0.51062	335.97096	0.41248	14.26479	0.1521	4.8039	0.13692	4.0069
6	1	0.50437	673.78885	0.32218	18.68083	0.06533	5.98879	0.05575	5.17337
8	1	0.49892	1539.47218	0.26899	23.81945	0.02877	6.69943	0.0234	5.93344
2	1.25	0.57424	172.61848	0.71184	9.18568	0.51755	4.86743	0.49794	4.4804
4	1.25	0.56545	257.06349	0.55253	11.77956	0.27764	4.69481	0.25712	4.34834
6	1.25	0.55831	435.91252	0.45774	14.2338	0.15644	5.70303	0.13935	5.2524
8	1.25	0.55204	826.86337	0.39576	16.62997	0.09043	6.4082	0.07711	5.78516
2	1.5	0.63357	136.5053	0.79749	9.20049	0.64204	5.41786	0.62073	4.94577
4	1.5	0.62356	178.86462	0.6679	10.48083	0.42263	4.9906	0.39591	4.70358
6	1.5	0.6158	259.92647	0.58176	12.0577	0.28691	5.72898	0.26053	5.38581
8	1.5	0.60918	414.76238	0.5193	13.33468	0.19791	6.19506	0.17302	5.61372
(b)									
2	0.5	0.38265	99.2853	0.33333	17.7189	0.12764	4.8366	0.12769	4.7610
4	0.5	0.37382	252.8343	0.21778	33.5398	0.02126	8.3810	0.0213	8.3596
6	0.5	0.36675	822.3960	0.16372	60.0764	0.00423	11.9897	0.00422	11.8726
8	0.5	0.36115	3172.0605	0.12808	116.6000	0.00096	17.7468	0.00095	17.3835
2	0.75	0.47808	110.6025	0.45823	16.6995	0.25277	5.6279	0.25312	5.7390
4	0.75	0.47171	209.3109	0.34522	28.3451	0.07768	8.4008	0.0779	8.4731
6	0.75	0.46636	474.9036	0.30097	44.0538	0.0272	11.0589	0.02712	10.9802
8	0.75	0.46175	1242.7993	0.27648	72.1209	0.01015	14.0679	0.01011	13.9514
2	1	0.53541	128.0932	0.54619	14.7611	0.39007	6.4553	0.39063	6.5981
4	1	0.52923	209.1868	0.41504	21.9765	0.17644	8.7716	0.17653	8.7715
6	1	0.52433	396.6731	0.36658	30.8997	0.08776	10.8329	0.08749	10.7356
8	1	0.52021	852.2415	0.34432	44.2901	0.04627	13.1512	0.04592	12.9635
2	1.25	0.58474	132.2916	0.62796	12.5012	0.51917	7.4699	0.51993	7.7352
4	1.25	0.57753	192.4844	0.48606	17.2045	0.30338	9.6580	0.30372	9.7313
6	1.25	0.57157	317.2975	0.42189	22.0471	0.1894	11.2471	0.18953	11.2849
8	1.25	0.56667	583.5887	0.38978	28.3116	0.12305	12.8640	0.12297	12.8647
2	1.5	0.63666	116.7465	0.70131	10.8822	0.63048	8.2936	0.63144	8.6476
4	1.5	0.62934	152.5812	0.56571	14.6265	0.43754	10.5977	0.43784	10.6622
6	1.5	0.6236	220.7266	0.49391	17.6316	0.3177	11.7906	0.3174	11.7735
8	1.5	0.61855	350.3109	0.45106	20.8481	0.2373	12.9141	0.23662	12.8509

are in agreement with the findings of Hsieh (1991) who examines weekly returns of the S&P500 from 1962 to 1989. Overall, the BDS statistic leads to the conclusion that non-linearities exist at the weekly time-aggregation level and the index portfolio aggregation level and across all countries for all series examined.

Correlation Integral Values

All indices examined exhibit similar (approximately equal), correlation integral values at each embedding dimension and resolution parameter value. This consistency translates to identical dependencies across all countries and for all series examined. In other words, the average local spatial correlations, as measured by the correlation integral, are of the same type for all countries.

Values for the raw price series range from 0.3 to 0.6 as the resolution parameter increases. These values remain essentially constant as the embedding dimension increases for each given resolution parameter value. The detrended counterpart exhibits similar behavior, although the values decrease as the embedding dimension increases. Hence we conclude that these series pass the Residual Brock Test.

The raw return series lack the convergence present in the raw price levels. However, the return series pass the Brock Residual Test, since their detrended counterpart shows similar behavior. Willey (1992) focuses on U.S. market data and finds that only the S&P100 Index passes this test.

V. CONCLUSIONS

In summary, the dependencies at a weekly time aggregation level are very similar across all major stock indices of six European, two North American and two Far Eastern countries. The spatial characteristics of all series examined (prices and returns) are also similar. However, price series appear more relevant candidates for investigating further the existence of strange attractors. Evidence of low dimensional structure as a plausible alternative to modeling complex and random appearing weekly index levels cannot be inferred from the above analysis due to the scarcity of the data limitations (which induces a bias in the estimates of correlation dimensions). Based on Hsieh's (1991) findings, the evidence detected is not due to structural changes (non-stationarity). Furthermore, Brock, Dechert, and Scheinkman (Brock and Malliaris (1989)) have shown that GARCH processes generate zero bispectra, which are inconsistent with the evidence of non-zero bispectra of stock returns cited in bispectral analysis studies (Hinich and Patterson (1985, 1988)). In effect, although there exists no statistical test under the null of chaos, sophisticated stochastic non-stationary specifications do not seem sufficient for accounting for the observed variability. A comparison of the present results and those found by Willey (1992) indicates that the dependencies detected are more prominent and uniform across all countries at a weekly time-aggregation level rather than at a daily holding period. Furthermore, the similarity of the results across European and non-European indices supports the hypothesis of integrated national markets, at least in the sense that the price dynamics of the markets are similar.

ENDNOTES

1. Other studies have examined rates of return on silver and gold (Frank and Stengos (1989)), daily foreign exchange rates (Hsieh (1989)), and futures prices for commodities and for financial assets (Blank (1991)).

2. We offer a brief analysis to motivate the empirical test. A detailed presentation may be found in Pilarinu (1993) and Malliaris and Philippatos (1992).

3. Philippatos and Pilarinu (1993) analyze in detail the behavior of the exponential logistic map.

4. The structure in such series cannot even be detected by many standard statistical tests.

5. The correlation dimension is a lower bound to the information dimension, that is based on the unconditional probability distribution constructed by embedding the true space in a probability space through an invariant probability measure.

6. Usually less than 2,000 observations.

7. $R_t = 100 * (\log (P_t) - \log (P_{t-1}))$.

8. Due to space limitations Tables 2-6 present embedding dimensions 2,4,6,8. Detailed results for embedding dimensions from 2 to 10 are available from the authors upon request.

9. The authors have recently obtained a database with daily data for numerous world stock indices and are planning to investigate this issue further.

REFERENCES

Anderson, P., Arrow, K., and D. Pines. (1988), *The Economy as an Evolving Complex system*, Santa Fe Institute Studies in the Sciences and Complexity, Vol. V, Addison-Wesley Publishing Company.

Baumol, W. J. and J. Benhabib (1989), "Chaos: Significance, Mechanism and Economic Applications." *Journal of Economic Perspectives*, Vol. 3, No. 1.

Benhabib, J. and R. H. Day. (1981), "Rational Choice and Erratic Behavior." *Review of Economic Studies*, Vol. 48.

Blank, C. Steven (1991), "Chaos in Futures Markets? A Nonlinear Dynamical Analysis." *The Journal of Futures Markets*, Vol. 11, No. 6.

Brock, A. W. (1987), "Nonlinearity and Complex Dynamics in Economics and Finance." In the *Economy as an Evolving Complex System*, edited by P. W. Anderson, K. J. Arrow, and D. Pines. Addison-Wesley Publishing Company.

Brock, A. W. (1992), "Understanding Macroeconomic Series Using Complex Systems Theory." In the *Structural Change and Economic Dynamics*, edited M. Landesmann at Cambridge University, England.

Brock, W. A. and W. D. Dechert (1986), "Theorems on distinguishing Deterministic from Random Systems." In *Dynamic Econometric Modeling*, edited by W. A. Barnett, E. R. Berndt, H. White.

Brock, W. A. and W. D. Dechert (1989), "Statistical Inference Theory for Measures of Complexity in Chaos Theory and Nonlinear Science." In *Measures of Complexity and Chaos*, edited by N. B. Abraham, A. M. Alfonso, A. Passamante, and P. E. Rapp, NATO ASI Series.

Brock, W. A., D. Hsieh, and B. LeBaron (1991), *Nonlinear Dynamics, Chaos, and Instability: Statistical Theory and Economic Evidence*. MIT Press.

Brock, W. A. and A. Malliaris (1989), *Differential Equations, Stability, and Chaos in Dynamic Economics*. North-Holland.

Bunov, B. and G. Weiss (1979), "How Chaotic is Chaos? Chaotic and Other "Noisy" Dynamics in the Frequency Domain." *Mathematical Biosciences* 47.

Dana, R. A. and P. Montrucchio (1986), "Dynamic Complexity in Duopoly Games." *Journal of Economic Theory*, Vol. 40.

Day, R. H. (1983), "The Emergence of Chaos from Classical Economic Growth." *Quarterly Journal of Economics*, Vol. 98.

Fischer, K. P. and A. P. Palasvirta (1990), "High Road to a Global Marketplace: The International Transmission of the Stock Market Fluctuations." *The Financial Review*, Vol. 25.

Frank, M. and T. Stengos (1989), "Measuring the Strangeness of Gold and Silver Rates of Return." *Review of Economic Studies*, Vol. 40.

Gaertner, W. (1988), "Periodic and Aperiodic Consumer Behavior." Unpublished paper cited by Kesley D. in The Economics of Chaos or the Chaos of Economics. *Oxford Economic Papers*, Vol. 40.

Genotte, G. and T. Marsh (1986), Variations in Ex Ante Risk Premium on Capital Assets. University of California, Berkeley, Business School, Unpublished.

Grassberger, P. and I. Procaccia (1983), "Measuring the Strangeness of Strange Attractors." *Physica D*, Vol. 9.

Hinich, J. M. and D. M. Patterson (1985), "Evidence of Nonlinearity in Daily Stock Returns." *Journal of Business & Economic Statistics*, Vol. 3, No. 1.

Hinich, J. M. and D. M. Patterson (1988), "Evidence of Nonlinearity in the Trade-by-Trade Stock Market Return Generating Process." In the *Economic Complexity: Chaos, Sunspots, Bubbles and Nonlinearity*, edited by W. A. Barnett, J. Geweke, K. Shell.

Hsieh, A. D. (1989), "Testing for Nonlinear Dependence in Daily Foreign Exchange Rates." *Journal of Business*, Vol. 63, No. 3.

Hsieh, A. D. (1991), "Chaos and Nonlinear Dynamics: Application to Financial Markets." *The Journal of Finance*, Vol. XLVL, No. 5.

Lorenz, H. W. (1989), *Non Linear Dynamical Economics and Chaotic Motion*, Springer-Verlag.

Lorenz, H. W., "Strange Attractors in a Multisector Business Cycle Model." *Journal of Economic Behavior and Organization* (forthcoming).

Malliaris, G. A. and G. C. Philippatos (1992), "Random Walk vs. Chaotic Dynamics in Financial Economics." Proceedings of the Conference on Chaos in the Social Sciences, Springer-Verlag.

Martell, T. F. and G. C. Philippatos (1974), "Adaptation, Information, and Dependence in Commodity Markets." *Journal of Finance*, Vol. XXIX.

May, R. H. (1974), Biological Populations with Nonoverlapping Generations, Stable Points, Limit Cycles, and Chaos. *Science*, Vol. 186.

Philippatos, C. G. and E. Pilarinu (1994), "Instabilities and Chaotic Behavior of Stock Prices in International Capital Markets." *Managerial Finance* (forthcoming).

Philippatos, C. G. and C. J. Wilson (1972), "Entropy, Market Risk, and the Selection of Efficient Portfolios." *Applied Economics*, Vol. 4.

Pilarinu, E. (1993), "A Chaotic Approach to the Analysis of Financial Data." Ph.D. Dissertation, University of Tennessee, Knoxville.

Ramsey, J. B. and H. Yuan (1989), "Bias and Error Bars in Dimension Calculations and their Evaluation in Some Simple Models." *Physics Letters A*, Vol. 134, No. 5.

Ramsey, J. B., C. Sayers, and P. Rothman (1990), "The Statistical Properties of Dimension Calculations Using Small Data Sets: Some Economic Applications." *International Economic Review*, Vol. 31, No. 4.

Scheinkman, J. A. and B. LeBaron (1989), "Nonlinear Dynamics and Stock Returns." *Journal of Business*, Vol. 62, No. 3.

Shaffer, S. (1991), "Structural Shifts and the Volatility of Chaotic Markets." *Journal of Economic Behavior and Organization*, Vol. 15.

Takens, F. (1983), "Distinguishing Deterministic and Random Systems." In *Non Linear Dynamics and Turbulence*, G. Borenblatt, G. Iooss, and D. Joseph.

Willey, T. (1992), "Testing for Nonlinear Dependence in Daily Stock Indices." *Journal of Economics and Business*, Vol. 44.

EUROPEAN STOCK MARKET FLUCTUATIONS: SHORT AND LONG TERM LINKS

A.G. Malliaris
Jorge L. Urrutia

Abstract. *The paper uses a error correcting model to examine long-term links and short-run causality for five major European capital markets. The empirical results report statistically significant relationships. These findings indicate that the European markets tend to move together and adjust to each other's movements. The results imply limitations in the role of portfolio diversification and confirm a high degree of integration among European equity markets.*

JEL Classifications: C32, G15
Key Words: European stock markets, Granger causality

1. INTRODUCTION

During the past two to three decades, world stock markets have become more integrated, primarily because of financial deregulation and advances in computer technology. Financial researchers have examined various aspects of the evolution of this particular aspect of world integration. For example, the early studies by Grubel (1968), Levy and Sarnat (1970), Grubel and Fadner (1971), Agmon (1972, 1973), Ripley (1973), Solnik (1974a, 1974b), and Lessard (1973, 1974, 1976) have investigated the benefits from international portfolio diversification. While some studies, such as Solnik (1974b), were exclusively theoretical in extending the capital asset pricing model to a world economy, others such as Levy and Sarnat (1970) used

---

A. G. Malliaris is Walter F. Mullady, Sr. Professor of Business Administration, Department of Economics, and Jorge L. Urrutia is Associate Professor, Department of Finance, both at Loyola University of Chicago, Chicago, IL. *An earlier version of the paper was presented at the First Annual Conference on Multinational Financial Issues. The authors are very grateful to George Papaioannou for his excellent comments that helped to greatly improve the paper.*

both theory and empirical testing to confirm the existence of financial benefits from international diversification.

Similar benefits were also confirmed by Grubel (1968), Grubel and Fadner (1971), Ripley (1973), Lessard (1973, 1974, 1976), Agmon (1972, 1973), Makridakis and Wheelwright (1974), and others, who studied the relations among equity markets in various countries. Specifically, Agmon (1972, 1973) investigated the relationships among the equity markets of the U.S., United Kingdom, Germany and Japan, while Lessard (1973) considered a group of Latin American Countries.

By 1976, eight years after the pioneering work of Grubel (1968), enough knowledge had been accumulated on this subject to induce Panton, Lessig and Joy (1976) to offer a taxonomy. It seems reasonable to argue that although these studies had used different methodologies and diverse data from a variety of countries, their main conclusions confirmed that correlations among national stock market returns were low and that world portfolio diversification offered significant benefits.

2. REVIEW OF RECENT LITERATURE

Theoretical developments on continuous time stochastic processes and arbitrage theory were quickly incorporated into international finance. Stulz (1981) developed a continuous time model of international asset pricing, while Solnik (1983) extended arbitrage theory to an international setting. Adler and Dumas (1983) integrated international portfolio choice and corporate finance. Empirical research also continued to flow such as Hilliard (1979), Maldonado and Saunders (1981), Christofi and Philippatos (1987), Philippatos, Christofi and Christofi (1983) and more recently Grauer and Hakansson (1987), Schollhammer and Sand (1987), Wheatley (1988), Eun and Shim (1989), von Furstenberg and Jeon (1989), Becker, Finnerty and Gupta (1990), Fischer and Palasvirta (1990), French and Poterba (1991), Harvey (1991) and Philippatos and Pilarinu (1994). These numerous studies employ more recent methodologies and larger data bases than the earlier studies. In contrast to earlier results, several of these studies find high and statistically significant level of interdependence between national markets, supporting the hypothesis that global stock markets are becoming more integrated.

The interdependence of returns among various national stock markets has been recently extended to an analysis of the behavior of volatilities across such markets. Theodossiou (1994a) found that future returns in certain major international stock markets are predictable from past realized returns; thus, these stock market indices violate the Martingale model while others do not.

Panayiotis (1994b) used various GARCH models in predicting movements (returns) and volatility patterns in stock market indices of Australia, Belgium, Canada, France, Italy and Switzerland. Theodossiou and Lee (1993) explored the degree and nature of interdependence and the influence of volatility on expected returns in stock markets of U.S., Japan, United Kingdom, Canada and Germany. Koutmos, Lee and Theodossiou (1994) asserted that small capitalization markets show higher volatility persistence than large capitalization markets with market betas being time-dependent for many of the ten international stock markets examined.

In comparing the results of the earlier studies with those of the more recent ones, one could deduce that greater global integration implies less benefits from international portfolio diversification. If this is true, how can one explain the ever increasing flow of big sums of money invested in international markets? To put it differently, why are increasing amounts of funds invested in non-home equity markets? For instance, currently about 10% of all trading in U.S. equities takes place outside of the United States. The June 14, 1993 issue of Barron's reported that U. S. investors have tripled their ownership of foreign equities over the past five years, from $63 billion in 1988 to over $200 billion in 1993.

Having reviewed the relevant literature, we now explain our contribution in the form of a hypothesis. We postulate that national equity markets exhibit interdependencies in the short-run and in the long-run. We test our hypothesis using equity prices for European indexes. The remainder of the paper is organized as follows: section two presents the data, section three describes the methodology, section four analyzes the empirical results, and section five concludes the paper.

3. DATA

The data consist of daily closing prices for the following European equity market indexes: London FT-100, Frankfurt DAX, Paris CAC 40, Milan Stock Index, and Brussels Bel-20 Index. Data of 813 observations were collected from the WSJ for the time period January 3, 1989 through April 3, 1992.

As Roll (1992) has emphasized, the indexes we use heavily represent European industrial firms of large capitalization. However, these are the only indexes reported by the WSJ, and in general, the ones most often cited.

4. METHODOLOGY

This paper investigates long-run and short-run interdependencies among European equity markets. The methodology used is the error correcting model, ECM. Since the ECM is based on the concept of causality in the Granger sense and on the notion of cointegration, these two tests are described first.

a) Granger Causality Tests

Granger causality tests are essentially tests of the prediction ability of time series models. A time series of returns X_t causes another time series of returns Y_t in the Granger (1969) sense if current Y can be predicted better by using past values of X than by not doing so, considering also other relevant information, including past values of Y. More specially, X, is said to cause Y provided some coefficient a_i is not zero in the following equation:

$$Y_t = C_0 + \sum_{i=1}^{m} \alpha_i Y_{t-i} + \sum_{j=1}^{m} \beta_j X_{t-j} + \mu_t \quad (1)$$

Similarly, Y is causing X if some coefficient α_i is not zero in equation (2):

$$X_t = \alpha_0 + \sum_{i=1}^{m} \alpha_i Y_{t-i} + \sum_{j=1}^{m} \beta_j X_{t-j} + \mu_t \quad (2)$$

If both of these events occur, there is a feedback. The test for causality is based on an F-statistic that is computed by running the above regressions in both unconstrained (full model) and constrained (reduced model) forms.

$$F = [(SSE_r - SSE_f) / m] \; / \; [SSE_f / (T-2m-1)]$$

where SSE_r and SSE_f are the sum of squares of the residuals of the reduced model and full model, respectively, m is the number of lags and T is the number of observations.

Equations (1) and (2) capture short-term linkages between variables X and Y. This is so because in (1) the current daily observation of Y is regressed against daily observation of X up to m day lags, while in (2) the current daily observation of X is similarly regressed against daily observation of Y up to **m** daily lags. In carrying out (1) and (2) we use up to 5 lags or one week of trade. Only a small number of lags is needed to capture the short-term interdependence between the two variables.

b) Cointegration Tests

The notion of cointegration can be expressed as follows. If the time series X_t and Y_t are both non stationary in levels but the first differences of the variables are stationary, it is said variables X_t and Y_t are both integrated of order one, $I(1)$. Their linear combinations of the form $Z_t = X_t - \alpha Y_t$ (3) are generally also $I(1)$. However, if there is an α, such that Z_t is integrated of order zero, $I(0)$, the linear combination of X_t and Y_t is stationary and it is said the two variables are cointegrated. If the two variables are cointegrated, then there is some underlying long-term relationship between them.

Cointegration is a property of two non-stationary time series and the cointegration relationship $X_t - \alpha Y_t = 0$ represents a long-run equilibrium relationship between X_t and Y_t established over the entire sample period. The cointegration factor Z_t can be used to measure the deviation from this long-run relationship. Engle and Granger (1987) suggest to estimate the value of α by running the regression:

$$X_t = \gamma + \alpha Y_t + \epsilon_t \tag{4}$$

By knowing α, the cointegration factor can easily be estimated from equation (3).

c) Error Correcting Model, ECM

By integrating the concept of causality in the Granger sense and the notion of cointegration, it is possible to develop a model that allows to test for both short-term and long-term relationships between variables X_t and Y_t. This model is known as the error correcting model, ECM (Engle and Granger (1987)). The following ECM model investigates the potential long-run and short-run impacts of the variable X on the variable Y:

$$Y_t - Y_{t-1} = a_0 + a_1 \hat{Z}_{t-1} + \sum_{i=1}^{m} c_i (X_{t-i} - X_{t-i-1}) + \sum_{j=1}^{m} d_j (Y_{t-j} + Y_{t-j-1}) + \varepsilon_t \tag{5}$$

where $\hat{Z}_{t-1} = X_{t-1} - \hat{\alpha} Y_{t-1}$ as defined in (3).

The ECM model of equation (5) decomposes the dynamic adjustments of the dependent variable Y into two components: i) A long-run component given by the cointegration term $a_1\hat{Z}_{t-1}$, also known as the error-correction term. The correction adjustments of Y_t to a disequilibrium error from the previous period Z_{t-1} can spread over several periods of time, with the coefficient a_1 indicating the speed of the correction mechanism. ii) A short-term component, given by the summation terms in the right hand side of equation (5). These two terms represent past changes in the variables X and Y and characterize the short-run dynamics because of the small number of lags. Specifically, the first summation term in equation (5) gives the short-run impact of X on Y.

Similarly, the long-run and short-run impacts of Y on X can be expressed as:

$$X_t - X_{t-1} = \alpha_0 + \alpha_1\hat{Z}_{t-1} + \sum_{i=1}^{m}\phi_i(Y_{t-i} - Y_{t-i-1}) + \sum_{j=1}^{m}\theta_j(X_{t-j} + X_{t-j-1}) + \mu_t . \tag{6}$$

From equations (5) and (6) follows that the variables X_t and Y_t are cointegrated when at least one of the coefficients of a_1 or α_1 is different from zero. In this case, X_t and Y_t exhibit long-run comovements. If a_1 is different from zero but α_1 is zero, then Y_t follows and adjusts to X_t in the long-term. The opposite occurs when α_1 is different from zero but a_1 is zero. If both coefficients, a_1 and α_1, are non zero, a feedback exists and the two variables adjust to one another over the long-run.

The coefficients c_i's and ϕ_i's represent the short-term relationship between the variables X_t and Y_t. If c_i's are not all zero but all ϕ_i's are zero, then X is leading or causing Y in the short-run. The reverse is the case if ϕ_i's are not zero but all c_i's are zero. If both events occur, then there is a feedback and the two variables impact each other in the short-run.

5. ANALYSIS OF THE EMPIRICAL RESULTS

Prior to the implementation of the error correcting model, it is necessary to check if the prices time series are integrated of order one, I (1). This is a condition for the appropriateness of the ECM. The results of the Augmented Dickey-Fuller (1979), ADF, tests of stationary for prices and returns are presented in Table 1. For the price level, Panel A indicates that the null hypothesis of non-stationarity cannot be rejected at the five percent of confidence level. However, Panel B shows that returns are stationary. That is, the daily closing price for the five European equity market indexes are integrated of order one. Thus, the ECM is appropriate for examining relationship between the prices of these five national market indexes.

TABLE 1. Augmented Dickey-fuller Tests of Stationary

Panel A: Price Levels

Index	b_0	b_1	b_2	b_3	b_4	b_5	R^2
London	0.1007 (3.1013)*	-0.0134 (-2.005)	0.0252 (0.718)	0.0258 (0.737)	0.0220 (0.627)	0.0854 (2.434)*	0.0196 (3.204)*
Frankfurt	0.0678 (2.005)*	-0.0092 (-1.997)	-0.0288 (-0.817)	0.0001 (0.001)	0.0018 (0.050)	-0.0111 (-0.316)	0.006 (1.011)
Paris	0.0368 (1.779)	-0.0049 (-1.731)	0.0048 (0.138)	0.0153 (0.435)	-0.0035 (-0.099)	-0.0117 (-0.333)	0.004 (0.664)
Milan	0.0749 (2.134)*	-0.0108 (-2.1350)	0.0865 (2.4511)*	-0.0289 (-0.8182)	0.0336 (0.9488)	-0.0237 (-0.671)	0.014 (2.297)*
Brussels	0.0182 (0.028)	-0.0036 (-0.039)	0.3340 (0.396)	-0.4197 (-0.497)	-0.0410 (-0.049)	0.3190 (0.378)	0.001 (0.110)

Panel B: Returns

Index	b_0	b_1	b_2	b_3	b_4	b_5	R^2
London	0.0230 (0.685)	-0.8618 (-11.595)ª	-0.1160 (-1.703)	-0.0938 (-1.572)	-0.0755 (-1.532)	0.0072 (0.204)	0.0492 (154.876)*
Frankfurt	0.0295 (0.607)	-1.0630 (-13.026)ª	0.0300 (0.413)	0.0259 (0.413)	0.0235 (0.463)	0.0079 (0.224)	0.516 (170.892)*
Paris	0.1010 (1.169)	-0.9970 (-12.722)ª	0.0006 (0.0081)	0.0146 (0.240)	0.0100 (0.201)	-0.0027 (-0.078)	0.498 (159.203)*
Milan	-0.0014 (-0.0259)	-1.0183 (-13.584)ª	0.0978 (1.459)	0.0652 (1.114)	0.0911 (1.903)	0.0670 (1.902)	0.465 (139.198)*
Brussels	0.0042 (0.133)	-0.9195 (-11.991)ª	-0.0434 (-0.627)	-0.0634 (-1.057)	-0.0588 (-1.201)	-0.0170 (-0.482)	0.482 (149.354)*

NOTES

The model is:

$$LnX_t - LnX_{t-1} = b_0 + b_1 LnX_{t-1} + b_2(LnX_{t-1} - LnX_{t-2}) + b_3(LnX_{t-2} - LnX_{t-3}) + b_4(LnX_{t-3} - LnX_{t-4}) + b_5(LnX_{t-4} - LnX_{t-5}) + \epsilon_t$$

where X represents daily prices for Panel A and daily returns for Panel B.

--The null hypothesis is: H_o: $b_1 = 0$ (X is not stationary). The critical t-statistic for the b_1 coefficient at the 5% of confidence level is -2.86 (from Dickey-Fuller (1979), Table 8. 5. 2.).

--An "a" indicates rejection of the null hypothesis of non-stationarity.

--An asterisk "*" indicates the regression coefficient is statistically significant different from zero at the 5% of confidence level.

The results of the ECM are reported in Table 2. The regressions are run using the natural logarithm of daily prices. The main rows contain the regression efficient of the independent variables of equations (5) and (6). The corresponding t-statistics are given in parenthesis in the second rows. The last two columns to the right of Table 2 report the F-statistics which test for short-term relationships, and for either short-term or long-term relationship, respectively. The coefficients a_1's are all significantly different from zero at the five percent of confidence level. Therefore, there is a two way long-term relationship between each pair of European equity indexes. That is, these markets impact and adjust to each other changes over the long-run.

A plausible economic interpretation of our empirical finding is as follows: The five European stock markets under investigation belong to countries that are members of the European Union. Thus, these countries have significant economic integration. More specifically, during the period under investigation from January 3, 1989 through April 3, 1992 the Exchange Rate Mechanism had functioned reasonably well and these five economies followed coordinated macroeconomic policies.[1] Therefore, the significant long-term linkages reported in this paper between Germany, France, Belgium, England and Italy probably reflect the strong economic similarities that prevailed in these countries during our sample period and also their coordinated macroeconomic policies under a stable Exchange Rate Mechanism.

The coefficients c_1's are all statistically significant at the five percent level, suggesting that there is also short-term causality in both directions for each pair of indexes, thus, the markets affect to each other in the short-term with one day lag. These short-term interrelationships reflect arbitrage activities among the European stock markets. Since the economies are integrated to a high degree because of the European Union, short-term divergences are corrected by arbitragers who buy the undervalued index and sell the overvalued one. Such arbitrage activity induces the indexes to exhibit short-term linkages and is initiated quite often by both independent speculators and fund managers who invest in Europe.

Finally, the hypothesis of neither long-term nor short-term relationship is also strongly rejected for all pair of national indexes at the five percent of confidence level. Therefore, some short-term or long-term relationship is always present among these European equity markets.

---

[1] The reader may recall that by 1993, Germany had hiked interest rates quite substantially to fight increasing inflation arising from its unification. The German monetary policy eventually contributed to speculate attacks on the British pound and the collapse of the Exchange Rate Mechanism during August of 1993. But this happened after the time period covered by our sample.

TABLE 2. Error Correction Model (Ecm) for Testing for Short-term and Long-term Linkages among European Equity Markets

Dependent Variable	Independent Variable	a_1	c_1	c_2	c_3	c_4	c_5	No Short term Impact	Neither Short Term nor Long Term Impact
London	Paris	0.0005 (52.879)^a	0.0822 (11.992)*	-0.0035 (-0.372)	0.0014 (0.147)	0.0018 (0.190)	-0.0047 (-0.693)	479.322^a	470.311^a
Paris	London	0.0003 (19.957)^a	0.5849 (7.156)*	0.0532 (0.487)	-0.1297 (-1.185)	0.0628 (0.574)	-0.0060 (-0.077)	74.466^a	67.613^a
London	Milan	0.0003 (28.750)^a	0.3011 (16.738)*	-0.0428 (-1.898)	0.0119 (0.527)	0.0018 (0.079)	-0.0081 (-0.523)	164.088^a	141.420^a
Milan	London	0.0007 (33.649)^a	0.6050 (15.013)*	-0.0235 (-0.449)	-0.0293 (-0.560)	0.0629 (1.201)	-0.0466 (-1.264)	206.362^a	190.542^a
London	Frankfurt	0.0005 (39.677)^a	0.2669 (15.504)*	0.0272 (1.265)	-0.0098 (-0.456)	0.0001 (-0.004)	-0.0111 (-0.698)	277.681^a	266.738^a
Frankfurt	London	0.0005 (38.823)^a	0.5687 (16.234)*	-0.0488 (-1.0476)	0.0252 (0.498)	0.0359 (0.770)	-0.0254 (-0.755)	297.265^a	260.271^a
London	Brussels	0.0004 (37.371)^a	0.1257 (5.223)*	0.0090 (-0.272)	0.0121 (0.368)	0.0152 (0.466)	-0.0200 (-0.871)	172.454^a	236.544^a
Brussels	London	0.0048 (122.260)^a	0.3684 (1.988)*	0.9072 (3.490)*	0.1709 (0.650)	0.3289 (1.252)	-0.3760 (-1.965)*	727.802^a	264.664^a
Paris	Milan	0.0004 (30.299)^a	-0.2223 (-5.385)*	0.0013 (0.0207)	0.0178 (0.289)	0.0151 (0.252)	-0.0275 (-0.700)	110.453^a	153.827^a
Milan	Paris	0.0008 (54.003)^a	-0.0636 (-6.202)*	0.0401 (2.659)*	-0.0123 (-0.810)	0.0127 (0.833)	-0.0119 (-1.140)	255.287^a	528.791^a
Paris	Frankfurt	0.0002 (14.348)^a	0.6217 (8.860)*	0.1179 (1.465)	-0.0656 (-0.815)	-0.0740 (-0.920)	0.0174 (0.293)	43.587^a	36.594^a
Frankfurt	Paris	0.0005 (38.989)^a	0.2071 (15.927)*	-0.0067 (-0.390)	-0.0023 (-0.134)	0.0068 (0.398)	-0.0045 (-0.365)	291.210^a	257.878^a

Table 2. Continued

Dependent Variable	Independent Variable	a_1	c_1	c_2	c_3	c_4	c_5	No Short term Impact	Neither Short Term nor Long Term Impact
Paris	Brussels	0.0002 (20.797)^{a}	-0.3228 (-3.929)*	0.0126 (0.112)	0.0526 (0.464)	0.1303 (-1.155)	0.0838 (1.057)	63.233^{a}	72.553^{a}
Brussels	Paris	0.0048 (115.695)^{a}	-0.7063 (-9.266)*	0.1659 (1.565)	0.0996 (0.936)	0.0336 (0.316)	0.0284 (0.369)	612.104^{a}	237.583^{a}
Milan	Frankfurt	0.0008 (42.251)^{a}	0.1866 (7.946)*	-0.0156 (-0.491)	0.0066 (0.207)	0.0087 (0.274)	0.0029 (0.124)	235.500^{a}	300.486^{a}
Frankfurt	Milan	0.0005 (43.522)^{a}	0.2126 (11.289)*	-0.0299 (-1.123)	0.0031 (0.118)	0.0104 (0.390)	0.0061 (0.336)	211.914^{a}	319.204^{a}
Milan	Brussels	0.0002 (14.980)^{a}	0.2318 (4.065)*	-0.0953 (-1.202)	0.0172 (0.217)	0.0595 (0.750)	-0.0547 (-0.979)	29.041^{a}	38.059^{a}
Brussels	Milan	0.0047 (103.543)^{a}	2.7107 (19.297)*	-0.2845 (-1.425)	0.2519 (1.261)	-0.1155 (-0.579)	0.0860 (0.623)	161.074^{a}	791.388^{a}
Frankfurt	Brussels	0.0002 (20.256)^{a}	0.1704 (3.398)*	-0.0028 (-0.041)	-0.0625 (-0.926)	0.1034 (1.532)	-0.0447 (-0.922)	60.928^{a}	69.390^{a}
Brussels	Frankfurt	0.0048 (125.777)^{a}	1.1229 (8.303)*	0.2381 (1.319)	0.2750 (1.524)	0.1698 (0.941)	-0.0384 (-0.280)	232.057^{a}	391.077^{a}

NOTES
The model is:

$$LnX_t = a_0 + a_1\hat{Z}_{t-1} + b_1LnX_{t-1} + b_2LnX_{t-2} + b_3LnX_{t-3} + b_4LnX_{t-4} + b_5LnX_{t-5} + c_1LnY_{t-1} + c_2LnY_{t-2} + c_3LnY_{t-3} + c_4LnY_{t-4} + c_5LnY_{t-5} + \mu_t$$

where X and Y represent daily prices.
The null hypotheses are:
i) the variable Y has no long-term impact in the variable X.
ii) the variable Y has no short-term impact in the variable X.
iii) the variable Y has neither short-term nor long-term impact in the variable X.

–An "a" indicates rejection of the null of no impact at the 5% of confidence level.
–An "asterisk "*" indicates the regression coefficient is statistically significantly different from zero at the 5% level.

6. SUMMARY AND CONCLUSIONS

This paper investigates short-term and long-tern relationships among five European equity markets. The data correspond to daily closing prices for the following national indexes: London FT-100, Frankfurt DAX, Paris CAC 40, Milan Stock Index and Brussels Bel-20 Index. The time period extends from January 3, 1989 to April 3, 1992.

Augmented Dickey-Fuller tests of stationarity allow us to conclude that prices are non-stationary in levels but they are stationary in first difference or returns. Thus, prices are integrated of order one, I (1) and the use of the error correcting model, ECM, is appropriate for testing for long-run and short-run linkages.

The empirical results of the ECM show statistically significant long-term links and short-term causal relationships. These findings imply that these markets are not independent but they move together. They adjust to each other in the long-run and they lead or lag each other in the short-run.

Short-term causality for national equity markets has been reported previously (as in Malliaris and Urrutia (1992, 1993)) and elsewhere. The long-run interdependency is puzzling. We offer the following explanation: we have concentrated our analysis to equity markets of five European countries that are members of the European Union. The implementation of institutional agreements of the European Union concerning equity markets has facilitated the multiple listing of domestic stocks in foreign exchanges. Furthermore, because of the Exchange Rate Mechanism, monetary policies were partially coordinated among the five countries during the time period of our sample. These factors have increased the integration of these European markets. If this trend continues, it is expected that these markets will constitute, for all practical purposes, one single equity market with exchanges in every country.

The results reported in this paper have obvious implications for the alleged benefits of diversifying internationally among the several European markets. In effect, the strong short-term causality and long-term linkages among these national indexes would prevent investors from greatly reducing the risk and/or increasing the return of their portfolio by diversifying among these countries. However, our empirical results of the strong short and long term linkages do not necessarily imply substantial reduction of the diversification benefits among these European markets. Indeed, it is very probable that security index prices in a stock market of an advanced economically country are interdependent because of the underlying economic fundamentals, yet various security cash flows may co-vary less than perfectly across different states of the economy. This can occur because different securities may have varying degrees of business and financial risk. Thus, the notions of market cointegration and diversification benefits are not mutually exclusive.[2] In other words, the presence of cointegration in European stock

---

[2] We are grateful to George Papaioannou for clarifying this distinction. This section incorporates several of his comments.

markets may reduce but certainly does not completely eliminate the benefits of international diversification among these countries.

In light of the above remarks we can raise a final key question: what are the reasons of the statistically documented links among the five European markets? The answer we offered in earlier section traces the cause to the supranational trade, industrial and financial policies of the European Union with its complementary macroeconomic coordination. A secondary cause may be the specific nature of the five indexes utilized which have greater similarities by representing major industrial firms. Roll's (1992) remarks that national market indexes exhibit stronger correlations when they have high concentration in similar industries represented in these indexes. This technical observation is certainly relevant as a cause of the presence of the links.

REFERENCES

Adler, M. and B. Dumas, 1983, "International Portfolio Choice and Corporation Finance: A Synthesis", *Journal of Finance*, 38, pp. 925-984.

Agmon, T., 1972, "The Relations Among Equity Markets: A Study of Share Price Co-movements in the United States, United Kingdom, Germany and Japan", *Journal of Finance*, 27, pp. 839-855.

Agmon, T., 1973, "Country Risk: Significance of Country Factor for Share Price Movements in the United Kingdom, Germany, and Japan", *Journal of Business*, 46, pp. 24-32.

Becker, K.G., J.E. Finnerty and M. Gupta, 1990, "The Intertemporal Relation Between the U.S. and Japanese Stock Markets", *Journal of Finance*, 45, pp. 1297-1306.

Christofi, A.C., and G.C. Philippatos, 1987, "An Empirical Investigation of the International Arbitrage Pricing Theory", *Management International Review*, 27, pp. 13-22.

Dickey, D. and W. Fuller, (1979), "Distribution of the Estimators for Autoregressive Time Series with a Unit Root", *Journal of the American Statistical Association*, 74, pp. 427-431.

Engle, R., and C. W. J. Granger, (1987), "Co-Integration and Error Correction: Representation, Estimation, Testing," *Econometrica*, 55, pp. 251-276.

Eun, C. and S. Shim, 1989, "International Transmission of Stock Market Movements", *Journal of Financial and Quantitative Analysis*, 24, pp. 241-256.

Fischer, K.P. and A.P. Palasvirta, 1990, "High Road to a Global Marketplace: The International Transmission of Stock Market Fluctuations", *Finance Review*, 25, pp. 371-494.

French, K. and J. Poterba, 1991, "Investor Diversification and International Equity Markets", *American Economic Review*, 81, pp. 222-226.

Granger, C.W.J., 1969, "Investigating Causal Relations by Econometric Models and Cross Spectral Methods", *Econometrics*, 37, pp.428-438.

Grauer, R.R. and N.H. Hakansson, 1987, "Gains From International Diversification: 1968-85 Returns on Portfolios of Stocks and Bonds", *Journal of Finance*, 42, pp. 721-741.

Grubel, H. G., 1968, "Internationally Diversified Portfolios: Welfare Gains and Capital Flows", *The American Economic Review*, 58, pp. 1299-1314.

Grubel, H. G. and K. Fadner, 1971, "The Interdependence of International Equity Markets", *Journal of Finance*, 26, pp. 89-94.

Harvey, C.R., 1991, "The World Price of Covariance Risk", *Journal of Finance*, 46, pp. 111-157.

Hilliard, J., 1979, "The Relationship Between Equity Indices on World Exchanges", *Journal of Finance*, 34, pp. 103-114.

Koutmos, Gregory, Unro Lee and Panayiotis Theodossiou, 1994, "Time-Varying Betas and Volatility Persistence in International Stock Markets", *Journal of Economics and Business*, Vol. 46, pp. 101-112.

Lessard, D. R., 1973, "International Portfolio Diversification: A Multivariate Analysis for a Group of Latin American Countries", *Journal of Finance*, 28, pp. 619-633.

Lessard, D. R., 1974, "World, National and Industry Factors in Equity Returns", *Journal of Finance*, 24, pp. 379-391.

Lessard, D. R., 1976, "World, Country, and Industry Relationships in Equity Returns", *Financial Analysts Journal*, 32, pp. 2-8.

Levy, H. and M. Sarnat, 1970, "International Diversification of Investment Portfolios", *American Economic Review*, 50, pp. 668-675.

Makridakis, S. G. and S. C. Wheelwright, 1974, "An Analysis of the Interrelationships among the Major World Stock Exchanges", *Journal of Business, Finance and Accounting*, Summer, pp. 195-215.

Maldonado, R, and A. Saunders, 1981, "International Portfolio Diversification and the Inter-Temporal Stability of International Stock Market Relationships", *Financial Management*, 10, pp. 54-63.

Malliaris, A. G. and J. L. Urrutia, 1992, "The International Crash of October 1987: Causality Tests", *Journal of Financial and Quantitative Analysis*, 27, pp. 353-363.

Malliaris, A. G. and J. L. Urrutia, 1993, "The Impact of the Persian Gulf Crisis on National Equity Markets", *Advances in International Banking and Finance*, Forthcoming.

Panton, D. B., V. P. Lessig, and O. M. Joy, 1976, "Comovement of International Equity Markets: A Taxonomic Approach", *Journal of Financial and Quantitative Analysis*, 11, pp. 415-432.

Philippatos, G. C., A. C. Christofi and P. Christofi, 1983, "The Inter-Temporal Stability of International Stock Market Relationships: Another View ", *Financial Management*, 12, pp. 63-69.

Philippatos, George and Efi Pilarinu, 1994, "Instabilities and Chaotic Behavior of Stock Prices in International Capital Markets", *Managerial Finance*, Vol. 20, No. 5/6, pp. 14-42.

Ripley, T. M., 1973, "Systematic Elements in the Linkage of National Stock Market Indices", *Review of Economics and Statistics*, 55, pp. 356-361.

Roll, R., 1992, "Industrial Structure and the Comparative Behavior of International Stock Market Indices", *Journal of Finance*, 47, pp. 3-41.

Schollhammer, H. and O. C. Sand, 1987, "Lead-lag Relationships Among National Equity Markets : An Empirical Investigation", In S, J. Khoury and A. Ghosh (eds.), *Recent Developments in International Banking and Finance*, Vol. 1, Lexington Books: Lexington, MA.

Solnik, B. H., 1974a, "Why not Diversify Internationally Rather than Domestically?", *Financial Analyst Journal*, 30, pp. 91-135.

Solnik, B. H., 1974b, "An Equilibrium Model of The International Capital Market", *Journal of Economic Theory*, 8, pp. 500-524.

Solnik, B. H., 1983, "International Arbitrage Pricing Theory", *Journal of Finance*, 38, pp. 449-457.

Stulz, R., 1981, "A Model of International Asset Pricing", *Journal of Financial Economics*, 9, pp. 383-406.

Theodossiou, Panayiotis, 1994a, "Models for Predicting Prices and Volatility Patterns in Major International Stock Markets", *Managerial Finance*, Vol. 20, No. 5/6, pp. 5-13.

Theodossiou, Panayiotis, 1994b, "Models for Predicting Prices and Volatility Patterns in Major International Stock Markets", *Managerial Finance*, Vol. 20, Number 5/6, pp. 5-13.

Theodossiou, Panayiotis and Unro Lee, 1993, "Mean and Volatility Spillovers Across Major National Stock Markets: Further Empirical Evidence", *The Journal of Financial Research*, Vol. 16, No. 4, pp. 337-350.

Von Furstenberg, G. M. and B. N. Jeon, 1989, "International Stock Price Movements: Links and Messages", *Brookings Papers on Economic Activity*, No. 1, pp. 125-167.

Wheatley, S., 1988, "Some Tests of International Equity Integration", *Journal of Financial Economics*, 21, pp. 177-212.

Multi-Fractality in Foreign Currency Markets

Marco Corazza
University Ca' Foscari of Venice, Italy

A. G. Malliaris
Loyola University Chicago, U.S.A.

Several empirical studies have shown the inadequacy of the standard Brownian motion (sBm) as a model of asset returns. To correct for this evidence some authors have conjectured that asset returns may be independently and identically Pareto-Lévy stable (PLs) distributed, whereas others have asserted that asset returns may be identically - but not independently - fractional Brownian motion (fBm) distributed with Hurst exponents, in both cases, that differ from 0.5. In this article we empirically explore such non-standard assumptions for both spot and (nearby) futures returns for five foreign currencies: the British Pound, the Canadian Dollar, the German Mark, the Swiss Franc, and the Japanese Yen.

Keywords: exponent of Hurst, fractional Brownian motion, multi-fractal market hypothesis, Pareto-Lévy stable process, R/S analysis.

I. Introduction

The standard hypothesis concerning the behavior of asset returns in financial markets claims that they are independently and identically lognormally distributed ($\ln[P(t + dt) - \ln[P(t)] \sim N(\mu dt, \sigma^2 dt)$). The

---

*The first draft of this article was written when Marco Corazza was a Visiting Research Associate in the Department of Economics at Loyola University Chicago. Earlier versions of this article were presented in the Asset and Liability Management Conference, The University of British Columbia, Vancouver, B.C., Canada, August 14-16, 1998 and at the Eighth Annual Conference of the Multinational Finance Society in Verona, Italy, June 23-27, 2001. The authors are grateful to two anonymous referees for several helpful suggestions, to Carolyn Tang and Robert Gyorgy for editorial assistance and to Peter Theodossiou for his generous encouragement.

(*Multinational Finance Journal*, 2002, vol. 6, no. 2, pp. 65–98)

corresponding underlying stochastic process is characterized by a quantity, called the Hurst exponent H, which is related to some fractal aspects of the process itself.[1] In particular, for a standard Brownian motion (sBm) the Hurst exponent is $H = 0.5$.

Several empirical studies have supported the independent and identical lognormal behavior of asset returns, but others have shown its inadequacy as a model of asset returns. This inadequacy is often caused by the existence of many outliers, nonstationarity in the variance level, presence of asymmetry, and short and long-term dependence. Authors such as Lo and MacKinlay (1988), Lo (1991), Peters (1991, 1994), Evertsz (1995a, 1995b), Evertsz and Berkner (1995), Corazza (1996), Campbell, Lo and MacKinlay (1997) and Corazza, Malliaris and Nardelli (1997) provide statistical evidence that asset prices do not follow random walks.

To account for this discrepancy, some authors have conjectured that financial returns may be independently and identically Pareto-Lévy stable (PLs) distributed, whereas others have conjectured that asset returns may be identically, but not independently, fractional Brownian motion (fBm) distributed.[2,3] Both of these conjectures are characterized by exponents of Hurst such that $H \neq 0.5$.

In this article we consider such non-standard hypotheses about returns for both spot and (nearby) futures for five foreign currency markets: the British Pound, the Canadian Dollar, the German Mark, the Swiss Franc and the Japanese Yen. We assume the Hurst exponent H belongs to a suitable neighborhood of 0.5, that is, we (indirectly) assume that the stochastic process generating exchange rate returns can be either a PLs or a fBm motion. This assumption provides a more flexible theoretical framework to examine if the so-called Fractal Market

---

1. There is extensive literature on fractality from a mathematical point of view, such as Mandelbrot and Van Ness (1968) and Falconer (1990). Applications of fractality in finance are presented in Evertsz (1995a, 1995b), Evertsz and Berkner (1995), and Corazza, Malliaris and Nardelli (1997).

2. See Mittnik and Rachev (1993) and Campbell, Lo and MacKinlay (1997).

3. Representative references include Lo (1991), Peters (1991, 1994), Corazza (1996), Evertsz (1995a, 1995b), Evertsz and Berkner (1995), Belkacem, Levy Vehel, and Walter (1996), Ostasiewicz (1996), Campbell, Lo and MacKinlay (1997) and Corazza, Malliaris and Nardelli (1997).

Hypothesis (FMH), as proposed in Peters (1991, 1994), is a reasonable generalization of the standard Efficient Market Hypothesis (EMH), initially elaborated in Fama (1970). Of course, when $H = 0.5$ the FMH coincides with the EMH. Furthermore, we also assume that the Hurst exponent is a function of time, $H = H(t)$, allowing the foreign currency markets structures to vary over time. The introduction of this dynamic dimension permits the generalization of the FMH into the MultiFractal Market Hypothesis (MFMH).

Briefly, the MFMH provides a theoretical framework to account for changes from "regular" to "irregular" phases of the capital markets and vice versa. In general, in such markets traders have investment horizons with similar or different lengths. If the matching between the asset demand and supply is relatively equal, then both the liquidity and regularity of the markets are ensured, otherwise the opposite holds.[4,5] Of course, when $H = 0.5$, for all suitable t, then the MFMH coincides with the EMH.

The remainder of the article is organized as follows: in section 2 we give a brief review of the literature; in sections 3 and 4 we present some theoretical and empirical aspects that are essential to our analysis; section 5 describes the data and section 6 reports the results of the multifractal analysis. In section 7 we offer an economic interpretation of our results, and finally, in section 8, we summarize our concluding remarks.

II. Review of the Literature

Market efficiency has been the most celebrated theory of financial markets during the past three decades. In its simplest formulation this theory claims that changes in asset prices reflect fully and instantaneously the release of all new relevant information. Furthermore, because such a flow of information cannot be anticipated between the current trading period and the next one, asset price changes, in efficient markets, are serially independent. In other words, the release of

4. Notice that the peculiarities of such a matching depends on the stochastic process generating the asset returns.

5. These concepts are discussed in detail in Pancham (1994), Corazza (1996), Belkacem, Vehel, and Walter (1996) and also in section 6 of this article.

unanticipated information moves asset prices randomly. The textbook by Campbell, Lo and MacKinlay (1997, section 8) explains various versions of the random walk hypothesis.

The efficient market theory, from its earliest formulation by Samuelson (1965) and Fama (1970), has been refined in several directions. Analytically, the concept of information has been rigorously defined. Statistically, the notion of random walk has been generalized to Itô processes. Moreover, the efficient market hypothesis has been extensively tested. Fama (1991) traces the evolution of the market efficiency theory during its first two decades and skillfully cites numerous studies that offer empirical support as well as empirical rejection of the EMH.

In this article we conduct an empirical investigation of the return behavior of five foreign currencies in order to detect possible discrepancies between the actual behavior of such currencies and the classical random walk. Note that we do not claim that foreign currency markets are inefficient nor do we assert that the EMH does not hold. We acknowledge that market efficiency is currently the central theory of financial economics, at least until a new theory is proposed as a better explanatory paradigm of asset prices behavior. We merely wish to emphasize the need for revising the EMH and provide empirical evidence to this end.

The existing literature proposes several approaches for verifying whether a foreign exchange market is more or less efficient. In the remainder of this section we briefly review some of most significant findings.

From an econometric standpoint, Cornell (1977), Frankel (1980), Chiang and Jiang (1995), and Zhou (1996) examine whether the current spot, the forward rate or the futures price can be used as an unbiased predictor of the spot rate itself at some future date. From the same point of view, it is possible to use the recent time series tools of cointegration, ARCH and GARCH techniques to detect possible market inefficiencies. Kao and Ma (1992), Leachman and El Shazly (1992), Chan, Gup and Pan (1992) and Alexakis and Apergis (1996) utilize such methodologies.

A more operative approach consists of devising certain trading rules concerning these markets and determining their profitability, as in Taylor (1992), Levich and Thomas (1993), and Kho (1992).

A third class of techniques looks for deterministic nonlinear and chaotic dynamics in foreign currency market data. Hsieh (1988, 1992), and

Bleaney and Mizen (1996) follow these methodologies.

Finally, a recent "inter disciplinary" approach is the fractal one which is linked to both stochastic and deterministic aspects of the underlying process generating the price changes. The tools of fractal analysis are employed by Liu and Hsueh (1993), Fang, Lai and Lai (1994), Evertsz (1995a, 1995b), Evertsz and Berkner (1995), Van de Gucht, Dekimpe and Kwok (1996), Corazza, Malliaris and Nardelli (1997) and in this article. A detailed presentation of these techniques is given in Shubik (1997).

III. Theoretical Aspects

The current literature proposes different stochastic processes to describe the behavior of financial returns. The most common approaches are the fractional Brownian motion (fBm), and some of the Pareto-Levy stable (PLs) distribution sub-families. In general, these stochastic processes can be characterized by the same Hurst exponent, $H \neq 0.5$, as explained in Taqqu (1986), Evertsz (1995a, 1995b), and Evertsz and Berkner (1995). In fact, if such stochastic processes are independently and identically distributed with exponentially decaying power-law tails, as for example the PLs, then $H \in (0.5, 1)$, whereas if they are identically, but not independently distributed, as for example the fBm, then $H \in (0, 1)$.[6]

In order to conduct our analysis and consequently to test the MultiFractal Market Hypothesis (MFMH), we need a set of mathematical and statistical tools to formally define and estimate the long-term dependence of asset returns and to determine the value of the Hurst exponent. In particular, in this section we first define the fBm and PLs motions and present some of their properties. Second, we describe some tests for detecting long-term memory in time series and we introduce some algorithms for estimating the Hurst exponent, H.

A. Fractional and MultiFractional Brownian Motion

The fBm is a term coined by Mandelbrot and Van Ness (1968) to

6. Notice that the interval (0.5, 1) is obtained as the intersection of the ones characterizing each of the different PLs distribution sub-families. Taqqu (1986) includes in these subfamilies, the symmetric, the fractional and the log-fractional one, among others.

describe an almost everywhere continuous Gaussian stochastic process of index $H \in (0,1)$, $\{B_H(t),\ t \geq 0\}$, defined by a Riemann-Liouville stochastic integral, such that $B_H(0) = 0$ with probability 1, and that $B_H(t_2) - B_H(t_1) \sim N(0, \sigma^{2H}(t_2 - t_1)^{2H})$, with $0 \leq t_1 < t_2 < +\infty$ and $\sigma > 0$. In particular, if $H \neq 0.5$ then the increments are stationary but not independent, and they show a long-term memory depending on both H and $t_2 - t_1$. If $H \in (0, 0.5)$, there is a negative dependence between the increments. In this case the stochastic process has an anti-persistent behavior. If $H \in (0.5, 1)$, there is a positive dependence between the increments and in this case the process has a persistent behavior. The case $H = 0.5$ is the sBm that has independent increments. Moreover, this stochastic process is statistically self-similar, that is $\{B_H(t),\ t \geq 0\}$ and $\{a^{-H}B_H(at),\ t \geq 0\}$, with $a > 0$, have the same distribution law. Further details for the fBm can be found in Falconer (1990), Evertsz (1995a, 1995b), Evertsz and Berkner (1995) and Corazza, Malliaris and Nardelli (1997).

In 1995, Peltier and Levy (1995) proposed an extension of the fBm by substituting the constant over time Hurst exponent, H, with a suitable time dependent function, $H(t)$. Unlike the fBm, this new stochastic process, called multifBm (mfBm), allows us to formally model the irregularities of the process trajectory. As such, this stochastic process can be fruitfully utilized to describe non-stationarity in financial asset price variations.[7]

B. Pareto-Lévy Stable Stochastic Process

The PLs motion, originally introduced by Lévy (1925) as a generalization of the sBm, is a stochastic process, $\{L_\alpha(t),\ t \geq 0\}$, characterized by a distribution, $S_{\alpha,\beta}(\mu,\sigma)$, depending on four parameters: the so-called characteristic exponent $\alpha \in (0, 2]$, the skewness parameter $\beta \in [-1, 1]$, the location parameter $\mu \in (-\infty, +\infty)$, and the scale coefficient $\sigma \in [0, +\infty)$.[8] This stochastic process is such that $L_\alpha(0) = 0$ almost-surely, and its increments $L_\alpha(t_2) - L_\alpha(t_1)$, with $0 \leq t_1 < t_2 < +\infty$, whose distribution is $S_{\alpha,\beta}(0, (t_2 - t_1)^{1/\alpha})$, are independent and stationary. In particular, if α

---

7. For details, see Cheung and Lai (1993), Corazza (1996) and Belkacem, Levy and Walter (1996).

8. If $\alpha \in (0,1)$ the distribution does not have a finite mean or a finite variance. If $\alpha \in [1,2)$ the distribution has only a finite mean and if $\alpha = 2$, the distribution has both finite mean and finite variance.

$\in (0, 2)$ then the tails of such a process decay slower than the tails of an fBm process, and if $\alpha = 2$ it is possible to prove that $\{2^{-1/2} L_2(t), t \geq 0\} \equiv \{B_{0.5}(t), t \geq 0\}$, which is the sBm. Moreover, if the distribution $S_{\alpha,\beta}(\mu, \sigma)$ is symmetric, that is if $\beta = 0$, then the corresponding PLs process is statistically self-similar.[9] Taking $\{L_\alpha(t), t \geq 0\}$ and $\{a^{-1/\alpha} L_\alpha(at), t \geq 0\}$, with $a > 0$, results in the same distribution law. In such a case it is possible to prove that the Hurst exponent equals $H = 1/\alpha$.[10]

IV. Empirical Aspects

Although a large empirical literature exists confirming the presence of long-run memory or long-range dependence in asset prices, there are no universally accepted quantitative methodologies that make it possible to detect such long-term dependence in (finite) time series as argued by Taqqu, Teverovsky and Willinger (1995). Moreover, some of the methodologies used show considerable limitations. Thus, in order to overcome the shortcomings of each methodology, we follow two different inferential approaches and compare the corresponding results. The methodologies employed are the classical modified range over standard deviation statistic, *R/S*, and the periodogram approach.[11]

A. Tests for Long-Term Dependence

i. The Modified R/S Test

Lo (1991) proposes a modification of a test based on the classical range over standard deviation statistic, *R/S*. To test for no long-term dependence in financial time series consider:

$$Q_r(q) = \frac{R_T / S_T(q)}{\sqrt{T}}, \tag{4.1}$$

---

9. From a financial standpoint it is not restrictive to assume that $\beta = 0$. In fact, most of the skewness parameters estimated from asset returns time series, though different from 0, are quite close to it.

10. See Taqqu (1986) and Corazza, Malliaris and Nardelli (1997).

11. We are grateful to an anonymous referee for suggesting that we use both methodologies.

where T is the time series size, q is the possible short-term dependence (integer) length, $R_T(q)$ is the sample range of partial sums of deviations of the time series from its sample mean, and $S_T(q)$ is the modified standard deviation of the time series including the autocovariances weighted up to lag q. This new methodology is described in detail in both Lo (1991) and Campbell, Lo and MacKinlay (1997). Precisely, this statistic is able to test the null hypothesis of no long-term dependence.[12] In particular, unlike the corresponding statistic based on the classical *R/S*, it is robust to short-term memory, conditional heteroscedasticity, and non-normal innovation. Furthermore, it also has well-defined distributional properties as described in Lo (1991) and Campbell, Lo and MacKinlay (1997), although the related (asymptotic) distribution is neither standard, nor easily tractable.

Of course, this statistic is crucially influenced by the statistical structure of short-term dependence. In order to accommodate this aspect, we apply two different approaches. In the first approach we specify in a nonparametric way the short-term memory structure determining the optimal value of q by the use of the Andrews' (1991) data-dependent rule $q^* = [(3T/2)^{1/3}[\rho/(1-\rho^2)]^{2/3}]$, where the operator $[\cdot]$ denotes the greatest integer less than or equal to the argument, and ρ is the sample first-order autocorrelation coefficient. In the second approach, we take into account the remarks of Lo (1991) and Jacobsen (1996) stating that, in general, there is little guidance in determining the optimal value of q. In this article, we follow the Jacobsen's (1996) procedure, and perform the test in two steps. First, we impose some specific models for the short-term dependence structure, namely an AR(1) one and a MA(1) one.[13] Second, we apply the statistic $Q_T(q^*)$, with $q^* = 0$, to the time series of the corresponding residuals.

Finally, by using the fractiles of the distribution of $Q_T(q)$ as in Lo

12. Notice that a rejection of such a null hypothesis does not necessarily imply that long-range dependence is present but, merely, that the underlying stochastic process does not simultaneously satisfy all the conditions stated by Lo (1991). However, such conditions are satisfied by many of the recently proposed stochastic processes for long-term dependence.

13. Notice that such an arbitrary way of choosing an AR(1) model and a MA(1) one is not particularly restrictive because, in general, such models are standard for handling short-term memory in financial returns time series.

(1991), it is possible to determine critical values for different significance levels in this two-sided test. At 10, 5 and 1 percent they are 1.747, 1.862, and 2.098, respectively.

ii. The Periodogram-based Test

Lobato and Savin (1998) employ a suitable approximation to the Lagrange multiplier test in order to develop the no long-term dependence in the following time series statistic that is based on a periodogram and is given as such:

$$LM_T(m) = m\left(\frac{\sum_{j=1}^{m} v_j I(\lambda_j)}{\sum_{j=1}^{m} I(\lambda_j)}\right), \tag{4.2}$$

where m is an (integer) bandwidth,

$$v_j = \ln(j) - \left[\sum_{j=1}^{m} \ln(j)\right] \Big/ m,$$

and

$$I(\lambda_j) = \left[\left|\sum_{t=1}^{T} x_t \exp(it\lambda_j)\right|\right] \Big/ (2\pi T),$$

is the periodogram computed at frequency $\lambda_j = (2\pi j)/T$, in which x_t, with $t = 1,\dots, T$, is the time series, and $i = \sqrt{-1}$. More specifically, this statistic tests the null hypothesis H_0: $H = 0.5$ rather than the alternative one H_A: $H \neq 0.5$. Moreover, this test is characterized by a well-known and quite tractable (asymptotic) distribution which is the χ_1^2.

Of course, in this statistic, the bandwidth m plays a crucial role. In order to determine its optimal value, we need to verify that certain proper assumptions hold (such as the Gaussianity of x_t, with $t = 1, \dots, T$). We use the iterative algorithm presented in Delgado and Robinson (1996) to estimate m. We could also apply the widely used "rule of thumb" that sets $m = \sqrt{T}$.

Finally, by using the fractiles of the χ_1^2 distribution, it is possible to determine the critical values for different significance levels for this two-sided test.

B. Procedure for Estimating the Hurst Exponent

i. The Modified R/S Estimation Procedure

The Hurst exponent is linked to the modified *R/S* statistic by $\lim_{t\to+\infty} E[R_T/S_T(q)]/(aT^H) = 1$, with $a > 0$. With this link it is possible to obtain the following approximate relationship: $\ln\{E[R_T/S_T(q)]\} \cong \ln(a) + H\ln(t)$. In order to estimate the value of the Hurst exponent, H, we have modified and improved the standard techniques described in Peters (1991, 1994), Corazza (1996) and Corazza, Malliaris and Nardelli (1997).

To do so, we first determine a series of estimates of the Hurst exponent $\{H_j, j = 1, ..., T^* < T\}$ by fitting an ordinary least square regression between $\{\ln[R_{T,l}/S_{T,l}(q)]\}, l = 1, ..., j\}$ and $\{\ln(l), l = 1, ..., j\}$, for every $j = 2, ..., T^*$, where $R_{T,l}$ and $S_{T,l}(q)$ are quantities related to R_T and $S_T(q)$ respectively. Then, we choose the optimal estimate in this series. Figures 1A and 1B illustrate the corresponding results for some of the analyzed time series by plotting H_j versus j, with $j = 2, ..., T^*$. In particular, this estimation procedure is robust, although possibly subject to bias, when the data generating process follows a highly non-normal distribution as argued by Lo (1991), Cheung and Lai (1993), Robinson (1994b), and Campbell, Lo and MacKinlay (1997). It is possible to prove its almost-sure convergence for stochastic processes with infinite variance. Consider for example the PLs distribution with $\alpha \in (0,2)$. Furthermore, Robinson (1994b) argues that the *R/S* estimation procedure is suboptimal when the data generating process follows a Gaussian distribution because such a procedure does not depend on second moments.

Overall, the *R/S*-based estimation procedure described in this section offers the possibility to estimate the Hurst exponent without complete information, and without strong a priori assumptions on the distributional properties of the considered stochastic process.[14]

---

14. See Pancham (1994), Peltier and Levy (1994) and Taqqu, Teverovsky and Willinger (1995) for a different methodology.

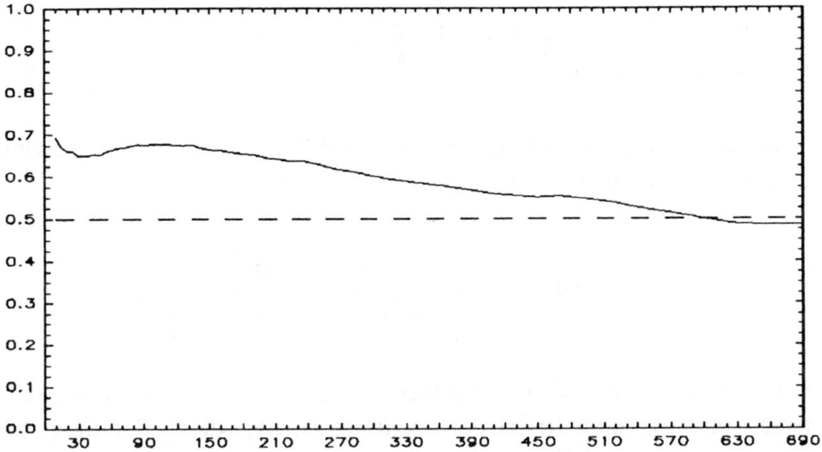

FIGURE 1A—*H* versus *j* for Canadian Dollar S. (08/76-01/82): The AR(1)case (T^{*}=690).

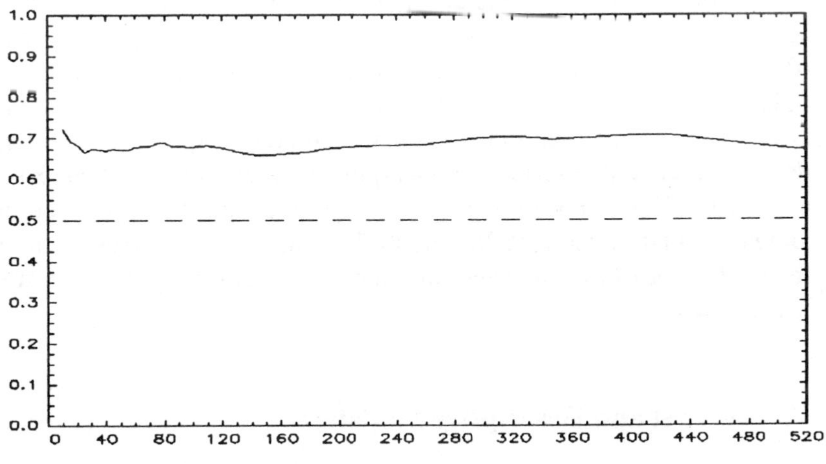

FIGURE 1B—*H* versus *j* for British Pound F. (06/72-07/76): The $q = \#$ case (T^{*}=520)

ii. The Periodogram-based Estimation Procedure

From a spectral density point of view, the Hurst exponent is linked to the discretely averaged periodogram:

$$F(\lambda) = 2\pi \left[\sum_{j=1}^{\lfloor \lambda T/2\pi \rfloor} I(\lambda_j) \right] \Big/ T.$$

Starting from this relationship, Robinson (1994a) proposed the following closed form semi-parametric estimator for H:

$$H(m,r) = 1 - \frac{1}{2\ln(r)} \ln\left[\frac{F(r\lambda_m)}{F(\lambda_m)} \right], \tag{4.3}$$

where m is the bandwidth introduced earlier and $r \in (0,1)$ is a suitable user-chosen variable. In particular, under the hypothesis that the data-generating process follows a Gaussian distribution, it is possible to prove that this estimator is consistent and that it has well-defined (asymptotic) distributional properties both normal and non-normal, depending on the estimated value of $H(m, r)$.[15, 16]

Of course r, plays a crucial role in this estimator. In particular, if some proper assumptions hold, among them the restrictions that $H \in (0.5, 0.75)$, then it is possible to determine its optimal value as discussed in Lobato and Robinson (1996). Thus, since both m and r depend on $H(m, r)$, in order to optimally estimate the Hurst exponent, we must determine a suitable series of converging estimates of H, $\{H_j(m_j, r_j), j = 1, ..., J\}$. This can be done using the iterative algorithm proposed in Delgado and Robinson (1996). Figure 1C illustrates the corresponding results for one of the analyzed time series by plotting $H_j(m_j, r_j)$ versus j, with $j = 1, ..., J$.

V. Data Set and Descriptive Statistics

The data we analyze are the time series of the daily returns using closing prices of exchange rates expressed in US Dollars, that is, $100\{\ln[P(t+1)] - \ln[P(t)]\}$. We use data from June 1972 to September 1994, for the following five spot and (nearby) futures foreign currency markets:

15. See Robinson (1994a).

16. See Lobato and Robinson (1996).

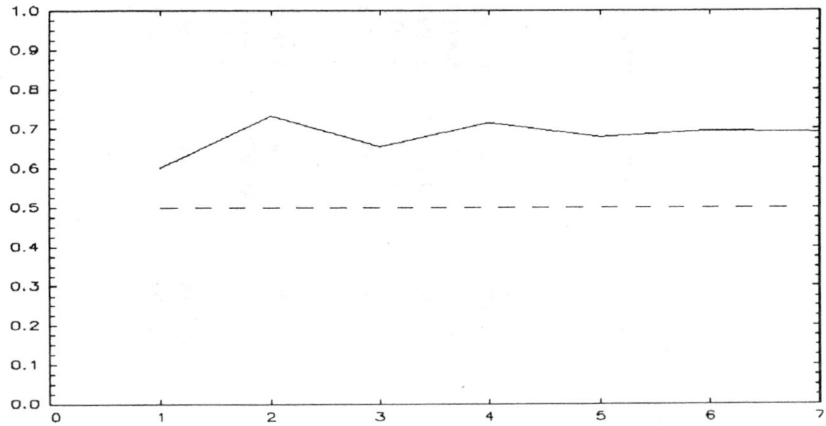

FIGURE 1C—*H versus j* for German Mark F. (06/72-07/76): The Periodogram case (J=7)

British Pound, Canadian Dollar, German Mark, Swiss Franc and Japanese Yen. In particular, in order to implement our multifractal analysis, we assume that the dynamic Hurst exponent $H(t)$is a stepwise constant function whose intervals are determined by splitting up each time series into four non-overlapping sub periods: June 1972 to July 1976; August 1976 to January 1982; February 1982 to June 1987; and July 1987 to September 1994. The choice of these four time sub-periods is driven by the (relative) homogeneity of the economic and political conditions in each geographical region.

In table 1A to table 1F, we report some standard descriptive statistics. The quantities reported indicate the number of observations, the minimum and maximum values of the time series, the means, the medians, the standard deviations, the skewness, and the kurtosis.

Generally, all the considered time series qualitatively denote to some degree a departure from normality. This is evidenced by the medians that differ from the corresponding means, skewness values, and particularly, kurtosis values. These departures are also confirmed by the performance of a simple χ^2-type test for distribution fitting, which rejects the null hypothesis of normality for all the time series at 1% significance level.

From a short and medium-term autocorrelation point of view, we investigate the sample autocorrelation function up to lag 22 (about a one-month trading period). In general, with the exception of certain time

TABLE 1. Descriptive Statistics

Time Period	N. Obs.	Min	Max	Mean	Median	St. Dev.	Skew.	Kurtosis
A. British Pound								
i. Spot								
06/72–07/76	1033	−3.0589	3.1812	−0.0369	0.0000	0.4470	−0.2436	9.0562
08/76–01/82	1382	−4.6623	3.7496	0.0037	0.0057	0.6302	−0.6097	6.8748
02/82–06/87	1377	−3.0175	4.5942	−0.0110	0.0000	0.7392	0.4208	3.3990
07/87–09/94	1894	−4.0900	3.2656	−0.0010	0.0000	0.7313	−0.2248	2.5073
06/72–09/94	5686	−4.6623	4.5942	−0.0088	0.0000	0.6659	−0.0857	4.3772
ii. (Nearby) Futures								
06/72–07/76	1045	−2.2103	2.8738	−0.0374	0.0000	0.4694	−0.5182	5.1612
08/76–01/82	1384	−3.4467	3.6057	0.0044	0.0000	0.6541	−0.4975	4.0314
02/82–06/87	1369	−2.7369	4.5529	−0.0113	0.0000	0.7714	0.4842	3.4082
07/87–09/94	1844	−4.4760	3.4748	−0.0010	0.0215	0.7714	−0.2628	2.5643
06/72–09/94	5642	−4.4760	4.5529	−0.0089	0.0000	0.6963	−0.0749	3.7279

TABLE 1. Descriptive Statistics

B. Canadian Dollar								
i. Spot								
06/72–07/76	1034	−1.5467	1.1957	0.0006	0.0000	0.1467	−0.5417	17.3788
08/76–01/82	1382	−1.8677	0.8678	−0.0148	−0.0212	0.2439	−0.4324	3.9179
02/82–06/87	1374	−1.6555	1.4323	−0.0078	−0.0122	0.2571	−0.2355	5.0739
07/87–09/94	1895	−1.9088	1.9971	−0.0006	0.0119	0.2735	−0.3115	4.3041
06/72–09/94	5685	−1.9088	1.9971	−0.0056	0.0000	0.2436	−0.3453	5.4804
ii. (Nearby) Futures								
06/72–07/76	1045	−1.1974	0.7754	0.0006	0.0000	0.1622	−0.2832	6.6126
08/76–01/82	1384	−1.1939	1.1851	−0.0144	−0.0118	0.2643	0.0482	1.5593
02/82–06/87	1369	−1.7946	1.6525	−0.0079	−0.0122	0.2745	−0.1552	5.1085
07/87–09/94	1844	−1.7811	1.9916	−0.0005	0.0230	0.3026	−0.5787	4.1179
06/72–09/94	5642	−1.7946	1.9916	−0.0055	0.0000	0.2651	−0.3262	4.5511

TABLE 1. (Continued)

C. German Mark								
i. Spot								
06/72–07/76	1033	−4.3193	6.0458	0.0219	0.0000	0.6695	0.5869	12.4245
08/76–01/82	1381	−7.0967	3.1639	0.0060	0.0000	0.6367	−0.7251	13.3480
02/82–06/87	1374	−3.2019	4.9899	0.0177	0.0000	0.7338	0.4353	2.5384
07/87–09/94	1894	−3.4661	3.1659	0.0090	0.0000	0.7149	−0.0533	1.8184
06/72–09/94	5682	−7.0967	6.0458	0.0127	0.0000	0.6933	0.0658	5.7780
ii. (Nearby) Futures								
06/72–07/76	1046	−1.8976	3.8037	0.0219	0.0000	0.5649	0.7705	4.1370
08/76–01/82	1384	−3.6945	3.4361	0.0064	0.0000	0.6416	0.2582	3.3015
02/82–06/87	1369	−3.2351	4.8321	0.0177	0.0000	0.7647	0.5001	2.5882
07/87–09/94	1844	−3.3125	3.6013	0.0088	0.0000	0.7392	−0.0997	1.7442
06/72–09/94	5643	−3.6945	4.8321	0.0128	0.0000	0.6932	0.2497	2.7370

TABLE 1. (Continued)

D. Japaneese Yen								
i. Spot								
06/72–07/76	1033	–6.2566	8.7260	0.0035	0.0000	0.4816	3.9312	133.7888
08/76–01/82	1382	–5.2644	3.5703	0.0182	–0.0224	0.6890	0.1337	4.3757
02/82–06/87	1374	–2.3846	5.4055	0.0321	0.0000	0.6558	0.7768	5.2895
07/87–09/94	1894	–4.0991	3.8777	0.0204	–0.0220	0.6953	0.0755	3.5482
06/72–09/94	5683	–6.2566	8.7260	0.0196	0.0000	0.6502	0.5588	11.6583
ii. (Nearby) Futures								
06/72–07/76	1046	–5.6660	5.5346	0.0027	0.0000	0.5526	–0.2844	26.8716
08/76–01/82	1384	–2.7504	4.8110	0.0189	0.0000	0.7290	0.5778	2.8046
02/82–06/87	1369	–2.3653	5.3327	0.0320	0.0000	0.6677	0.7597	4.6245
07/87–09/94	1844	–4.2073	4.7533	0.0208	0.0000	0.7008	0.1364	3.8295
06/72–09/94	5643	–5.6660	5.5346	0.0197	0.0000	0.6751	0.3821	5.8022

TABLE 1. (Continued)

E. Swiss Franc								
i. Spot								
06/72–07/76	1033	–4.3367	3.7346	0.0427	0.0249	0.7248	0.1778	6.3538
08/76–01/82	1379	–7.0054	4.4466	0.0210	0.0000	0.8356	0.4140	8.8837
02/82–06/87	1372	–3.9302	5.3094	0.0145	0.0000	0.8187	0.3038	2.6768
07/87–09/94	1891	–3.5750	3.4613	0.0087	0.0000	0.7797	0.0465	1.4185
06/72–09/94	5675	–7.0054	5.3094	0.0193	0.0000	0.7938	0.0003	4.6543
ii. (Nearby) Futures								
06/72–07/76	1047	–3.2377	4.6886	0.0424	0.0000	0.6461	0.4319	5.0734
08/76–01/82	1384	–3.9371	4.3620	0.0213	–0.0173	0.8098	0.4728	2.8961
02/82–06/87	1369	–3.6919	5.5361	0.0144	0.0000	0.8640	0.4471	2.5081
07/87–09/94	1844	–3.6227	3.1341	0.0086	0.0000	0.8074	–0.0210	1.2281
06/72–09/94	5644	–3.9371	5.5361	0.0194	0.0000	0.7953	0.2906	2.5401

TABLE 1. (Continued)

	06/72–07/76	08/76–01/82	02/82–06/87	07/87–09/94	06/72–09/94
F. Short Term Dependence Analysis					
British Pound (Spot)	9, 14	9	11	6, 10, 18	9, 11, 20
British Pound (Fut.)	9	–	6	6, 15, 18	1, 15
Canadian Dollar (Spot)	1, 2, 7, 10	1, 5	1, 2, 3, 12, 16	4, 16	1, 4, 5, 7, 16
Canadian Dollar (Fut.)	–	5	1, 2, 3, 12, 13	12, 15	1, 2
German Mark (Spot)	2, 3, 5, 7, 9, 10, 11, 14	3, 10	10	10	3, 9, 10
German Mark (Fut.)	10, 13, 18	10	3, 8, 11, 16	15	15, 20
Japanese Yen (Spot)	1, 10, 20, 21	1, 9, 10, 13	3, 5, 6	6, 10, 14	9, 10
Japanese Yen (Fut.)	4	10, 20, 21	6	6, 10, 14	8, 9, 10, 14, 21
Swiss Franc (Spot)	2, 7	10	–	10	9, 12
Swiss Franc (Fut.)	1, 8	1, 2, 20	16	2, 15	15

series, such an autocorrelation structure is negligible. In table 1F, we report the lag(s) for which the corresponding autocorrelation coefficient is significantly different from 0 at the 5% significance level for each time series under observation.[17]

Finally, some authors, such as Lobato and Savin (1998), suggest that evidence of long-term memory could be spuriously caused by non-stationarity in the time series itself. To test for non-stationarity, we perform the basic Dickey-Fuller test and its properly augmented version.[18] For all the considered series, both tests reject the null hypothesis of non-stationarity (more precisely the tests reject the presence of a unit root in the autoregressive representation) at the 2% significance level.[19]

VI. Empirical Results of MultiFractal Analysis[20]

The empirical results obtained are reported in table 2A to table 2E. In particular, the results relative to each of the considered single time periods are presented in four rows. The first three rows are devoted to the modified *R/S*-based approach, and the fourth row is devoted to the periodogram-based approach. In the columns labeled "*" we report the information concerning the assumed short-term dependence structure (in the first three rows relative to each period), and the bandwidth value (in the fourth row relative to each period). In the columns labeled "H_0" we report the results of the test for no long-term dependence (acceptance or non-rejection is indicated by "A", rejection is indicated by its significance level), and in the columns labeled "H" we report the values of the Hurst exponent.[21]

---

17. Such as the the Canadian Dollar spot, the Canadian Dollar futures, the German Mark spot, the Japanese Yen spot, and the Swiss Franc futures in some sub and full-sample periods.

18. For more details see Dickey and Fuller (1979, 1981).

19. The 2% significance level is the lowest boundary of the significance levels tabulated in Dickey and Fuller (1979).

20. Statistical computations were performed by Marco Corazza.

21. Notice that, although for completeness of exposition we also report the cases when the null hypothesis is rejected at the 20% significance level, practically we consider such rejections as acceptances in table 2F.

TABLE 2. Multifractal Analysis

Spot				(Nearby) Futures			
Time Period	*	H_0	H	Time Period	*	H_0	H
A. British Pound							
06/72–07/76	$q = 1$	5%	0.5991	06/72–07/76	$q = 1$	5%	0.7079
	AR(1)	10%	0.6798		AR(1)	5%	0.7057
	MA(1)	10%	0.6838		MA(1)	5%	0.7474
	$m = 258$	A	0.5828		$m = 261$	A	0.5816
08/76–01/82	$q = 1$	1%	0.5466	08/76–01/82	$q = 2$	5%	0.5499
	AR(1)	20%	0.6408		AR(1)	20%	0.6253
	MA(1)	20%	0.6343		MA(1)	20%	0.6027
	$m = 326$	A	0.5139		$m = 326$	5%	0.4844
02/82–06/87	$q = 1$	5%	0.6446	02/82–06/87	$q = 0$	5%	0.6424
	AR(1)	A	0.5990		AR(1)	A	0.5906
	MA(1)	A	0.5881		MA(1)	A	0.5940
	$m = 324$	A	0.4821		$m = 323$	A	0.4565
07/87–09/94	$q = 2$	20%	0.5022	07/87–09/94	$q = 2$	10%	0.4854
	AR(1)	A	0.6255		AR(1)	A	0.6181
	MA(1)	A	0.6046		MA(1)	A	0.5942
	$m = 419$	A	0.5206		$m = 410$	A	0.5137
06/72–09/94	Q=2	1%	0.6780	06/72–09/94	$q = 2$	1%	0.6778
	AR(1)	1%	0.6336		AR(1)	5%	0.6658
	MA(1)	1%	0.6499		MA(1)	1%	0.6228
	$m = 1009$	5%	0.5399		$m = 1003$	A	0.5305

TABLE 2. (Continued)

B. Canadian Dollar

06/72–07/76	$q = 4$	10%	0.6175	06/72–07/76	$q = 1$	20%	0.6273
	AR(1)	A	0.6523		AR(1)	20%	0.6089
	MA(1)	10%	0.6083		MA(1)	20%	0.6026
	m=258	20%	0.6216		$m = 261$	A	0.5287
08/76–01/82	$q = 4$	20%	0.4449	08/76–01/82	$q = 2$	10%	0.4497
	AR(1)	20%	0.4890		AR(1)	10%	0.4671
	MA(1)	20%	0.4384		MA(1)	10%	0.4476
	$m = 326$	10%	0.6216		$m = 326$	20%	0.5855
02/82–06/87	$q = 3$	10%	0.6123	02/82–06/87	$q = 5$	20%	0.5947
	AR(1)	A	0.6116		AR(1)	A	0.5916
	MA(1)	20%	0.5805		MA(1)	A	0.5601
	$m = 324$	A	0.5244		$m = 323$	20%	0.4430
07/87–09/94	$q = 1$	10%	0.5873	07/87–09/94	$q = 2$	10%	0.5072
	AR(1)	A	0.6046		AR(1)	20%	0.5178
	MA(1)	A	0.5833		MA(1)	A	0.5130
	$m = 419$	A	0.4929		$m = 410$	A	0.4217
06/72–09/94	$q = 4$	5%	0.5937	06/72–09/94	$q = 4$	10%	0.5896
	AR(1)	10%	0.6080		AR(1)	20%	0.5997
	MA(1)	10%	0.5957		MA(1)	20%	0.5935
	$m = 1009$	A	0.5494		$m = 1003$	A	0.5033

TABLE 2. (Continued)

C. German Mark

06/72–07/76	$q = 0$	20%	0.7105	06/72–07/76	$q = 2$	5%	0.6999
	AR(1)	20%	0.7141		AR(1)	10%	0.7440
	MA(1)	20%	0.7105		MA(1)	5%	0.6919
	$m = 258$	A	0.6199		$m = 261$	1%	0.6910
08/76–01/82	$q = 1$	5%	0.6123	08/76–01/82	$q = 2$	5%	0.5918
	AR(1)	20%	0.5825		AR(1)	10%	0.5620
	MA(1)	20%	0.5738		MA(1)	10%	0.5345
	$m = 326$	A	0.5810		$m = 326$	20%	0.5729
02/82–06/87	$q = 0$	1%	0.6519	02/82–06/87	$q = 2$	1%	0.6208
	AR(1)	20%	0.5711		AR(1)	A	0.6391
	MA(1)	A	0.4088		MA(1)	A	0.6036
	$m = 324$	10%	0.5799		$m = 323$	10%	0.5797
07/87–09/94	$q = 0$	A	0.6356	07/87–09/94	$q = 2$	A	0.6157
	AR(1)	A	0.6342		AR(1)	A	0.6340
	MA(1)	A	0.6356		MA(1)	A	0.6140
	$m = 419$	A	0.4930		$m = 410$	A	0.4753
06/72–09/94	$q = 0$	1%	0.6600	06/72–09/94	$q = 2$	1%	0.6563
	AR(1)	10%	0.6175		AR(1)	10%	0.6161
	MA(1)	10%	0.6179		MA(1)	10%	0.6120
	$m = 1009$	5%	0.5832		$m = 1003$	5%	0.5795

TABLE 2. (Continued)

D. Japanese Yen							
06/72–07/76	$q = 2$	A	0.6087	06/72–07/76	$q = 2$	A	0.6133
	AR(1)	A	0.6546		AR(1)	A	0.6317
	MA(1)	A	0.6022		MA(1)	A	0.6103
	$m = 258$	20%	0.6133		$m = 261$	A	0.5800
08/76–01/82	$q = 2$	1%	0.7173	08/76–01/82	$q = 1$	1%	0.7321
	AR(1)	10%	0.6572		AR(1)	10%	0.6418
	MA(1)	10%	0.6340		MA(1)	10%	0.6389
	$m = 326$	A	0.5724		$m = 326$	A	0.5509
02/82–06/87	$q = 1$	5%	0.6314	02/82–06/87	$q = 1$	5%	0.6330
	AR(1)	10%	0.6589		AR(1)	10%	0.6581
	MA(1)	10%	0.6616		MA(1)	10%	0.6129
	$m = 324$	5%	0.6512		$m = 323$	5%	0.6145
07/87–09/94	$q = 1$	A	0.6211	07/87–09/94	$q = 1$	A	0.6200
	AR(1)	A	0.6287		AR(1)	A	0.6267
	MA(1)	20%	0.6215		MA(1)	A	0.6194
	$m = 419$	A	0.5026		$m = 410$	A	0.4897
06/72–09/94	q = 1	1%	0.6245	06/72–09/94	$q = 1$	5%	0.6200
	AR(1)	1%	0.6297		AR(1)	5%	0.6224
	MA(1)	1%	0.5320		MA(1)	5%	0.6199
	$m = 1009$	1%	0.6077		$m = 1003$	10%	0.5849

TABLE 2. (Continued)

E. Swiss Frank							
06/72–07/76	$q = 0$	20%	0.6877	06/72–07/76	$q = 3$	10%	0.6670
	AR(1)	20%	0.6925		AR(1)	10%	0.7114
	MA(1)	20%	0.6877		MA(1)	10%	0.6593
	$m = 258$	20%	0.5806		$m = 261$	20%	0.6127
08/76–01/82	$q = 2$	5%	0.6224	08/76–01/82	$q = 3$	10%	0.6119
	AR(1)	20%	0.6451		AR(1)	20%	0.6386
	MA(1)	20%	0.6268		MA(1)	A	0.5897
	$m = 325$	A	0.5466		$m = 326$	5%	0.5517
02/82–06/87	$q = 1$	5%	0.6604	02/82–06/87	$q = 2$	5%	0.6436
	AR(1)	20%	0.5512		AR(1)	20%	0.5417
	MA(1)	20%	0.5470		MA(1)	20%	0.5131
	$m = 325$	A	0.5405		$m = 323$	A	0.5246
07/87–09/94	$q = 1$	20%	0.6306	07/87–09/94	$q = 2$	20%	0.6225
	AR(1)	20%	0.6362		AR(1)	A	0.6421
	MA(1)	20%	0.6303		MA(1)	20%	0.6217
	$m = 418$	A	0.4988		$m = 410$	A	0.4819
06/72–09/94	$q = 1$	1%	0.6550	06/72–09/94	$q = 2$	1%	0.6517
	AR(1)	10%	0.5991		AR(1)	10%	0.6015
	MA(1)	10%	0.5956		MA(1)	10%	0.5933
	$m = 1008$	A	0.5473		$m = 1003$	A	0.5495

TABLE 2. (Continued)

Time Period	B. Pound Spot	B. Pound Fut.	C. Dollar Spot	C. Dollar Fut.	G. Mark Spot	G. Mark Fut.	J. Yen Spot	J. Yen Fut.	S. Franc Spot	S. Franc Fut.
F. Comparative MultiFractal Analysis										
6/72-07/76	fBm	fBm	fBm	Pls	PLs	fBm	PLs	PLs	PLs	fBm
	fBm	fBm	PLs	PLs	PLs	fBm	PLs	PLs	PLs	fBm
	fBm	fBm	fBm	PLs	PLs	fBm	PLs	PLs	PLs	fBm
	PLs	PLs	PLs	PLs	PLs	fBm	PLs	PLs	PLs	PLs
08/76-01/82	fBm	fBm	?	fBm	fBm	fBm	fBm	fBm	fBm	fBm
	PLs	PLs	?	fBm	PLs	fBm	fBm	fBm	PLs	PLs
	PLs	PLs	?	fBm	PLs	fBm	fBm	fBm	PLs	PLs
	PLs	fBm	fBm	PLs	PLs	PLs	PLs	PLs	PLs	fBm
02/82-06/87	fBm	fBm	fBm	PLs	fBm	fBm	fBm	fBm	fBm	fBm
	PLs	PLs	PLs	PLs	PLs	PLs	fBm	fBm	PLs	PLs
	PLs	PLs	PLs	PLs	?	PLs	fBm	fBm	PLs	Pls
	?	?	PLs	?	fBm	fBm	fBm	fBm	PLs	Pls
07/87-09/94	PLs	fBm	fBm	fBm	PLs	PLs	PLs	PLs	PLs	PLs
	PLs	PLs	PLs	PLs	PLs	PLs	PLs	PLs	PLs	PLs
	PLs	PLs	PLs	PLs	PLs	PLs	PLs	PLs	PLs	PLs
	PLs	PLs	?	?	?	?	PLs	?	?	?
06/72-09/94	fBm	fBm	fBm	fBm	fBm	fBm	fBm	fBm	fBm	fBm
	fBm	fBm	fBm	PLs	fBm	fBm	fBm	fBm	fBm	fBm
	fBm	fBm	fBm	PLs	fBm	fBm	fBm	fBm	fBm	fBm
	fBm	PLs	PLs	PLs	fBm	fBm	fBm	fBm	PLs	PLs

Generally, from the results reported in Table 2A to Table 2E, we observe that for the 66% of the considered time periods, both the modified *R/S*-based and the periodogram-based-tests qualitatively agree to accept or reject the null hypothesis of no long-term memory.[22]

We also wish to note that, in general, the estimates of *H* based on the modified *R/S* approach are greater than the corresponding estimates based on the periodogram approach. This is in accordance with the findings of Mandelbrot and Wallis (1969) and Jacobsen (1996), which confirm that the modified *R/S*-based estimation procedure overestimates the value of *H* when the true value is lower than 0.72 (as it seems to be in the majority of our cases).

Again, for all time periods and for both spot and (nearby) futures foreign currency markets, the corresponding value of the dynamic Hurst exponent $H(t)$ is neither equal to 0.5 nor constant over time. This provides us with important empirical evidence for the MFMH or, at least, for the need to revise the EMH. In particular, the dynamic dimension is well supported by the test for no long-term dependence results. In fact, both the spot and (nearby) futures foreign currency markets are characterized over time by different underlying stochastic processes: the fBm, the PLs motion and an undetectable one.[23]

Almost all the fBms describing the stochastic behavior of a wide percentage of the time sub-periods show a persistent long-term dependence, that is $H \in (0.5, 1)$, and all the PLs motions describing the stochastic behavior of another wide percentage of the time sub-periods are distinguished by the non-finiteness of the variance, that is by $\alpha \in (1, 2)$ (by $\alpha = 1/H$). Coupling both these aspects, that is, long-term dependence/independence and variance finiteness/non-finiteness, it follows that the structure of financial risk can vary widely from one time sub-period to the next.

In general, the spot and the (nearby) futures foreign currency

---

22. There are instances when at least two of the three sub-cases of the modified R/S-based approach (q = #, AR(1), and MA(1)) qualitatively agree with the only accept/reject decision given by the periodogram-based approach.

23. For these processes jointly characterized by $H \in (0,0.5)$ and long-term independence, some authors, such as Evertsz (1995a, 1995b), suggest suitable mixtures of fBms and PLs motions. Others, like Zou (1996) suggest that some proper PLs distribution sub-families, such as a fractional distribution may be suitable. These issues have not been settled and are beyond the scope of this work.

markets for each currency are characterized by similar dynamic stochastic structures, especially from a short and long-term dependence/independence point of view.

VII. Economic Interpretations

In general, all the analyzed foreign currency markets exhibit a behavior over time influenced by their Hurst exponent and by their long-term independence/dependence. This behavior provides empirical support for the MFMH as a reasonable extension of the EMH. In fact, different stochastic processes describe the foreign currency markets during various periods. We distinguish three phases characterizing the conjectured MFMH (instead of the two standard ones): a "regular" phase, a new phase that we identify as "semi-regular" and an "irregular" phase.

The "regular" phase is associated with the fBm via long-term dependence, that is, with the Hurst exponent $H \in (0.5, 1)$. In fact, the characteristics of the financial risk described by the corresponding distributional law are such as to permit a relatively simple matching between the demand and supply for two reasons:

First, the statistical self-similarity characterizing the fBms guarantees that the risk associated with investments of different horizon lengths t and at, with $a > 0$, are evaluated in the same proportion by their corresponding investors. Actually, $\{B_H(t), t \geq 0\}$ and $\{a^{-H}B_H(at), t \geq 0\}$, with $a > 0$, have the same distributional law.[24] Because of this, the demands and supplies of these investors with different horizon lengths match, and thus ensure a certain liquidity for the foreign currency markets. Notice that the statistical self-similarity implicitly asserts the existence of some relationships between the Hurst exponent, H, and the liquidity level.

Second, the long-term persistent memory distinguishing these foreign currency markets makes it possible to partially forecast future returns, and consequently, *ex ceteris paribus*, to manage a lower risk than in the classical independently and identically log-normally distributed

---

24. Notice that a^{-H} plays the role of a proportionality factor.

environment.[25] This lowering of long-run risk may explain the attractiveness of longer investment horizons by some investors in an fBm regime.

In particular, in order to explain such long-term persistent memory, we can conjecture that the analyzed foreign currency markets are characterized by the regular arrival of new information confirming underlying economic trends. Of course, this reduces the spread between the ability of economic agents to make optimal decisions and the complexity of decisions made under uncertainty.

The "semi-regular" phase is associated with the PLs motion, that is distinguished both by the non-finiteness of the variance because of $\alpha \in (1, 2)$, and by the no long-term dependence. The characteristics of the financial risk arising from the corresponding distributional law permit, again, the matching between the demand and the supply, but to a lower degree as compared to the "regular" phase. In fact, in the current case, the only source of attractiveness for investors who value lengthy horizons is the statistical self-similarity. In particular, notice that the values of the Hurst exponents, characterizing the "regular" and the "semi-regular" phases are within a limited range and, so, their impacts on the liquidity levels are quite similar for both phases. At least, no significant differences are apparent. To the contrary, the unpredictability of future returns due to the absence of some long-term dependence puts the "semi-regular" phase volatility in a higher risk class than does the unpredictability of the "regular" phase (however, *ex ceteris paribus*, both normal). Furthermore, the distributional properties of the underlying stochastic process put this PLs volatility in a higher risk class than the normal one.[26] Of course, this latter financial risk characteristic causes a lower participation of investors in the "semi-regular" foreign currency market than in the "regular" foreign currency market and, in particular, a lower participation of investors having long horizon lengths that are associated with highest risk. Because of this, in the corresponding "semi-regular" foreign currency market there are both a lower liquidity level, and a lower average investment horizon length than in the "regular" phase foreign currency one.

---

25. Notice that, because of the trend due to long-term dependence, the standard deviation of the considered fBms provides an over-evaluation of the actual volatility of the corresponding foreign currency markets.

26. Recall that the tails of the PLs motions with $\alpha \in (0,2)$ decay slower than the fBm ones.

In order to explain such a higher risk level distinguishing the "semi-regular" phase, we can conjecture that the corresponding foreign currency markets are characterized by an irregular arrival of exogenous noise. Of course, this makes it difficult for investors to detect any trends that may exist in the fundamentals of the economy and thus may influence their ability to make rational decisions.

The "irregular" phase is associated with an undetectable stochastic process, that may be a suitable mixture of fBms and PLs motions, or which may belong to some proper PLs distribution sub-family. Although such lack of detection is possible, the (generic) identifiable characteristics of the corresponding distributional law (and, consequently, of the financial risk) are such as to prevent a simple matching between the demand and supply. In fact, in this "irregular" phase, volatility belongs to a risk class quite similar to the one that characterizes the "semi-regular" phase. Again, this causes primarily a lower participation of investors having long horizon lengths (who are associated with a higher level of risk) and, consequently, a lower liquidity level and a lower average investment horizon length than in the "regular" phase foreign currency markets. Moreover, the underlying stochastic process may or may not be characterized by the statistical self-similarity. In the first case, for the "irregular" phase, the corresponding Hurst exponent, H, is lower than that for the "regular" and "semi-regular" phases. It is simple to prove, under a reasonable assumption on a, that the proportionality factor a^{-H} is higher for these latter phases.[27] In the second case different horizon length investors do not evaluate investments in the same proportional way, and so their demands and supplies do not match.

In particular, in order to explain such a financial environment, we can conjecture that the corresponding foreign currency markets are characterized by the arrival of conflicting information. This causes very different and, often, incompatible behavior among the economic agents.

VII. Concluding Remarks

All the foreign currency markets studied in this article exhibit a Hurst exponent that is statistically different from 0.5 in the majority of the samples studied. Furthermore, it is also found that the Hurst exponent is

27. A simple proof of this claim may be obtained from the authors.

not fixed but it changes dynamically over time. The interpretation of these results is that the foreign currency returns follow either a fractional Brownian motion or a Pareto-Levy stable distribution. The key question is: what are the implications of such findings on the Efficient Market Hypothesis? Both in its original formulation and in the recent more sophisticated elaborations of the random walk hypothesis found in Campbell, Lo and MacKinlay (1997), the efficient market hypothesis is associated with returns that follow a Brownian motion with Hurst exponent equal to 0.5. Rogers (1997) has shown that a market where the asset returns follow a fractional Brownian motion cannot be efficient since there always exists an arbitrage strategy. Our approach has been to use the statistical evidence in this article to support the proposed Multi-Fractal Market Hypothesis. Needless to say, this extension of the traditional Efficient Market Hypothesis needs a further elaboration that goes beyond the general ideas we have offered in the previous sections. In particular, we need to develop theoretical explanations for both long-term positive and negative dependence as well as explanations for the transition of distributions from Brownian to fractally Brownian or Pareto-Levy stable.

References

Alexakis, P., and Apergis, N. 1996. ARCH effects and cointegration: Is the foreign exchange market efficient? *Journal of Banking and Finance* 20 (4): 687-697.

Andrews, D.W.K. 1991. Heteroscedasticity and autocorrelation consistent covariance matrix estimation. *Econometrica* 59 (5): 817-858.

Belkacem, L.; Levy Vehel, J.; and Walter, C. 1996. CAPM, risk and portfolio selection in stable markets. *Rapport de Recherche* n. 2776, INRIA, Le Chesnay Cedex.

Bleaney, M., and Mizen, P. 1996. Nonlinearities in exchange rate dynamics: Evidence from five currencies. 1973-1994. *Economic Record* 72(216): 36-45.

Campbell, J.Y.; Lo, A.W.; and MacKinlay, A.C. 1997. The econometrics of financial markets. Princeton University Press, Princeton.

Chan, K.; Gup, B.; and Pan, M.S. 1992. Market efficiency and cointegration tests for foreign currency futures markets. *Journal of International Financial Markets, Institutions & Money* 2(1): 78-89.

Cheung, Y.-W., and Lai, K.S. 1993. Do gold market returns have long memory? *The Financial Review* 28(2): 181-202.

Chiang, T.C., and Jiang, C.X. 1995. Foreign exchange returns over short and long horizons. *International Review of Economics and Finance* 4(3): 267-282.

Corazza, M. 1996. Long-term memory stability in the Italian stock market. *Economics & Complexity* 1(1): 19-28.

Corazza, M.; Malliaris, A.G.; and Nardelli, C. 1997. Searching for fractal structure in agricultural futures Markets. *The Journal of Futures Markets* 17(4): 433-473.

Cornell, B. 1977. Spot rates, forward rates and exchange market efficiency. *Journal of Financial Economics* 5: 55-65.

Delgado, M.A., and Robinson, P.M. 1996. Optimal spectral bandwidth for long memory. *Statistica Sinica* 6(1): 97-112.

Dickey, D.A., and Fuller, W.A. 1979. Distribution of the estimators for autoregressive time series with a unit root. *Journal of the American Statistical Association* 74: 427-431.

Dickey, D.A., and Fuller, W.A. 1981. Likelihood ratio statistics for autoregressive time series with a unit root. *Econometrica* 49: 1057-1072.

Evertsz, C.J.G. 1995a. Fractal geometry of financial time series. *Fractals* 3(3): 609-616.

Evertsz, C.J.G. 1995b. Self-Similarity of high-frequency USD-DEM exchange rates. Proceedings of the First International Conference on High Frequency Data in Finance, Zurich.

Evertsz, C.J.G., and Berkner, K. 1995. Large deviation and self-similarity analysis of graphs: DAX stock prices. *Chaos, Solitons & Fractals* 6: 121-130.

Falconer, K. 1990. Fractal geometry. John Wiley & Sons, New York.

Fama, E.F. 1970. Efficient capital markets: Review of theory and empirical work. *The Journal of Finance* 25: 383-417.

Fama, E.F. 1991. Efficient capital markets: II. *The Journal of Finance* 46(5): 1575-1617.

Fang, H.; Lai, K.S.; and Lai, M. 1994. Fractal structure in currency futures price dynamics. *The Journal of Futures Markets* 14(2): 169-181.

Frankel, J.A. 1980. Tests of rational expectations in the forward exchange market. *Southern Economic Journal* 46: 1083-1101.

Hsieh, D.A. 1989. Testing for nonlinear dependence in daily foreign exchange rates. *Journal of Business* 62(3): 339-368.

Hsieh, D.A. 1992. A Nonlinear stochastic rational expectations model of exchange rates. *Journal of International Money and Finance* 11(3): 235-250.

Jacobsen, B. 1996. Long term dependence in stock returns. *Journal of Empirical Finance* 3: 393-417.

Kao, G.W., and Ma, C. 1992. Memories, heteroskedasticity, and price limit in currency futures markets. *Journal of Futures Markets* 12(6): 679-692.

Kho, B.C. 1996. Time varying risk premia, volatility, and technical trading rule profits: Evidence from foreign currency futures markets. *The Journal of Financial Economics* 41(2): 249-290.

Leachman, L.L., and El Shazly, M. R. 1992. Cointegration analysis, error correction models and foreign exchange market efficiency. *Journal of International Financial Markets, Institutions & Money* 2(1): 57-77.

Levich, R.M., and Thomas, L.R. 1993. The Significance of technical trading rule profits in the foreign exchange markets: A bootstrap approach. *Journal of International Money and Finance* 12(5):451-474.

Lévy, P. 1925. Calcul des probabilites. Gauthier-Villars, Paris.

Liu, Y. A.; Pan, M.S.; and Hsueh, L.P. 1993. A modified R/S Analysis of long-term dependence in currency futures prices. *Journal of International Financial Markets, Institutions & Money* 3(2): 97-113.

Lo, A.W. 1991. Long-term memory in stock market prices. *Econometrica* 59(5): 1279-1313.

Lo, A.W., and MacKinlay, A.C. 1988. Stock Market Prices Do not follow random walks: Evidence from a simple specification test. *Review of Financial Studies* 1: 41-66.

Lobato, I., and Robinson, P.M. 1996. Averaged periodogram estimation of long memory. *Journal of Econometrics* 73: 303-324.

Lobato, I.N., and Savin, N.E. 1998. Real and spurious long memory properties of stock market data. preprint, University of Iowa, Iowa City.

Machones, M.; Mase, S.; Plunkett, S.; and Thrash, R. 1994. Price prediction using nonlinear techniques. *The Magazine of Artificial Intelligence in Finance* Fall: 51-56.

Mandelbrot, B.B., and Van Ness J.W. 1968. Fractional Brownian motions, fractional noises and applications. *SIAM Review* 10(4): 422-437.

Mandelbrot, B.B., and Wallis, J.R. 1969. Robustness of the rescaled range R/S in the measurement of noncyclic long run statistical dependence. *Water Resources Research* 5: 967-988.

Mittnik, S., and Rachev, S.T. 1993. Reply to comments on modeling asset returns with alternative stable distributions and some extensions. *Economic Review* 12: 347-390.

Ostasiewicz, W. 1996. Advanced financial techniques. *Badania Operacyine i Decyzje* 3-4: 161-178.

Pancham, S. 1994. Evidence of the multifractal market hypothesis using wavelet transforms. mimeo, Florida International University, Miami (downloadable from the web site: http://home.nyc.rr.com/spancham).

Peltier, R.F., and Levy Vehel, J. 1994. A new method for estimating the parameter of fractional Brownian motion *Rapport de Recherche* n. 2396, INRIA, Le Chesnay Cedex.

Peltier, R.F., and Levy Vehel, J. 1995. MultiFractional Brownian motion: Definition and preliminary results. *Rapport de Recherche* n. 2645, INRIA, Le Chesnay Cedex.

Peters, E.E. 1991. Chaos and order in the capital markets. John Wiley & Sons, New York.

Peters, E.E. 1994. Fractal market analysis. John Wiley & Sons, New York.

Robinson, P.M. 1994. Semiparametric analysis of long-memory time series. *Annals of Statistics* 22: 515-539.

Robinson, P.M. 1994a. Rates of convergence and optimal spectral bandwidth for long range dependence. *Probability Theory and Related Fields* 99: 443-473.

Robinson, P.M. 1994b. Time series with strong dependence, in sims. C.A. (ed.) *Advances in Econometrics. Sixth World Congress* 1, Cambridge University Press: 47-95.

Rogers, L.C.G. 1997. Arbitrage with fractional Brownian motion. *Mathematical Finance* 7: 95-105.

Samuelson, P.A. 1965. Proof that properly anticipated prices fluctuate randomly. *Industrial Management Review* 6: 41-49.

Shubik, M. 1997, Proceedings of a conference on risks involving derivatives and other new financial instruments. *Economic Notes* 26: 169-443.

Taqqu, M.S. 1986. A bibliographical guide to self-similar processes and long-range dependence. In Eberlein, E. and Taqqu, M.S. (eds.) *Dependence in Probability and Statistics*, Birkhauser, Boston: 137-162.

Taqqu, M.S.; Teverovsky, V.; and Willinger, W. 1995. Estimators for long-range dependence: An empirical study. *Fractals* 3(4): 785-798.

Taylor, S.J. 1992. Rewards available to currency futures speculators: Compensation for risk or evidence of inefficient pricing? *Economic Record*, Supplement: 105-116.

Van De Gucht, L.M.; Dekimpe, M.G.; and Kwok, C.Y. 1996. Persistence in foreign exchange rates. *Journal of International Money and Finance* 15(2): 191-220.

Zhou, B. 1996. High frequency data and volatility in foreign-exchange rates. *Journal of Business and Economic Statistics* 14(1): 44-52.

Asset Bubbles

ARE THERE RATIONAL BUBBLES IN THE U.S. STOCK MARKET? OVERVIEW AND A NEW TEST

Ramaprasad Bhar and A. G. Malliaris

ABSTRACT

A speculative bubble is usually defined as the difference between the market value of a security and its fundamental value. Although there are several important theoretical issues surrounding the topic of asset bubbles, the existence of bubbles is inherently an empirical issue that has not been settled yet. This paper reviews several important tests and offers one more methodology that improves upon the existing ones. The new test is applied to the annual U.S. stock market data spanning over a century and at the monthly frequency covering the post-war period. Although we find evidence of stock price bubble in both cases, the post-war period exhibit only positive component whereas the annual data exhibit some episode of negative bubble.

I. INTRODUCTION

During the past 30 years, theoretical models and empirical testing in asset pricing have been motivated by market efficiency. This theory claims that the price of an asset today reflects correctly the future random payoffs of this asset

---

Asset Price Bubbles: Implications for Monetary and Regulatory Policies, Volume 13, pages 125–144.

ISBN: 0-7623-0845-1

conditioned on today's information and appropriately discounted by a stochastic factor. The opportunity to make a riskless profit using arbitrage strategies ensures that markets are efficient. Campbell (2000) articulates this paradigm in detail.

Many economists accept market efficiency as the well-established paradigm of financial economics but also acknowledge that asset prices are too volatile. For example, NASDAQ, from its peak on March 10, 2000 when it stood at 5048.62 to its low of 1638.80 on April 4, 2001, it declined by 67.5%. Is this significant decline due to substantial revisions of the expected payoffs and/or changes in the discount factor?

This paper considers the rational bubble approach as an alternative to the present value model of market efficiency. We make a clear distinction between the speculative past famous bubble episodes that involved specific assets, such as tulips, John Law's Mississippi Bubble or even the stock market of the 1920s, all of which ended in a crash and what the current literature defines as "rational bubbles". Section II reviews the general ideas of rational bubbles and Section III identifies two key statistical tests proposed by economists. In Section IV we offer a modification of the existing tests and apply it to the U.S. stock market. We find evidence of rational bubbles in annual data spanning over a century as well as in monthly data covering the post-war period. In Sections V and VI we elaborate in detail our methodological procedures to test for bubbles and compare this with a no-bubble solution. Our main findings and the conclusions are given in the last two sections.

II. SPECULATIVE BUBBLES

Economists have long conjectured that movements in stock prices may involve speculative bubbles, as trading is often said to generate over-priced markets. Some economists, however, believe that stock price fluctuations reflect changes in the values of the underlying market fundamentals. The standard definition of fundamental value is the summed discounted value of all future cash flows. The difference, if any, between the market value of the security and its fundamental value is termed a speculative bubble. Yet confusion persists about what factors generate bubbles. Fads and irrationality have always figured prominently, and the hypothesis that these factors are important has gained some empirical support from the literature on asset price volatility. Another bubble-producing factor is the structure of information in the market. In a partial-equilibrium setting, Allen and Gorton (1988) showed that rational bubbles can exist with a finite number of agents who had asymmetric information.

The existence of bubbles is inherently an empirical issue that has not been settled yet. A number of studies such as Blanchard and Watson (1982) and West (1988) have argued that dividend and stock price data are not consistent with the "market fundamentals" hypothesis, in which prices are given by the present discounted values of expected dividends. These results have often been construed as evidence for the existence of bubbles or fads.

According to Shiller (1981), and LeRoy and Porter (1981) the variability of stock price movements is too large to be explained by the present value of future earnings. Over the past century U.S. stock prices are five to thirteen times more volatile than can be justified by new information about future dividends. Campbell and Shiller (1988a, b) and West (1987, 1988) remove the assumption of constant discount rate. But a variable discount rate provides only marginal support in explaining stock price volatility. They reject the null hypothesis of no bubbles. See also Rappoport and White (1993, 1994).

A major problem with such arguments is that evidence for bubbles can be reinterpreted in terms of market fundamentals that are unobserved by the econometricians (Flood & Garber, 1980; Hamilton & Whiteman, 1985; Hamilton, 1986; Diba & Grossman, 1984, 1988a, b), have recommended the alternative strategy of testing for rational bubbles by investigating the stationarity properties of asset prices and observable fundamentals.

In essence, the argument for equities is that if stock prices are not more explosive than dividends, then it can be concluded that rational bubbles are not present, since they would generate an explosive component in stock prices. Using unit-root tests, autocorrelation patterns, and cointegration tests to implement this procedure, several authors reach the conclusion that stock prices do not contain explosive rational bubbles (see Dezhbakhsh & Demirgue-Kunt, 1990).

Evans (1991) criticizes tests for bubbles based on an investigation of the stationarity properties of stock prices and dividends. By Monte-Carlo simulations he demonstrates that an important class of rational bubbles cannot be detected by these tests even though the bubbles are explosive.

Froot and Obstfeld (1991), introduce the concept of *intrinsic bubble* which they define as exclusively dependent on market fundamentals and not on extraneous events. Assuming that a stock price should go to zero as dividends go to zero, they derive a bubble solution composed of stable and unstable components. This bubble is unstable and implies an explosive price-dividend ratio. They find significant evidence of such a bubble and demonstrate that incorporating an intrinsic bubble into the simple present-value model helps account for the long-run variability of the U.S. stock data. Furthermore, as their bubble is a deterministic function of dividends, once the bubble gets started, it will never burst as long as dividends remain positive. In practice, tests for intrinsic bubbles are very easily implemented only when dividends are assumed to follow a very simple process, for example, a geometric random walk. When a more general dynamic specification, such as ARIMA (p, 1, q) process is introduced for dividends, the test procedure for intrinsic bubbles becomes virtually intractable.

Using a stochastic dividend-growth model, Ikeda and Shibata (1992) specify the stock price as a function of dividends (i.e. market fundamentals) as well as of time. The resulting bubble solution will bridge a gap between time-driven bubbles (Flood & Garber, 1980) and bubbles exclusively depending on fundamentals (Froot & Obstfeld, 1991). Depending on a parameter that decides relative degrees of fundamental dependency and time dependency, the bubble solution obtained exhibits various dynamic properties that cannot be derived by combining linearly the two special solutions.

Wu (1997) examines a stochastic bubble, able to burst and restart continuously. The specification is parsimonious and allows easy estimation. The model fits the data reasonably well, especially during several bull and bear markets in this century. Much of the deviation of U.S. stock prices from the simple present-value model can be explained by such rational stochastic bubbles.

A rational speculative bubble is nonnegative by definition: it represents what an investor might be willing to pay to buy a stock forever stripped of its dividends. As soon as either dividends or discount rates depend on the presence or absence of a bubble, however, the fundamental is affected by the presence of a bubble. For instance, the existence of a bubble may lead to an increase in interest rates which so depresses the fundamental that the sum of the positive bubble and the bubbly fundamental falls short of the nonbubbly fundamental. Hence, a positive rational bubble may in fact decrease the overall price of a stock, contrary to what is commonly believed. Empirical tests of this hypothesis are provided, for example by Weil (1990).

Most of the references above address issues of rational bubbles either theoretically or in the context of a mature economy. To complete this rapid bibliographical review we need to mention two additional trends in this literature. First several studies have tested for the existence of bubbles in emerging markets. For example, Richards (1996) claims that emerging markets have not consistently been subject to fads or bubbles. Chan and coauthors (1998) test for rational bubbles in Asian stock markets and Chen (1999) specializes his search for bubbles in the Hong Kong market. Sarno and Taylor (1999) find evidence of bubbles in all East Asian economies. Significant increases in cross-markets linkages after a shock have now become a topic of important research under the term "contagion". Several important papers collected in Claessens and Forbes (2001) discuss both methodological issues and case studies of contagion.

Beyond the existence or not of bubbles, economists have also studied in detail the implications of a stock market bubble to the economy at large. Biswanger (1999) offers a comprehensive review of these issues and Chirinko and Schaller (1996) argue that bubbles existed in the U.S. stock market but real investment decisions were based on fundamentals.

III. REVIEW OF TWO KEY EMPIRICAL PAPERS

To motivate our methodological contribution we review two influential papers.

Ikeda and Shibata (1992)

Using a stochastic dividend-growth model, the paper provides a general analysis of fundamental-dependent bubbles in stock prices. Given that dividends follow a continuous Markov process, a stock price is specified as a function of dividends as well as of time. The authors derive a partial differential equation with respect to this price function from an arbitrage equation. Provided that a free-disposal condition is satisfied, a fundamental price process is defined as the forward-looking particular solution of this equation and a price bubble as the general solution of the corresponding homogeneous equation.

Lets consider a stock share which yields dividends D(t) at time t. These dividends follow a geometric Brownian motion with positive drift:

$$dD(t) = gD(t)dt + oD(t)dz(t),\ D(0) = D_0,\ g - o^2/2 > 0,\ o > 0 \tag{1}$$

Constant g and σ are, respectively, the expected value and the standard deviation of the instantaneous rate of dividend growth. dz is an independent increment of a standard Wiener process, z, with the initial condition z(0) = 0. Since lnD follows a normal distribution, the time series of dividend payments have a positive trend.

Stochastic dividend-payment process (1) is the only source of randomness. Supposing risk neutrality of investors and free disposability of the stock, we assume that the cum-dividend stock price is determined by the following two conditions:

$$E[dP(t)|\Omega_t]/dt + D(t) = rP(t) \tag{2}$$

$$P(t) \geq 0, \text{ with } r > 0\ \forall t \in [0,\infty] \text{ w.p.1}, \tag{3}$$

where $E[\cdot|\Omega_t]$ represents mathematical expectations conditional on Ω, and parameter r denotes the riskless interest rate which is assumed to be constant.

The rational expectations stochastic process of the stock price is obtained then by solving nonhomogeneous partial differential Eq. (2), subject to the dividend payment process (1) and the price positivity condition (3).

The author finds that the fundamentals dependency stabilizes bubble dynamics and that stock prices with fundamentals-dependent bubbles can be less volatile than fundamentals. Furthermore, fundamentals-dependent bubbles exhibit various transition patterns, such as nonmonotonic movements and monotonic shrinkage in magnitude and volatility.

Wu (1997)

The paper estimates a rational stochastic bubble using the Kalman filtering technique. The bubble grows at the discount rate in expectation and it can collapse and restart continuously, allowing for the possibility of a negative bubble. The log dividends follow a general ARIMA (p, 1, q) process. The model for stock prices with the bubble component, the dividend process and the bubble process are expressed in the state-space form with the bubble being treated as an unobserved state vector. The model parameters are estimated by the method of maximum likelihood and obtain optimal estimates of stochastic bubbles through the Kalman filter.

Lets consider the standard linear rational expectations model of stock price determination:

$$[E_t(P_{t+1} + D_t) - P_t]/P_t = r, \tag{4}$$

where p = real stock price at time t
D = the real dividend at time t
E = the mathematical expectation conditional on information available at time t
r = the required real rate of return, $r > 0$.

The log-linear approximation of (6) can be written as follows:

$$q = k + \psi E_t P_{t+1} + (1 - \psi)d_t - p_t, \tag{5}$$

where q = required log gross return rate
Ψ = average ratio of the stock price to the sum of the stock price and the dividend
k = $-\ln(\Psi) - (1 - \Psi)\ln(1/\Psi - 1)$
p = $\ln(P)$
d = $\ln(D)$.

The general solution to (7) is given by:

$$p_t = (k - q)/(1 - \psi) + (1 - \psi)\sum_{1=0}^{\infty} \psi^i E_t(d_{t+i}) + b_t = p_t^f + b_t \qquad (6)$$

where b_t satisfies the following homogeneous difference equation:

$$E_t(b_{t+i}) = (1/\psi)^i b_t. \qquad (7)$$

In Eq. (5), the no-bubble solution p is exclusively determined by dividends, while b can be driven by events extraneous to the market and is referred to as a rational speculative bubble. After defining the stock price equation, the parametric bubble process and the dividend process in a state-space form, the bubble is treated as an unobserved state vector, which can be estimated by the Kalman filtering technique.

The author finds statistically significant estimate of the innovation variance for the bubble process. During the 1960s bull market the bubble accounts for between 40% to 50% of the actual stock prices. Negative bubbles are found during the 1919–1921 bear market, in which the bubble explains between 20% to 30% of the decline in stock prices.

IV. OUR CONTRIBUTION

The purpose of our study is to search empirically for bubbles in national stock markets using state-of-the-art methodology such as Wu (1995, 1997) with emphasis on the U.S., over different sample period and different data frequency. We analyze the market at the monthly frequency over the post-war period as opposed to Wu (1997), which concentrates on only the annual data series dating back to 1871. The monthly returns data of the S&P 500 ranges from January 1951 to December 1998, that is, 576 observations. All data are converted to real values using the corresponding CPI measures and Global Financial Data provided the data. In order to establish the soundness of our methodology we attempted to reproduce the results from Wu (1997) using annual U.S. data (also obtained from Global Financial Data) covering the period 1871–1998.

Although we employ the unobserved component modeling approach similar to Wu (1997), our implementations of the state space form (or the Dynamic Linear Model, DLM, (Shumway & Stoffer, 2000, p. 306) is quite different from that of Wu. We treat both the dividend process and the bubble process as part of the unobserved components, that is the state vector. The state equations also include their own system error, which are assumed uncorrelated. The measurement vector in this case contains the price and the realized dividend without any measurement errors. The advantage of this way modeling is that the comparison with the no bubble solution becomes much more straightforward. Wu (1997) had to resort to alternative way (GMM) of estimating the no bubble solution and the model adequacy tests are not performed there. Besides, the precise moment conditions used in the GMM estimation are not reported there. On the other hand, in our approach we are able to subject both the bubble and the no bubble solutions to a battery of diagnostics test applicable to state space systems. In the following sections we describe in detail the mathematical structures of our models and the estimation strategies.

V. DYNAMIC LINEAR MODELS FOR BUBBLE SOLUTIONS

Our starting point in this approach are the Eqs (6) and (7) described earlier. As our preliminary investigations reveal that both the log real price and log real dividend series are non-stationary, we choose to work with the first differenced series. Thus, the Eq. (6) becomes,

$$\Delta p_t = \Delta p_t^f + \Delta b_t \tag{8}$$

where, $\Delta p_t^f \equiv (1-\psi)\sum_{i=0}^{\infty}\psi^i E_t(d_{t+i}) - (1-\psi)\sum_{i=0}^{\infty}\psi^i E_t(d_{t-1+i})$.

Assuming the following parametric representation of Eq. (9),

$$b_{t+1} = \frac{1}{\psi} b_t + \varepsilon_\eta, \quad \varepsilon_\eta \sim N(0, \sigma_\eta^2) \tag{9}$$

$$\Delta b_t = \frac{1}{\psi}(b_t - b_{t-1}). \tag{10}$$

In order to express the fundamental component of the price, Δp_t^f, in term of the dividend process, we fit an appropriate AR model of sufficient order so that the information criterion AIC is minimized. We find that for the annual data an AR(2) model is sufficient whereas for the monthly data we need an AR(3) model. The infinite sums in the expression for Δp_t^f may be expressed in terms of the parameters of the dividend process once we note the following conditions:

- The differenced log real dividend series is stationary, therefore the infinite sum converges,
- Any finite order AR process can be expressed in companion form (VAR of order 1) by using extended state variables, that is, suitable lags of the original variables as in Campbell, Lo and MacKinlay (1997, p. 280),
- Using demeaned variables the VAR(1) process can be easily used for multi-period ahead forecast.

Assuming the demeaned log real dividend process has the following AR(3) representation,

$$\Delta d_t = \phi_1 \Delta d_{t-1} + \phi_2 \Delta d_{t-2} + \phi_3 \Delta d_{t-3} + \varepsilon_\delta,\ \varepsilon_\delta \sim N(0, \sigma_\delta^2), \tag{11}$$

the companion form may be written as,

$$\begin{bmatrix} \Delta d_t \\ \Delta d_{t-1} \\ \Delta d_{t-2} \end{bmatrix} = \begin{bmatrix} \phi_1 & \phi_2 & \phi_3 \\ 1 & 0 & 0 \\ 0 & 1 & 0 \end{bmatrix} \begin{bmatrix} \Delta d_{t-1} \\ \Delta d_{t-2} \\ \Delta d_{t-3} \end{bmatrix} + \begin{bmatrix} \varepsilon_\delta \\ 0 \\ 0 \end{bmatrix}, \text{ or} \tag{12}$$

$$X_t = \Phi X_{t-1} + \Xi_t, \tag{13}$$

where, the definitions of X_t, Φ, and Ξ_t are obvious from comparison of Eqs (12) and (13). Following Campbell, Lo and MacKinlay (1997, p. 280), Δp_t^f may be expressed as, with I being the identity matrix of the same dimension as Φ

$$\Delta p_t^f = \Delta d_t + \psi\Phi(I - \psi\Phi)^{-1}\Delta X_t. \tag{14}$$

We can now express Eq. (8) in terms of fundamental component and the bubble component,

$$\Delta p_t = \Delta d_t + e'\psi\Phi(I - \psi\Phi)^{-1}\Delta X_t + \Delta b_t, \tag{15}$$

where $e' \equiv [1 \quad 0 \quad 0]$.

The Eq. (15) represents the measurement equation of the DLM and we need to suitably define the state equation for the model. An examination of the Eq. (10) and (12) suggests that the following state equation adequately represent the dynamics of the dividend and the bubble process:

$$\begin{bmatrix} \Delta d_t \\ \Delta d_{t-1} \\ \Delta d_{t-2} \\ \Delta d_{t-3} \\ b_t \\ b_{t-1} \end{bmatrix} = \begin{bmatrix} \phi_1 & \phi_2 & \phi_3 & 0 & 0 & 0 \\ 1 & 0 & 0 & 0 & 0 & 0 \\ 0 & 1 & 0 & 0 & 0 & 0 \\ 0 & 0 & 1 & 0 & 0 & 0 \\ 0 & 0 & 0 & 0 & \frac{1}{\psi} & 0 \\ 0 & 0 & 0 & 0 & 1 & 0 \end{bmatrix} \begin{bmatrix} \Delta d_{t-1} \\ \Delta d_{t-2} \\ \Delta d_{t-3} \\ \Delta d_{t-4} \\ b_{t-1} \\ b_{t-2} \end{bmatrix} + \begin{bmatrix} \varepsilon_\delta & 0 \\ 0 & 0 \\ 0 & 0 \\ 0 & 0 \\ 0 & \varepsilon_\eta \\ 0 & 0 \end{bmatrix}, \tag{16}$$

$$\begin{pmatrix} \varepsilon_\delta \\ \varepsilon_\delta \end{pmatrix} \sim N\left(\begin{bmatrix} 0 \\ 0 \end{bmatrix}, \begin{bmatrix} \sigma_\delta^2 & 0 \\ 0 & \sigma_\eta^2 \end{bmatrix}\right). \tag{16'}$$

We are in a position now to define the measurement equation of the DLM in term of the state vector in Eq. (16). This is achieved by examining Eq. (15) and defining a row vector, $M \equiv e'\psi\Phi(I - \psi\Phi)^{-1} = [m_1, m_2, m_3]$, as follows:

$$\Delta p_t = \Delta d_t + [m_1, m_2, m_3]\begin{bmatrix} \Delta d_t & - & \Delta d_{t-1} \\ \Delta d_{t-1} & - & \Delta d_{t-2} \\ \Delta d_{t-2} & - & \Delta d_{t-3} \end{bmatrix} + \Delta b_t\text{, or}$$

$$\begin{bmatrix} \Delta p_t \\ \Delta d_t \end{bmatrix} = \begin{bmatrix} (1+m_1) & (m_2 - m_1) & (m_3 - m_2) & -m_3 & 1 & -1 \\ 1 & 0 & 0 & 0 & 0 & 0 \end{bmatrix} \begin{bmatrix} \Delta d_t \\ \Delta d_{t-1} \\ \Delta d_{t-2} \\ \Delta d_{t-3} \\ b_t \\ b_{t-1} \end{bmatrix} \tag{17}$$

The Eq. (17) determines the measurement equation of the DLM without any measurement error. In other words, the evolution of the state vector in Eq. (16) results in the measurement of the measurement vector through Eq. (17).

We have now set up the DLM for the bubble solution for the monthly data given by Eqs (16) and (17). For the annual data since the dividend process is an AR(2), these equations need to be appropriately redefined. The parameters of the models embedded in these equations and the filtered and the smoothed estimates of the bubble series are to be estimated from the observed price and the dividend series. In the next section we proceed to set up the DLMs for the no-bubble solutions.

VI. DYNAMIC LINEAR MODELS FOR NO-BUBBLE SOLUTIONS

In order to compare the performance of the bubble solution discussed in the previous sub-section we develop the DLM for a no-bubble solution. We maintain the same framework so that comparison is more meaningful. This is opposed to the approach taken in Wu (1997) where the no-bubble solution was estimated in the GMM framework. We also note that the model should account for the correlations in the variance of the stock return series. This is done by incorporating the GARCH(1,1) effect in the price Eq. (8) without the bubble component. In this context we adopt the methodology of Harvey, Ruiz and Sentana (1992) and follow Kim and Nelson (1999, p. 144) to suitably augment the state vector of the DLM.

For the monthly data set the state Eq. (16) becomes,

$$\begin{bmatrix} \Delta d_t \\ \Delta d_{t-1} \\ \Delta d_{t-2} \\ \Delta d_{t-3} \\ \varepsilon_{p,t} \end{bmatrix} = \begin{bmatrix} \phi_1 & \phi_2 & \phi_3 & 0 & 0 & 0 \\ 1 & 0 & 0 & 0 & 0 & 0 \\ 0 & 1 & 0 & 0 & 0 & 0 \\ 0 & 0 & 0 & 1 & 0 & 0 \\ 0 & 0 & 0 & 0 & 0 & 0 \end{bmatrix} \begin{bmatrix} \Delta d_{t-1} \\ \Delta d_{t-2} \\ \Delta d_{t-3} \\ \Delta d_{t-4} \\ \varepsilon_{p,t-1} \end{bmatrix} + \begin{bmatrix} \varepsilon_\delta & 0 \\ 0 & 0 \\ 0 & 0 \\ 0 & 0 \\ 0 & \varepsilon_{p,t} \end{bmatrix}, \quad (18)$$

$$\begin{pmatrix} \varepsilon_\delta \\ \varepsilon_{p,t} | \omega_{t-1} \end{pmatrix} \sim N\left(\begin{bmatrix} 0 \\ 0 \end{bmatrix}, \begin{bmatrix} \sigma_\delta^2 & 0 \\ 0 & h_t \end{bmatrix} \right), \quad h_t = \alpha_0 + \alpha_1 \varepsilon_{p,t-1}^2 + \beta_1 h_{t-1}, \quad (18')$$

and ω_{t-1} is the information set at time $t-1$. The corresponding measurement equation becomes,

$$\begin{bmatrix} \Delta p_t \\ \Delta d_t \end{bmatrix} = \begin{bmatrix} (1+m_1) & (m_2 - m_1) & (m_3 - m_2) & -m_3 & 1 \\ 1 & 0 & 0 & 0 & 0 \end{bmatrix} \begin{bmatrix} \Delta d_t \\ \Delta d_{t-1} \\ \Delta d_{t-2} \\ \Delta d_{t-3} \\ \varepsilon_{p,t} \end{bmatrix} \quad (19)$$

For the annual data again with an AR(2) dividend process, the no-bubble DLM will have to be appropriately defined by modifying the Eqs (18) and (19). In the no-bubble solutions the parameters to be estimated are those of the dividend process and the GARCH(1,1) coefficients.

VII. RESULTS AND DISCUSSIONS

First we discuss the estimations results of the dynamic linear model with the bubble solution for the annual U.S. data series. In Table 1 we find all the parameter estimates are statistically significant. The significance of the parameter, σ_η, implies highly variable bubble component of the price through out the period 1871 to 1998. The parameters describing the real dividend process are very close to the univariate estimation (not included) results of the dividend series. Besides, the discount parameter, ψ, is close to its sample value.

In Table 2 we present the estimates of the no-bubble solution with a GARCH (1,1) error structure for the price equation for the same U.S. annual data. Here also, most of the parameters are statistically significant. The significance of the GARCH parameter, β_1, implies persistence in the residual volatility. This model is used to compare the results of the bubble solution. We would like to stress the fact we implemented the GARCH(1,1) model also in the state space framework so that the comparison with the bubble solution would be more realistic. This is, however, not the case with Wu (1997), which uses the GMM methodology. This approach also allows us to check the performance of both the models

Table 1. Parameter Estimates from the State Space Model Using Kalman Filter Bubble Solution.

	ψ	σ_η	ϕ_1	ϕ_2	ϕ_3	σ_δ
Yearly						
	0.9830*	0.1857*	0.1929*	−0.2016*		0.1289*
	(0.0203)	(0.0110)	(0.0711)	(0.0656)		(0.0049)
Monthly						
	0.9964*	0.0416*	−0.7218*	−0.3553*	−0.0969*	0.0287*
	(0.0020)	(0.0009)	(0.0350)	(0.0453)	(0.0387)	(0.0007)

Estimates reported here are obtained from maximising the innovation form of the likelihood function. Numerical optimisation procedure in GAUSS is used without any parameter restriction. The standard errors (reported below the parameters in parentheses) are obtained from the Hèssian matrix at the point of convergence. These estimates are robust to different starting values including different specification of the prior covariance matrix. Significance at 5% level is indicated by *.

Table 2. Parameter Estimates from the State Space Model Using Kalman Filter No Bubble Solution with GARCH(1,1) Error for Price Equation.

	ψ	ϕ_1	ϕ_2	ϕ_3	σ_δ	α_0	α_1	β_1
Yearly								
	0.6195*	0.2170*	-0.2164*		0.1290*	0.0073	0.1754	0.6054*
	(0.1327)	(0.0867)	(0.0856)		(0.0081)	(0.0062)	(0.1279)	(0.2649)
Monthly								
	0.3189*	-0.7213*	-0.3271*	-0.0901*	0.0288*	0.0001*	0.0657*	0.8365*
	(0.0344)	(0.0413)	(0.0484)	(0.0400)	(0.0008)	(4.62e-5)	(0.0274)	(0.0533)

Estimates reported here are obtained from maximising the innovation form of the likelihood function. Numerical optimisation procedure in GAUSS is used without any parameter restriction. The standard errors (reported below the parameters in parentheses) are obtained from the Hessian matrix at the point of convergence. These estimates are robust to different starting values including different specification of the prior covariance matrix. GARCH(1,1) error for state space system implemented following Harvey, Ruiz, Sentana (1992). Significance at 5% level is indicated by *.

by analyzing the residual diagnostics. We present these test results in Table 3. The portmanteau tests support the whiteness of the residuals and the ARCH tests indicate no remaining heteroscedasticity in the residuals. Besides, the Kolmogorov-Smirnov tests support the normality of the residuals. These three tests overwhelmingly support the modeling approach adopted here and, therefore, the conclusions drawn are statistically meaningful.

In addition to the three tests just outlined above, we also include two additional tests particularly designed for recursive residuals produced by the dynamic linear systems developed in this study. The modified von-Neumann ratio tests against serial correlations in the residuals where as the recursive *t*-test is used to check for correct model specification. As the entries Table 3 suggest both the models, i.e. the dynamic linear models of the bubble and the no-bubble solution, both perform extremely well in respect of these two tests. There is overwhelming support for the adequacy of the models in describing the price process.

In view of the battery of tests discussed in the preceding two paragraphs we can now proceed to analyze the other observations. As discussed in Wu (1997), the rational stochastic bubble can alternate between positive and negative values. It is argued there that the securities may be overvalued when the participants are bullish and these may be undervalued when the participants are bearish. Figure 1 shows negative bubble in the very early part of the sample as well as during the early 1920s. It is obvious though that the stochastic bubbles account

Table 3. Residual Diagnostics and Model Adequacy Tests.

	Portmanteau	ARCH	KS Test	MNR	Recursive T
Yearly					
Bubble	0.035	0.385	0.138	0.531	0.952
No Bubble	0.033	0.519	0.119	0.422	0.931
Monthly					
Bubble	0.377	0.327	0.048	0.425	0.894
No Bubble	0.353	0.283	0.047	0.418	0.846

Entries are p-values for the respective statistics except for the KS statistic. These diagnostics are computed from the recursive residual of the measurement equation, which corresponds to the real dividend process. The null hypothesis in portmanteau test is that the residuals are serially uncorrelated. The ARCH test checks for no serial correlations in the squared residual up to lag 26. Both these test are applicable to recursive residuals as explained in Wells (1996, page 27). MNR is the modified Von Neumann ratio test using recursive residual for model adequacy (see Harvey, 1990, Ch. 5). Similarly, if the model is correctly specified then Recursive T has a Student's t-distribution (see Harvey, 1990, p. 157). KS statistic represents the Kolmogorov-Smirnov test statistic for normality. 95% and 99% significance levels in this test are 0.121 and 0.145 respectively for annual data. When KS statistic is less than 0.121 or 0.145 the null hypothesis of normality cannot be rejected at the indicated level of significance. For the monthly data these significance levels are at 0.057 and 0.068 respectively.

for a substantial percentage of the stock price in the sample. It is also interesting to note that in spite of the drop in the bubble percentage during the oil shock of the 1970s and the stock market crash of 1987 there has been a upward trend of the bubble percentage through out the later part of the sample period considered. This particular feature is most clearly visible in the lower panel of Fig. 1, which separates the stock price in the fundamental and the bubble components.

Next, we compare the performance of the bubble and the no-bubble solutions by examining the in sample fitting the stock prices. In Table 4 we display the criteria used and these are defined as,

$$\mathrm{RMSE} = \frac{1}{T}\sum_{t=1}^{T}(\hat{p}_t - p_t)^2, \ \mathrm{MAE} = \frac{1}{T}\sum_{t=1}^{T}|\hat{p}_t - p_t|,$$

where $\hat{p}_t$ is the fitted price and T is the number of observations. The entries in Table 4 clearly demonstrate the superiority of the bubble solution to capture the price process over the sample period.

We next proceed to analyze the monthly data, covering the post war period. Table 1 also presents the estimation results of the bubble solutions and it is clear that most of the parameters are statistically significant. The discount

Yearly Data

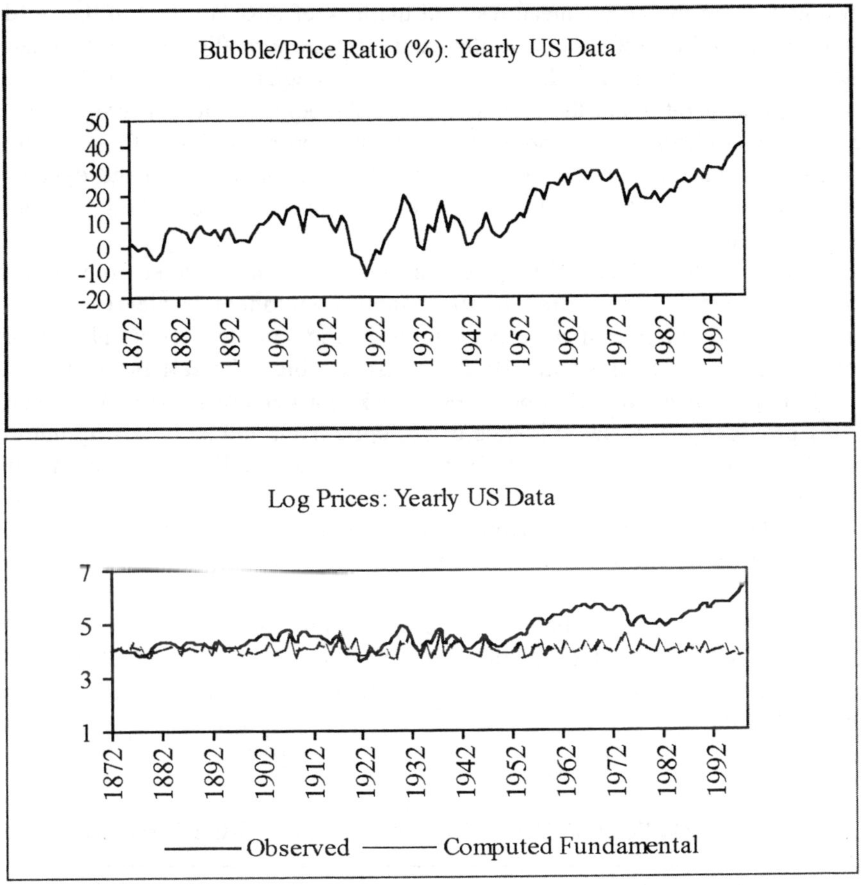

Fig. 1. Plots using the Smoothed Estimates of the Bubble from the State Space Model.

parameter, ψ, as before is close to the respective sample values while the significant σ_η implies highly variable bubble components. Needless to say that the estimated parameters of the dividend processes are close to their respective univariate estimation (not reported here) results. As evident from Table 2, the significant ARCH and the GARCH parameters indicate appropriateness of the error specification for the log price difference series. There is substantial persistence in the variance process.

The residual diagnostics for the monthly data series indicate whiteness of residuals from the portmanteau test and the lack of ARCH effect in the residuals from ARCH test results. It also supports the normality of the residuals. More importantly though the tests for model adequacy are captured by the von-Neumann ratio and the recursive t-test. As pointed out in Harvey (1990, p. 157) von-Neumann test provides the most appropriate basis for a general test of misspecification with recursive residuals. In this context the dynamic linear models for the bubble and the no-bubble solutions both perform extremely well.

Figure 2 plots the bubble price ratio for the monthly sample period and the substantial variation of the bubble component is clearly visible. There is no evidence of negative bubble in the sample period. The effect of the oil price shock of the 1970s is also visible. The fall in the bubble percentage during the October 1987 stock market crash is also evident. This provides the visual evidence of the collapsing and self-starting nature of the rational stochastic bubble we have attempted to capture in this study.

In order to quantify the performance improvement of the bubble solution compared to the no-bubble case with GARCH(1,1) errors we note the in sample fitting statistics, RMSE and MAE, in Table 4. The entries prove beyond doubt that the bubble solution does a credible job in terms of both metrics. For example, the bubble solution reduces the metric RMSE to 7% and the metric MAE to 52% of the no-bubble solution respectively, for the monthly data.

Table 4. Bubble Solution Versus No Bubble with GARCH Error Compared.

	RMSE	MAE
Yearly		
Bubble	0.25	0.34
No Bubble GARCH(1,1)	1.37	1.42
Monthly		
Bubble	0.117	0.895
No Bubble GARCH(1,1)	1.734	1.735

RMSE and MAE stand for 'root mean squared error' and 'mean absolute error' respectively. These are computed from the differences between the actual log prices and the fitted log prices from the corresponding estimated model. Additional details are in the text.

Monthly Data

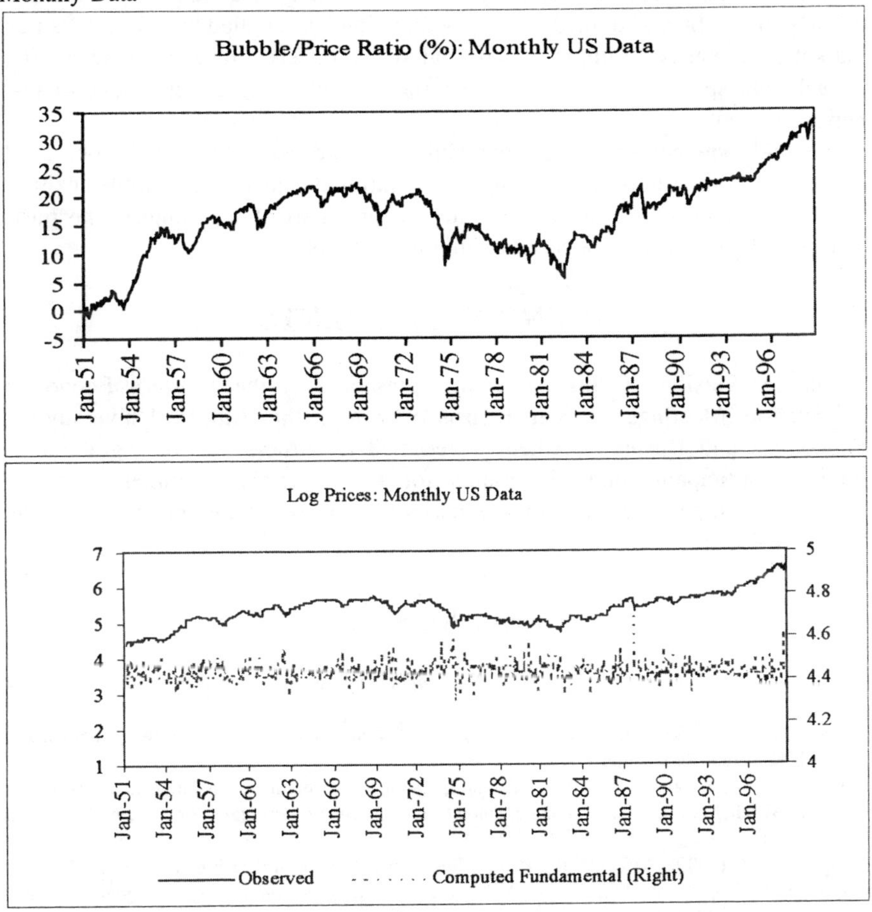

Fig. 2. Plots using the Smoothed Estimates of the Bubble from the State Space Model.

VIII. CONCLUSION

Economists have long conjectured that movements in stock prices may involve speculative bubbles because trading often generates over-priced markets. A speculative bubble is usually defined as the difference between the market value of a security and its fundamental value. Although there are several important theoretical issues surrounding the topic of asset bubbles, the existence of bubbles is inherently an empirical issue that has not been settled yet. This paper reviews several important tests and offers a new methodology that improves upon the existing ones. In addition, the new methodology is applied to the U.S. stock market data over two sample periods and at two different data frequencies. The annual data spans over a century and the monthly data covers the post-war period.

We find evidence of bubbles explaining a large percentage of the observed prices in both samples. Although the rational stochastic bubble exhibit negative episode in the annual data in the early part of the century, the post-war period exhibit only positive bubble component.

ACKNOWLEDGMENTS

An earlier version of this paper was presented at the Western Economic Association Meetings in San Fransisco and at the Athens University of Economics and Business, Athens, Greece. The authors are very grateful to seminar participants and discussants for their valuable comments and to Professor George Kaufman for the invitation to contribute this paper to the current volume.

REFERENCES

Allen, F., & Gorton, G. (1988). *Rational Finite Bubbles.* mimeo, The Wharton School, University of Pennsylvania.

Binswanger, M. (1999). *Stock Markets, Speculative Bubbles and Economic Growth.* Cheltenham, U.K.: Elgar Publishing.

Blanchard, O. J., & Watson M. (1982). Bubbles, Rational Expectations and Financial Markets. In: P. Wachel (Ed.), *Crises in the Economic and Financial Structure.* Lexington: Lexington Books.

Campbell, J. Y. (2000). Asset Pricing at the Millennium. *The Journal of Finance, 55,* 1515–1568.

Campbell, J., Lo, A., & MacKinlay, A. C. (1997). *The Econometrics of Financial Markets.* Princeton, New Jersey: Princeton University Press.

Campbell, J. Y., & Shiller R. J. (1988a). The Dividend-Price Ratio and the Expectations of Future Dividends and Discount Factors. *Review of Financial Studies, 1,* 195–228.

Campbell, J. Y., & Shiller, R. J. (1988b). Stock Prices, Earnings and Expected Dividends. *Journal of Finance, 43,* 661–676.

Chan, K., McQueen, G., & Thorley, S. (1998). Are there Rational Speculative Bubbles in Asian Stock Markets? *Pacific-Basin Finance Journal, 6,* 125–151.

Chen, J. (1999). When the Bubble Is Going to Burst. *International Journal of Theoretical and Applied Finance, 2,* 285–292.

Chirinko, R., & Schaller, H. (1996). Bubbles, Fundamentals, and Investment: A Multiple Equation Testing Strategy. *Journal of Monetary Economics, 38,* 47–76.

Claessens, S., & Forbes, K. (Eds) (2001). *International Financial Contagion.* Amsterdam: Kluwer Academic Publishers.

Dezhbakhsh, H., & Demirguc-Kunt, A. (1990). On the Presence of Speculative Bubbles in Stock Prices. *Journal of Financial and Quantitative Analysis*, *25*, 101–112.

Diba, B. T., & Grossman, H. I. (1984). Rational Bubbles in the Price of Gold, National Bureau of Economic Research, Working Paper No. 1300.

Diba, B. T., & Grossman, H. I. (1988a). The Theory of Rational Bubbles in Stock Prices. *Economic Journal*, *98*, 746–754.

Diba, B. T., & Grossman, H. I. (1988b). Explosive Rational Bubbles in Stock Prices. *American Economic Review*, *78*, 520–530.

Evans, G. E. (1991). Pitfalls in Testing for Explosive Bubbles in Asset Prices. *American Economic Review*, *81*, 922–930.

Flood, R. P., & Garber, P. M. (1980). Market Fundamentals versus Price Level Bubbles: The First Tests. *Journal of Political Economy*, *88*, 745–770.

Froot, K. A., & Obstfeld, M. (1991). Intrinsic Bubbles: The Case of Stock Prices. *American Economic Review*, *81*, 1189–1214.

Hamilton, J. D. (1986). On Testing for Self-Fulfilling Speculative Price Bubbles. *International Economic Review*, *27*, 545–552.

Hamilton J. D., & Whiteman, C. H. (1985). The Observable Implications of Self-Fulfilling Expectations. *Journal of Monetary Economics*, *16*, 353–373.

Harvey, A. C. (1990). *The Econometric Analysis of Time Series* (2nd ed.). Cambridge, Massachusetts: The MIT Press.

Harvey, A., Ruiz, E., & Sentana, E. (1992). Unobserved Component Time Series Models with ARCH Disturbances. *Journal of Econometrics*, *52*, 129–157.

Ikeda, S., & Shibata, A (1992). Fundamentals-Dependent Bubbles in Stock Prices. *Journal of Monetary Economics*, *30*, 143–168.

Kim, C., & Nelson, C. R. (1999). *State Space Models with Regime Switching: Classical and Gibbs-Sampling Approach with Applications*. Cambridge: The MIT Press.

LeRoy, S., & Porter, R. D. (1981). The Present Value Relation: Tests Based on Implied Variance Bounds. *Econometrica*, *49*, 555–574.

Lutkepohl, H. (1993). *Introduction to Multiple Time Series Analysis* (2nd ed.). New York: Spinger-Verlag.

McCarthy, J., & Najand, M. (1995). State Space Modelling of Linkages among International Markets. *Journal of Multinational Financial Management*, *5*, 1–9.

Pierce, d. A., & Haugh, L. D. (1977). Causality in Temporal Systems: Characterizations and a Survey. *Journal of Econometrics*, *5*, 265–293.

Rappoport, P., & White, E. N. (1993). Was There a Bubble in the 1929 Stock Market? *Journal of Economic History*, *53*, 549–574.

Rappoport, P., & White, E. N. (1994). The New York Stock Market in the 1920s and 1930s: Did Stock Prices Move Together Too Much? NBER Working Paper, No. 4627.

Richards, A. (1996). Volatility and Predictability in National Stock Markets: How do Emerging and Mature Markets Differ? *International Monetary Fund Staff Papers*, *43*, 461–501.

Sarno, L., & Taylor, M. (1999). Moral Hazard, Asset Price Bubbles, Capital Flows and the East Asian Crisis: The First Test. *Journal of International Money and Finance*, *18*, 637–657.

Shiller, R. J. (1981). Do Stock Price Move too Much to be Justified by Subsequent Changes in Dividends? *American Economic Review*, *71*, 421–436.

Shumway, R. H., & Stoffer, D. S. (2000). *Time Series Analysis and Its Applications*. New York: Springer.

Tirole, J. (1982). On the Possibility of Speculation under Rational Expectations. *Econometrica*, *50*, 1163–1181.

Tirole, J. (1985). Asset Bubbles and Overlapping Generations. *Econometrica*, *53*, 1499–1528.
Weil, P. (1990). On the Possibility of Price Decreasing Bubbles. *Econometrica*, *58*, 1467–1474.
Wells, C. (1996). *The Kalman Filter in Finance*. Amsterdam: Kluwer Academic Publishers.
West, K. D. (1988). Bubbles, Fads, and Stock Price Volatility Tests: A Partial Evaluation. National Bureau of Economic Research, Working Paper No. 2574.
West, K. D. (1987). A Specification Test for Speculative Bubbles. *Quarterly Journal of Economics*, *102*, 553–580.
Wu, Y. (1995). Are There Rational Bubbles in Foreign Exchange Markets? *Journal of International Money and Finance*, *14*, 27–46.
Wu, Y. (1997). Rational Bubbles in the Stock Market: Accounting for the U.S. Stock-Price Volatility. *Economic Inquiry*, *35*, 309–319.

IS THE FEDERAL RESERVE STOCK MARKET BUBBLE-NEUTRAL?

Marc D. Hayford and A. G. Malliaris

ABSTRACT

This paper argues that the Fed was not stock market bubble-neutral during the last several years. This nonneutrality implies two options: first, the Fed has used monetary policies to prevent the building of the stock market bubble or, second, the Fed has contributed to its development and subsequent deflation. We supply representative quotes from the FOMC transcripts to establish that the Fed has paid significant attention to the valuation of the stock market. These quotes confirm that the stock market's valuation was an important variable in the Fed's decision-making and its conduct of monetary policy. We also conduct econometric modeling, by extending the Taylor rule and using data for the 1987–2000 period, to argue that the Fed, perhaps unintentionally, has contributed to the stock market's overvaluation and subsequent decline.

I. INTRODUCTION

The question "Is the Fed stock market bubble-neutral?" is controversial for at least two reasons. First, economists have difficulty defining what is a stock market bubble because there are no universally accepted models of stock market valuation. Second, how can one define the neutrality of the Fed's monetary

---

Asset Price Bubbles: Implications for Monetary and Regulatory Policies, Volume 13, pages 229–243.

ISBN: 0-7623-0845-1

policies with respect to the stock market? Most macroeconomic variables, such as GDP, rate of unemployment, rate of inflation and stock market valuation are interrelated. In practice, it is very difficult to separate the impact of monetary policies on inflation from their influence on the stock market.

Before March 2000, very few analysts talked about a stock market bubble. The ones who expressed concerns were reminded that the economic conditions during 1995–2000 were different. Today, the issue of a stock market bubble is no longer controversial. With NASDAQ having declined by about 65% from its high on March 2000 and both the S&P 500 and the Dow Jones in bear territory, both economists and analysts agree that we had a bubble and that this bubble has been burst. Even those who do not wish to use the word "bubble" acknowledge that we are no longer in the old bull market. Thus, even if we do not know exactly how to value the market, reality has shown us that its value a year ago was too high. What one could not see as an overvaluation a year ago, it has become obvious today. Bubbles are always obvious after they burst.

If we accept the observation that we had a bubble in the stock market and that this bubble has been deflated, what can we say about the role of the Fed during the growing and collapsing of the bubble? If one can argue that the Fed had absolutely nothing to do with feeding the bubble and also nothing to do with reducing it, then analysts would need to search elsewhere for an explanation of this recent bubble phenomenon.

We wish to argue, with modesty, that the Fed was not bubble-neutral during the last several years. For those who remain skeptical about the existence of a stock market bubble and its subsequent collapse, we wish to show that the Fed was not stock market neutral. This nonneutrality implies two options: the Fed used monetary policies to prevent the building of a bubble or the Fed, perhaps unintentionally, contributed to its development and subsequent deflation.

II. FIRST THINGS FIRST

The Employment Act of 1946 requires the U.S. Federal government, including the Federal Reserve System, to pursue economic policies that generate maximum employment and price stability. The Humphrey-Hawkins Act of 1978 further directs the Federal Reserve System to aim at both low unemployment and price stability. Observe that price stability in both Acts means keeping the price *level* rather than the rate of inflation constant. In other words price stability means that the rate of inflation is to be stabilized at zero rather than at some positive or negative rate. There is no mention anywhere that price stability extends to asset prices.

In contrast to the U.S. Federal Reserve Bank, both the European and Japanese Central Banks are not required to pursue monetary policies that yield low unemployment. They need however, to exclusively pursue monetary policies that lead to price stability. Thus, it appears that the U.S. Federal Reserve Bank has a more challenging task than both the European and Japanese Central Banks since it has the mandate to achieve the twin goals of price stability and low unemployment simultaneously.

Chairman Alan Greenspan, in his testimony of June 17, 1999, before the Joint Economic Committee of the U.S. Congress on "Monetary Policy and the Economic Outlook", remarked "[t]his all leads to the conclusion that monetary policy is best primarily focused on stability of the general level of prices of goods and services as the most credible means to achieve sustainable economic growth." Elsewhere in the same testimony, Mr. Greenspan said "[a]s recent experiences attest, a prolonged period of price stability does help to foster economic prosperity".

In the July 22, 1997 Semiannual Monetary Report before the Committee on Banking, Housing and Urban Affairs, Greenspan revisited the dual goals of monetary policy by stating that "[o]ur objective has never been to contain inflation as an end in itself, but rather as a precondition for the highest possible long-run growth of output and income – the ultimate goal of macroeconomic policy". It is reasonable to conclude, both from these brief quotations and also from reading the numerous other testimonies of Chairman Greenspan, that he believes that price stability is the foremost goal of monetary policy because such price stability contributes to sustainable economic growth of output and employment.

But what is price stability? Beyond the abstract definition given above emphasizing stability of the price *level*, Greenspan, in his December 5, 1996 Lecture to the American Enterprise Institute for Public Policy Research, reflects by saying "[b]ut where do we draw the line on what prices matter? Certainly prices of goods and services now being produced – our basic measure of inflation – matter. But what about futures prices or more importantly prices of claims on future goods and services, like equities, real estate, or other earning assets? Is stability of these prices essential to the stability of the economy?"

Having raised this important question, Chairman Greenspan, in the same December 5, 1996 presentation, offers an answer in the form of both reflections and questions. He writes: "But how do we know when *irrational exuberance* has unduly escalated asset values, which then become subject to unexpected and prolonged contractions as they have in Japan over the past decade? And how do we factor that assessment into monetary policy? We, as central bankers, need not be concerned if a collapsing financial asset bubble does not threaten to impair the real economy, its production, jobs and price stability. Indeed, the sharp stock market break of 1987 had few negative consequences for the economy. But we should not underestimate or become complacent about the complexity of the interactions of asset markets and the economy. Thus, evaluating shifts in balance sheets generally, and in asset prices particularly, must be an integral part of the development of monetary policy".

In addition to the above remarks linking price stability to asset inflation, Greenspan has revisited the topic of asset inflation several times during the past five years. For example, in July 22, 1997, Greenspan reflected that "[w]ith the economy performing so well for so long, financial markets have been buoyant, as memories of past business and financial cycles fade with time. Soaring prices in the stock market have been fueled by moderate long-term interest rates and expectations of investors that profit margins and earnings growth will hold steady, or even increase further, in a relatively stable, low-inflation environment". Also on June 17, 1999, Greenspan opined "[s]hould volatile asset prices cause problems, policy is probably best positioned to address the consequences when the economy is working from a base of stable product prices."

III. JUST RHETORIC OR ACTION

Numerous statements made by Chairman Greenspan, beyond the ones highlighted above, indicate that he believes that soaring stock prices create imbalances in the economy that threaten long-run economic growth. It is reasonable to wonder if these concerns by the Chairman have been activated into monetary policy decisions. Were the Chairman's worries about rapidly increasing asset prices opinions that did or did not translate into any active monetary policy? Put differently: were soaring stock market valuations a critical variable in the conduct of monetary policy? Equivalently, was the Fed stock market bubble-neutral?

Furthermore, beyond what actually did happen, we also have the normative question: should the Fed be concerned with the stock market, particularly in view of its clearly specified goals. In other words, should the Fed be stock market neutral? The academic literature does not offer a decisive answer to this question. Some economists have argued that a central bank dedicated to a policy of flexible inflation targeting should pay little attention to asset inflation because a proper setting of interest rates to achieve the desired inflation target will also stabilize asset prices. Others have argued exactly the opposite: central bankers can improve economic performance by paying attention to asset prices.

IV. EVIDENCE FROM FOMC TRANSCRIPTS

Having read very carefully numerous FOMC transcripts we wish to offer support for our opinion that the Fed has been concerned with the stock market bubble, wished to control it but contrary to its intentions, actually contributed to its growth.

For example, a reading of the FOMC transcripts suggests that Greenspan and other members of the FOMC felt the stock market was overvalued at the beginning of 1994. The press also echoed such a belief: "Many of the world's stock markets (including it should be said, America's) are at near record levels . . . American shares are trading at an historically high . . .. 17 times forecasted earning for this year . . .." ["Stock markets: Flying high" *Economist* January 8, 1994 pp. 72–73]. This belief that the market was overvalued was supported by a comparison of the p/e ratio and the implied equity premium to their historic values. Did the Fed increase the federal funds rate at this time to pop or deflate a speculative bubble in the stock market? Our reading of the transcripts suggests that this was not the case.

On February 4, 1994 the FOMC increased the target federal funds rate for the first time in five years. This is longest period of no increases in the federal funds rate since the end of World War II. From June 6, 1989 to September 4, 1992 there were 40 months of decline with the federal funds rate target falling from 9.81% to 3.00%, a fall of 681 basis points. For all of 1993, the target federal funds rate remained constant at 3%. Then on February 4, 1994, the FOMC increased the target Federal Funds rate 25 basis points to 3.25%. From the vantage point of January 1994, inflation had been fairly steady in the 3% range for the previous two years while unemployment had been rapidly falling since the middle of 1992.

By the beginning of 1994, unemployment was in the range of contemporaneous estimates of the natural rate of unemployment. Monetary policy had been 'loose' for all of 1993, because with an inflation rate of around 3%, the real federal funds rate was about zero. At the time observers of the U.S. economy felt, as did members of the FOMC, that the U.S. stock market was potentially overvalued. The p/e ratio of the S&P 500 was above its historic average and above the level it had been prior to the 1987 stock market crash; the first major financial crisis faced by Alan Greenspan after becoming chairman of the Federal Reserve Board in August 1987.

The transcripts of the February 3rd and 4th 1994 FOMC meeting show there was a consensus that accelerating inflation was a risk. While some members of the FOMC wanted a 50 basis point increase, Greenspan strongly pushed for an unanimous vote for a 25 basis point increase. Greenspan was afraid a 50 basis point increase could cause a stock market crash:

Chairman Greenspan: "*Well, I've been around a long time watching markets behave and I will tell you that if we do 50 basis points today, we have a very high probability of cracking these markets. I think that would be very unwise procedure. It is far easier for us to start the process with a smaller move. And, as Dick Syron says, there's a very large announcement effect. Having stuck with an unchanged policy for so long, it is going to be far easier for us to get on an accelerated path if we need to a later time. To go more than 25 at this point I think would be a bad mistake. It could generate surprising counter-productive responses in this market*" (p. 53).

"*Look, the stock market is at an elevated level at this stage by any measure we know of. We could set off a sequence of events here that I think could make the policy path that we have been developing here a difficult one*" (p. 53).

Governor LaWare: "*I certainly buy the fact that this is the time to make a change in policy forward more constraint. But I really favor of the 50 basis point move at this point, and I respectfully disagree with the assessment that such a move would crack the markets. I think the markets have already discounted a 25 basis point move and are still burning away at a great rate. I would like to see a stronger move than 25 basis points simply to damp down without a crash the stock market particularly. I think it is getting increasingly dangerous because of the way it has been running. I believe a 50 basis point move will send an unmistakable message that will damp this enthusiasm in the stock market without causing it to crash*" (p. 54).

Chairman Greenspan: "*You know, I rarely feel strongly about an issue, and I very rarely sort of press this committee. But let you tell me something about what's gnawing at me here. I am very sympathetic with the view that we've got to move and that we're going to have an extended period moves, assuming the changes that are going on now continue in the direction of strength. It is very unlikely that the recent rate of economic growth will not simmer down largely because some developments involved in this particular period are clearly one shot factors* . . ..

"*I would be very concerned if this committee went 50 basis points now because I don't think markets expect it. You want to hit the market when it needs to be hit; there is no significant evidence at this stage of an imbalance that require the type of action that a number of us have discussed. Were we to go the 50 basis points with the announcement effect and the shock effect, I'm telling you that these markets will not hold still. I've been in the economic forecasting business since 1948, and I've been on Wall Street since 1948, and I'm telling you I have a pain in the pit of my stomach, which in the past*

I've been very successful in alluding to. I am telling you – and I've seen these markets – this is not the time to do this. I think there will be a time; and if the staff's forecast is right, we can get to 150 basis points pretty easily. We can do it with a couple of ½ point jumps later when the markets are in the position to know what we are doing and there's continuity. I really request that we do not do this" (p. 55).

Mr. Jordan: "*I'm willing to defer to your judgment on the market reaction, but the logic of that position is that if 50 basis points really would be the correct move except for constraints of the market, then once we've done the 25 basis points and overcome any concerns about market reaction we would come in with the second installment fairly promptly*" (p. 57).

Chairman Greenspan: "*Let me make the suggestion then that we move 25 basis points with symmetry, that we watch this process very closely, and that evidence suggests that this situation is not simmering down, that we can have a telephone conference at the appropriate time.*"

"*I would request that, if we can, we act unanimously. It is a very potent message out in the various communities with which we deal if we stand together. If we are going to get a split in the vote, I think it will create a problem for us, and I don't know how it will play out. I rarely ask this, as you know. This is one of the times when we really are together and I'd hate to have our vote somehow implies something other than the agreement for a tightening move that in fact exists in this committee*" (p. 57). (*Source*: transcripts of the February 3rd and 4th 1994 FOMC meeting.)

The FOMC voted unanimously for a 25 basis point increase. So, did the Fed tighten in February 1994 to pop a stock market bubble? The answer seems to be no. The evidence indicates that the FOMC raised the target fed funds rate to preempt what they perceived as inflationary pressure. Members of the FOMC also believed that the stock market was probably overvalued. However, Greenspan was clearly concerned that too large a move to tighter monetary policy would induce a stock market crash. The stock market's reaction was considered to be a constraint on the perceived need to move to a tighter monetary policy.

How did the stock market react to the tighter monetary policy? The move was signaled prior to the February FOMC meeting by Greenspan in testimony to congress and the increase was anticipated at the time in the financial press [see e.g. "The Economy: Subtle Levitation" *Economist*, February 5, 1994 p. 24]. Hence the rate increase was not a complete surprise to financial market participants. Nonetheless, the market did react. As reported at the time by *The*

Economist: "*When the Federal Reserve raised the federal funds rate on February 4th by a quarter of a percentage point, the first tightening in American monetary policy for five years, investors reckoned that more would follow . . .. This consensus, conceived quickly when the Fed raised its rate, still more speedily dissolved. A 96 point (2.4%) decline in the DJIA on the day of the central bank's announcement triggered steep stock market declines in Europe and East Asia. But the panic subsided quickly and most markets stabilized. An unexpected* $^1/_2$ *point reduction in British rates on February 8th contributed to a calmer mood.*" (*Source*: "Stock markets: On second thought . . ." *Economist*, February 12, 1994, pp. 78–80.)

The rate increase resulted in a large drop in the S&P 500 p/e ratio. Between February and March 1994, the ratio fell from 23.24 to 20.98, a decrease of 9.7%. The only larger month to month drops in the P/E ratio are associated with: (1) the October 1987 crash, −12.5% and −18.3% drops from September to October and from October to November respectively; and (2) October to September 1988 drop of −10.2%. At the next meeting of the FOMC, Chairman Greenspan was clearly happy with the outcome:

Chairman Greenspan: "*When we moved on Feb 4th [1994], I think our expectation was that we would prick the bubble in the equity markets*" (p. 41).

"*So the question is, having very consciously and purposely tried to break the bubble and upset markets in order to sort of break the cocoon of capital gains speculation, we are now in a position – having done that and in a sense succeeded perhaps more than we had intended – to try to restore some degree of confidence in the System*" (p. 44). (*Source*: transcripts of the March 22, 1994 FOMC meeting.)

Perhaps it makes sense that Greenspan could talk about "prick[ing] the bubble". The target federal funds rate only increased by 25 basis points but it is the first increase since May 17, 1989 and signaled further tightening to come. As a consequence, the response of the financial markets was larger than if it had been anticipated to be a one-time increase.

Discussions at FOMC meetings later in 1999 are informative concerning FOMC members views on financial markets in general. Clearly members of the FOMC believe that there are episodes of bubbles or irrationally in stock, bond and foreign exchange markets. Further they believe that it can be appropriate at times for a central bank and the Fed in particular to attempt to push the market toward what the Fed would perceive as its fundamental value. While members of the FOMC, Chairman Greenspan included, hold these beliefs, have these beliefs systematically influenced monetary policy? Has the Fed tried to systematically deflate perceived speculative bubbles? The econometric evidence presented in the next section suggests they have not. In fact, the results are consistent with the Fed accommodating rapidly increasing stock market prices.

V. THE TAYLOR RULE EVIDENCE

There is a long debate in monetary economics on the topic of "rules versus discretion" in monetary policy. Some economists, such as Tobin, have argued that a mechanical rule blind to actual economic developments could not work. Greenspan in various testimonies has reflected that "because monetary policy works with a significant lag, policy actions are directed at a future that may not be clearly evident in current experience. This leads to policy judgements that are by their nature calibrated to relative probabilities of different outcomes" (July 22, 1997). Elsewhere, Greenspan has said "I wish I could say that there is a bound volume of immutable instructions on my desk on how effectively to implement policy to achieve our goals of maximum employment, sustainable economic growth, and price stability. Instead, we have to deal with a dynamic, continuously evolving economy whose structure appears to change from business cycle to business cycle . . ." (December 5, 1996).

On the other hand, John Taylor has argued that "if there is anything about which modern macroeconomics is clear . . . – and on which there is substantial consensus – it is that policy rules have major advantages over discretion in improving economic performance". Taylor believes that a major reason for applying rules instead of discretion is to sustain credibility by the policy makers and thus to avoid dynamic inconsistency.

To test the empirical relationship between monetary policy and the stock market, we augment Taylor's monetary policy rule with a target for the stock market:

$$i_t = \pi_t + r^* + \alpha_1(\pi_t - \pi^*) + \alpha_2 y_t + \alpha_3 (\rho_t - \rho^*) \quad (1)$$

where i_t denotes the current nominal federal funds rate, π_t is the average inflation rate over the contemporaneous and prior three quarters measured by the GDP deflator, r^* is the long run equilibrium real federal funds rate, π^* is the target inflation rate, and y_t is the output gap, that is, 100 times (Real GDP – Potential GDP)/Potential GDP. The Taylor rule implies that the Fed sets the Federal funds rate to hit a target inflation rate and a target for real GDP that equals potential GDP. Monetary policy is "stable", that is, offsets increases in inflation by increasing the real funds rate if $\alpha_1 > 0$. To test whether monetary policy is responsive to the valuation of the stock market we add to Taylor's rule, ρ_t, that denotes the price earnings ratio, commonly written as P/E, of the

S&P 500 Index. Presumably, the Fed would set ρ^* equal to an estimate of the fundamental value of ρ_t. If monetary policy is aiming at reducing an estimated bubble, then $\alpha_3 > 0$, that is, a stock market overvaluation leads the Fed to increase the Fed funds rate. However, if monetary policy is accommodating a stock market overvaluation, as judged by the long run average value of the S&P 500 P/E ratio, then $\alpha_3 < 0$.

There are several data issues and at least one important econometric decision in estimating Eq. (1). The first data issue concerns the periodicity of the data: quarterly or monthly? Taylor (1993) uses quarterly data. Other researchers have used monthly data. The FOMC meets approximately every six weeks and sometimes adjusts the Fed funds target between meetings. We decided to follow Taylor and use quarterly data. A second data issue is what is the appropriate measure of the excess demand. Either gap between the unemployment rate and NAIRU or the GDP gap can be used. Taylor uses the recent revised data for real GDP and calculates potential GDP using the Hodrick-Prescott filter. Orphanides (2000) argues that using real time estimates of potential GDP that would be available at the time the FOMC was meeting is more appropriate and that doing so reduces the explanatory power of Taylor's rule. Evans (1998) argues that using the gap between unemployment and an estimate of the natural rate of unemployment comes closer to real time data than using revised values of real GDP. In this paper we use the CBO's estimate of the real GDP gap.

A third issue is what measures of the inflation should be used? Again, one can evaluate the advantages and shortcomings of the CPI and the GDP deflator. In this paper we use the GDP price deflator as a better proxy of the economy's overall rate of inflation.

Finally in estimating Eq. (1) one needs to select an appropriate measure of stock market valuation. As is indicated earlier, we choose to use the well-accepted P/E ratio of the S&P500 Index as a measure of the stock market's valuation.

One econometric decision in estimating Eq. (1) as specified, is that it results in serially correlated errors. This does not seem to bother Taylor (1999). Other researchers, such as Evans (1998), Judd and Rudebusch (1998) and Bernanke and Gertler (1999) have combined Eq. (1) with an equation that allows the Fed funds target to adjust slowly. The result of this approach is a "dynamic" specification of Taylor's rule that results in serially uncorrelated errors. In this paper, we report estimates of Taylor's rule with both 'static' and 'dynamic' specifications.

The econometric specification of Eq. (1), is as follows

$$i_t^* = c_1 + c_2\pi_t + c_3 y_t + c_4\rho_t \tag{2}$$

Table 1. Variable Definitions and Sample Statistics.

Sample period: 1987:3 to 2000:2

	Mean	Std. Dev	Max	Min
Fedfunds	5.74	1.76	9.73	2.99
Inflation	2.54	0.89	4.21	1.17
CBOGAP	−0.40	1.85	3.97	−3.47
PE	20.81	6.40	35.77	11.70

Notes:
Fedfunds = Federal funds rate.
Inflation = Growth in the GDP deflator, year over year.
CBOGAP = CBO estimate of GDP gap, using data available in year 2000.
PE = S&P 500 price earnings ratio.

where

$c_1 = r^* - \alpha_1\pi^* - \alpha_3\rho^*$
$c_2 = 1 + \alpha_1 > 1$ if monetary policy is stable
$c_3 = \alpha_2$
$c_4 = \alpha_3$

Table 2 reports estimates of Eq. (2). All coefficients are statistically significant at the usual significance levels. Model 1 reports estimates of Eq. (2) without including the P/E ratio. The estimated parameters for inflation and excess demand are consistent with those reported by Taylor (1999). Monetary policy is found to be stable during this period, with the Federal funds rate estimated to increase by 1.6 percentage points for every 1 percentage point increase in inflation, using the CBOGAP as the measure of excess demand.

Model 2 gives the estimate of Eq. (2) including the P/E ratio. The negative coefficient on the P/E ratio indicates that the Fed, during the sample period, controlling for inflation and GDP gap, was lowering the Federal funds rate as the market became overvalued. Are the estimated effects of the stock market overvaluation on the Federal funds rate large or small? Model 2 estimates suggest that an increase in the P/E ratio of 10 (approximately a 1.5 standard deviation increase) results in a decrease in the Fed funds rate of 80 basis points. Such effects seem to us to be large.

The inclusion of the P/E ratio in the static Taylor rule reduces the magnitude of the inflation coefficient from 1.56 to 1.16. Obviously, the P/E ratio depends on interest rates so the regression result reflects, perhaps, some simultaneity bias. To address this problem we estimated Eq. (2) using the method of instrumental variables. As instruments for the measures of stock

Table 2. Static Taylor Rules.

	Model 1	Model 2	Model 3
Constant: c_1	2.01	4.82	1.91
	(6.04)	(6.43)	(1.50)
Inflation: c_2	1.56	1.16	1.58
	(12.40)	(7.80)	(7.20)
CBOGAP: c_3	0.60	0.64	0.69
	(9.87)	(11.86)	(9.33)
P/E: c_4		−0.08	0.003
		(−4.06)	(0.085)
$\bar{R}^2$	0.80	0.85	0.81
DW	0.25	0.36	0.25

Notes: OLS estimation for Models 1 and 2 and Instrumental Variables estimation for Model 3. Instruments for Model 3 are inflation, CBOGAP, Growth rate of real GDP from year ago (lags 0–2).
Dependent Variable: Federal funds rate (mean = 5.74, variance = 1.75).
Sample: 1987:3 to 2000:2, *t*-statistics in parenthesis.

market overvaluation we use zero to two lags of the growth rate of real GDP from the previous year. We use these instruments because the lag between changes in the Fed funds rate and output growth is long and variable. In addition, over the sample period, the correlation between current real GDP growth and the level of the Fed funds rate is −0.04. This suggests that the growth rate of current and past real GDP is uncorrelated with the current level of the Fed funds rate.

Model 3 in Table 2 shows the instrumental variables estimates of equation (2). The estimate of the P/E ratio is now positive, small and statistically insignificant, implying that monetary policy was not responding to the stock market.

The low Durban Watson statistic implies the regression errors are serially correlated. Following other researchers such as Judd and Rudebusch (1998), we address this issue by estimating a "dynamic Taylor rule". Following Judd and Rudebusch (1998) and including a target for the stock market, we write the target for the nominal Federal funds rate as:

$$i_t^* = \pi_1 + r^* + \alpha_1 (\pi_t - \pi^*) + \alpha_2 y_t + \alpha_3 (\rho_t - \rho^*) \tag{3}$$

with the actual changes in the Fed funds rate following:

$$\Delta i_t = \gamma_1 (i^* - i_{t-1}) + \gamma_2 \Delta i_{t-1} \tag{4}$$

where γ_1 measures the speed of adjustment of the actual Fed funds rate to the target. Instantaneous adjustment would imply that γ_1 is infinite. Combining Eqs (3) and (4) results in the regression equation:

$$\Delta i_t = c_1 + c_2\Delta i_{t-1} + c_3[c_4\pi_t + c_5 y_t + c_6\rho_t - i_{t-1}] \tag{5}$$

where:

$c_1 = \gamma_1\ [r^* - \alpha_1\pi^* - \alpha_3\rho^*]$
$c_2 = \gamma_2$
$c_3 = \gamma_1$ adjustment parameter
$c_4 = 1 + \alpha_1 > 1$ if monetary policy is stable.
$c_5 = \alpha_2$
$c_6 = \alpha_3$

Table 3 reports estimates of Eq. (5). The Q-statistics suggest that the regression errors are serially uncorrelated. The results for Model 4 are similar to the static Model 1 in terms of the size of the parameters on inflation and the CBOGAP. Model 5 gives the estimates of Eq. (5) including the P/E ratio. The negative coefficient on the P/E ratio is 2 times larger than in the static regressions and statistically significant. Also, the coefficient on inflation implies that monetary policy was not stable. Model 6 reports the results using the method of instrumental variables. In Model 6, the estimated coefficient on the P/E ratio is similar in sign and magnitude to those of the OLS results reported in Table 2. The coefficient is also statistically significant at standard levels and larger than the estimates in the static Taylor rule regression.

Note that the instruments used in Model 6 are the same as in Model 3. To summarize the estimated dynamic regression results reported in Table 3 are consistent with the results of Table 2. Adding the P/E ratio to either static or dynamic Taylor rule results in negative correlation between the Fed funds rate and the stock market overvaluation after controlling for inflation and a measure of excess aggregate demand for all estimated equations except one. This empirical evidence does not support the hypothesis that the Greenspan Fed has been systematically trying to deflate apparent speculative bubbles in the stock market. Rather a case can be made that the FOMC has at least accommodated the stock market overvaluation in the mid to late 1990s.

VI. CONCLUSIONS

Chairman Greenspan has repeatedly expressed concerns about the stock market overvaluation. Were these concerns translated into policy actions, or were they

Table 3. Dynamic Taylor Rules.

	Model 4	Model 5	Model 6
Constant: c_1	0.53	2.03	1.40
	(3.57)	(6.08)	(2.77)
Δ Fedfunds-$_1$:	0.53	0.27	0.38
c_2	(5.41)	(2.86)	(3.23)
Adjust. Param.	0.21	0.27	0.25
c_3	(4.80)	(7.00)	(5.82)
Inflation: c_4	1.41	0.71	0.96
	(6.49)	(3.28)	(3.38)
CBOGAP	0.73	0.84	0.80
	(6.09)	(9.63)	(7.98)
P/E	–	−0.16	−0.10
		(−4.68)	(−1.96)
$\bar{R}^2$	0.60	0.73	0.71
DW	1.91	1.95	2.05
Q-statistic			
4 lags	3.37	3.85	0.05
(Prob)	(0.50)	(0.43)	(0.83)

Notes: OLS estimates for Models 4 and 5 and Instrumental Variables estimates for Model 6.
Dependent Variable: Federal funds rate (mean = −0.01, variance = 0.45).
Sample: 1987:3 to 2000:2.
t-statistics in parenthesis.

mere rhetorical remarks? In other words, has the Greenspan Fed been stock market neutral?

The question is very difficult to answer because the economic complexities are enormous. It is no surprise that there is no agreement among economists on whether monetary policy should or should not target asset prices. This paper examines empirically if monetary policy, during the past few years, has been influenced by the high valuation of the stock market.

We use two different approaches to offer empirical evidence that the valuation of the stock market was an important variable in setting monetary policy. First, we review the transcripts of the early 1994 FOMC meetings. Second, we augment the Taylor rule using the P/E ratio as a measure of stock market valuation to examine the impact of market valuations the Federal funds rate.

The regression results of the augmented Taylor rule suggest that rather than the Greenspan FOMC using the Federal funds rate policy to offset increases in the value of the stock market above estimates of fundamentals, Federal funds policy has, perhaps inadvertently, on average accommodated the apparent stock market bubble. Chairman Greenspan's 'jaw boning' of the stock market since

December 1996 may be an attempt to find another policy instrument to influence the stock market in the direction of estimates of fundamentals. The 1994 FOMC transcripts, consistent with Taylor's rule, suggest the Federal funds rate target has largely been set in response to inflation and measures of excess demand and at least has not been *increased solely* to offset a potential stock market bubble. However a case can be made that the Fed has contributed to the stock market bubble. So, has the Fed been "bubble-neutral"? Our results suggest, not quite.

ACKNOWLEDGMENTS

Earlier versions of this paper were presented at the Federal Reserve Bank of Chicago, Northern Illinois University and the European Financial Management Associations Meetings in Lugano, Switzerland. We are thankful to numerous seminar participants for their valuable comments. We wish in particular to acknowledge the help of Charles Evans and Marsha Courchane. Maryanthe Malliaris offered several useful comments that improved the exposition of our ideas. We also thank George Kaufman for the invitation to include the paper in this book.

REFERENCES

Bernanke, B., & Gertler, M. (1999). *Monetary Policy and Asset Price Volatility in New Challenges for Monetary Policy*. Federal Reserve Bank of Kansas City.

Cecchetti, S., Genber, H., Lipsky, J., & Wadhwani, S. (2000). *Asset Prices and Central Bank Policy*. London: International Center for Monetary and Banking Studies.

Chappell, H. Jr., & McGregor, R. R. (2000). A Long History of FOMC Voting Behavior. *Southern Economic Journal*, *66*, 906–922.

Evans, C. (1998). Real-Time Taylor rules and the Federal Funds Futures Market. *Economic Perspectives*, Federal Reserve Bank of Chicago, 3rd Quarter, 44–55.

Filardo, A. (2000). Monetary Policy and Asset Prices. *Federal Reserve Bank of Kansas City Review*, *85*, 11–37.

Gordon, M. J. (1962). *The Investment, Financing and Valuation of the Corporation*. Homewood IL: Irwin.

Gordon, R. (2000). *Macroeconomics*. Addison Wesley Longman.

Judd, J. P., & Rudebusch, G. R. (1998). Taylor's rule and the Fed: 1970–1997. *FRBSF Economic Review*, *3*, 3–16.

Orphanides, A. (2000). Activist Stabilization Policy and Inflation: The Taylor rule in the 1970s. Working paper. Board of Governors of the Federal Reserve System.

Taylor, J. (1999). *A Historical Analysis of Monetary Policy Rules*. In: J. B. Taylor (Ed.), *Monetary Policy Rules*. Chicago: The University of Chicago Press.

Taylor, J. (1993). Discretion versus policy rules in practice. *Carnegie-Rochester Conference Series on Public Policy*, *39*, 195–214.

World Economic Outlook International Monetary Fund, April 2000.

Available online at www.sciencedirect.com
SCIENCE @ DIRECT®

European Journal of Operational Research 163 (2005) 20–29

EUROPEAN JOURNAL OF OPERATIONAL RESEARCH

www.elsevier.com/locate/dsw

How did the Fed react to the 1990s stock market bubble? Evidence from an extended Taylor rule

M.D. Hayford *, A.G. Malliaris

Economics, School of Business Administration, Loyola University, Chicago, 820 N. Michigan Avenue, Chicago, IL 60611, USA

Available online 26 February 2004

Abstract

How did the Federal Reserve Bank react to the stock market bubble of the late 1990s? At a Symposium sponsored by the Federal Reserve Bank of Kansas City in Jackson Hole, Wyoming on August 30, 2002, Chairman Alan Greenspan remarked that economists do not currently have a way to measure a stock market bubble convincingly. He also argued that in the absence of such a measure, it was difficult for the Fed to justify, with some degree of certainty, a preemptive tightening that would likely be necessary to neutralize such a bubble. This paper extends the Taylor Rule methodology to include three measures of stock market overvaluation and confirms Greenspan's statement that the Fed did not neutralize the bubble. However, the extended Taylor Rule methodology also shows that the Fed, perhaps unintentionally, by keeping the Fed funds rate below those suggested by the Taylor Rule, may have actually contributed to the growth of the bubble.

Keywords: Economics; Finance; Stock market bubbles; Monetary policy; Taylor rules

1. Introduction

From the standpoint of 2002, many economists view the run up in the US stock market in the late 1990s as a bubble. Both before and since the collapse of the bubble, beginning with the NASDAQ Composite Index in March 2000, economists have debated the appropriate role of monetary policy in addressing apparent stock market overvaluations. For example, Cecchetti (1998), Cecchetti et al. (2000) and Cecchetti and Krause (2000) argue that central bankers can identify stock market bubbles as readily as they can recognize inflationary pressures of positive output gaps and consequently can and should respond to stock market bubbles. Other economists, such as Bernanke and Gertler (1999, 2001), Blanchard (2000) and Svensson (2002), argue that central banks should consider stock price bubbles only to the extent that they impact on the primary monetary policy goals of price stability and output growth. The preeminent practitioner of monetary policy, Alan Greenspan (2002), maintains that central banks can neither identity asset prices bubbles ex ante nor use monetary policy to successfully deflate asset price bubbles without also endangering the real economy.

* Corresponding author.
E-mail addresses: mhayfor@luc.edu (M.D. Hayford), tmallia@luc.edu (A.G. Malliaris).

0377-2217/$ - see front matter
doi:10.1016/j.ejor.2003.12.002

During the late 1990s, there was contemporaneous concern at the Fed about the level of the stock market. In an earlier paper, Hayford and Malliaris (2001) quote evidence from the FOMC transcripts of the concerns raised by Fed officials, as early as 1994, about the stock market valuation. The most noted concern was expressed in December 1996 by Chairman Greenspan with his famous "irrational exuberance" remark.

In this paper we focus on the positive question of how monetary policy responded to the stock market from 1987 up to the beginning of bubble collapse 2000. Given the numerous statements made by Chairman Greenspan during the 1990s that soaring stock prices create imbalances in the economy that may threaten long-run economic growth, it is natural to ask: Were these concerns by the Chairman activated into monetary policy decisions? Or, were the Chairman's worries about asset inflation mere opinions that did not translate into any active monetary policy?

There are at least three approaches to answering these questions. First, one can review and evaluate the transcripts of the FOMC meetings. Hayford and Malliaris (2001) follow this approach by looking at the FOMC transcripts. A second approach is found in Rigobon and Sack (2001) who use an identification technique based on the heteroskedasticity of stock market returns to identify the reaction of monetary policy to the stock market. In this paper we use a third approach, namely, we extend the Taylor Rule (1993) to include measures of stock market valuation to estimate the impact of stock market valuation on Federal funds rate during the period 1987–2000.

2. Measures of stock market valuation

We use three related measures of stock market overvaluation for the S&P 500: the P/E ratio, the implied equity premium and a measure promoted by Yardeni (2000) which he calls the "Fed's Stock Valuation Market Model". The P/E ratio is the most commonly used measure. Using this approach the stock market is appropriately valued if the P/E ratio equals the inverse of some appropriately risk adjusted return. This assumes of course that earnings and interest rates are expected to be constant at current levels into the future. Typically, economists just compare the P/E ratio to its historic average. If a P/E ratio is above its historic average it often signals a potential overvaluation.

The 'Gordon Equation' (Gordon, 1962) is used to calculate the implied equity premium. Stock prices are assumed to equal the expected present value of future earnings discounted at the long-term government bond rate plus an equity premium. If nominal earnings are expected to grow at the current growth rate g, and the nominal long-term government bond rate and the equity premium are expected to be constant, then the stock price is given as

$$P_t = \frac{E_t(1+g_t)}{i_t + \rho_t - g_t},$$

where P_t is the stock price, E_t is earnings, and g is the growth rate of earnings. Solving for the implied equity premium results in

$$\rho = (1+g)\frac{E_t}{P_t} - i + g$$

or in real terms

$$\rho = (1+rg_t)(1+\pi_t)\frac{E_t}{P_t} - i + rg_t + \pi_t + rg_t \times \pi_t.$$

To calculate the implied equity premium (following the World Economic Outlook, International Monetary Fund, April, 2000) we use the growth rate of potential real GDP for rg, recent inflation for π, the inverse of the S&P 500 price/earnings rate for E/P and the 10-year constant maturity treasury bond rate for i.

Yardeni's measure of market overvaluation is based on the idea that if the stock market is appropriately valued, the P/E ratio should equal the inverse of the risk adjusted interest rate. Yardeni defines the "fair-value price" for the S&P 500 as the ratio of $I/B/E/S$ consensus estimates of earnings over the coming 12 months divided by the 10-year treasure note yield. The measure of overvaluation is then just the percent difference between the actual S&P 500 index and the 'fair-value price'.

Fig. 1 compares these three measures of market valuation. The mean for the S&P 500 P/E ratio for the period 1948 to 1993 is about 14. Hence by

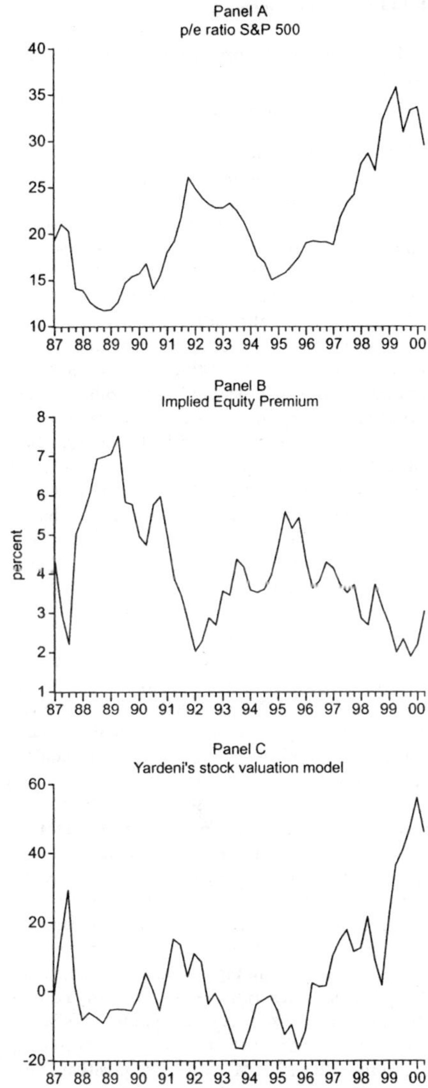

Fig. 1. (a) P/E ratio S&P 500; (b) implied equity premium and (c) Yardeni's stock valuation model.

historic standards, a P/E ratio in excess of 14 would indicate a potentially overvalued market. The historic average of the implied equity premium from 1960 to 1993 is 8%. An equity premium below this value could signal overvaluation. Yardeni's stock valuation model implies the market is overvalued when it is above zero and undervalued when below zero.

By all three measures the stock market was overvalued prior to the 1987 crash. For 1993 and the beginning of 1994 the three measures of the stock market valuation disagree. The P/E and equity premium imply an overvalued market while Yardeni's stock valuation model suggests the stock market was undervalued. However, all measures agree that from 1996 to 2000 the market was overvalued.

3. Extended Taylor rule evidence

To test the empirical relationship between monetary policy and the stock market, we augment Taylor's (1993, 1999) monetary policy rule with a target for the stock market:

$$i_t = \pi_t + r^* + \alpha_1(\pi_t - \pi^*) + \alpha_2 y_t + \alpha_3(\rho_t - \rho^*), \quad (1)$$

where i_t denotes the current nominal Federal funds rate, π is the average inflation rate, r^* is the long run equilibrium real Federal funds rate, π^* is the target inflation rate, and y a measure of excess demand. The Taylor rule implies that the Fed sets the Federal funds rate to hit a target inflation rate and to set excess demand to zero. Monetary policy is "stable", i.e. offsets increases in inflation by increasing the real Federal funds rate if $\alpha_1 > 0$. In the empirical results reported below, ρ_t is either the P/E ratio, the implied equity premium or the Yardeni valuation model and ρ^* is its target value. Presumably, the Fed would set ρ^* equal to an estimate of ρ_t fundamental value. If ρ_t is the price earnings ratio or the Yardeni valuation model and it is above its target value, a monetary policy aimed at reducing the estimated bubble would involve increasing the Federal funds rate, so $\alpha_3 > 0$. If monetary policy is contributing to a stock market bubble then $\alpha_3 < 0$. If instead ρ_t is implied equity premium and it is below its target value, a monetary policy aimed at reducing the estimated bubble would involve decreasing the Federal funds rate, so $\alpha_3 < 0$. If monetary policy is accommodating a stock market bubble then $\alpha_3 > 0$.

Following Taylor (1993) we use quarterly data to estimate Eq. (1) and use a four-quarter moving average of the growth rate of the GDP deflator as the measure of inflation. We use two alternative measures of excess demand: the CBO's estimate of the real GDP gap and the deviation of Gordon's (2000) measure of the natural rate of unemployment from the actual unemployment rate. As discussed above, we employ three alternative measures of stock market valuation: *P*/*E* ratio, equity premium and Yardeni's stock valuation model.

Estimating Eq. (1) as specified results in serially correlated errors, a fact that is not addressed by some researchers, for example Taylor (1999). Specifying a "dynamic" Taylor's rule, as done for example by Evans (1998), Judd and Rudebusch (1998) and Bernanke and Gertler (1999), results in serially uncorrelated errors. Estimates of Taylor's rule with both 'static' and 'dynamic' specifications are reported in Sections 4 and 5. Sample statistics are given in Table 1.

Table 1
Variable definitions and sample statistics

	Mean	Std. dev.	Max	Min
Sample period: 1987:3 to 2000:2				
Fedfunds	5.74	1.76	9.73	2.99
Inflation	2.54	0.89	4.21	1.17
CBOGAP	−0.40'	1.85	3.97	−3.47
UNEMPGAP	0.16	0.77	1.20	−1.53
P/*E*	20.81	6.40	35.77	11.70
SVM	4.95	16.91	56.00	−16.83
PREMIUM	4.12	1.44	7.51	1.89

Fedfunds = Federal funds rate.
Inflation = Growth in the GDP deflator, year over year.
CBOGAP = CBO estimate of GDP gap, using data available in year 2000.
UNEMPGAP = Gordon's (2000) estimate of NAIRU minus actual unemployment rate.
P/*E* = S&P 500 price earnings ratio.
SVM = Yardeni's stock market valuation model.
PREMIUM = Implied equity premium on the S&P 500.

4. Static specifications

The econometric specification of Eq. (1), is as follows:

$$i_t = c_1 + c_2\pi_t + c_3 y_t + c_4 \rho_t, \tag{2}$$

where $c_1 = r^* - \alpha_1\pi^* - \alpha_3\rho^*$; $c_2 = 1 + \alpha_1 > 1$ if monetary policy is stable; $c_3 = \alpha_2$ and $c_4 = \alpha_3$.

The estimated Eq. (2), for two measures of excess demand and three measures of stock market valuation, is reported in Table 2. Model 1 and Model 2 presented in columns 2 and 3 of Table 2 report the estimates of Eq. (2) using CBOGAP and UNEMPGAP as alternative measures of excess demand without including a measure of stock market valuation. The estimated parameters for inflation and excess demand are similar to those reported by Taylor (1999). Monetary policy is stable during this period, with the Federal funds rate estimated to increase by 1.6 percentage points for every 1 percentage point increase in inflation, if the CBOGAP is the measure of excess demand (Model 1). If UNEMPGAP is used (Model 2), the Federal funds rate is less responsive to inflation but monetary policy is still stable over the period. All coefficients are statistically significant at the usual significance levels.

Fig. 2 shows the actual Federal funds rate and the predicted Federal funds rate from Model 1 and Model 2. Using UNEMPGAP as the measure of excess demand gives a slightly better fit to the actual Federal funds rate. Neither model predicts the drop in the Federal funds rate in the Fall Quarter of 1998. This is no surprise since at the time the Fed was lowering the Federal funds rate in response to the Russian Debt and LTCM crisis, two events that are not included in the Taylor Rule.

Models 3–8 in Table 2 (columns 4–9) report estimates of equation (2) using various measures of stock market valuation and the two measures of excess demand. In all regressions the coefficient on the price earnings ratio (*P*/*E*) and on Yardeni's measure of stock valuation model (SVM) are negative, while the coefficient on the implied equity premium (PREMIUM) is always positive. The *t*-statistics indicate that the coefficients are statistically significant at the usual levels. The results suggest that, controlling for inflation and the GDP

Table 2
Static Taylor rules, OLS estimation

	Model 1	Model 2	Model 3	Model 4	Model 5	Model 6	Model 7	Model 8
Constant: c_1	2.01 (6.04)	2.17 (8.23)	4.82 (6.43)	2.37 (6.82)	1.55 (4.98)	4.53 (7.84)	2.45 (8.83)	1.83 (7.10)
Inflation: c_2	1.56 (12.40)	1.31 (13.44)	1.16 (7.80)	1.47 (11.81)	1.12 (7.34)	0.96 (8.35)	1.22 (12.13)	1.02 (8.24)
Measure of excess demand: c_3								
CBOGAP	0.60 (9.87)	–	0.64 (11.86)	0.69 (10.16)	0.54 (9.99)	–	–	–
UNEMPGAP	–	1.53 (13.56)	–	–	–	1.58 (16.34)	1.66 (13.79)	1.40 (12.91)
Measure of stock market valuation: c_4								
P/E	–	–	−0.08 (−4.06)	–	–	−0.07 (−4.44)	–	–
SVM	–	–	–	−0.02 (−2.49)	–	–	−0.01 (−2.40)	–
PREMIUM	–	–	–	–	0.38 (4.17)	–	–	0.27 (3.42)
$\bar{R}^2$	0.80	0.88	0.85	0.82	0.85	0.91	0.89	0.90
DW	0.25	0.36	0.36	0.33	0.37	0.46	0.42	0.44

Dependent variable: Federal funds rate (mean = 5.74, variance = 1.75).
Sample: 1987:3 to 2000:2.
t-statistics in parenthesis.

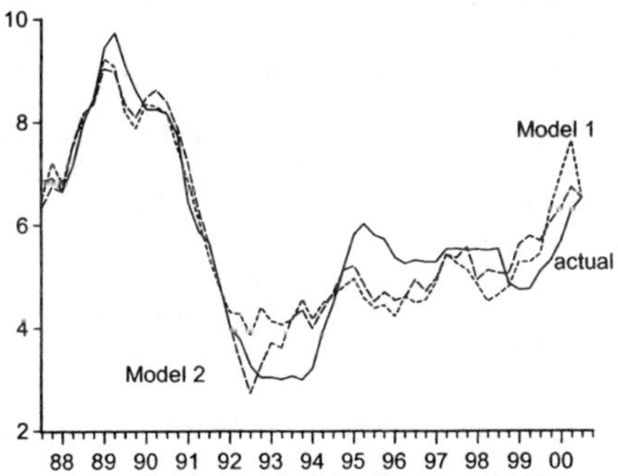

Fig. 2. Static Taylor rules: Model 1 versus 2.

gap, the Fed tended to be lowering the Federal funds rate as the market became more overvalued.

The magnitude of the response of the Fed funds rate to changes in the stock market valuation seem to be large for the P/E ratio and small for Yardeni's stock valuation model. To see this, note that estimated models 3 and 6 imply that an increase in the P/E ratio of 10 (approximately 1.5 standard deviation increase)—a reasonable magnitude over the sample—results in a decrease in the Fed funds rate of 70–80 basis points. Estimated models 4 and 7 suggest that, an increase in Yardeni's stock valuation model of 20 (an approximately 1.5 standard deviation increase) results in a decrease in the Fed funds rate from 10 to 20 basis points. Models 5 and 8 indicate that decrease in the implied equity premium by 2.2 (an approximately 1.5 standard deviation decrease) results in a decrease in the Fed funds rate by 40–50 basis points.

The inclusion of measures of stock market valuation in the static Taylor Rule in most cases reduced the magnitude of inflation coefficient (c_2). In Model 6, which uses UNEMPGAP as the measure of excess demand, including P/E as the measure of stock market overvaluation, results in unstable monetary policy that is $c_2 < 1$. This is almost the case as well for Model 8, which also uses UNEMPGAP as the measure of excess demand and PREMIUM as the measure of stock market overvaluation.

The measures of stock valuation, of course are partly endogenous, since they depend on interest rates. Thus the regression results reported in Table 2, may in part be a consequence of a simultaneity bias. To address this issue, we re-estimated Eq. (2) using instrumental variables (IV). We used zero to two lags of the growth rate of real GDP from the previous year as instruments for the measures of stock market overvaluation. We choose these instruments for two reasons: first, stock prices will be correlated to current real GDP growth if market participants forecast future earnings based on what they observe in the present. Empirically, current real GDP growth is correlated with the measures of market overvaluation, 0.23, 0.30 and −0.16 for *P*/*E*, SVM and PREMIUM, respectively. Second, changes in the Federal funds rate influence output growth with a lag (which the Fed estimates to be 12–18 months). The correlation between current real GDP growth and the level of the Federal funds rate, for the sample period 1987–2000 is −0.04. This suggests that current level of the Federal funds rate is uncorrelated with the growth rate of current and past real GDP.

Table 3 shows the estimates of Eq. (2) with the two measures of excess demand and three measures of market overvaluation. Compared with the OLS estimates, the inflation coefficient are larger and greater than 1 in all regressions implying a stable monetary policy. The coefficient estimates on the measures of excess demand do not change. The dramatic differences are with the coefficient estimates on the measures of stock market overvaluation. Using current and lagged output growth as instruments, result in statistically insignificant estimates. In four out of six cases (Models 4, 5, 6 and 8) the magnitude of the coefficients are 2–4 times smaller than the OLS estimates. For Model 7 the instrumental variables (IV) estimate of the SVM coefficient is the same as the OLS estimate. For Model 3 the IV estimate of the *P*/*E* coefficient is positive but very small. Issues of statistical significant aside, the IV estimates of Models 3 and 6 suggest that an increase in the *P*/*E* ratio of 10, controlling for inflation and excess aggregate demand, results in a change in the Federal funds rate between +3 and −20 basis points. The IV estimates of Models 4 and 7 imply that an increase in Yardeni's stock valuation model by 20, results in a decrease in the Federal funds rate by −20 basis points. The IV estimates of Models 5 and 8 imply that a decrease in the implied equity premium by 2.2 results in a decrease in the Federal funds rate by −15 to −33 basis points. So the IV estimates, except for estimated coefficients for SVM, imply a much smaller decrease in the Federal funds rate in response stock market overvaluation.

To sum up the results of Tables 2 and 3, adding a measure of stock market valuation to the "static" Taylor Rule results in a negative correlation, although statistically weak for the IV regressions, between the Federal funds rate and measures of stock market overvaluation after controlling for inflation and measures of excess aggregate demand. Taken seriously, this result indicates that the Greenspan monetary regime, rather than deflating apparent speculative bubbles, accommodated them.

Table 3
Static Taylor rules, IV estimation

	Model 3	Model 4	Model 5	Model 6	Model 7	Model 8
Constant: c_1	1.91 (1.50)	2.19 (5.39)	1.83 (5.07)	2.94 (2.44)	2.28 (6.29)	2.08 (6.61)
Inflation: c_2	1.58 (7.20)	1.52 (11.19)	1.39 (6.53)	1.20 (6.04)	1.27 (10.07)	1.23 (6.56)
Measure of excess demand: c_3						
CBOGAP	0.60 (9.33)	0.64 (7.30)	0.58 (9.55)	–	–	–
UNEMPGAP	–	–	–	1.55 (14.43)	1.59 (9.85)	1.50 (11.58)
Measure of stock market valuation: c_4						
P/*E*	0.003 (0.085)	–	–	−0.02 (−0.66)	–	–
SVM	–	−0.01 (−0.71)	–	–	−0.01 (−0.45)	–
PREMIUM	–	–	0.15 (0.97)	–	–	0.07 (0.48)
$\bar{R}^2$	0.81	0.82	0.83	0.89	0.88	0.88
DW	0.25	0.33	0.28	0.40	0.38	0.37

Instruments: Inflation, CBOGAP (Models 3–5), UNEMPGAP (Models 6–8), Growth rate of real GDP from year ago (lags 0–2).
Dependent variable: Federal funds rate (mean = 5.74, variance = 1.75).
Sample: 1987:3 to 2000:2.
t-statistics in parenthesis.

At this point some readers may be concerned about the low Durbin Watson statistic with its implication that the errors in the above regression equations are serially correlated. Following other researchers, such as Judd and Rudebusch (1998), we address this issue by estimating a "dynamic Taylor Rule".

5. Dynamic specifications

Following Judd and Rudebusch (1998) and including a target for the stock market, write the target for the nominal Federal funds rate as

$$i_t^* = \pi_t + r^* + \alpha_1(\pi_t - \pi^*) + \alpha_2 y_t + \alpha_3(\rho_t - \rho^*) \quad (3)$$

with the actual changes in the Fed funds rate following

$$\Delta i_t = \gamma_1(i_t^* - i_{t-1}) + \gamma_2 \Delta i_{t-1}, \quad (4)$$

where γ_1 measures the speed of adjustment of the actual Fed funds rate to the target. Instantaneous adjustment would imply that γ_1 is infinite. Combining Eqs. (3) and (4) results in

$$\Delta i_t = \gamma_1[\pi_t + r^* + \alpha_1(\pi_t - \pi^*) + \alpha_2 y_t + \alpha_3 y_{t-1} + \alpha_4(\rho_t - \rho^*) + \alpha_5(\rho_{t-1} - \rho^*) - i_{t-1}] + \gamma_2 \Delta i_{t-1},$$

resulting in the regression equation

$$\Delta i_t = c_1 + c_2 \Delta i_{t-1} + c_3[c_4 \pi_t + c_5 y_t + c_6 \rho_t - i_{t-1}], \quad (5)$$

where $c_1 = \gamma_1[r^* - \alpha_1 \pi^* - \alpha_3 \rho^*]$; $c_2 = \gamma_2$; $c_3 = \gamma_1$; $c_4 = 1 + \alpha_1 > 1$ if monetary policy is stable; $c_5 = \alpha_2$ and $c_6 = \alpha_3$.

Estimates of Eq. (5) for the two measures of excess demand and three measures of stock market overvaluation are reported in Table 3. The regressions errors for all models, are indicated by the Q-statistics, are serially uncorrelated. Models 9 and 10 reported in columns 2 and 3 of Table 3 report the estimate of Eq. (5) using CBOGAP and UNEMPGAP as alternative measures of excess demand without including a measure of stock market valuation. The results for Model 9 are similar to the static Model 1 in terms of the size of the parameters on inflation and the CBOGAP. Using UNEMPGAP as the measure of excess demand results in a smaller response of the Federal funds rate to inflation although monetary policy is still stable.

Fig. 3 shows the actual Federal funds rate and the predicted Federal funds rate from Models 10 and 11. The picture is very similar to that of Fig. 2. However the dynamic models, which assume the Fed adjusts the Federal funds rate gradually to the desired targeted value, estimate as one would expect, a smoother path for the Federal funds rate.

Models 11–16 (Table 4 columns 4–9) estimate equation (5) with the two alternative measures of excess demand and the three alternative measures of stock market overvaluation. In four out of six regressions monetary policy is unstable (i.e. $c_4 < 1$). This result is a bit troublesome since there seems to be a consensus in the literature that the Greenspan years have been characterized by stable monetary policy. Our regression estimates show that the use of UNEMPGAP, which is probably a more accurate measure of the real time perception of excess demand (see Evans, 1998) rather than CBOGAP, reduces the responsiveness of the Federal funds rate to inflation. Adding measures of stock market valuation lowers the response even more. This might be the consequence of a simultaneity bias.

The response of the Federal funds rate to changes in CBOGAP and the UNEMPGAP are of

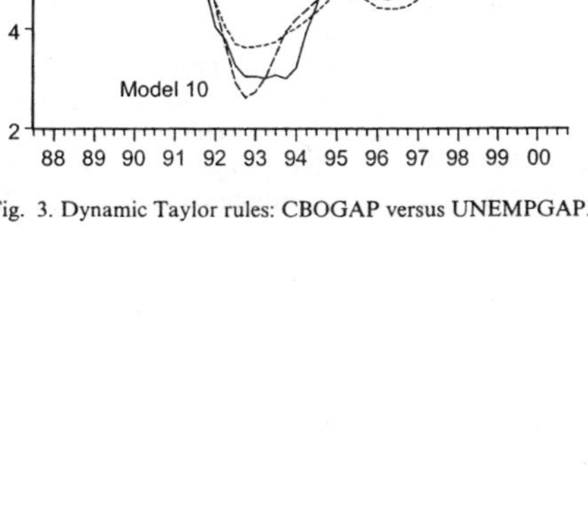

Fig. 3. Dynamic Taylor rules: CBOGAP versus UNEMPGAP.

Table 4
Dynamic Taylor rules

	Model 9	Model 10	Model 11	Model 12	Model 13	Model 14	Model 15	Model 16
Constant: c_1	0.53 (3.57)	0.71 (4.55)	2.03 (6.08)	0.62 (3.72)	0.47 (3.33)	2.09 (6.25)	0.78 (4.35)	0.67 (4.35)
Δ Fed funds$_{-1}$: c_2	0.53 (5.41)	0.52 (5.57)	0.27 (2.86)	0.48 (4.49)	0.38 (3.48)	0.31 (3.34)	0.50 (4.94)	0.41 (3.98)
Adjust. Parameters: c_3	0.21 (4.80)	0.28 (5.48)	0.27 (7.00)	0.23 (4.98)	0.26 (5.75)	0.35 (7.53)	0.30 (5.48)	0.32 (6.03)
Inflation: c_4	1.41 (6.49)	1.17 (7.48)	0.71 (3.28)	1.34 (6.34)	0.92 (3.74)	0.66 (3.89)	1.13 (6.89)	0.87 (4.32)
Measure of excess demand: c_5								
CBOGAP	0.73 (6.09)	–	0.84 (9.63)	0.82 (5.94)	0.68 (7.43)	–	–	–
UNEMPGAP	–	1.64 (8.44)	–	–	–	1.79 (12.48)	1.72 (7.98)	1.55 (9.06)
Measure of stock market valuation: c_6								
P/E	–	–	−0.16 (−4.68)	–	–	−0.11 (−4.48)	–	–
SVM	–	–	–	−0.02 (−1.24)	–	–	−0.01 (−0.81)	–
PREMIUM	–	–	–	–	0.46 (2.90)	–	–	0.28 (2.19)
$\bar{R}^2$	0.60	0.63	0.73	0.60	0.65	0.73	0.62	0.65
DW	1.91	1.87	1.95	1.94	1.83	1.78	1.87	1.78
Q-statistic 4 lags (Prob.)	3.37 (0.50)	3.63 (0.46)	3.85 (0.43)	3.09 (0.54)	2.82 (0.59)	1.82 (0.77)	2.95 (0.57)	2.06 (0.73)

Dependent variable: Δ Federal funds rate (mean = −0.01, variance = 0.45).
Sample: 1987:3 to 2000:2.
t-statistics in parenthesis.

similar magnitude and expected sign as in the estimates of the static Taylor rules and suggests that the FOMC increases the Federal funds rate in respond to increases in excess aggregate demand. As with the static regressions, the coefficients of *P/E* and SVM are consistently negative and of PREMIUM consistently positive. The magnitude of the coefficient on *P/E* is 1.5–2 times larger than in the static regressions. The magnitude on the coefficient on SVM is the same as in the static regression, however, it is no longer statistically significant at the usual levels. The coefficients on PREMIUM are roughly the same in the dynamic regressions as in the static regressions.

Next we re-estimated Eq. (5) using current and past real GDP as instruments for the measures of stock market valuation to attempt to account for the possibility of the valuation measures being endogenous in Eq. (5). The results are reported in Table 5. The estimated coefficients on inflation using instrumental variables imply monetary policy is more likely to have been stable during the sample period. The inflation coefficients are larger than the OLS results and greater than one in four out of six models. The estimated response of the Federal funds rate to measures of excess demand is the same for IV and OLS estimates.

In Models 11 and 14, the estimated coefficients on *P/E* ratio are similar in sign and magnitude to the OLS results reported in Table 4. The coefficients are also statistically significant at standard levels and larger than the estimates in the static Taylor Rule regressions. The IV estimated coefficient on SVM in Model 12 is the same sign as the OLS estimate, 1.5 larger and still statistically insignificant. The IV estimated SVM coefficient in Model 15 is same as the OLS estimate in terms of sign, magnitude and statistical significant. The IV coefficient estimates on PREMIUM are the same sign and smaller than the OLS estimates: for Model 14 the OLS estimates are 1.3 times larger and for Model 16, the OLS estimates are three times larger. While the OLS estimates are statistically significant at the standard levels for Models 14 and 16, the IV estimates are not.

Note that the estimated dynamic regressions reported in Tables 4 and 5 are similar to the results of the static regressions reported in Table 2 and 3. With the exception of one regression,

Table 5
Dynamic Taylor rules, IV estimation

	Model 11	Model 12	Model 13	Model 14	Model 15	Model 16
Constant: c_1	1.40 (2.77)	0.70 (3.57)	0.48 (3.34)	2.36 (2.87)	0.78 (2.98)	0.70 (4.32)
Δ Fedfunds$_{-1}$: c_2	0.38 (3.23)	0.43 (3.62)	0.41 (3.08)	0.27 (1.77)	0.50 (3.96)	0.49 (3.47)
Adjust. Parameters: c_3	0.25 (5.82)	0.24 (4.94)	0.25 (4.81)	0.36 (6.27)	0.30 (4.79)	0.29 (4.85)
Inflation: c_4	0.96 (3.38)	1.30 (6.06)	1.02 (2.99)	0.58 (2.10)	1.13 (5.52)	1.08 (3.09)
Measure of excess demand: c_5						
CBOGAP	0.80 (7.98)	0.88 (5.60)	0.69 (6.90)			–
UNEMPGAP				1.81 (11.77)	1.72 (5.64)	1.61 (7.69)
Measure of stock market valuation: c_6						
P/E	−0.10 (−1.96)			−0.13 (−2.43)		
SVM		−0.03 (−1.46)			−0.01 (−0.33)	–
PREMIUM			0.36 (1.34)			0.09 (0.29)
$\bar{R}^2$	0.71	0.60	0.64	0.73	0.62	0.63
DW	2.05	1.90	1.88	1.65	1.87	1.86
Q-statistic 4 lags (Prob)	0.05 (0.83)	0.10 (0.75)	0.11 (0.74)	1.09 (0.30)	0.20 (0.65)	0.23 (0.63)

Instruments: Δ Fedfunds$_{-1}$, Fedfunds$_{-1}$, Inflation, CBOGAP (Models 11–13), UNEMPGAP (Models 14–16), Growth rate of real GDP from year ago (lags 0–2).
Dependent variable: Δ Federal funds rate (mean = −0.01, variance = 0.45).
Sample: 1987:3 to 2000:2.
t-statistics in parenthesis.

adding a measure of stock market valuation to either the static or dynamic Taylor Rule, after controlling for inflation and measures of excess aggregate demand, results in a negative correlation between the Federal funds rate and measures of stock market overvaluation. This finding suggests that the Greenspan Fed did not systematically try to deflate apparent speculative bubble in the late 1990s stock market. Instead one could argue, that the Fed, in the mid and late 1990s, accommodated the growing stock market bubble.

6. Conclusions

How did the Federal Reserve Bank react to the stock market bubble of the late 1990s? At the Symposium sponsored by the Federal Reserve Bank of Kansas City in Jackson Hole, Wyoming on August 30, 2002, Chairman Alan Greenspan (2002) remarked that economists do not currently have a way to measure a stock market bubble convincingly. Thus in the absence of such a measure, it was difficult for the Fed to justify, with some degree of certainty, a preemptive tightening that would likely be necessary to neutralize such a bubble. Furthermore, Mr. Greenspan (2002) has also argued that even if the Fed had certainty about the existence of a bubble, neutralizing it could not be achieved without considerable increases in the Fed funds rate and potentially significant damage to the real economy. From these remarks of Mr. Greenspan, it is reasonable to conclude that the Fed did not actually react to the stock market bubble. This paper, extends the Taylor Rule methodology to include measures of stock market overvaluations and concludes that the Fed not only avoided neutralizing the bubble but may, probably unintentionally, have contributed to the growth of the stock market bubble.

Acknowledgements

An earlier version of this paper was presented at the XXX Meeting of the Euro Working Group on Financial Modelling, May 2–4, 2002 in Capri,

ITALY. We are thankful to Professor Rita D'Ecclesia for the invitation to participate and to numerous conference participants for useful comments. We also wish to thank Charles Evans and George Kaufman for useful comments on an earlier draft.

References

Bernanke, B., Gertler, M., 1999. Monetary policy and asset price volatility, new challenges for monetary policy, Federal Reserve Bank of Kansas City.

Bernanke, B., Gertler, M., 2001. Should central banks respond to movements in asset prices? American Economic Review: Papers and Proceedings 91, 253–257.

Blanchard, O., 2000. Bubbles, liquidity traps, and monetary policy: Comments on Jinushi et al., and on Bernanke. Working paper, Department of Economics, MIT.

Cecchetti, S., 1998. Policy rules and targets: Framing the Central Banker's problem. Economic Policy Review of the Federal Reserve Bank of New York, June, pp. 1–14.

Cecchetti, S., Genber, H., Lipsky, J., Wadhwani, S., 2000. Asset Prices and Central Bank Policy. International Center for Monetary and Banking Studies, London.

Cecchetti, S., Krause, S., 2000. Financial structure, macroeconomic stability and monetary policy. In: Paper Presented at the XII Symposium of Moneda y Credito, Madrid, Spain.

Evans, C., 1998. Real-time Taylor rules and the federal funds futures market, economic perspectives. Federal Reserve Bank of Chicago, 3rd Quarter, pp. 44–55.

Greenspan, A., 2002. Remarks on "Economic Volatility" at the "Rethinking Stabilization Policy". In: Symposium Sponsored by the Federal Reserve Bank of Kansas City, Jackson Hole, Wyoming, August 29–31, 2002. Available from <http://www.federalreserve.gov/boarddocs/speeches/2002/20020830/default.htm>.

Gordon, M.J., 1962. The Investment, Financing and Valuation of the Corporation. Irwin, Homewood, IL.

Gordon, R., 2000. Macroeconomics. Addison-Wesley/Longman, Reading, MA/New York.

Hayford, M., Malliaris, A.G., 2001. Is the federal reserve stock market bubble-neutral. In: Kaufman, G. (Ed.), Asset Price Bubbles: Implications for Monetary and Regulatory Policies. JAI Press, New York, pp. 229–243.

Judd, J.P., Rudebusch, G.D., 1998. Taylor's rule and the Fed: 1970–1997. Federal Reserve Bank of San Fransisco Economic Review 1998 (3), 3–16.

Rigobon, R., Sack, B., 2001. Measuring the reaction of monetary policy to the stock market. Working paper, Department of Economics, MIT and the Board of Governors of the Federal Reserve System.

Svensson, L.E.O., 2002. Monetary Policy and Real Stabilization. In: Presented at the Rethinking Stabilization Policy Symposium sponsored by the Federal Reserve Bank of Kansas City, Jackson Hole, Wyoming, August 29–31, 2002. Available from <http://www.kc.frb.org/Publicat/sympos/2002/pdf/Svensson.912.pdf>.

Taylor, J., 1999. A historical analysis of monetary policy rules. In: Taylor, J.B. (Ed.), Monetary Policy Rules. The University of Chicago Press, Chicago.

Taylor, J., 1993. Discretion versus policy rules in practice. In: Carnegie–Rochester Conference Series on Public Policy, vol. 15, pp. 151–200.

World Economic Outlook, International Monetary Fund, April 2000.

Yardeni, E., 2000. Fed's Stock Valuation Model, in: yardeni@yardeni.com.

MONETARY POLICY AND THE U.S. STOCK MARKET

MARC D. HAYFORD and A. G. MALLIARIS*

What is the influence of stock market valuations on monetary policy? We use a forward-looking Taylor rule model to examine if monetary policy since the 19 October 1987 stock market crash has been influenced by the valuation of the stock market. We estimate the model using revised and real-time data and find no empirical evidence that the Federal Reserve policy attempted to moderate stock market valuations during the late 1990s despite the "irrational exuberance" comments by Chairman Greenspan. Actually, the empirical evidence suggests that the Fed accommodated the high valuations of the stock market during this period. (*JEL* E52, G12)

I. INTRODUCTION

The monetary policy goals of the Federal Reserve System, as often stated in publications and testimony of Fed officials, are "price stability" and "sustainable economic growth." Recently, Fed officials and academic economists have addressed the question of whether in addition to price level stability, a central bank should also consider the stability of assets prices. As Federal Reserve Chairman Alan Greenspan (1996) asked,

> where do we draw the line on what prices matter? Certainly prices of goods and services now being produced—our basic measure of inflation—matter. But what about futures prices or more importantly prices of claims on future goods and services, like equities, real estate, or other earning assets? Is stability of these prices essential to the stability of the economy?

Greenspan (1996) answered his own question in the form of both reflections and additional questions: "But how do we know when *irrational exuberance* has unduly escalated asset values, which then become subject to unexpected and prolonged contractions as they have in Japan over the past decade? And how do we factor that assessment into monetary policy?"

In response to these statements, the academic literature has addressed both the normative question "should monetary policy react to asset bubbles?" as well as the positive question "does monetary policy react to asset bubbles?" After a review of the academic literature in section II, this article focuses on the positive question of whether monetary policy since 1987 has been influenced by the high valuation of the stock market. As mentioned earlier, Greenspan (1996) indicated he believed that soaring stock prices might create imbalances that would threaten the goals of general price level stability and sustainable economic growth. Such warnings, however, were followed by speeches by Greenspan (1998, 1999a, 1999b, 2002b), in which due to the

*Earlier versions of this article were presented at an economics seminar at the Brown Bag Macroeconomics Seminar of the Federal Reserve Bank of Chicago; at the European Financial Management Association Meetings in Lugano, Switzerland; the Euro Financial Modeling Group in Capri, Italy; and at the University of Northern Illinois. We are grateful to seminar and conference participants for their numerous helpful suggestions. We are especially thankful to Philip Bartholomew, Elijah Brewer, Marsha Courchane, Charles Evans, Lars Hansen, George Kaufman, James Moser, and Francois Velde for their valuable comments that assisted us in improving our work. We are also grateful to two anonymous referees of *Economic Inquiry* who made several valuable suggestions that improved the methodology of our article. All remaining errors are our own responsibility.

Hayford: Associate Professor of Economics, Loyola University Chicago, 820 N Michigan Ave., Chicago, IL 60611. Phone 1-312-915-6073, Fax 1-312-915-8508, E-mail mhayfor@luc.edu

Malliaris: Professor of Economics and Finance, Loyola University Chicago, 820 N Michigan Ave., Chicago, IL 60611. Phone 1-312-615-6063, Fax 1-312-915-8508, E-mail tmallia@luc.edu

ABBREVIATIONS

FOMC: Federal Open Market Committee
GDP: Gross Domestic Product
GMM: General Method of Moments
P/E: Price/Earnings
S&P: Standard & Poors
VAR: Vector Autoregressive

Economic Inquiry
(ISSN 0095-2583)
Vol. 42, No. 3, July 2004, 387–401

DOI: 10.1093/ei/cbh068

high rates of productivity of the "new economy," Greenspan hinted that share prices might not be overvalued after all. Beyond issues of a "new economy" and high levels of productivity due to information technologies, Greenspan (2002a) also reflected that lower risk premiums might rationalize higher stock market valuations than in the past.

Greenspan's views about share prices clearly evolved over time and show his intellectual interest in the implications of stock market valuations for monetary policy. It is natural to ask: Did the chairman's concerns about the stock market actually influence monetary policy decisions? Put differently, considering the two competing assessments made by the chairman of irrational exuberance (and its logical implication that stock market prices were unsustainably high) or the new economy (justifying high share prices because of high productivity gains and low inflation), it is important to clarify which view ultimately guided monetary policy.

It is the purpose of this article to present empirical evidence that indicates that the new economy rhetoric won out over concerns about irrational exuberance. In section III we use the price/earnings ratio as a signal of potential overvaluation, and in section IV we give a brief overview of the evidence from the FOMC minutes to ground our empirical analysis on the Fed's deliberations. In section V, we present and estimate a forward-looking Taylor rule model using revised and real-time data. In section VI we revisit the question of Fed policy in response to stock market overvaluation using the vector autoregressive (VAR) methodology. The last section summarizes our conclusions.

II. NORMATIVE VERSUS POSITIVE ISSUES

How should monetary policy react to a stock market bubble? Using the language of control theory, we can ask the more technical question: Should monetary policy target the level of equity prices, measured by an index such as the Standard & Poor (S&P) 500 Index? Most economists consider these normative questions as meaningless because there is little agreement on how to recognize a bubble ex ante. Defining a bubble as the difference between the actual market price and the fundamental price is a relative statement that becomes operational provided one could compute the fundamental price. If the fundamental price cannot be computed, then one cannot talk about the existence and the magnitude of the bubble. Shiller (1989) and, more recently, Salge (1997) offer an extensive review of the literature on market volatility and discuss both the theoretical and empirical issues associated with bubbles.

At the risk of oversimplification, one finding of this literature is that bubbles are easier to identify ex post rather than ex ante. For example, it is difficult to find economists who would argue today that the stock market increase in Japan in the late 1980s or the NASDAQ increase in the late 1990s reflected only fundamentals. The fact that in both cases these markets declined significantly is ex post evidence of the existence of a bubble, yet there was no consensus among economists prior to its dramatic collapse that a bubble was present in these two markets.

If we cannot ascertain the existence of a bubble, how can we decide what should the reaction of the monetary policy be in regard to it? One way to simplify the analysis is to follow Blanchard (2000) who, for the sake of argument, assumes that the central bank recognizes that there is a bubble in the stock market. In other words, suppose the Fed discerns that the current price of stocks exceeds fundamentals and also recognizes the bubble will eventually collapse and stock prices will return to fundamentals. How should monetary policy respond under these assumptions?

Economists have proposed two answers. One group, represented by Bernanke and Gertler (1999, 2001), argues that monetary policy that targets the rate of inflation is best, independent of whether a bubble exists or not. Put differently, the existence of a bubble should not cause the central bank to change its policy of targeting inflation. Another group, represented by Cecchetti (1998), argues that the central bank can improve economic performance by paying attention to asset prices. Next, we present a brief elaboration of these arguments.

Bernanke and Gertler (1999) argue that a central bank dedicated to a policy of flexible inflation targeting should pay little attention to asset inflation because a proper setting of interest rates to achieve the desired inflation target will also stabilize asset prices. These authors (1999, 18) "view price stability and financial stability as highly complementary and mutually consistent objectives to be pursued within a unified policy framework." Elsewhere they (1999, 18) state that "trying to stabilize asset prices *per se* is problematic for a variety of reasons, not the least of which is that it is nearly impossible to know for sure whether a given change in asset values results from fundamental factors, non-fundamental factors, or both."

The sufficiency of targeting inflation can be argued as follows. Keeping both current and expected inflation at a constant level is equivalent to maintaining output at its natural level. The existence of a bubble can either cause no change in aggregate demand or cause it to increase because of the wealth effect or some other reason. In either case, the monetary rule of inflation targeting guides the central bank to act appropriately, either by doing nothing in the case the bubble causes no change in aggregate demand or by tightening in the case the bubble increases aggregate demand via the wealth effect.

Blanchard (2000) finds the analysis of Bernanke and Gertler powerful but also argues that their model works provided the bubble affects some components of spending more than others. For example, if the bubble increases consumption, via the wealth effect, that puts pressure on inflation, then Fed tightening guided by inflation targeting can be optimal. But what if the bubble causes publicly traded firms, whose equity has increased because of the bubble, to increase their investment? If investment depends on the bubble, among other economic factors, then with output at its natural level, an increase in investment can occur only by an equivalent decrease in consumption. Hence, although inflation targeting keeps inflation constant, the composition of output tilts more in favor of investment, and thus the bubble may cause excessive capital accumulation. When ultimately the bubble bursts, this excessive capital accumulation deters firms from investment and postpones economic growth. Thus, inflation targeting does not address issues related to the impact of a bubble on the composition of output and the long-run impact of the bubble on investment, capital accumulation, and growth.

Others who have also evaluated the model of Bernanke and Gertler (1999) are Bordo and Jeanne (2001). They argue that asset price reversals can be very costly in terms of declining output, as in the United States in the early 1930s and Japan during the 1990s. They go further to argue that traditional monetary policy may be unable to correct such asset price disturbances, and therefore monetary policy should attempt primarily to discourage the emergence and growth of bubbles, rather than act after they burst in an effort to stabilize the economy.

Mishkin (2000) also acknowledges that the most serious economic downturns are often associated with financial instability but does not discuss specifically the impact of a stock market crash on the economy. The implication of Mishkin's argument is that monetary policy should attempt to avoid financial instabilities such as the 1929 U.S. stock market crash or the Japanese stock market decline of the 1990s. However, Cogley (1999) argues that deliberate attempts to puncture asset price bubbles may destabilize the economy and thus monetary policy may generate instabilities that are similar to the ones arising from the burst of a bubble.

Bullard and Schaling (2002) use a simple macroeconomic model to study the implications of targeting inflation, output, and equity prices. They show that a policy that reacts to equity price increases can be counterproductive because it can interfere with the policy maker's ability to minimize inflation and output variability. They also show that under certain conditions, a policy of targeting stock market prices can lead to an indeterminate rational expectations equilibrium and hence a more unpredictable volatility than would be achieved if asset prices were ignored. They conclude that targeting the stock market degrades the effectiveness of monetary policy and can do real damage, and such damage could be avoided by concentrating on inflation and output targeting. Thus, monetary policy should ignore the stock market.

Goodfriend (2003) reaches a similar conclusion. He argues that the direction and size of the unconditional correlation between asset price movements and real short-term interest rates is not stable. Therefore, in principle, the appropriate direction and size of the interest rate response to equity prices would be difficult to discern in practice. Finally, Filardo (2000, 2001) also explores the role of monetary policy in an economy with asset bubbles by developing a small-scale macroeconomic model and running various simulations. He finds that if there is no uncertainty about the role of asset prices in determining output and inflation, then monetary policy should respond to asset prices. However, if the monetary authority is sufficiently uncertain about the macroeconomic consequences of stock prices, then it is preferable for monetary policy to remain neutral.

In contrast to Bernanke and Getler and the other authors who recommend that monetary policy should not respond to stock market bubbles, it was mentioned earlier that Cecchetti (1998) argues that monetary policy should take into account asset prices. The logic behind his argument is the idea that the policy maker must often trade off variability in output for variability in prices because it is generally not possible to stabilize both. More specifically, Cecchetti et al. (2000) argue that central bankers can improve economic performance by paying attention to asset prices. Cecchetti and Krause (2000) examine in detail the connection between the dramatic changes in the financial structure (a concept much more general than stable asset prices) of numerous countries and conclude that these changes have contributed to the stability of both economic growth and low inflation.

In a recent paper, Cecchetti et al. (2003) revisit the same question and argue that there are sound theoretical reasons for an inflation-targeting monetary policy to improve the economy's performance by reacting to asset price misalignments. They emphasize that policy reactions to stock price bubbles must be qualitatively different from reactions to stock price increases driven by fundamentals, such as increases in productivity and earnings. The concern with stock market bubbles is both their inevitable collapse but also the encouragement of overinvestment and excessive borrowing by households and firms before the bubble collapses. As a result, bubbles can cause, both during their rapid growth and also after their collapse, serious economic imbalances that can generate either inflation or deflation. One reason that Cecchetti et al. (2003) support the opposite conclusion than the other authors is because they explore a larger family of policy reaction functions.

What is the tentative answer to the normative question: Should monetary policy react to an asset bubble? The answer depends on the timing of the bubble. There is strong consensus that after the bubble bursts, monetary policy should always act to stabilize the economy. However, before the collapse of the asset bubble, there is no consensus on what monetary policy should do because it is not clear how to identify a bubble, estimate its size, and predict when it will burst. Governor Bernanke (2002) adds that "even putting aside the great difficulty of identifying bubbles in asset prices, monetary policy cannot be directed finely enough to guide asset prices without risking severe collateral damage to the economy."

Next, we move on from the normative to the positive question: What does monetary policy do in response to asset prices. Tarhan (1995) finds evidence that the Fed affects asset prices. Filardo (2000) carefully reviews the literature on including asset prices in inflation measures and finds little evidence that by paying attention to asset prices the Fed would reliably improve economic stability. Fair (2000) uses a macroeconomic model to offer quantitative evidence that the Fed may be unable to correct asset price disturbances. Fair shows that the negative effects from the loss of wealth following a stock market crash dominate the positive effects from the Fed lowering interest rates immediately after such a crash.

Rigobon and Sack (2003) use an identification technique based on the heteroscedasticity of stock market returns to identify the reaction of monetary policy to the stock market. They find that monetary policy reacts significantly to stock market movements, with a 5 percent rise (fall) in the S&P 500 Index increasing the likelihood of a 25-basis-point tightening (easing) by about half. The authors decompose both daily and weekly movements in interest rates and stock prices from approximately 1985 to 1999. Their results suggest that stock market movements have a significant impact on short-term interest rates, driving them in the same direction as the change in stock prices. The authors attribute this response to the anticipated reaction of monetary policy to stock market increases. They acknowledge that this interpretation should be taken a bit cautiously. Hayford and Malliaris (2001, 2004) also empirically investigate how the Fed has responded to stock prices using quarterly data and conclude that the Fed was not bubble-neutral.

In contrast to the above-cited literature, this article takes three approaches to answering the positive question: Has monetary policy during the Greenspan Fed been stock market–neutral? Our first approach is to the review of the minutes of the FOMC meetings. This is the closest we can come to directly asking the FOMC members if the stock market influences their decision

FIGURE 1
P/E Ratio, S&P 500

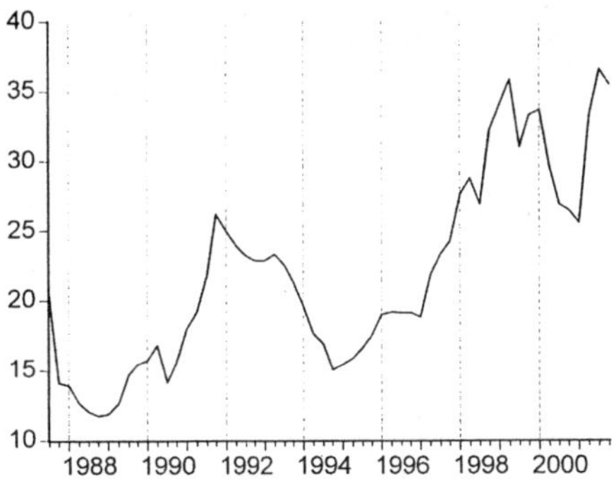

with respect to the target for the Fed funds rate and how. Our second approach is to augment Clarida et al.'s (2000) forward-looking Taylor rule with a measure of stock market valuation and estimate the rule using both revised and real-time data. Finally, we estimate a VAR model to address the question of whether the Fed set the Fed funds rate in response to the stock market. A brief summary and its major findings are presented in the last section.

III. MEASURING STOCK MARKET VALUATION

We use the S&P 500 price/earnings (P/E) ratio in addressing the question of whether monetary policy has responded to stock market overvaluation. A P/E ratio above its historic average is often used to signal a potential overvaluation. Shen (2000) finds strong historical evidence that disappointing stock market performance follows high price-earnings ratios. Figure 1 shows the P/E ratio from 1987:3 to 2001:4. The mean of the S&P 500 P/E ratio for the period 1948 to 1993 is about 14. Hence, by historical standards, a P/E ratio in excess of 14 would indicate a potentially overvalued market. Comparing the P/E ratio to its historical average indicates the stock market was overvalued prior to the 1987 crash and that from 1996 to 2001 the market was overvalued also.

IV. EVIDENCE FROM FOMC MINUTES

Our first approach in addressing whether monetary policy during the Greenspan period was influenced by the stock market is to the review of the minutes of the FOMC meetings. The minutes of the FOMC meetings are available on the Federal Reserve Board's Web site six weeks after each meeting. The minutes clearly show that sometimes the Fed does consider the stock market when determining the stance of monetary policy. For example, the minutes of the FOMC meeting on 3 November 1987, the first meeting after the October 1987 stock market crash, document the fact that the Fed increased bank reserves in response to the decline in the stock market. The concern of the members of the FOMC was the fragility of financial markets in the wake of the crash and the potential negative wealth effect on aggregate demand. From 1988 to September 1993, the minutes show little discussion of the stock market other than to mention what happened to stock prices in the inter-meeting periods. Table 1 provides a rough summary of mentions of the stock market in the FOMC minutes from 1993 to January 2002. The second column of Table 1 gives the number of meetings at which FOMC members expressed concern about the potential overvaluation of the stock market. For example in 1996, in four out of eight meetings, members expressed such a concern that is consistent with Greenspan giving his irrational exuberance speech in December 1996. The third column gives the number of meetings where the FOMC minutes mention the stock market in the context of its wealth effect on consumption and/or its effect on the cost of capital. From 1998 to 2000 the stock market wealth effect was in the minutes of every meeting. The last column in Table 1 gives the number of meetings where the minutes report concern about the reaction of the stock market to monetary policy.

A careful reading of the minutes suggests that the central goals of monetary policy are price stability and sustainable economic growth. Furthermore, the minutes suggest that the stock market is considered to the extent that members of the FOMC feel that its overvaluation may influence aggregate demand and hence output and inflation. Consistent with a speech given by Federal Reserve Board Governor Gramlich (2001), there is no evidence from the minutes that the FOMC has an implicit target for the stock market independent of the FOMC goals for inflation and growth. However, the FOMC minutes suggest that monetary policy may respond to the stock

TABLE 1
Summary of Discussion of Stock Market in FOMC Meetings

Year	Concern about Value of Stock Market or Possible Correction	Concern or Discussion of Effect of Stock Market on Aggregate Demand	Concern or Discussion of Stock Market as a Constraint on Monetary Policy
1993	1	1	1
1994		6	
1995		7	
1996	4	5	
1997	2	4	
1998	1	8	1
1999	2	8	
2000	2	8	
2001		8	

market indirectly through the wealth effect of the stock market on aggregate demand.

V. FORWARD-LOOKING TAYLOR RULE EVIDENCE

In our second approach to the question of whether monetary policy has systematically responded to the stock market, we augment Clarida et al.'s (2000) forward-looking Taylor (1993) monetary policy rule with a target for the stock market:

$$(1)\quad i_t^* = \pi^* + r^* + \alpha_1\left[E(\pi_{t,k}|\Omega_t) - \pi^*\right] + \alpha_2 E(y_{t,q}|\Omega_t) + \alpha_3[E(\rho_{t,v}|\Omega_t) - \rho^*],$$

where i^* is the target Federal funds rate; π^* is the target inflation rate; r^* is the "natural" real interest rate; $E(\cdot|\Omega_t)$ is the expectations operator, conditioned on the information set of the Fed at time t, Ω_t; $\pi_{t,k}$ is the rate of inflation from t to $t+k$; $y_{t,q}$ is the average excess demand from t to $t+q$; $\rho_{t,v}$ is the average P/E ratio from t to $t+v$; and ρ^* is the target P/E ratio. This forward-looking policy rule implies that the Fed, based on expectations of future inflation, output, and potential output, sets the Federal funds rate preemptively to hit a target inflation rate and to set real gross domestic product (GDP) equal to potential GDP. Monetary policy is stable, that is, it offsets increases in inflation by increasing the real Fed funds rate, if $\alpha_1 > 1$. If the goals of monetary policy include systematically influencing the stock market, the Fed funds rate will be set to make the expected value of the P/E ratio, $E(\rho_{t,v}|\Omega_t)$, equal to its target value ρ^*. Presumably the target value for the P/E ratio would be an estimate of what the P/E ratio should be, based on economic fundamentals. A monetary policy aimed at reducing an apparent bubble, $E(\rho_{t,v}|\Omega_t) > \rho^*$, would increase the Fed funds rate, implying $\alpha_3 > 0$. However, if monetary policy contributes or accommodates a stock market bubble, then $\alpha_3 \leq 0$.

The actual Fed funds rate is assumed to adjust dynamically to the target Fed funds rate according to

$$(2)\quad i_t = \lambda i_{t-1} + (1-\lambda) i_t^* + \mu_t,$$

where $0 \leq \lambda < 1$ is the adjustment parameter and μ_t is a zero mean exogenous shock to the nominal Federal funds rate. If $\lambda = 0$ then the Fed funds adjusts instantaneously to the target Fed funds rate.

Combining equations (1) and (2) results in the regression equation:

$$i_t = (1-\lambda)\{\pi^* + r^* + \alpha_1\left[E(\pi_{t,k}|\Omega_t) - \pi^*\right] + \alpha_2 E(y_{t,q}|\Omega_t) + \alpha_3\left[E(\rho_{t,v}|\Omega_t) - \rho^*\right]\} + \lambda i_{t-1} + \mu_t$$

or

$$(3)\quad i_t = \alpha_0 + \lambda i_{t-1} + (1-\lambda)\alpha_1 \pi_{t,k} + (1-\lambda)\alpha_2 y_{t,q} + (1-\lambda)\alpha_3 \rho_{t,v} + \varepsilon_t,$$

where $\alpha_0 = (1-\lambda)(r^* + (1-\alpha_1)\pi^* - \alpha_3\rho^*)$ and $\varepsilon_t = -(1-\lambda)\{\alpha_1[\pi_{t,k} - E(\pi_{t,k}|\Omega_t)] + \alpha_2[y_{t,q} - E(y_{t,q}|\Omega_t)] + \alpha_3[\rho_{t,v} - E(\rho_{t,v}|\Omega_t)]\} + \mu_t$. Equation (3) is estimated using the general method of moments (GMM) as in Hansen (1982). The error term in equation (3), ε_t, is composed partly of forecast errors and hence is orthogonal to information known at time t, that is, $E(\varepsilon_t|\Omega_t) = 0$. Therefore, the information set, Ω_t, plays the role of instruments in the estimation of equation (3). Also according to the model, ε_t will be serially correlated and follow an MA process with order $= \max(k,q,v) - 1$. In the estimation, k was set equal to either 1 or 4, q equal to 1 or 2, and v equal to 1. To account for possible serially correlated errors, an autocorrelation consistent covariance matrix is used as a weighting matrix in the GMM estimation.

We estimated equation (3) using both revised data, as done by Clarida et al.'s (2000) and real-time data, following Orphanides (1998), Evans (1998), and others. With the exception of the P/E ratio, the revised data for inflation, unemployment, real GDP, and the Fed funds rate are from the Federal Reserve Bank of St. Louis, FRED data set. The S&P 500 P/E ratio is obtained from Standard and Poor's.

In this article, we use two alternative measures of excess demand: the GDP gap and the unemployment gap. Following Clarida et al.'s (2000) and using revised data, the GDP gap is calculated as the detrended log of real GDP. We calculated trend real GDP as the fitted value from a regression of the log of real GDP on a constant, time trend, and time trend squared. The output gap is calculated as log of real GDP minus the log of the trend real GDP. The unemployment gap is measured as the detrended unemployment rate. The trend unemployment rate was estimated as the fitted values from regressing unemployment on a constant, time trend, and time trend squared. The unemployment gap was then calculated as the trend rate of unemployment minus the actual unemployment rate. The inflation rate is calculated using the revised data for the GDP deflator.

The real-time data for the GDP deflator, unemployment, and real GDP are from the real-time data set maintained by the Federal Reserve Bank of Philadelphia. Croushore and Stark (2001) describe this data set. In general, data on economic variables become available with a lag and are subject to revision. At any point in time there is a data set on past economic activity. This data set changes as time passes and new data are added and old data are revised. Using real-time data in estimating equation (3) allows us to use data that is closer to what was available to monetary policy makers at the time they made decisions than when we use the latest revised data. Following Croushore and Stark (2001) we use the term *vintage* to refer to the data set that was available at a particular date. For 1987 to 2002 the Philadelphia Fed has 60 vintage data sets, one for each quarter. We use a left subscript on variable names to denote the *vintage* of the data. For example, ${}_{t+k+1}\pi_{t,k}$ is the rate of inflation, that is, the growth rate of the GDP deflator, from t to $t+k$, for vintage data set (i.e., what was known at) $t+k+1$. The lead subscript is $t+k+1$, because the GDP deflator is known with a lag of one quarter. Hence, our real-time data for inflation from t to $t+1$, that is, one quarter ahead inflation, is denoted ${}_{t+2}\pi_{t,1}$ where $t = 1987{:}3$ to 2001:4. So for example, the real-time data set inflation rate from 1987:3 to 1987:4 is based on vintage data set of 1988:1. Our real-time data for inflation from t to $t+4$, that is, four quarters ahead inflation, is denoted ${}_{t+5}\pi_{t,4}$, for $t = 1987{:}3$ to 2001:4. Hence, the real-time data set inflation rate from 1987:3 to 1988:3 is based on vintage data set of 1988:4, and for inflation from 1987:4 to 1988:4 it is based on the vintage data set of 1989:1, and so on.

To construct real-time measures of the GDP gap, first we calculated trend real GDP as the fitted values from a regression of the log of real GDP on a time trend and time trend squared for each of the 60 vintages of the real-time data sets from 1987:3 to 2001:4. The output gap for each vintage data set, for $q = 1$ or 2 was then calculated as log of real GDP minus the log of the trend real GDP for each vintage. A real-time data set for the output gap was constructed as the most recent estimate for the most recent vintage, that is, ${}_{t+2}y_{t,1}$ and ${}_{t+3}y_{t,2}$, for $t = 1987{:}3$ to 2001:4. A similar procedure was followed in constructing the real-time unemployment gap.

In equation (3) the future values of inflation and excess demand are used as proxies for their expected values. When equation (3) is estimated using real-time data, the first vintage for which the future inflation rate, the output, and unemployment gap can be calculated is used as the proxy for the expected value.

Table 2 gives the summary statistics for both the revised and real-time data sets. The summary statistics for inflation are similar for both real-time and revised data. The big differences occur with measures of the output gap and the unemployment gap. This finding is consistent with that found by other researchers, such as

TABLE 2
Variable Definitions and Sample Statistics

i_t = Federal funds rate at time t.
$\rho_{t,1}$ = average P/E ratio from t to $t+1$.
For the variables below, the data is either revised or real-time:
$\pi_{t,1}$ = inflation from t to $t+1$.
$\pi_{t,4}$ = inflation from t to $t+4$.
$y_{t,1}$ = either average GDP or unemployment gap from t to $t+1$.
$y_{t,2}$ = either average GDP or unemployment gap from t to $t+2$.

Sample period: 1987:3 to 2001:4

Variable	Mean	SD	Max	Min
i_t	5.70	1.71	9.72	2.99
$\rho_{t,1}$	21.72	6.77	35.96	11.75
Revised data				
$\pi_{t,1}$	2.42	1.07	4.65	−0.51
$\pi_{t,4}$	2.39	0.90	4.20	0.76
GDP gap: $y_{t,1}$	−0.12	2.28	4.14	−3.36
GDP gap: $y_{t,2}$	−0.11	2.26	4.06	−3.31
Unemployment gap: $y_{t,1}$	0.31	0.81	1.25	−1.53
Unemployment gap: $y_{t,2}$	0.31	0.80	1.25	−1.45
Real-time data				
$\pi_{t,1}$	2.37	1.20	5.46	−0.33
$\pi_{t,4}$	2.53	0.97	4.80	0.89
GDP gap: $y_{t,1}$	2.01	1.88	6.01	−1.42
GDP gap: $y_{t,2}$	1.90	1.77	5.60	−1.56
Unemployment gap: $y_{t,1}$	1.19	0.78	2.43	−0.59
Unemployment gap: $y_{t,2}$	1.17	0.72	2.53	−0.40

Orphanides (1998). With the revised data the mean gap is zero, whereas the real-time measures have positive means. The standard deviations are roughly the same for revised and real-time data estimates of excess demand.

Table 3 reports estimates of equation (3) without the P/E ratio, using the revised data, two measures of excess demand, and the different assumptions regarding how forward-looking monetary policy is. The results are consistent with Taylor (1999) and Clarida et al.'s (2000) in that monetary policy is found to be stable during this period ($\alpha_1 > 1$) and statistically significant, with the Federal funds rate estimated to increase by 1.39–2.18 percentage points for every 1-percentage-point increase in inflation. The response of the Fed funds rate to inflation is larger, if monetary policy is assumed to target inflation four rather than one quarter ahead. The coefficients for both measures of excess demand and $q = 1$ or 2 are positive ($\alpha_2 > 0$) and statistically significant, indicating that the Fed funds rate increases if the Fed expects an increase in future excess demand.

Table 4 reports the estimated parameters of equation (3) using the revised data, with the P/E ratio included as a measure of stock market valuation. Including the P/E ratio, results in coefficients on inflation that no longer consistently imply a stable monetary policy. For models 8 to 10, the inflation coefficient is statistically insignificantly different from zero, whereas for model 7 the coefficient is negative and statistically significant. The results for models 11 and 12 imply that monetary policy is stable, with the inflation coefficient greater than one and statistically significant. The coefficients on the measures of excess demand are consistent with the previous results and indicate an increase in the Fed funds rate in response to expected increases in excess demand. The coefficients of the P/E ratio are all negative and statistically significant. Estimated models 7 to 12 imply that an increase in the P/E ratio by 2 (approximately 10% of the mean value of the P/E ratio from 1987 to 2001), results in a decrease in the Fed funds rate by 30 to 66 basis points. One interpretation of these results is that during the sample period,

TABLE 3
Estimates of Equation (3), Revised Data, without the P/E Ratio (Dependent Variable: Federal Funds Rate)

	Model 1	Model 2	Model 3	Model 4	Model 5	Model 6
Constant: α_0	0.16	0.08	0.03	0.53	0.31	0.24
	(0.60)	(0.31)	(0.12)	(2.42)	(1.30)	(1.07)
Adjustment parameter: λ	0.88	0.81	0.80	0.69	0.63	0.66
	(18.16)	(14.31)	(14.41)	(9.37)	(10.53)	(11.93)
Inflation: α_1						
$\pi_{t,1}$	1.72			1.39		
	(2.15)			(5.91)		
$\pi_{t,4}$		2.10	2.18		1.77	1.82
		(5.05)	(5.24)		(8.87)	(9.01)
Measure of excess demand: α_2						
GDP gap: $y_{t,1}$	0.61	0.50				
	(2.40)	(3.59)				
GDP gap: $y_{t,2}$			0.51			
			(3.66)			
Unemployment gap: $y_{t,1}$				1.67	1.47	
				(8.07)	(8.09)	
Unemployment gap: $y_{t,2}$						1.58
						(7.61)
$\bar{R}^2$	0.92	0.93	0.93	0.92	0.94	0.94
J-statistic (probability)	0.17	0.16	0.16	0.17	0.11	0.11
	(0.70)	(0.66)	(0.64)	(0.71)	(0.37)	(0.35)

Notes: Sample: 1987:3 to 2001:4 (*t*-statistics in parentheses).

The instrument list is lags 1 to 4 of the Fed funds rate, inflation, and the appropriate measure of excess demand. The *J*-statistic tests the null hypothesis that the instruments are orthogonal to the error term of regression. The probability, in parentheses, is the probability of observing the value of the *J*-statistic if the null hypothesis is true. In all cases the *J* statistic fails to reject the null hypothesis under standard levels of significance.

controlling for inflation and excess demand, the Fed was lowering the Federal funds rate as the stock market became more overvalued.

Tables 5 and 6 report estimates of equation (3) using real-time data. Table 5 reports the models that exclude the P/E ratio. The results show that monetary policy was stable for models 14, 15, 17, and 18 that assume the Fed targets inflation four quarters ahead. The sign on the excess demand measures is positive (as expected) and statistically significant, with the exception of model 13.

Table 6 reports the estimated parameters for equation (3) using real-time data with the P/E ratio included. The coefficient on inflation is positive although less than one for models 22, 23, and 24, which suggests an unstable monetary policy. For models 19 and 21, the inflation coefficient is not statistically significantly different from zero, and for model 20 the coefficient is slightly greater than one. Responses of the Fed funds rate to measures of expected excess demand are consistently positive and statistically significant. Similar to the revised data estimates, the sign on the P/E is negative but not statistically significant for models 22 and 24. Estimated models 19 to 24 imply that an increase in the P/E ratio by 2 (approximately 10% of the mean value of the PE ratio from 1987 to 2001), results in a decrease in the Fed funds rate in the range of 8–60 basis points.

To sum up the results of Tables 4 and 6, controlling for inflation and measures of excess aggregate demand, adding the P/E ratio to a forward-looking monetary policy rule results in a negative correlation between the Fed funds rate and the P/E measure of stock market valuation. Taken seriously, this result indicates that the Greenspan monetary regime, rather than deflating apparent speculative bubbles, in the period 1987 to 2001 perhaps accommodated them. The results, at least, do not support the hypothesis that the Greenspan Fed has been systematically trying to deflate apparent speculative bubbles in the stock market. Rather, a case can be made that the FOMC at least accommodated the apparent stock market bubble in the mid- and late 1990s. Another interpretation is

TABLE 4
Estimates of Equation (3), Revised Data, with the P/E Ratio (Dependent Variable: Federal Funds Rate)

	Model 7	Model 8	Model 9	Model 10	Model 11	Model 12
Constant: α_0	5.87	4.66	4.23	2.60	1.78	1.35
	(12.18)	(13.01)	(13.01)	(8.36)	(6.27)	(4.90)
Adjustment parameter: λ	0.58	0.63	0.66	0.71	0.68	0.76
	(14.77)	(19.11)	(29.49)	(16.64)	(14.61)	(17.51)
Inflation: α_1						
$\pi_{t,1}$	−0.59			−0.28		
	(−4.19)			(−1.33)		
$\pi_{t,4}$		0.04	0.18		1.23	1.41
		(0.23)	(0.91)		(5.73)	(5.08)
Measure of excess demand: α_2						
GDP gap: $y_{t,1}$	0.91	0.87				
	(13.84)	(18.39)				
GDP gap: $y_{t,2}$			0.89			
			(19.71)			
Unemployment gap: $y_{t,1}$				1.43	2.03	
				(8.74)	(10.64)	
Unemployment gap: $y_{t,2}$						2.40
						(7.93)
P/E ratio: α_3	−0.33	−0.31	−0.32	−0.17	−0.15	−0.17
	(−12.66)	(−11.96)	(−12.55)	(−4.01)	(−6.04)	(−4.81)
$\bar{R}^2$	0.93	0.95	0.95	0.95	0.95	0.95
J-statistic (probability)	0.11	0.12	0.11	0.16	0.12	0.13
	(0.13)	(0.18)	(0.12)	(0.38)	(0.19)	(0.26)

See notes for Table 3.

TABLE 5
Estimates of Equation (3), Real-Time Data, without the P/E Ratio (Dependent Variable: Federal Funds Rate)

	Model 13	Model 14	Model 15	Model 16	Model 17	Model 18
Constant: α_0	0.33	−0.62	0.02	0.68	−0.02	−0.02
	(1.74)	(−4.15)	(0.13)	(6.94)	(−0.11)	(−0.12)
Adjustment parameter: λ	0.95	0.73	0.86	0.89	0.72	0.71
	(16.72)	(11.14)	(19.56)	(18.22)	(13.02)	(12.35)
Inflation: α_1						
$\pi_{t,1}$	−2.17			−2.28		
	(−0.60)			(−1.23)		
$\pi_{t,4}$		2.57	1.66		1.30	1.26
		(9.05)	(3.87)		(6.77)	(5.69)
Measure of excess demand: α_2						
GDP gap: $y_{t,1}$	1.84	0.62				
	(1.06)	(5.62)				
GDP gap: $y_{t,2}$			1.20			
			(3.54)			
Unemployment gap: $y_{t,1}$				5.37	2.10	
				(2.73)	(5.80)	
Unemployment gap: $y_{t,2}$						2.37
						(5.59)
$\bar{R}^2$	0.91	0.88	0.93	0.91	0.94	0.93
J-statistic (probability)	0.15	0.13	0.14	0.12	0.12	0.11
	(0.64)	(0.49)	(0.58)	(0.46)	(0.46)	(0.38)

See notes to Table 3.

TABLE 6

Estimates of Equation (3), Real-Time Data, with the P/E Ratio (Dependent Variable: Federal Funds Rate)

	Model 19	Model 20	Model 21	Model 22	Model 23	Model 24
Constant: α_0	1.82 (8.39)	1.48 (5.65)	2.05 (7.47)	0.81 (3.14)	1.36 (5.82)	0.46 (1.73)
Adjustment parameter: λ	0.84 (31.81)	0.77 (22.28)	0.77 (20.83)	0.71 (14.90)	0.58 (11.43)	0.71 (15.14)
Inflation: α_1						
$\pi_{t,1}$	−0.74 (−1.67)			0.47 (2.30)		
$\pi_{t,4}$		1.06 (4.14)	−0.39 (−1.07)		0.71 (4.50)	0.92 (3.75)
Measure of excess demand: α_2						
GDP gap: $y_{t,1}$	1.09 (6.16)	0.91 (7.27)				
GDP gap: $y_{t,2}$			0.88 (6.82)			
Unemployment gap: $y_{t,1}$				2.21 (9.59)	1.74 (10.72)	
Unemployment gap: $y_{t,2}$						2.38 (8.16)
P/E ratio: α_3	−0.30 (−4.42)	−0.24 (−5.29)	−0.20 (−3.80)	−0.05 (−1.45)	−0.06 (−3.43)	−0.04 (−1.45)
$\bar{R}^2$	0.96	0.95	0.94	0.96	0.95	0.94
J-statistic	0.24 (0.74)	0.24 (0.76)	0.26 (0.81)	0.29 (0.89)	0.28 (0.86)	0.26 (0.81)
(probability)						

See notes to Table 3.

that the "new economy" rhetoric won out in the conduct of monetary policy over concerns about "irrational exuberance."

VI. VAR SPECIFICATION

As a final approach to the question of whether monetary policy has been systematically influenced by valuation of the stock market, we estimate the following VAR model:

$$(4)\quad \begin{bmatrix} 1 & 0 & 0 & 0 \\ -a_{21} & 1 & 0 & 0 \\ -a_{31} & -a_{32} & 1 & 0 \\ -a_{41} & -a_{42} & -a_{43} & 1 \end{bmatrix} A(L) \begin{bmatrix} \pi_t \\ y_t \\ i_t \\ PE_t \end{bmatrix} X_t = \begin{bmatrix} b_{11} & 0 & 0 & 0 \\ 0 & b_{22} & 0 & 0 \\ 0 & 0 & b_{33} & 0 \\ 0 & 0 & 0 & b_{44} \end{bmatrix} \begin{bmatrix} \varepsilon_{AS,t} \\ \varepsilon_{IS,t} \\ \varepsilon_{MP,t} \\ \varepsilon_{SM,t} \end{bmatrix}$$

where the vector $[\pi, y_t, i_t, PE_t]'$, consists of inflation, a measure of the output gap, the Fed funds rate, and the P/E ratio, respectively. The $[\varepsilon_{AS,t}, \varepsilon_{AD,t}, \varepsilon_{MP,t}, \varepsilon_{SM,t}]'$ is a vector of structural disturbances that we interpret as shocks to the aggregate supply curve, the aggregate demand curve, monetary policy, and the stock market, respectively. $A(L)$ is a matrix polynomial in the lag operator L. The recursive structure of equation (4) can be given the following structural interpretation. In the first equation, the only contemporaneous variables that inflation depends on are contemporaneous shocks to inflation. This can be interpreted as a horizontal aggregate supply curve in inflation-output gap space. The second equation can be interpreted as an aggregate demand curve that depends contemporaneously on inflation. This allows shocks to inflation to have contemporaneous effects on output. The third equation represents monetary policy with the Fed funds rate depending contemporaneously on inflation and the output gap. This is Taylor's rule for monetary policy and assumes that the stock market only influences monetary policy contemporaneously through the effects it has on the inflation and output gap. The fourth

FIGURE 2
Impulse Response Functions for Equation (4), Sample 1987:3 to 2001:4

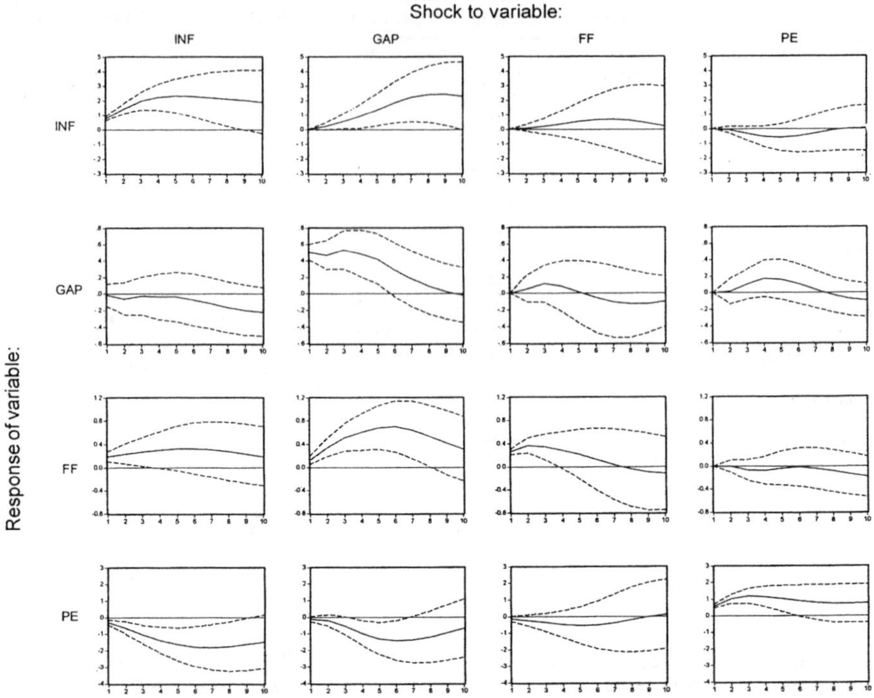

equation represents the stock market, where the P/E ratio depends on contemporaneous shocks to inflation, the output gap and the Fed funds rate, which is appealing because stock market participants presumably look at all available and relevant information when determining the appropriate price of stocks.

The VAR is estimated with four lags of each variable (i.e., $A(L)$ is of order 4) and a constant in each equation. The data definitions are the same as in section V. To summarize the VAR results, Figure 2 shows the graphs of the impulse response functions for the Greenspan sample period 1987:3 to 2001:1. For comparison with the Greenspan period, Figure 3 gives the results for the sample period 1960:1 to 1987:2.

Discussion of the Pre-Greenspan Sample Period 1960:1 to 1987:2

Figure 3, row 1 shows the responses of inflation to shocks to inflation, output gap, Fed funds rate, and the P/E ratio. Inflation responds positively to an output gap shock. The inflation response to a Fed funds shock shows what is called the price puzzle in the SVAR literature, namely, that a positive shock to the Fed funds rates results in an increase in inflation. This apparent anomalous result may be the outcome of the Fed increasing the Fed funds rate in anticipation of higher inflation. Shocks to the P/E ratio have little effect on inflation.

Row 2 shows the response the output gap to shocks to inflation, Fed funds rate, and the P/E ratio. The results are consistent with economic theory. An inflation shock causes a decline in the output gap, as does a shock to the Fed funds rate. The gap increases when there is a shock to the P/E ratio, which is consistent with a wealth effect running from the stock market to consumption and finally to output. Row 4 gives the responses of the P/E ratio to shocks to inflation,

FIGURE 3

Impulse Response Functions for Equation (4), Sample 1960:1 to 1987:2

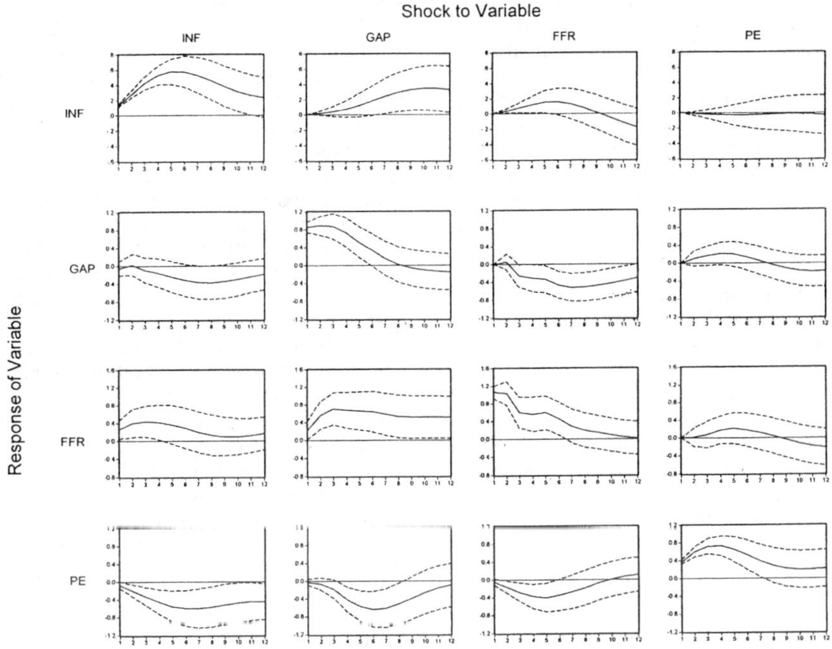

gap, and Fed funds rate. Positive shocks to inflation result in a decline in the P/E ratio. The same is true of gap shocks that are somewhat surprising. However perhaps a positive gap shock, given that it is temporary, increases current earnings more than stock prices. A positive shock to the Fed funds rate results in a decrease in the P/E ratio. In summary, from 1960 to 1987 the response of the P/E ratio to inflation gap and Fed funds rate shocks is consistent with what one would expect from economic theory.

Row 3 shows that the Fed funds rate responds positively to inflation and gap shocks that are consistent with Taylor's monetary policy rule. The Fed funds rate also responds positively to shocks to the P/E ratio, although the effects are insignificantly different from zero. These results suggest that in the sample period 1960 to 1987, monetary policy (as measured by the Fed funds rate) was responding positively to inflation and output gap shocks and also positively to P/E shocks, although the estimated effect is statistically insignificant.

Discussion of the Greenspan Sample Period 1987:3 to 2001:1

Figure 2, row 1 shows that the response of inflation to an output gap shock is similar to Figure 3. However, shocks to the Fed funds rate now have little effect on inflation (so there is no price puzzle), and shocks to the P/E result in decreases in inflation. This is consistent with the new economy interpretation that increases in the P/E ratio in the late 1990s corresponded to positive productivity shocks. Row 2, Figure 2, shows that for the Greenspan sample period the output gap seems to be responding mainly to shocks to the output gap, with shocks to inflation, Fed funds, and P/E having little impact on the output gap. Row 4 gives the response of P/E to inflation and gap shocks. The results are similar to those presented in Figure 3. In the 1987–2002 sample period, however, Fed funds shocks have little effect on the P/E ratio. Row 3, Figure 2, presents the responses of monetary policy to shocks. Both inflation and output gap shocks result in an increase in the Fed funds rate.

Interestingly and in contrast to Figure 3, the Fed funds rate responds negatively (but not statistically significantly) to a positive shock to the P/E. This result suggests that monetary policy was not systematically responding to changes in stock market valuation and thus tacitly accommodated the emerging stock bubble in the late 1990s. Similar results were obtained for impulse response functions with the variable ordering gap, inflation, Fed funds rate, and P/E ratio.

VII. CONCLUSIONS

The review of the literature does not offer a conclusive answer of whether and how the Fed should respond to asset bubbles. Stock market bubbles are very difficult to identify ex ante with sufficient certainty. Even if one could identify such a bubble, it is not clear that the Fed can deflate it without serious economic risks. Therefore, there is no consensus among economists about the optimal response of the Fed to a stock market bubble.

In contrast to the inconclusiveness of the normative question "should monetary policy respond to stock market overvaluation?" the positive question "has monetary policy responded to stock market overvaluation?" can be answered by exploring the data. This article examines empirically if monetary policy under Greenspan has been influenced by the high valuation of the stock market using three different methodologies: a review of FOMC minutes, estimates of a forward-looking Taylor rule model, and a VAR model.

The results suggest that rather than the Greenspan FOMC using the Fed funds rate policy to offset increases in the value of the P/E ratios as a measure of the stock market overvaluation, Fed funds policy has, perhaps unintentionally, on average accommodated the apparent stock market overvaluation. Greenspan's jaw boning of the stock market in the late 1990s may have been an attempt to find another policy instrument to influence the stock market in the direction of estimates of fundamentals. The econometric evidence suggests that the Fed funds rate target has largely been set in response to inflation and measures of excess demand and, at least, has not been *increased solely* to offset a potential stock market overvaluation. The augmented forward-looking Taylor rule estimated with both revised and real-time data indicates that the Fed funds rates might have been slightly higher had the Fed completely ignored the overvaluation of the market as measured by the P/E ratio of the S&P500 Index. This evidence suggests that the Fed has not taken the risk of increasing Fed funds aggressively to reduce speculation, at least during the 1995–99 period, being aware of the potential overreaction of the stock market. The data suggest that the Greenspan Fed has had no intentions, beyond the rhetoric of irrational exuberance, to actually orchestrate a rapid correction of the stock market's overvaluation because of the potential destabilizing effects of declining asset prices on the economy. Thus, one is left with the conclusion that either the Fed ultimately adopted the new economy paradigm that justified higher stock market prices due to trend increases in productivity generated by the information technology innovations or, as Greenspan (2002a) remarked, that the nonexistence of a low-risk, low-cost incremental monetary tightening rule that can reliably deflate a bubble led the Fed to accommodation.

REFERENCES

Bernanke, B. "Asset-Price 'Bubbles' and Monetary Policy." Remarks by Governor Ben S. Bernanke before the New York Chapter of the National Association for Business Economics, New York. Federal Reserve Board, 15 October 2002.

Bernanke, B., and M. Gertler. "Monetary Policy and Asset Price Volatility." *Federal Reserve Bank of Kansas City Economic Review*, 84(4), 1999, 17–51.

———. "Should Central Banks Respond to Movements in Asset Prices?" *American Economic Review: Papers and Proceedings*, 91(2), 2001, 253–57.

Blanchard, O. "Bubbles, Liquidity Traps, and Monetary Policy: Comments on Jinushi et al, and on Bernanke," in *Japan's Financial Crisis and its Parallels to the U.S. Experience*. Institute for International Economics, 2000.

Bordo, M., and O. Jeanne. "Asset Prices, Reversals, Economic Instability and Monetary Policy." Paper presented at the Allied Social Science Association Meetings in New Orleans, LA, 2001.

Bullard, J., and E. Schaling. "Why the Fed Should Ignore the Stock Market." *Review of the Federal Reserve Bank of St. Louis*, 84, 2002, 35–41.

Cecchetti, S. "Policy Rules and Targets: Framing the Central Banker's Problem." *Economic Policy Review of the Federal Reserve Bank of New York*, June 1998, 1–14.

Cecchetti, S., and S. Krause. "Financial Structure, Macroeconomic Stability and Monetary Policy." Paper presented at the XII Symposium of Moneda y Credito, 2000, Madrid, Spain.

Cecchetti, S., H. Genber, J. Lipsky, and S. Wadhwani. *Asset Prices and Central Bank Policy*. London: International Center for Monetary and Banking Studies, 2000.

Cecchetti, S., H. Genberg, and S. Wadhwami. "Asset Prices in a Flexible Inflation Targeting Framework," in *Asset Price Bubbles: The Implications of Monetary, Regulatory and International Policies*, edited by W. Hunter, G. Kaufman, and M. Pomerleano. Cambridge, MA: MIT Press 2003, 427–44.

Clarida, R., J. Gali, and M. Gertler. "Monetary Policy Rules and Macroeconomic Stability: Evidence and Some Theory." *Quarterly Journal of Economics*, February 2000, 147–80.

Cogley, T. "Should the Fed Take Deliberate Steps to Deflate Asset Price Bubbles?" *Economic Review of the Federal Reserve Bank of San Francisco*, 1999, 42–52.

Croushore, D., and T. Stark. "A Real-Time Data Set for Macroeconomists." *Journal of Econometrics*, November 2001, 111–30.

Evans, C. "Real-Time Taylor Rules and the Federal Funds Futures Market." *Economic Perspectives of the Federal Reserve Bank of Chicago*, 3rd Quarter 1998, 44–55.

Fair, R. "Fed Policy and the Effects of a Stock Market Crash on the Economy." *Business Economics*, April 2000, 7–14.

Filardo, A. "Monetary Policy and Asset Prices." *Federal Reserve Bank of Kansas City Review*, 85, 2000, 11–37.

Filardo, A. "Should Monetary Policy Respond to Asset Price Bubbles? Some Experimental Results," in *Asset Price Bubbles: Implications for Monetary Policy and Regulatory Policies*, edited by G. Kaufman. New York: JAI Press, 2001, 99–118.

Goodfriend, M. "Interest Rate Policy Should Not React Directly to Asset Prices," in *Asset Price Bubbles: The Implications of Monetary, Regulatory, and International Policies*, edited by W. Hunter, G. Kaufman, and M. Pomerleano. Cambridge, MA: MIT Press, 2003, 445–57.

Gramlich, E. M. "Asset Prices and Monetary Policy." Speech given at the New Technologies and Monetary Policy International Symposium, Bank of France, Paris. Federal Reserve Board, 30 November 2001.

Greenspan, A. "The Challenge of Central Banking in a Democratic Society." Remarks by Chairman Alan Greenspan at the Annual Dinner and Francis Boyer Lecture of the American Enterprise Institute for Public Policy Research, Washington, DC. Federal Reserve Board, 5 December 1996.

———. "Question: Is There a New Economy?" Remarks by Chairman Alan Greenspan at the Haas Annual Business Faculty Research Dialogue, University of California, Berkeley, California. Federal Reserve Board, 4 September 1998.

———. "High Tech Industry in the U.S. Economy." Testimony of Chairman Alan Greenspan before the Joint Economic Committee, U.S. Congress. Federal Reserve Board, 14 June 1999a.

———. "Information, Productivity, and Capital Investment." Remarks by Chairman Alan Greenspan before the Business Council, Boca Raton, Florida. Federal Reserve Board, 28 October 1999b.

———. "Economic Volatility." Remarks by Chairman Alan Greenspan at a Symposium Sponsored by the Federal Reserve Bank of Kansas City, Jackson Hole, Wyoming. Federal Reserve Board, 30 August 2002a.

———. "Productivity." Remarks by Chairman Alan Greenspan at the U.S. Department of Labor and American Enterprise Institute Conference, Washington, DC. Federal Reserve Board, 23 October 2002b.

Hansen, L. P. "Large Sample Properties of Generalized Method of Moments Estimators." *Econometrica*, 50(4), 1982, 1029–54.

Hayford, M., and A. G. Malliaris. "Is the Federal Reserve Stock Market Bubble-Neutral?," in *Asset Price Bubbles: Implications for Monetary Policy and Regulatory Policies*, edited by G. Kaufman. New York: JAI Press, 2001, 229–43.

———. "How Did the Fed React to the 1990s Stock Market Bubble? Evidence from an Extended Taylor Rule." *European Journal of Operational Research*, forthcoming 2004.

Mishkin, F. "What Should Central Banks Do?" *Review of the Federal Reserve Bank of St. Louis*, November/December 2000, 1–13.

Orphanides, A. "Monetary Policy Rules Based on Real-Time Data." Finance and Economics Discussion Series, Division of Research and Statistics and Monetary Affairs, Board of Governors of the Federal Reserve System, 1998.

Rigobon, R., and B. Sack. "Measuring the Reaction of Monetary Policy to the Stock Market." *Quarterly Journal of Economics*, 118(2), 2003, 639–69.

Salge, M. *Rational Bubbles*. New York: Springer, 1997.

Shen, P. "The P/E Ratio and Stock Market Performance." *Economic Review of the Federal Reserve Bank of Kansas City*, 4th Quarter 2000, 23–36.

Shiller, R. *Market Volatility*. Cambridge, MA: MIT Press, 1989.

Tarhan, V. "Does the Federal Reserve Affect Asset Prices?" *Journal of Economic Dynamics and Control*, 19(5–7), 1995, 1199–222.

Taylor, J. "Discretion versus Policy Rules in Practice." *Carnegie-Rochester Conference Series on Public Policy*, 15, 1993, 151–200.

Taylor, J. "A Historical Analysis of Monetary Policy Rules," in *Monetary Policy Rules*, edited by John B. Taylor. Chicago: University of Chicago Press, 1999, 319–48.

Crashes and Instabilities

The International Crash of October 1987: Causality Tests

A. G. Malliaris and Jorge L. Urrutia*

Abstract

The paper analyzes lead-lag relationships for six major stock market indexes: New York S&P 500, Tokyo Nikkei, London FT–30, Hong Kong Hang Seng, Singapore Straits Times, and Australia All Ordinaries, for time periods before, during, and after the October 1987 market crash. Unidirectional and bidirectional causality tests are conducted by means of the Granger methodology. Practically no lead lag relationships are found for the pre-crash and post-crash periods. However, important feedback relationships and unidirectional causality are detected for the month of the crash. There is also an increase in contemporaneous causality during and after the month of the crash. In general, our findings suggest that the October 1987 market crash probably was an international crisis of the equity markets and that it might have begun simultaneously in all the national stock markets.

I. Introduction

The international stock market crash of October 1987 has raised several important questions for financial analysts. To motivate our contribution, we identify three such questions:

- (i) What were the causes of the crash?
- (ii) What are the implications of the crash for international market efficiency?
- (iii) How and why did the stock market crash propagate internationally?

*Department of Economics and Department of Finance, respectively, Loyola University of Chicago, 820 N. Michigan Avenue, Chicago, IL 60611. Earlier versions of this paper were presented at the Financial Management Association, the Midwest Finance Association, the North America Economics and Finance Association annual meetings, and the University of Illinois at Chicago and Loyola University of Chicago Finance Workshops. The authors thank George Kaufman for valuable comments and useful expository changes and Paul Newbold for sharing his knowledge of cointegration models. The authors also thank an anonymous **JFQA** referee and **JFQA** Managing Editor Jonathan Karpoff for suggestions, Wichai Saenghirunwattana for computer assistance, and Jane Merikas for data collection. Any remaining errors are the authors' responsibility. Jorge Urrutia acknowledges the financial support provided by a Loyola University of Chicago summer research grant.

Numerous papers and commission reports have attempted to answer these and other questions.[1] Briefly, one could summarize the answers provided to the first question as belonging in two categories: macroeconomic and microeconomic causes. Among the macroeconomic causes, the existence of the twin deficits both in the federal budget and the balance of payments are cited most often. Portfolio insurance, speculative activities in derivative markets, such as futures and options markets, the introduction in the U.S. Congress of a tax bill that would have severely penalized corporate takeovers and leveraged buyouts, and the possible existence of speculative bubbles are listed as candidate microeconomic causes. In a well-documented survey paper, Roll (1989) reviews and critically evaluates some of these answers to the first question and concludes that empiricists have found it difficult to confirm the validity of any of these causes.

Since the first question is so difficult to answer, what can be said about the second? Efficiency in the conventional sense means that security prices, at any time, discount all information then publicly available about subsequent cash flows. This notion of market efficiency has been extended to international markets, whereby world stock market prices reflect all current information of world economic activity. Because the world markets received no obvious new information in the days immediately preceding the October 19, 1987, international crash, the academic community is challenged to consider the implications of such a crash to the notion of market efficiency. Friedman (1990) surveys some 50 papers that study U.S. market efficiency. Again, the evidence is mixed. There are numerous approaches that attack market efficiency, but there are also attempts to reconcile observed patterns of stock returns with standard notions of efficient markets.

The purpose of this paper is to analyze the third question. More specifically, we provide statistical evidence regarding the international propagation of the stock market crash. The questions of causality or lead-lag relationships are empirically investigated for several major national equity markets by means of Granger (1969) methodology. The paper is organized as follows. Section II describes the methodology used in testing the hypotheses. Section III describes the data and discusses the important problem of synchronization. Section IV presents the tests of cointegration. The empirical results and main findings of the causality tests are given in Section V. Finally, the last section briefly summarizes and concludes the paper.

II. Granger Causality Tests

The empirical tests are based on the Granger causality tests. These are essentially tests of the predictive ability of time series models. A time series $\{Y_t\}$ causes another time series $\{X_t\}$ in the Granger sense if present X can be predicted better by using past values of Y than by not doing so, considering also

[1] See, i.e., Blume and MacKinlay (1989), Brady et al. (1988), Greenwald and Stein (1988), Leland and Rubinstein (1988), and Miller et al. (1987).

other relevant information, including past values of X. More specifically, X is said to cause Y, provided some α_i is not zero in Equation (1),

$$(1) \qquad Y_t = \delta_0 + \sum_{i=1}^{m} \alpha_i X_{t-i} + \sum_{j=1}^{m} \beta_j Y_{t-j} + \mu_t.$$

Similarly, Y is causing X if some a_i is not zero in Equation (2),

$$(2) \qquad X_t = c_0 + \sum_{i=1}^{m} a_i Y_{t-i} + \sum_{j=1}^{m} b_j X_{t-j} + e_t.$$

If both of these events occur, there is feedback.[2] The test for causality is based on an F-statistic that is calculated by estimating the above expression in both unconstrained and constrained forms (full and reduced models),

$$F_1 = \frac{(SSE_r - SSE_f)/m}{SSE_f/(T - 2m - 1)},$$

where SSE_r, SSE_f = residual sum squares of the reduced and full models, respectively,
T = total number of observations,
m = number of lags.

F_1 follows a χ^2/m distribution and corresponds to a Wald test.[3]

This methodology is used to study potential links between international stock markets before, during, and after the crash of October 1987. Our approach differs from that in Roll (1988), who uses regression techniques and argues that the U.S. market was not the first to decline sharply on October 19, 1987. In effect, Roll (1988) indicates that non-Japanese Asian markets began a severe decline on October 19 on their time and this decline was echoed first by a number of European markets, then by North America, and finally by Japan.

III. Data Description

The data consist of daily closing prices for the following major equity market indexes: New York S&P 500, Tokyo Nikkei, London FT–30, Hong Kong Hang Seng, Singapore Straits Times, and Australia All Ordinaries. The prices have been collected from the *Wall Street Journal* for the time period May 1, 1987, through March 31, 1988.

To investigate the lead-lag relationships between the six stock market indexes before, during, and after the market crash of October 19, 1987, the data are divided into three sets:

[2] A more detailed description of the several testable forms of Granger's causality can be found in Pierce and Haugh (1977), Geweke, Meese, and Dent (1983), and Guilkey and Salemi (1982).

[3] For details see, Guilkey and Salemi (1982), Schmidt (1976), and Geweke, Meese, and Dent (1983).

(i) May 1, 1987, through September 30, 1987: the period before the market crash;
(ii) October 1, 1987, through October 31, 1987: the period of the market crash;
(iii) November 1, 1987, through March 31, 1988: the period after the market crash.

Tests of unidirectional and bidirectional (feedback) Granger causal relationships are conducted in the three data sets, assuming 5 lags (5 trading days).

Testing for lead-lag relationships between international markets presents a problem of data synchronization due to time-zone shift differences. Addressing this issue is of primary importance in the execution and interpretation of the empirical tests conducted in this paper.

The data reported in the *Wall Street Journal* for the several indexes are closing prices for the same trading day. Since the Journal is published after the closing of the New York Stock Exchange, data for closing prices are available for all world exchanges. Exhibit 1 shows the trading hours of the national stock exchanges in Greenwich Mean Time, local time, and New York time. The last column of Exhibit 1 indicates that in any given trading day the closing prices for the several foreign exchanges analyzed in our sample are known by the time the NYSE closes for the day. With daily data available for the six national exchanges, daily returns are defined as

$$R_t = [\text{log of closing price index at } t\text{–log of closing price index at } t-1]\times 100,$$

where log denotes natural logarithm. Daily returns are computed for all six exchanges and a superscript is used to denote the return of a given exchange (i.e., R_t^{NY} and R_{t+1}^{T} correspond to the New York return at time t and Tokyo return at time $t+1$, respectively).

EXHIBIT 1

Market Time Tables

Stock Markets	Hours (Greenwich Mean Time)	Hours (Local Time)	Hours (New York Time)
Sydney	Midnight–2:15 a.m./ 4:00 a.m.–5:15 a.m.	10:00 a.m.–12:15 p.m./ 2:00 p.m.–3:15 p.m.	7:00 p.m.–9:15 p.m./ 11:00 p.m.–0:15 a.m.
Tokyo	Midnight–2:00 a.m./ 4:00 a.m.–6:00 a.m.	9:00 a.m.–11:00 a.m./ 1:00 p.m.–3:00 p.m.	7:00 p.m.–9:00 p.m./ 11:00 p.m.–1:00 a.m.
Hong Kong	2:00 a.m.–4:30 a.m./ 6:30 a.m.–7:30 a.m.	10:00 a.m.–12:30 p.m./ 2:30 p.m.–3:30 p.m.	9:00 p.m.–11:30 p.m./ 1:30 a.m.–2:30 a.m.
Singapore	2:00 a.m.–4:30 a.m./ 6:30 a.m.–8:00 a.m.	10:00 a.m.–12:30 p.m./ 2:30 p.m.–4:00 p.m.	9:00 p.m.–11:30 p.m./ 1:30 a.m.–3:00 a.m.
London	9:00 a.m.–5:00 p.m.	9:00 a.m.–5:00 p.m.	4:00 a.m.–12:00 noon
New York	2:30 p.m.–9:00 p.m.	9:30 a.m.–4:00 p.m.	9:30 a.m.–4:00 p.m.

Source: *Directory of World Stock Exchanges.*

Now, let us suppose that a major world event occurs in Japan (such as a political crisis or changes in monetary policy, trade agreements, etc.) and is announced at 7:00 p.m. New York time on a given Tuesday. The Tuesday New York returns on the S&P 500 Index will not reflect this information. Observe from Exhibit 1 that at 7:00 p.m. New York time, Wednesday trading begins in Tokyo. Wednesday Tokyo returns will incorporate the information of this event and when Wednesday trading begins in New York, after 14½ hours from the announcement, New York Wednesday returns will also be affected. This illustrates that returns at time t in Japan affect returns in New York the same calendar day t. Therefore, a Granger regression investigating if Tokyo is leading New York looks as follows,

$$R_t^{NY} = c_0 + \sum_{i=1}^{m} a_i R_{t-i}^T + \sum_{j=1}^{m} b_j R_{t-j}^{NY} + e_t. \tag{1a}$$

On the other hand, suppose that important U.S. economic data are released on a given day at 8:00 a.m. New York time. Their impact will be reflected in the same day returns in New York but at Tokyo's following day returns. This illustrates that New York returns at time t may affect returns in Tokyo at time $t+1$ (and not at time t). That is, a Granger regression postulating that New York is leading Tokyo looks like this, after adjusting for time-zone differences,

$$R_{t+1}^T = \delta_0 + \sum_{i=1}^{m} \alpha_i R_{t-i}^{NY} + \sum_{j=0}^{m} \beta_j R_{t-j}^T + \mu_t. \tag{2a}$$

Because we are working with day-end prices, similar adjustments were made in testing for lead-lag relationships among other markets. Specifically, activities in the European market indexes today impact the U.S. market in the same calendar day but the Asian and Australian markets are impacted the following trading day. Also, today's activity in the New York market affects European, Asian, and Australian markets the following trading day. Finally, activities in the Asian and Australian markets impact the European and American markets the same calendar day. The complete details of these adjustments are motiviated by Exhibit 1, describing the market characteristics of the countries studied.

In Tables 1 and 2 the appropriate time dimension of the causality analysis is clearly specified. Observe that the dependent variable is indexed by τ, which takes the value t or $t+1$ depending upon the time zone shifts of the exchanges.

IV. Tests of Cointegration

It is also important to consider the cointegration among price movements on the different markets. In effect, Engle and Granger (1987) show that if two nonstationary variables are cointegrated, a vector autoregression in the first differences is misspecified. For example, if the natural logarithm of New York and Tokyo prices (i.e., $\text{Ln}\, P_{1t}$ and $\text{Ln}\, P_{2t}$) are both nonstationary (follow random walks), but the first differences of the natural logarithm of each price (i.e., $\text{Ln}\, P_{1t} - \text{Ln}\, P_{1,t-1}$ or $\text{Ln}(P_{1t}/P_{1,t-1})$, and $\text{Ln}\, P_{2t} - \text{Ln}\, P_{2,t-1}$ or $\text{Ln}(P_{2t}/P_{2,t-1})$), that is the returns, are stationary, it is said that prices are integrated of order one, denoted by $I(1)$. If each price is $I(1)$ and there is a linear combination of the New York prices and the Tokyo prices that is stationary, the two sets of prices are said to be cointegrated. The presence of cointegration can cause the Granger causality tests of Equations (1) and (2) to be misspecified. Therefore,

TABLE 1

Granger Causality Tests

Sample Period 1: May 1, 1987–September 30, 1987 (Pre-Crash Period)
Sample Period 2: October 1, 1987–October 31, 1987 (Month of the Crash Period)
Sample Period 3: November 1, 1987–March 31, 1988 (Post-Crash Period)

Models:

$$\text{I)}\quad Y_\tau = \delta_0 + \sum_{i=1}^{5} \alpha_i X_{t-i} + \sum_{j=1}^{5} \beta_j Y_{\tau-j} + \gamma\epsilon_{\tau-1} + \mu_\tau \qquad (X \to Y)‡$$

$$\text{II)}\quad X_\tau = c_0 + \sum_{i=1}^{5} a_i Y_{t-i} + \sum_{j=1}^{5} b_j X_{\tau-j} + d\epsilon_{\tau-1} + e_\tau \qquad (Y \to X)‡$$

Direction of Causality	τ	χ^2 for the Null: $H_0: \sum_{i=1}^{5} \alpha_i = 0,\ \sum_{i=1}^{5} a_i = 0$ Pre-Crash Period 5/1/87–9/30/87	Crash Period 10/1/87–10/31/87	Post-Crash Period 11/1/87–3/31/88
London → New York	t	0.7469	21.7581*	1.1091
New York → London	$t+1$	4.4202	29.9261*	0.4941
Singapore → New York	t	0.7734	3.8165	2.4689
New York → Singapore	$t+1$	0.9277	4.3614	0.6408
Hong Kong → New York	t	0.5106	230.0596*	1.5892
New York → Hong Kong	$t+1$	0.2310	24.1764*	0.5388
Tokyo → New York	t	0.2142	3.7410	1.1051
New York → Tokyo	$t+1$	1.0410	24.9239*	1.1160
Sydney → New York	t	1.8906	2.7351	0.0837
New York → Sydney	$t+1$	0.5907	9.4632	0.2905
Singapore → London	t	0.7281	14.7755*	1.8238
London → Singapore	$t+1$	0.4419	170.1973*	2.0772
Hong Kong → London	t	0.8406	6.2548	2.9746
London → Hong Kong	$t+1$	1.5336	269.6398*	0.7009
Tokyo → London	t	1.4324	124.5739*	1.0248
London → Tokyo	$t+1$	1.5884	188.9507*	2.9268
Sydney → London	t	2.0058	63.0430*	0.6733
London → Sydney	$t+1$	1.1865	15.5716*	1.0758
Hong Kong → Singapore	t	0.2109	48.0951*	2.9563
Singapore → Hong Kong	$t+1$	0.8129	3.0475	1.9582
Tokyo → Singapore	t	0.8226	33.6032*	2.2559
Singapore → Tokyo	$t+1$	2.5649	9.6592	2.7850
Sydney → Singapore	t	2.1629	71.4901*	0.3575
Singapore → Sydney	$t+1$	1.4586	5.2444	0.3258
Tokyo → Hong Kong	t	1.0193	4.1744	1.6568
Hong Kong → Tokyo	$t+1$	0.6221	77.4223*	3.5276
Sydney → Hong Kong	t	0.5004	8691.81*	0.9143
Hong Kong → Sydney	$t+1$	0.6621	52.9271*	0.5053
Sydney → Tokyo	t	2.7220	151.5554*	0.1318
Tokyo → Sydney	$t+1$	0.1407	70.2552*	0.1395

* Significant at the 5-percent confidence level, χ^2 crit at 5 percent = 11.07.
‡ $\gamma = 0$, $d = 0$ if no cointegration.

Equations I and II are Granger tests of causality. Equation I tests if X is causing $Y(X \to Y)$, Equation II tests if Y is causing $X(Y \to X)$. If both events occur there is feedback. The variable $\epsilon_{\tau-1}$ corresponds to the error-correcting term if cointegration is present. The index τ corrects for the synchronization problem by taking the values of t or $t+1$ depending upon the time zone shifts of the exchanges. The null hypotheses of no causality are $\Sigma\alpha_i = 0$ or $\Sigma a_i = 0$ for Equations I and II, respectively. The test for causality is based on an F-statistic calculated by estimating Equations I and II in both unconstrained and constrained forms,

$$F_1 = \frac{(SSE_r - SSE_f)/m}{SSE_f/(T-2m-1)},$$

F_1 follows a χ^2/m distribution. The computed F_1s are reported in the table for each pair of national markets.

it is necessary to test for cointegration before running the causality tests. If cointegration is found, an error-correcting model must be constructed.

Engle and Granger (1987) propose several test statistics for testing the null of no-cointegration. In this paper, we use the Augmented Dickey-Fuller test.[4]

[4]Engle and Granger (1987) propose several ways of testing for cointegration. They formally state the test statistics, construct tables of critical values, and compare the powers of the tests. The simplest test of cointegration is the cointegrating regression Durbin-Watson, CRDW, which works

The Dickey-Fuller test of cointegration consists of running first the following cointegrating regression,

$$\text{(3)} \qquad \operatorname{Ln} P_{1t} = c_0 + c_1 \operatorname{Ln} P_{2t} + \epsilon_t,$$

and then running the following auxiliary Dickey-Fuller regression on the residuals of (3),

$$\text{(4)} \qquad \epsilon_t - \epsilon_{t-1} = -b_1 \epsilon_{t-1} + \mu_t.$$

The null hypothesis is $H_0: b_1 = 0$; that is, $\operatorname{Ln} P_{1t}$ and $\operatorname{Ln} P_{2t}$ are not cointegrated. The tests of cointegration yield mixed results with the null of no-cointegration being rejected more often for the month of the crash and the post-crash period than for the pre-crash period.[5]

Given that the results of the tests of cointegration are mixed, we proceed as follows: when the variables are not cointegrated, the causality tests are conducted by running the Granger regressions appropriately adjusted to correct for the synchronization problem (as indicated in Equations (1a) and (2a)). However, if the Dickey-Fuller statistic rejects the null, we conclude that the variables are cointegrated and, therefore, the Granger regressions are misspecified. We correct the regressions by incorporating the residuals from the cointegrating regression (3) as an additional independent variable in the Granger regression equations.[6] For instance, when cointegration is present and no synchronization problem exists between two markets, Equations (1) and (2) become

$$Y_t = \delta_0 + \sum_{i=1}^{m} \alpha_i X_{t-i} + \sum_{j=1}^{m} \beta_j Y_{t-j} + \gamma \hat{\epsilon}_{t-1} + \mu_t,$$

$$X_t = c_0 + \sum_{i=1}^{m} a_i Y_{t-i} + \sum_{j=1}^{m} b_j X_{t-j} + d \hat{\epsilon}_{t-1} + e_t,$$

where $\hat{\epsilon}_{t-1}$ are the residuals from Regression (3).

V. Results of Granger Causality Tests

The main results of the Granger causality tests are presented in Table 1. Column 1 gives the direction of causality (i.e., New York → London indicates that we are testing if New York leads London). Columns 2, 3, and 4 contain the

well with first-order systems. However, the critical values of the CRDW test are very sensitive to the particular parameters within the null. Engle and Granger (1987) do not recommend the use of the CRDW for economic data because, for most economic data, the differences are not white noise, making it difficult to know what critical value to use. Engle and Granger (1987) find that the Augmented Dickey and Fuller test has essentially the same critical values and same good power properties for first-order and higher-order systems. They also indicate that it is the most powerful test and, therefore, it is the recommended approach. The CRDW is simple and easy to implement. For statistical completeness, we have performed both tests.

[5]For the sake of space, the tables containing the results of the tests of cointegration based on the Augmented Dickey and Fuller tests are not presented in the paper. The CRDW was also used. Results from both tests are available from the authors upon request.

[6]We thank Professor Newbold from the Economics Department, University of Illinois at Champaign, for suggesting these error-correcting regressions.

TABLE 2

Tests of Contemporaneous Causality

Models:

I) $Y_\tau = \delta_0 + \sum_{i=0}^{3} \alpha_i X_{t-i} + \sum_{j=1}^{3} \beta_j Y_{\tau-j} + \gamma\epsilon_{\tau-1} + \mu_\tau$ $(X \rightarrow Y)$‡

II) $X_\tau = c_0 + \sum_{i=0}^{3} a_i Y_{t-i} + \sum_{j=1}^{3} b_j X_{\tau-j} + d\epsilon_{\tau-1} + e_t$ $(Y \rightarrow X)$‡

Direction of Causality	τ	α_0, a_0 Regression Coefficients, Standard Error and t-Statistics in Parentheses: Pre-Crash Period 5/1/87–9/30/87	Crash Period 10/1/87–10/31/87	Post-Crash Period 11/1/87–3/31/88
London → New York	t	−0.0214 (0.1169) (−0.18)	2.3750 (0.6512) (3.65)*	0.9026 (0.1455) (6.20)*
New York → London	$t+1$	0.2010 (0.0908) (2.21)*	0.8254 (0.1664) (4.96)*	0.0724 (0.0784) (0.92)
Singapore → New York	t	0.1082 (0.0903) (1.20)	1.5035 (0.6190) (2.43)*	0.4403 (0.1515) (2.90)*
New York → Singapore	$t+1$	0.1316 (0.1173) (1.12)	1.2403 (0.1640) (7.56)*	0.4504 (0.0706) (6.38)*
Hong Kong → New York	t	0.1751 (0.1106) (1.58)	0.3267 (0.2127) (1.54)	0.2734 (0.1210) (2.26)*
New York → Hong Kong	$t+1$	0.1921 (0.0939) (2.05)*	−0.0129 (0.2836) (−0.04)	0.4192 (0.0898) (4.67)*
Tokyo → New York	t	0.0950 (0.0582) (1.63)	−1.0920 (4.3173) (−0.25)	0.4235 (0.2041) (2.07)*
New York → Tokyo	$t+1$	0.3959 (0.1794) (2.21)*	0.7572 (0.0358) (21.16)*	0.1429 (0.0547) (2.61)*
Sydney → New York	t	0.0094 (0.0039) (2.44)*	−2.2916 (1.4096) (−1.63)	−0.0123 (0.0393) (−0.31)
New York → Sydney	$t+1$	−2.3055 (2.7503) (−0.84)	1.2459 (0.0982) (12.69)*	0.4460 (0.2900) (1.54)
Singapore → London	t	0.0160 (0.0874) (0.18)	0.5176 (0.0891) (5.81)*	0.2430 (0.0893) (2.72)*
London → Singapore	$t+1$	0.1590 (0.1200) (1.32)	2.7929 (1.9078) (1.46)	0.4417 (0.1267) (3.49)*
Hong Kong → London	t	0.1433 (0.1047) (1.37)	0.9555 (0.3652) (2.62)*	0.1885 (0.0737) (2.56)*
London → Hong Kong	$t+1$	0.0086 (0.0976) (0.09)	−0.5452 (0.6883) (−0.79)	0.7335 (0.1407) (5.21)*
Tokyo → London	t	0.1464 (0.0541) (2.70)*	1.0098 (0.4040) (2.50)*	0.0542 (0.1396) (0.39)
London → Tokyo	$t+1$	0.1008 (0.1941) (0.52)	2.4605 (0.4718) (5.21)*	0.3140 (0.0813) (3.86)*
Sydney → London	t	−0.0036 (0.0039) (−0.93)	1.2766 (0.3435) (3.72)*	−0.0058 (0.0244) (−0.24)
London → Sydney	$t+1$	−1.7112 (2.7689) (−0.62)	3.5627 (0.4898) (7.27)*	0.5252 (0.4747) (1.11)

continued on next page

TABLE 2 (continued)
Tests of Contemporaneous Causality

Direction of Causality	τ	α_0, a_0 Regression Coefficients, Standard Error and t-Statistics in Parentheses Pre-Crash Period 5/1/87–9/30/87	Crash Period 10/1/87–10/31/87	Post-Crash Period 11/1/87–3/31/88
Hong Kong → Singapore	t	–0.0344 (0.1259) (–0.27)	–0.6857 (0.6353) (–1.08)	0.5615 (0.0600) (9.36)*
Singapore → Hong Kong	$t+1$	0.0470 (0.0819) (0.57)	–0.0725 (0.3215) (–0.23)	0.0555 (0.1800) (0.31)
Tokyo → Singapore	t	0.0485 (0.0702) (0.69)	1.3411 (0.2483) (5.40)*	0.6039 (0.1356) (4.45)*
Singapore → Tokyo	$t+1$	–0.2650 (0.1515) (–1.75)*	1.0986 (0.4330) (2.54)*	0.0167 (0.0835) (0.20)
Sydney → Singapore	t	0.0011 (0.0047) (0.24)	0.3486 (0.3883) (0.90)	0.0222 (0.0296) (0.75)
Singapore → Sydney	$t+1$	1.5707 (2.2602) (0.69)	1.2620 (0.7778) (1.62)	0.4546 (0.3886) (1.17)
Tokyo → Hong Kong	t	0.0463 (0.0539) (0.86)	–0.3595 (0.3560) (–1.01)	0.6643 (0.1714) (3.88)*
Hong Kong → Tokyo	$t+1$	0.2740 (0.1921) (1.42)	0.8694 (0.1335) (6.51)*	–0.0242 (0.0640) (–0.38)
Sydney → Hong Kong	t	0.0003 (0.0039) (0.08)	–0.5361 (0.1627) (–3.29)*	0.0493 (0.0372) (1.33)
Hong Kong → Sydney	$t+1$	0.7201 (2.7480) (1.36)	0.4831 (0.2306) (2.09)*	0.5646 (0.3100) (1.82)
Sydney → Tokyo	t	0.0167 (0.0066) (2.53)*	0.6315 (0.0406) (15.54)*	0.0201 (0.0205) (0.98)
Tokyo → Sydney	$t+1$	–1.6641 (1.5564) (–1.07)	6.0408 (2.2934) (2.63)*	0.1758 (0.5586) (0.31)

* Significant at the 5-percent confidence level.
‡ $\gamma = 0$, $d = 0$ if no cointegration.
Equations I and II are tests of contemporaneous causality. The current values of X and Y are incorporated in the right hand side of Equations I and II, respectively. Equation I tests if X is causing $Y(X \to Y)$. Equation II tests if Y is causing $X(Y \to X)$. If both events occur, there is a feedback. The variable $\epsilon_{\tau-1}$ corresponds to the error-correcting term if cointegration is present. The index τ corrects for the synchronization problem by taking the value of t or $t+1$, depending upon the time zone shifts of the exchanges. The contemporaneous equation models I and II test if X and Y affect each other contemporaneously through α_0 or a_0, respectively.

statistics for the null hypothesis of no causality ($H_0: \sum \alpha_i = 0$ or $\sum a_i = 0$) for the pre-crash period, month of the crash, and post-crash period, respectively. As the χ^2 statistics in columns 2 and 4 indicate, the null hypothesis of no-causality cannot be rejected and practically no lead-lag relationships are detected for the pre-crash and post-crash period.[7]

On the other hand, the χ^2 reported in Column 3 show a dramatic increase in causality for the month of the market crash, that is, for the time period October 1, 1987, through October 31, 1987. In fact, for the month of the crash, in 20 out

[7] Furthermore, for the periods before and after the market crash, most of the individual regression coefficients are not different from zero at the 5-percent level of significance. The complete tables containing all the individual coefficients, standard errors, and t-statistics are available upon request.

of the 30 lead-lag relationships analyzed, the null hypothesis of no-causality is rejected at the 5-percent confidence level. Bidirectional causality or feedback is detected among the following markets: New York and London, New York and Hong Kong, London and Singapore, London and Tokyo, London and Sydney, Hong Kong and Sydney, and Tokyo and Sydney. In addition, unidirectional causality is found among the following markets: New York leading Tokyo, London leading Hong Kong, Hong Kong leading Singapore, Tokyo leading Singapore, Sydney leading Singapore, and, finally, Hong Kong leading Tokyo.

The empirical results suggest that Tokyo played a passive role during the market crash of October 1987. In effect, no market lagged Tokyo except Singapore. On the other hand, no market led New York during the crash. However, with the exception of Tokyo, no market lagged New York, either. The results also indicate that Hong Kong played a leading role among the Asian markets by leading Tokyo and Singapore. Hong Kong, however, lagged the European market of London and showed feedback with New York. London and New York also exhibited feedback during the month of the crash.

Some studies, such as Roll (1988), have suggested that the equity market crash started in Asian countries other than Japan and from there spread to Europe, the United States, and finally reached Japan. On the other hand, Shiller (1987) and Shiller, et al. (1988) have indicated that the United States played a leading role. They postulate that the crash was initiated in New York and that the dramatic decline of U.S. stock prices spread the crash to other markets.

This paper provides evidence of the alleged passive role played by Tokyo during the market crash, but fails to confirm the alleged leading role played by New York or the non-Japanese Asian markets. In other words, our causality tests appear to reject both of the above hypotheses.

In order to get more insights about the relationships among the several markets before, during, and after the crash, we have run tests of contemporaneous causality. Models with contemporaneous causality can be constructed by including the current values of the independent variables X and Y in the right-hand side of Equations (1) and (2), respectively. The contemporaneous equation models imply that X and Y may affect each other contemporaneously through α_0 and a_0, respectively. The α_0 and a_0 regression coefficients are shown in Table 2. Little contemporaneous causality is observed for the pre-crash period. However, a substantial increase in contemporaneous causality is detected during and after the month of the crash.

The increase in feedback and contemporaneous causality among the national markets during the month of the crash suggests that the crash started more or less simultaneously in all countries. That is, according to our results, the market crash of October 1987 seems to have been a global crisis of the equity markets all around the world.

VI. Summary and Conclusions

The paper analyzes possible causal relationships among national stock markets around the October 1987 stock market crash. Lead-lag relationships among equity market indexes in six major countries are investigated: New York S&P

500, Tokyo Nikkei, London FT–30, Hong Kong Hang Seng, Singapore Straits Times, and Australia All Ordinaries. The study covers the time period May 1, 1987, through March 31, 1988. For analytical purposes, the data have been divided into three data sets: pre-crash period, month of crash, and post-crash period. Unidirectional and bidirectional causality relationships are analyzed based on the Granger tests.

Practically no lead-lag relationships are detected for the periods before and after the market crash. However, a dramatic increase in bidirectional and unidirectional causality is observed for the month of the crash. The empirical results show that during the month of the crash, Tokyo led no market except Singapore, and was also the only market lagging New York. No other national market led or lagged New York. New York also showed feedback with London and Hong Kong. London led Hong Kong, and Hong Kong led the other Asian markets. These results provide empirical evidence of the passive role played by Tokyo, but fail to confirm the leading role allegedly played by New York or the non-Japanese Asian markets during the October 1987 market crash.

Tests of contemporaneous causality indicate an increase of contemporaneous causality during and after the month of the crash. The increase in feedback and contemporaneous causality among the national stock markets during the month of the crash suggests that the crash probably started simultaneously in all the stock markets. Thus, the market crash of October 1987 seems to have been an international crisis of the equity markets.

References

Blume, M. E.; A. C. MacKinlay; and B. Terker. "Order Imbalances and Stock Price Movements on October 19 and 20, 1987." *Journal of Finance*, 44 (Sept. 1989), 827–848.

Brady, N. (chairman); J. Cotting; R. Kirby; J. Opel; H. Stein; and R. Glauber. *Report of The Presidential Task Force on Market Mechanisms* (1988).

Engle, R., and C. W. J. Granger. "Co-Integration and Error Correction: Representation, Estimation, Testing." *Econometrica*, 55 (March 1987), 251–276.

Friedman, B. "Financial Markets and Monetary Economics." *National Bureau of Economic Research Reporter* (Spring 1990), 1–7.

Geweke, J.; R. Meese; and W. Dent. "Comparing Alternative Tests of Causality in Temporal Systems." *Journal of Econometrics*, 21 (Feb. 1983), 161–194.

Granger, C. W. J. "Investigating Causal Relations by Econometric Models and Cross Spectral Methods." *Econometrica*, 37 (July 1969), 428–438.

Greenwald, B., and J. Stein. "The Task Force Report: The Reasoning behind the Recommendations." *Journal of Economic Perspectives*, 2 (Summer 1988), 3–23.

Guilkey, D. K., and M. K. Salemi. "Small Sample Properties of Three Tests for Granger Causal Ordering in a Bivariate Stochastic System." *The Review of Economics and Statistics*, 64 (Nov. 1982), 668–680.

Leland, H., and M. Rubinstein. "Comments on the Market Crash: Six Months After." *Journal of Economic Perspectives*, 2 (Summer 1988), 45–50.

Miller, M. H.; J. D. Hawke, Jr.; B. Malkiel; and M. Scholes. "Preliminary Report of the Committee of Inquiry Appointed by the Chicago Mercantile Exchange to Examine the Events surrounding October 19, 1987." Chicago Mercantile Exchange (1987).

Pierce, D. A., and L. D. Haugh. "Causality in Temporal Systems: Characterizations and a Survey." *Journal of Econometrics*, 5 (May 1977), 265–293.

Roll, R. "The International Crash of October 1987." *The Financial Analysts Journal*, 44 (Sept.–Oct. 1988), 19–35.

________________. "Price Volatility International Market Links and Their Implications for Regulatory Policies." Working Paper, Graduate School of Business, Univ. of California, Los Angeles (1989).

Schmidt, P. *Econometrics*. New York, N.Y.: Marcel Dekker, Inc. (1976).

Shiller, R. J. "Investor Behavior in the October 1987 Stock Market Crash: Survey Evidence." *National Bureau of Economic Research*, Working Paper No. 2446 (1987).

Shiller, R. J.; F. Konya; and Y. Tsutsui. "Investor Behavior in the October 1987 Stock Market Crash: The Case of Japan." *National Bureau of Economic Research*, Working Paper No. 2684 (1988).

THE IMPACT OF THE PERSIAN GULF CRISIS ON NATIONAL EQUITY MARKETS

A. G. Malliaris and Jorge L. Urrutia

ABSTRACT

This paper uses the mean-adjusted returns and the market and risk-adjusted returns event-study methodologies to analyze the response of national equity markets to the Persian Gulf Crisis. Daily cumulative abnormal returns are computed for 16 national stock markets and three portfolios of national markets. The main empirical findings are: (1) the Persian Gulf Crisis had a negative effect on equity prices; (2) the Oil Crisis had a greater negative effect on the European, Asian, and Australian markets than on the American and Canadian markets; (3) the initiation of the Gulf War had a much lesser impact in the equity market prices than the invasion of Kuwait; (4) the national markets reacted to both events, the invasion of Kuwait and the start of the Gulf War with lags of two to three days. The negative abnormal returns following the invasion of Kuwait seem to reflect investors' fear of a long armed conflict in the Middle East. On the other hand, the positive abnormal returns following the initiation of the War

Advances in International Banking and Finance, Volume 1, pages 43–65.

ISBN: 1-55938-318-6

suggest that investors expected a quick end to the Gulf War. Our results confirm the important role played by oil prices in the world economies and the limitations of international diversification. The efficiency of equity markets is also reflected in the fact that several national markets responded to the Persian Gulf Crisis according to the country's dependence on oil imports.

INTRODUCTION

The interrelationships of international stock markets have been extensively researched in the finance literature. The early emphasis of contributions such as Grubel (1968), Levy and Sarnat (1970), Lessard (1976), and Hilliard (1979), among others, was placed on the benefits of international portfolio diversification. For example, Levy and Sarnat (1970) use the theoretical models of portfolio selection developed by Harry Markowitz and James Tobin to examine the potential gains, if any, accruing from international diversification. In a sample of 28 countries during 1951–1967 they find that potential gains could be materialized from international diversification.

The financial logic of international diversification is straightforward. The degree to which international diversification can reduce risk depends upon the correlations among world stock returns. If such world returns are not correlated, then international diversification could eliminate risk. On the other hand, if world stock returns are perfectly correlated, such international diversification could not eliminate risk.

The simultaneous collapse of world stock market returns during the few days surrounding October 19, 1987 illustrates the limitations of international diversification. Although a satisfactory explanation of this crash is still not available, several recent studies, such as Roll (1988, 1989) and others, have emphasized the role of international market integration. Roll (1988) suggested that the 1987 crash was caused by some "worldwide triggering variable" or "some international underlying fundamental factor," both notions left unclarified. In their paper, von Furstenberg and Jeon (1989) provide an efficient market's framework to study the links and messages of international stock price returns, and outline a model that uses four variables to explain world stock price returns. These variables are interest rate differentials, exchange rates, the price of oil, and the price of gold.

We do not wish to pursue here the important topic of international portfolio diversification and its limitations caused by world integration. Rather, we wish to study the impact of the Gulf Crisis on the world stock market returns. Unlike Roll's (1988) unnamed world triggering variable or the four variables identified by von Furstenberg and Jeon (1989), the Persian Gulf Crisis with its dramatic impact on oil prices and world market stock returns is a specific event with great significance since it influenced the world economies. Furthermore, it was of such importance that it dominated for a period of about seven months almost all other economic variables. Seldom do social scientists have such ideal conditions for a financial experiment.

In studying the impact of the Persian Gulf Crisis on world stock markets, this paper attempts to shed light on several interrelated issues. First, we establish the significance played by oil in world stock markets. This means that oil, its price, production, and distribution all have significant consequences not only as industry specific effects but as global events affecting the entire economies of the world, of course, in various degrees.

Second, the impact of the Gulf Crisis on world stock markets essentially depended on the degree of world financial integration. Of course, the same experiment could not be repeated without world financial integration to allow for comparisons. However, it is not difficult to imagine that the impact of the Gulf Crisis would have been lesser without multiple stock listings in several national stock markets and without worldwide financial deregulation. In fact, the Gulf Crisis can be used to illustrate the limitations of international diversification.

The empirical results reported here confirm both the important role played by oil prices in the world economies and the limitations imposed on international diversification by the global integration of national financial markets. In effect, all the equity markets under study exhibit statistically significant negative abnormal returns on the days surrounding the invasion of Kuwait. Also the national stock markets responded to the crisis according to the importance of oil in their economies. Actually, European and Asian markets which are more dependent on oil imports were more affected than their American and Canadian counterparts.

The rest of the manuscript is organized as follows. The next section describes the data. The third presents the two event-study methodologies used in this paper. The measures of abnormal returns and the statistical tests are described in the fourth section. A detailed analysis of the empirical results is given in the fifth. Finally, the last section summarizes and concludes the paper.

DATA DESCRIPTION

Daily closing price indexes for the time period October 1, 1989 through January 31, 1991, are collected from the Wall Street Journal and elsewhere,[1] for the World Index and the following sixteen national markets: New York S&P 500, Toronto 300 Composite, London FT-100, Frankfurt DAX, Zurich Credit Suisse, Paris CAC 40, Milan Stock Index, Amsterdam ANP-CBS General, Stockholm Affarsvarlden, Brussels Bel-20 Index, Australia All Ordinaries, Hong Kong Hang Seng, Singapore Straits Times, Tokyo Nikkei Average, Seoul-Korean, and Taipei-Taiwan. Daily returns are computed as $R_t = 100*[\ln (P_t/P_{t-1})]$, where P_t and P_{t-1} are daily price indexes for days t and $t-1$, respectively. The data samples are divided into an "Estimation Period" from October 1, 1989 through May 31, 1990 ($t = -206$ to $t = -44$), and an "Event Period," from June 1, 1990 to January 31, 1991 ($t = -43$ to $t =$

+119). That is, both the estimation period and the event period contain 163 observations or trading days. The event day ($t = 0$) corresponds to August 2, 1990, the day Iraq invaded Kuwait. Other important dates in the data sample are January 16, 1991 ($t = +112$) the day the Allied Forces-Iraq war began, and January 24, 1991 ($t = +118$), the day the International Coalition launched the ground attack.

EXCESS OR ABNORMAL RETURN METHODOLOGIES

To determine if a security's returns are abnormal, it is necessary to compare them to a benchmark. This paper uses two methodologies to generate normal or ex-ante expected returns. They are the mean-adjusted return model and the market and risk-adjusted return model. For each method the excess return for a given security in any given time period is computed as the difference between its actual ex-post return and that which is predicted by the assumed model. A brief description of these two event-study procedures follows.

Mean-Adjusted Return Method

The mean-adjusted return method is a simple procedure, which makes no explicit risk adjustment. This method assumes that the ex-ante expected return of a security is equal to a constant, K_i, which can differ across securities. That is, under this approach a security is expected to generate the same return that it averaged during the estimation period. The security's excess return is equal to the difference between the observed return during the event period and a constant, which corresponds to the average return for the security during the estimation period.

The mean-adjusted return approach is consistent with the Capital Asset Pricing Model. In effect, under the assumption of constant systematic risk and stationary efficient frontier, the CAPM also predicts constant expected returns.

In this study, instead of individual securities we consider 16 national market indexes. Therefore, we need to emphasize that the consistency of the mean-adjusted return method must be interpreted in terms of a world version of the CAPM, such as the one proposed by Solnik (1974a), and extended by Stulz (1981).

Market and Risk-Adjusted Return Method

The market and risk-adjusted return method takes into account both the market-wide factors and the systematic risks of each security. This methodology presumes that the CAPM generates expected returns. It uses a regression model to predict the security's expected returns. This OLS regression procedure, known as the market model, consists in regressing the security's returns on the market's returns. The security's excess return is equal to the difference between the observed return during the event period and the return predicted by the OLS regression.

Again, as with the first method, we consider 16 national market indexes instead of individual stocks within one country. Given the nature of our data, it is not straightforward to identify the appropriate "market" portfolio. Fortunately, there exists a proxy for such a world market portfolio constructed by and reported daily in the *WSJ* as the World Index. Empirical studies in international finance such as those by Solnik (1974b), Stehle (1977), and Wheatley (1988) have shown that a world market factor is quite weak compared to national factors. For the validity of the results of the second method what matters most is not how strong or how weak is the relationship between national markets and the World Index but rather how stable are such relationships before and after the event. This issue is addressed subsequently where it is confirmed that these relationships are stable.

Comparison of the Two Methodologies

Brown and Warner (1980) indicate that the mean-adjusted return and the market and risk-adjusted return methodologies yield similar results. They also point out that the two approaches compare favorably against more complicated methodologies used in event studies. Brown and Warner (1980, 1985) find that the simple mean-adjusted return technique works well for both monthly and daily returns. However, Dyckman, Philbrick, and Stephan (1984) report that the mean-adjusted return method does not work as well as the market regression model. Moreover, Klein and Rosenfeld (1987) find that the mean-adjusted return produces upwardly (downwardly) biased residuals when many of the events occur during bull (bear) markets.

The market and risk-adjusted return method dominates the event study literature. In implementing this method several regression models have been used, among them the single-index market model, SIMM, and the zero-beta model of Fama and MacBeth (1973). Brenner (1979) examines several different approaches and finds that the simplest SIMM does as well as the more complicated methods. We use the SIMM version of the market and risk-adjusted return method because it seems to be the more widely accepted event study methodology, which has proved to work better than or at least as well as other approaches. Once again we observe that caution must be applied in extending the SIMM version from individual securities within a market to national indexes related to the World Index, particularly when such a global SIMM may be unstable.

Abnormal returns are computed using the mean-adjusted return method as in Masulis (1980). This method has its own flaws, as was indicated earlier, but it has also proven to be an effective event-study methodology. Moreover, the mean-adjusted returns method does not require the "world" or "market" portfolio, which, as was mentioned previously, is an important problem of the SIMM approach. By using both methodologies, the excess returns produced by the market and risk-adjusted approach can be compared to those generated by the mean-adjusted return method.

ABNORMAL RETURN MEASURES

Let $R_{i,t}$ designate the observed return for national market i at time t. Define $AR_{i,t}$ as the excess or abnormal return for national market i at day t. For every national market, the excess or abnormal return for each day in the event period is estimated using the formulas described here.

Mean-Adjusted Returns. These returns are defined by:

$$AR_{i,t} = R_{i,t} - \overline{R}_i \tag{1}$$

where $\overline{R}_i$ is a simple average of national market i's daily returns in the (–206, –44) estimation period. The daily abnormal returns for national market i are standardized:

$$SAR_{i,t} = \frac{AR_{i,t}}{S_i} \tag{2}$$

where $SAR_{i,t}$ is the standardized excess return for national market i at day t, and S_i is the standard deviation of returns for national market i, during the estimation period.

Market and Risk-Adjusted Returns. These are defined by:

$$AR_{i,t} = R_{i,t} - [\hat{\alpha}_i + \hat{\beta}_i R_{W,t}] \tag{3}$$

where $R_{W,t}$ is the observed return for the World Index at day t of the event period, (t = –43, +113), and $\hat{\alpha}_i$, $\hat{\beta}_i$ are the OLS values obtained by running the following regression for the estimation period (t = –206, –44):

$$R_{i,t} = \alpha_i + \beta_i R_{W,t} + \varepsilon_{i,t} \tag{4}$$

The standardized daily abnormal returns for national market i, $SAR_{i,t}$, are given by:

$$SAR_{i,t} = \frac{AR_{i,t}}{S_{i,t}} \tag{5}$$

where $S_{i,t}$ is the square root of national market i's estimated forecast variance, calculated by:

$$S_{i,t} = \left(S_i^2 \left[1 + \left(\frac{1}{163} \right) + \frac{(R_{W,t} - \overline{R}_W)^2}{\sum_{k=-206}^{-44} (R_{W,k} - \overline{R}_W)} \right] \right)^{1/2} \tag{6}$$

In (6), $R_{W,t}$ and $R_{W,k}$ denote observed return for the World Index at day t of the event period and day k of the estimation period, respectively, and $\overline{R}_W$ is the average return of the World Index for the estimation period.

Finally, S_i^2 is the residual variance for national market i, that corresponds to the mean-squared error of the OLS regression (4) and 163 is the number of observations in the estimation period.

Aggregating Abnormal Returns Across Time and National Markets. The cross-sectional average standardized daily abnormal return for a portfolio of national markets, at day t of the event period, $ASAR_t$, is given by:

$$ASAR_t = \frac{1}{N}\sum_{i=1}^{N} SAR_{i,t} \tag{7}$$

where N is the number of national markets in the portfolio. The $ASAR_t$'s can be accumulated over selected multi-day intervals of the event period using:

$$ASCAR_{t_1,t_2} = \sum_{t=t_1}^{t_2} ASAR_t \tag{8}$$

where $ASCAR_{t_1,t_2}$ denotes the average standardized cumulative abnormal return for a portfolio of national markets during the (t_1, t_2) interval of the event period.

Statistical Tests Under the Null Hypotheses. The null hypotheses to be tested are that the mean excess return for the t day of the event period (the average standardized daily abnormal return for a portfolio of national markets, $ASAR_t$), and the mean cumulative excess return over multi-day interval of the event period (the average standardized cumulative abnormal returns over a multi-day interval (t_1, t_2) of the event period, $ASCAR_{t_1,t_2}$) are equal to zero.

The Z-statistic for the average standardized daily abnormal returns for any event day t is computed as:

$$Z_t = ASAR_t\sqrt{N} \tag{9}$$

The Z-statistic for the average standardized cumulative abnormal returns over a multi-day interval (t_1, t_2) of the event period is calculated as:

$$Z_{t_1,t_2} = \frac{ASCAR_{t_1,t_2}\sqrt{N}}{\sqrt{t_2 - t_1 + 1}} \tag{10}$$

These statistics are very popular in event studies (see, e.g., Patell, 1976; Masulis, 1980; Dodd, 1980; Dann, 1981; Holthausen, 1981; Leftwich, 1981; Dodd and Warner, 1983; Brown and Warner, 1980, 1985). The assumptions required for the significance tests are also discussed in these references.

EMPIRICAL FINDINGS

Before computing abnormal returns, we test for possible shifts in alphas and betas of regression (6). Next, we empirically analyze the response of the equity market prices to the Persian Gulf Crisis by computing, first, abnormal returns for selected portfolios of national equity markets and second, by estimating excess returns for each individual national stock market.

Testing for Shifts in the Regression Coefficients

An important event such as the Persian Gulf Crisis could produce changes in the alpha and beta coefficients. The problem of alpha and beta shifts can be handled by means of a procedure suggested by Ruback (1982) and Alexander, Benson, and Kampmeyer (1984). In this approach, which is essentially the Gujarati (1970) technique, the parameters before the event date are estimated on data from a pre-event estimation period and those on and after the event data are estimated on data from a post-event estimation period. We test for alpha and beta shifts between the pre-event and post-event estimation periods using the following regression model:

$$R_{i,t} = \alpha_{i,0} + \alpha_{i,1}D_t + \beta_{i,1}R_{w,t} + \beta_{i,2}(D_tR_{w,t}) + \varepsilon_{i,t} \qquad (11)$$

where $R_{w,t}$ is the observed return for national market i on day t, $R_{w,t}$ World Index on day t and finally, D_t is a dummy variable that takes the value of 0 for the pre-event estimation period and 1 for the post-event estimation period.

In this regression if $\alpha_{i,1}$ and/or $\beta_{i,2}$ are statistically different from zero then there has been a parameter shift. In testing for parameter shifts, we define a pre-event estimation period including days –206 through –31, and a post-event estimation period including days +11 through +119 (observations on $R_{i,t}$ and $R_{w,t}$ during the event window –30 to +10 are excluded). The results are not shown here for the sake of space limitations. It was found that $\alpha_{i,1}$ were negative but statistically insignificant at the 5 percent level and also that most of the $\beta_{i,1}$ were positive but statistically insignificant at the 5 percent level. These results allow us to conclude that, generally, the shifts in alphas and betas are insignificant and they are not expected to have an important impact in the computation of abnormal returns.[2] Therefore, the results reported in this paper correspond to those obtained by estimating alphas and betas from the pre-event estimation period containing observations –206 through –44 (as defined previously in the paper).

Abnormal Return for Portfolios of National Equity Markets

Abnormal returns are computed for the following three portfolios of national equity markets:

1. "U.S. and Canada" portfolio, composed of the S&P 500 and the Toronto exchange
2. "Europe" portfolio, composed of the eight European markets: London, Frankfurt, Zurich, Paris, Milan, Amsterdam, Stockholm, and Brussels

3. "Asia and Australia" portfolio, composed of Tokyo, Hong Kong, Singapore, Seoul, Taipei and Australia

Excess returns for each of the three portfolios are generated by means of both the market and risk-adjusted return method and the mean-adjusted return method. The behavior of abnormal returns is analyzed for an event period containing –43 to +119 days relative to the initiation of the Persian Gulf Crisis ($t = 0$), which corresponds to August 2, 1990, the day Iraq invaded Kuwait.

Table 1 presents the daily average standardized abnormal returns produced by the market and risk-adjusted return method. The first column shows the event date, relative to the announcement day in terms of trading days (for the sake of space only a selected number of the –40 to +116 event dates are presented in this and subsequent tables). The second column contains the daily average standardized abnormal returns, *ASAR*'s, for the "U.S. and Canada" portfolio. The third column contains the *Z*-statistics corresponding to *ASAR*'s of the "U.S. and Canada" portfolio. The subsequent columns, that is, columns (4) and (5), columns (6) and (7), present the *ASAR*'s and the *Z*-statistics for the "Europe" portfolio, and the "Asia and Australia" portfolio, respectively.

The results shown in Table 1 suggest that the Persian Gulf Crisis has had a global negative effect on equity market prices. More specifically, by examining columns (3), (5) and (7) of Table 1, it can be observed that the adverse impact of the Oil Crisis is stronger in the European, Asian and Australian markets, and weaker in the American and Canadian markets. In effect, most of the *ASAR*'s of the "U.S. and Canada" portfolio are negative after the day $t = 0$ but they are not statistically significant. On the other hand, the *ASAR*'s for the "European" and "Asian and Australian" portfolios are statistically significantly negative in the dates immediately following day $t = 0$ (the day of the invasion of Kuwait) and day $t = +112$ (the day of the initiation of the Allied Forces-Iraq War). These results support the important role played by the production, distribution, and prices of oil in the world economies. Our findings also provide evidence of the limitations of the international diversification when stock markets are shocked by a global event, such as the Persian Gulf Crisis.

The average standardized cumulative abnormal returns, *ASCAR*'s, produced by the market and risk-adjusted return method, are presented in Table 2. The *ASCAR*'s are positive or negative for the dates before day $t = 0$, but not statistically significant. However, the *ASCAR*'s are negative and most of them statistically significant after day $t = 0$ for the portfolio of "Europe" and "Asia and Australia." After the invasion of Kuwait the *ASCAR*'s for the "U.S. and Canada" portfolio are also negative but insignificant. The *ASCAR*'s for the three portfolios produced by the market and risk-adjusted returns method, are plotted in Figures 1, 2 and 3. Clearly, the cumulative abnormal returns are less negative for the "U.S. and Canada" portfolio.

The daily average standardized abnormal returns, *ASAR*'s, and the average standardized cumulative abnormal returns, *ASCAR*'s, generated by the mean-

Table 1. Daily Average Standardized Abnormal Returns ($ASAR_t$) for Three Portfolios of National Markets, From 43 Days Before to 119 Days After the Invasion of Kuwait (Day '0' = August 2, 1990)
Market and Risk-Adjusted Return Method

	US and Canada		*Europe*		*Asia and Australia*	
Event Day	*ASAR*	*Z-Score*	*ASAR*	*Z-Score*	*ASAR*	*Z-Score*
–40	–0.0931	–0.1317	0.2217	0.6271	–0.1577	–0.3864
–30	0.3302	0.467	0.1544	0.4367	–0.6185	–1.5149
–20	0.802	1.1342	–0.0934	–0.2642	0.0168	0.0412
–10	–0.9722	–1.375	0.1273	0.3601	0.7486	1.8337
–5	0.5155	0.729	0.1486	0.4204	0.0378	0.0927
–4	–0.1605	–0.227	–0.1379	–0.3902	–0.1735	–0.4249
–3	–0.3182	–0.45	–0.3525	–0.9969	–0.1033	–0.253
–2	–0.0795	–0.1124	–0.3609	–1.0207	–0.3429	–0.8399
–1	1.5374	2.1742*	0.3223	0.9116	0.6187	1.5156
0	–0.2543	–0.3597	–0.1702	–0.4813	–0.0854	–0.2093
+1	–0.5011	–0.7087	–1.0618	–3.0032*	–0.8063	–1.975*
+2	–0.6009	–0.8499	–1.2884	–3.6441*	–1.2248	–3.0001*
+3	–1.0338	–1.462	–3.8353	–10.8478*	–3.129	–7.6645*
+4	–1.0118	–1.4309	0.811	2.2939*	–1.2037	–2.9484*
+5	0.5395	0.763	–0.8382	–2.3707*	0.5805	1.422
+10	0.7191	1.017	0.3786	1.0708	1.4967	3.6662*
+20	–0.016	–0.0227	0.1997	0.565	–1.0737	–2.6301*
+40	–0.8376	–1.1845	0.1573	0.4449	–0.2516	–0.6162
+60	0.3577	0.5059	–0.2136	–0.604	–0.3147	–0.771
+90	–0.3927	–0.5554	0.296	0.8372	0.7976	1.9537
+110	0.0776	0.1097	–0.0357	–0.1008	0.7557	1.8511
+111	–0.6538	–0.9247	–1.9113	–5.4061*	–1.0657	–2.6103*
+112	0.2348	0.3321	–0.0518	–0.1465	–0.6846	–1.6768
+113	–0.6798	–0.9614	–0.122	–0.345	–0.0335	–0.0821
+114	2.0398	2.8847*	4.1469	11.7291*	2.7993	6.8568*
+115	0.8106	1.1464	–0.2094	–0.5924	0.5957	1.4592
+116	–0.2096	–0.2965	–0.7534	–2.1309*	–0.476	–1.1659

Note: *significant at the 5% or better

adjusted returns method are presented in Tables 3 and 4, respectively. The ASCAR's estimated by the mean-adjusted return approach are also graphically illustrated in Figures 4, 5 and 6. In general, the results obtained by the mean-adjusted method are similar to those reported in Tables 1 and 2 for the market and risk-adjusted method. Indeed, both event-study procedures yield practically the same empirical results. Both methodologies reinforce each other, and the findings obtained by both methods allow us to conclude that the Persian Gulf

Table 2. Average Standardized Cumulative Abnormal Returns ($ASCAR_{t1,t2}$) for Three Portfolios of National Markets, From 43 Days Before to 119 Days After the Invasion of Kuwait (Day '0' = August 2, 1990)
Market and Risk-Adjusted Return Method

	US and Canada		*Europe*		*Asia and Australia*	
Event Day	*ASCAR*	*Z-Score*	*ASCAR*	*Z-Score*	*ASCAR*	*Z-Score*
–40	1.348	0.9532	0.7187	1.0164	0.6131	0.7509
–30	–0.1941	–0.0733	–0.1299	–0.0982	–1.8264	–1.1957
–20	1.0103	0.2916	0.6235	0.36	–1.916	–0.958
–10	1.2108	0.2937	1.2055	0.5847	0.303	0.1273
–5	0.89	0.2015	0.3182	0.1441	–0.2715	–0.1065
–4	0.7295	0.1631	0.1803	0.0806	–0.4449	–0.1723
–3	0.4113	0.0908	–0.1722	–0.0761	–0.5482	–0.2097
–2	0.3318	0.0724	–0.5331	–0.2326	–0.8911	–0.3368
–1	1.8692	0.4031	–0.2108	–0.0909	–0.2723	–0.1017
0	1.6149	0.3443	–0.3809	–0.1624	–0.3578	–0.1321
+1	1.1138	0.2348	–1.4427	–0.6083	–1.1641	–0.4251
+2	0.5129	0.1069	–2.7311	–1.139	–2.3888	–0.8627
+3	–0.5209	–0.1075	–6.5664	–2.7091*	–5.5179	–1.9715*
+4	–1.5327	–0.3129	–5.7554	–2.3496*	–6.7215	–2.3764*
+5	–0.9932	–0.2007	–6.5936	–2.6642*	–6.141	–2.1489*
+10	0.0737	0.0142	–7.6107	–2.9294*	–6.7996	–2.2665*
+20	–4.3288	0.7652	–10.9864	–3.8843*	–11.7404	–3.5948*
+40	–8.0239	–1.2381	–20.2452	–6.2478*	–17.9103	–4.7867*
+60	–9.3824	–1.3011	–16.5672	–4.5949*	–10.176	–2.4442*
+90	–4.2279	–0.5165	–17.3552	–4.2405*	–8.6899	–1.8388
+110	–4.6029	–0.5245	–20.9091	–4.7656*	–12.605	–2.488*
+111	–5.2567	–0.5971	–22.8204	–5.1845*	–13.6707	–2.6897*
+112	–5.0219	–0.5686	–22.8722	–5.1795*	–14.3552	–2.8153*
+113	–5.7018	–0.6435	–22.9942	–5.1906*	–14.3888	–2.8129*
+114	–3.662	–0.412	–18.8474	–4.241*	–11.5895	–2.2585*
+115	–2.8514	–0.3198	–19.0568	–4.2746*	–10.9938	–2.1356*
+116	–3.061	–0.3422	–19.8102	–4.4297*	–11.4698	–2.2211*

Note: * significant at the 5% or better

Crisis has had a greater negative impact in the European and Asian equity markets than in the American and Canadian stock markets. Since both event-study procedures produce similar results, the rest of the paper presents only the results generated by the mean and risk-adjusted return method.

To facilitate the comparison of the abnormal returns among the three portfolios, cumulative abnormal returns are computed for selected multi-day intervals constructed around the invasion of Kuwait (day $t = 0$) and the initiation of the Gulf War

Table 3. Daily Average Standardized Abnormal Returns ($ASAR_t$) for Three Portfolios of National Markets, From 43 Days Before to 119 Days After the Invasion of Kuwait (Day '0' = August 2, 1990) Mean-Adjusted Return Method

	US and Canada		*Europe*		*Asia and Australia*	
Event Day	*ASAR*	*Z-Score*	*ASAR*	*Z-Score*	*ASAR*	*Z-Score*
–40	–0.1392	–0.1968	0.2198	0.6216	–0.1612	–0.3948
–30	0.4006	0.5666	0.1601	0.4367	–0.6124	–1.5
–20	0.7637	1.0801	–0.0919	–0.26	0.0157	0.0385
–10	–0.9779	–1.383	0.1278	0.3614	0.7456	1.8264
–5	0.318	0.4497	0.1394	0.3942	0.0208	0.0508
–4	–0.3157	–0.4464	–0.1457	–0.4121	–0.1876	–0.4596
–3	–0.2541	–0.3593	–0.3497	–0.9892	–0.0977	–0.2393
–2	0.2357	0.3333	–0.3479	–0.9839	–0.3186	–0.7805
–1	1.4631	2.0692*	0.3198	0.9046	0.6144	1.505
0	–0.7884	–1.1149	–0.2029	–0.5738	–0.1323	–0.3241
+1	–0.8555	–1.2098	–1.0894	–3.0814*	–0.8438	–2.0669*
+2	–1.3086	–1.8507	–1.3778	–3.8971*	–1.3349	–3.2699*
+3	–1.1061	–1.5642	–3.8442	–10.8729*	–3.1354	–7.68*
+4	–0.9111	–1.2885	0.8179	2.3135*	–1.1986	–2.9358*
+5	0.5446	0.7702	–0.8433	–2.3853*	0.5832	1.4286
+10	0.3409	0.4822	0.3642	1.0302	1.4793	3.6236*
+20	0.0431	0.0609	0.2046	0.5787	–1.0705	–2.6221*
+40	–0.9378	–1.3262	0.1476	0.4176	–0.2595	–0.6356
+60	–0.0762	–0.1078	–0.2381	–0.6735	–0.3595	–0.8806
+90	–0.3172	–0.4485	0.2982	0.8435	0.8077	1.9785
+110	–0.1898	–0.2684	–0.0498	–0.1409	0.7394	1.8111
+111	–0.6653	–0.9409	–1.9162	–5.4197*	–1.0679	–2.6159*
+112	0.0528	0.0747	–0.0597	–0.1688	–0.7031	–1.7223
+113	0.388	0.5487	–0.073	–0.2064	0.062	0.152
+114	2.2815	3.2265*	4.1896	11.8498*	2.839	6.954*
+115	0.7266	1.0275	–0.2154	–0.6091	0.5865	1.4365
+116	–0.2159	–0.3053	–0.7531	–2.13*	–0.4762	–1.1665

Note: *significant at the 5% or better

(day $t = +112$). The *ASCAR*'s and the corresponding *Z*-scores are presented in Table 5. For the (–1,0) interval, that includes the day of the invasion of Kuwait, all ASCAR's are positive but statistically insignificant. On the other hand, for the (+1,+3) and (+1,+5) intervals, the ASCAR's are negative and significant, except for the "U.S. and Canada" portfolio. Negative abnormal returns in the days following the invasion of Kuwait seem to reflect investors' expectations for a long armed conflict.

Table 4. Average Standardized Cumulative Abnormal Returns ($ASCAR_{t1,t2}$) for Three Portfolios of National Markets, From 43 Days Before to 119 Days After the Invasion of Kuwait (Day '0' = August 2, 1990)
Mean-Adjusted Return Method

	US and Canada		*Europe*		*Asia and Australia*	
Event Day	*ASCAR*	*Z-Score*	*ASCAR*	*Z-Score*	*ASCAR*	*Z-Score*
−40	1.4004	0.9902	0.7184	1.016	0.621	0.7605
−30	−0.477	−0.1803	−0.1299	−0.1179	−1.8532	−1.2132
−20	1.0633	0.3069	0.6276	0.3623	−1.9102	−0.9551
−10	1.9862	0.4817	1.2473	0.6051	0.3703	0.1556
−5	0.8877	0.201	0.3208	0.1453	−0.2787	−0.1093
−4	0.572	0.1279	0.1751	0.0783	−0.4664	−0.1806
−3	0.3179	0.0702	−0.1746	−0.0771	−0.5641	−0.2158
−2	0.5536	0.1208	−0.5225	−0.228	−0.8827	−0.3336
−1	2.0167	0.4349	−0.2027	−0.0874	−0.2683	−0.1002
0	1.2284	0.2619	−0.4056	−0.1729	−0.4006	−0.1479
+1	0.3729	0.0786	−1.495	−0.6303	−1.2444	−0.4544
+2	−0.9357	−0.1951	−2.8728	−1.198	−2.5793	−0.9315
+3	−2.0418	−0.4212	−6.717	−2.7712*	−5.7147	−2.0418*
+4	−2.9529	−0.6028	−5.899	−2.4083*	−6.9133	−2.4442*
+5	−2.4083	−0.4866	−6.7424	−2.7243*	−6.33	−2.2151*
+10	−1.3371	−0.2573	−7.7662	−2.9892*	−6.9627	−2.3209*
+20	−6.4246	−1.1357	−11.1527	−3.9431*	−12.030	−3.686*
+40	−12.5379	−1.9346	−20.6105	−6.363*	−18.456	−4.9325*
+60	−11.3944	−1.5801	−16.7	−4.6317*	−10.504	−2.5229*
+90	−5.7259	−0.6995	−17.4594	−4.266*	−8.9594	−1.8958*
+110	−7.5711	−0.8628	−21.1233	−4.8144*	−13.019	−2.5698*
+111	−8.2364	−0.9356	−23.0394	−5.2342*	−14.087	−2.7716*
+112	−8.1836	−0.9266	−23.0991	−5.2309*	−14.79	−2.9006*
+113	−7.7956	−0.8799	−23.1721	−5.2307*	−14.728	−2.8792*
+114	−5.5141	−0.6204	−18.9825	−4.2714*	−11.889	−2.3169*
+115	−4.7876	−0.5369	−19.1979	−4.3063*	−11.303	−2.1957*
+116	−5.0034	−0.5594	−19.951	−4.4612*	−11.779	−2.281*

Note: *significant at the 5% or better

For the (+111, +112) interval, which includes the day of the initiation of the Gulf War, the *ASCAR*'s are also negative and significant for the "Europe" and "Asia-Australia" portfolios. In contrast, the *ASCAR*'s for the (+113, +114) and (+113, +116) intervals are all positive and significant, except for the "U.S. and Canada" portfolio. Positive abnormal returns for the days immediately after the initiation of the War suggest investors' expectations for a quick end to the War.

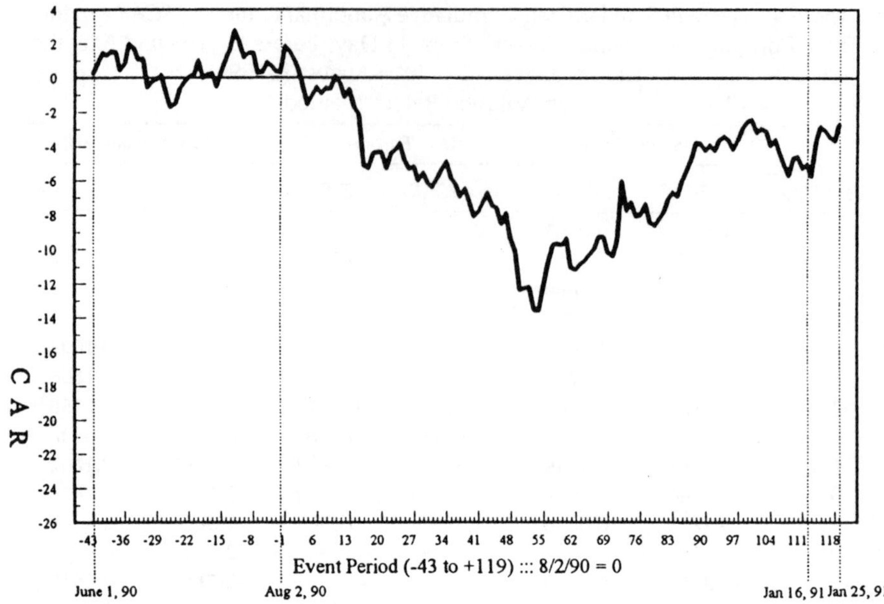

Figure 1. Cumulative Abnormal Returns, Market and Risk Adjusted Returns Method, U.S. and Canada

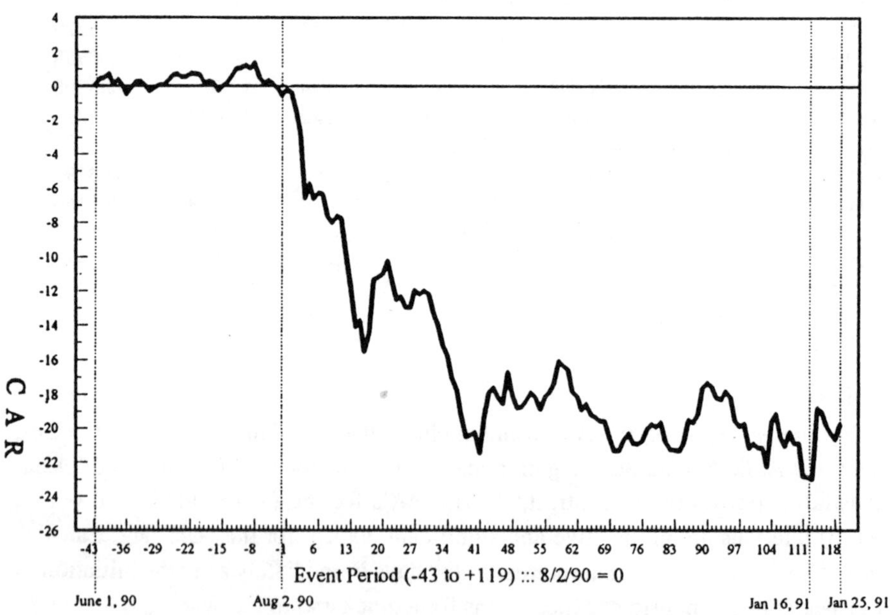

Figure 2. Cumulative Abnormal Returns, Market and Risk Adjusted Returns Method, Europe

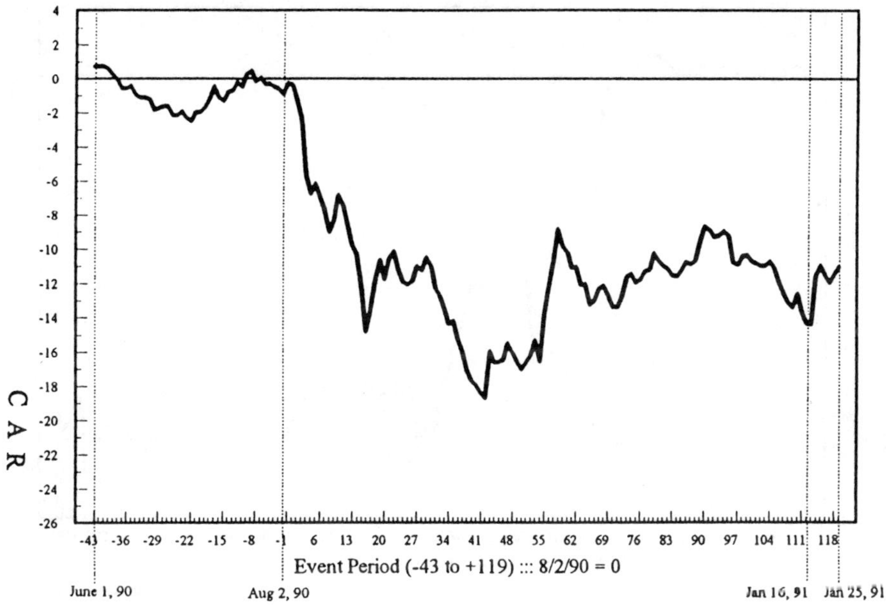

Figure 3. Cumulative Abnormal Returns, Market and Risk Adjusted Returns Method, Asia and Australia

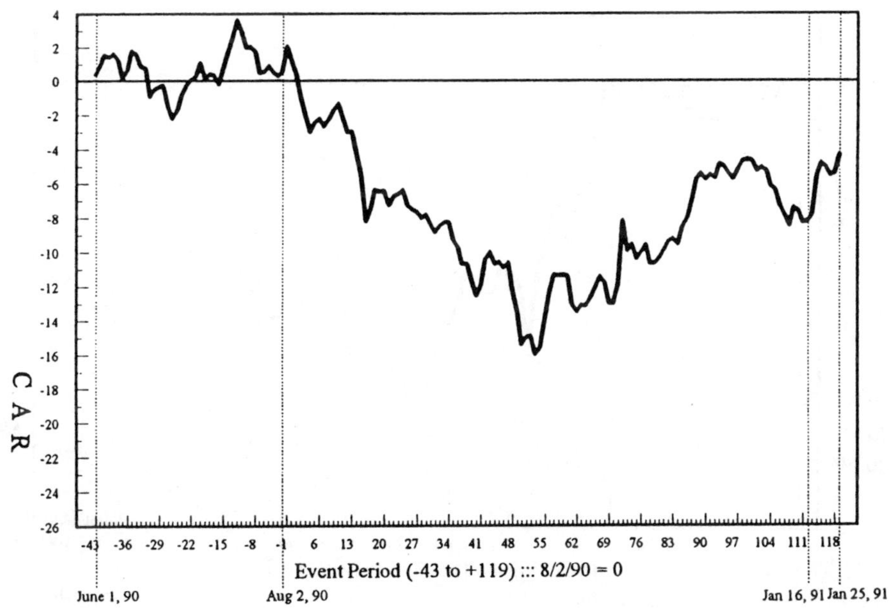

Figure 4. Cumulative Abnormal Returns, Mean Adjusted Returns Method, U.S. and Canada

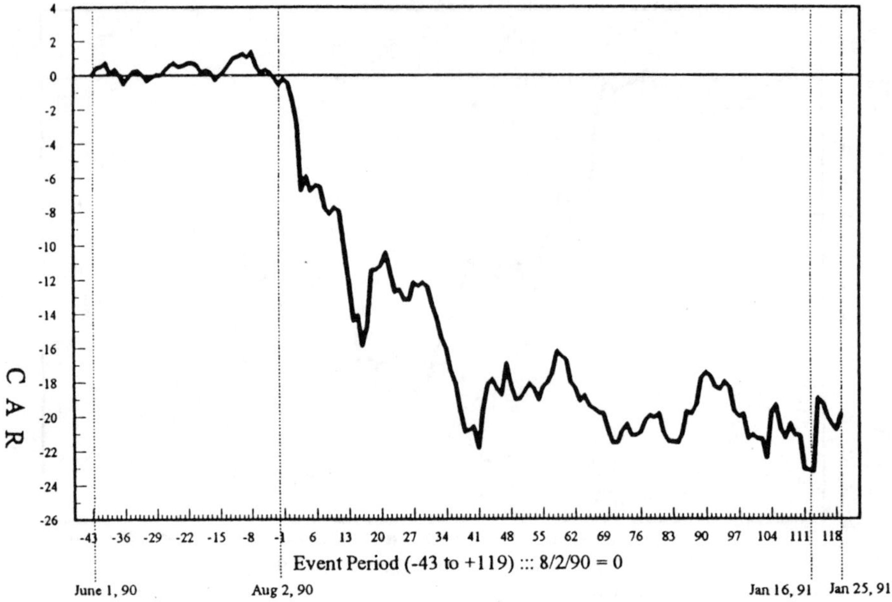

Figure 5. Cumulative Abnormal Returns, Mean Adjusted Returns Method, Europe

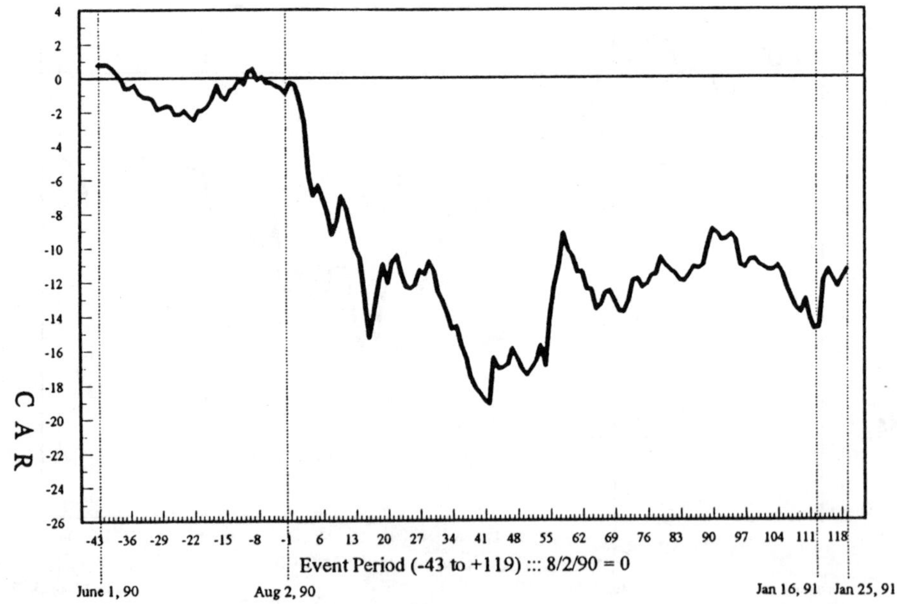

Figure 6. Cumulative Abnormal Returns, Mean Adjusted Returns Method, Asia and Australia

Table 5. Average Standardized Cumulative Abnormal Returns (*ASCAR*) for Three Portfolios of National Markets For Selected Multi-Day Intervals Around the Invasion of Kuwait (Day *t* = 0) and the Initiation of the USA-Iraq War (Day *t* = +112) Market and Risk-Adjusted Return Method

	US and Canada		*Europe*		*Asia and Australia*	
Multi-Day Interval	*ASCAR*	*Z-Score*	*ASCAR*	*Z-Score*	*ASCAR*	*Z-Score*
(–1,0)	1.2831	1.283	0.1521	0.304	0.5333	0.924
(+1,+3)	–2.1358	–1.744	–6.1855	–10.101*	–5.1601	–7.297*
(+1,+5)	–2.6081	–1.65	–6.2126	–7.858*	–5.7832	–6.335*
(+111,+112)	–0.419	–0.419	–1.9631	–3.926*	–1.7502	–3.031*
(+113,+114)	1.3599	1.36	4.0249	8.05*	2.7658	4.791*
(+113,+116)	1.9609	1.387	3.0621	4.33*	2.8855	3.534*

Note: *significant at the 5% or better

The results shown in Table 5 agree with those reported in Tables 1 to 4. Thus, the invasion of Kuwait has had a negative impact on national equity markets and this impact is more dramatic in the European and Asian countries than in the United States and Canada. On the other hand, all portfolios, exhibit a positive reaction to the initiation of the war.

Abnormal Returns for Individual National Stock Markets

Table 6 reports the abnormal returns for each of the 16 national equity markets. The table shows that the daily standardized abnormal returns, *SAR*'s for the (–40, –10) interval are more positive than negative but not significant in a statistical sense. For the time intervals (–5,+5) and (–1,+1), that contain day *t* = 0, the day of the invasion of Kuwait, more than 60 percent of the *SAR*'s are negative and about one-fourth of these are statistically significant. For the (+1,+5) interval, that is, the five-day period immediately following the invasion of Kuwait, about 75 percent of the *SAR*'s are negative and about half of these are significant. Interestingly, day = +3, three days after Iraq invaded Kuwait, all national markets except Toronto and Seoul, exhibit statistically significant negative abnormal returns.

With respect to the (+111,+113) interval that contains day *t* = +112, the day the Allied Forces-Iraq War started, we have that about 65 percent of the SAR's are negative, but only about 30 percent of these negative *SAR*'s are statistically significant. On the other hand, day *t* = +114, two days after the initiation of the war, all national markets exhibit statistically significant positive *SAR*'s.

Table 6. *Z*-Score for Daily Standardized Abnormal Returns (*SAR*), For Each National Equity Market, From 43 Days Before to 119 Days After the Invasion of Kuwait (Day '0' = August 2, 1990) Market and Risk–Adjusted Return Method

Event Day	*New York*	*Toronto*	*London*	*Frankfurt*	*Zurich*	*Paris*	*Milan*	*Amsterdam*
–40	–0.1276	–0.0586	0.0895	0.5555	0.2337	–0.8331	0.0055	–0.0899
–30	0.2499	0.4106	–0.3143	1.2198	–0.0925	0.5131	0.2182	0.2211
–20	0.1374	1.4666	–0.7957	0.245	0.5714	–0.6481	–0.7533	–0.214
–10	–0.6758	–1.2687	–0.6233	1.0536	–0.3476	0.4249	0.9935	–0.3247
–5	0.4349	0.5961	0.1713	–0.111	0.0944	0.0985	–0.2942	0.4501
–4	–0.1191	–0.2019	–0.5878	0.3045	–0.3549	–0.6882	0.4525	–0.2858
–3	–0.5956	–0.0408	–0.5763	–0.4449	–0.4424	–0.8904	0.0168	–0.5854
–2	0.1417	–0.3006	–0.561	–0.2577	–0.5671	–0.5047	–0.0011	–0.2372
–1	2.0409*	1.0339	0.4261	0.1625	0.5094	0.4442	0.3926	0.3753
0	–1.5056	0.9969	1.0356	–0.9151	0.081	–0.2976	–1.2285	0.3541
+1	–0.5414	–0.4608	–1.8641	–0.8293	–0.8271	–1.9865	–2.276	0.1929
+2	–0.7771	–0.4248	–0.2155	–1.0113	–1.0831	–2.3294*	–0.8961	–1.8494
+3	–2.2507*	0.1832	–3.4416*	–3.3342*	–4.5714*	–4.8407*	–3.4719*	–2.1278*
+4	–0.0027	–2.0209*	0.8774	0.9338	1.5912	1.9137	–0.2639	1.314
+5	0.7611	0.3179	0.0025	–1.6163	–1.7162	–2.8404*	0.5538	–1.2819
+10	0.4746	0.9637	0.7511	0.7996	1.0323	–0.0427	–0.2254	0.6494
+20	0.5969	–0.629	0.0377	0.6621	0.1074	0.9501	–0.5403	0.4183
+40	–0.9284	–0.7467	1.1545	–1.2645	0.3105	1.4648	0.9042	–0.1808
+60	–0.2002	0.9157	–0.8239	0.0288	–0.6415	–1.2006	–0.2639	0.0957
+90	–0.5271	–0.2584	0.2773	0.2704	–0.3232	–0.181	1.0645	–0.2819
+110	0.397	–0.2418	0.047	–0.1419	–0.5036	–0.7762	–0.0804	–0.0925
+111	–0.6537	–0.654	–1.0907	–2.4111*	–2.1141*	–3.3859*	–2.1948*	–1.0543
+112	0.4479	0.0217	–0.2613	–0.1777	0.0226	0.9775	0.0561	0.0182
+113	–0.4281	–0.9315	–1.9443	–0.0239	0.1257	0.0326	0.6288	–0.6836
+114	2.492*	1.5875	2.4088*	4.2205*	3.8468*	6.1762*	3.4699*	1.8791
+115	1.0241	0.5971	0.4193	–0.7954	–0.9789	–0.0454	–0.3618	–0.0129
+116	–0.2727	–0.1465	–0.9797	–0.6798	–1.0211	–0.4256	–1.0217	–0.8196

Note: *significant at the 5% or better

In short, only half of the national markets had negative abnormal returns in the day of the invasion of Kuwait (day $t = 0$), and the day of the initiation of the war (day $t = +112$). In addition, these *SAR*'s are insignificant. These results seem to suggest that the national markets reacted to these two events (the invasion of Kuwait and the beginning of the war) with lags of two and three days. The significant negative abnormal returns of day $t = +3$ occur, probably, in anticipation of a long armed conflict in the Middle East. On the other hand, the significant positive abnormal returns of day $t = +114$ reflect investors' expectations for a quick end of the Gulf War.

More insights of the reaction of the several national markets to the Persian Gulf Crisis can be obtained by computing Standardized Cumulative Abnormal Returns, *SCAR*'s, for several multi-day intervals, constructed around the invasion of Kuwait and the initiation of the January war. The *SCAR*'s and their *Z*-scores are presented in Table 7. Almost all *SCAR*'s for the (–1,0) interval are positive but insignificant. For the (+1,+3) and (+1,+5) intervals all *SCAR*'s are negative but statistically significant, except for Toronto, Seoul, and Australia. These results suggest that Canada and Australia reacted faster and were less affected by the invasion of

Table 7. *Z*-Score for Daily Standardized Abnormal Returns (*SAR*), For Each National Equity Market, From 43 Days Before to 119 Days After the Invasion of Kuwait (Day '0' = August 2, 1990)
Market and Risk-Adjusted Return Method

Event Day	*Stockholm*	*Brussels*	*Australia*	*Tokyo*	*Hong Kong*	*Singapore*	*Seoul*	*Taipei*
–40	1.0392	0.7733	0.3155	0.0543	0.079	–0.1162	–0.0767	–1.2023
–30	–0.1191	–0.4113	–0.322	–0.7399	0.7504	–0.5575	–0.6809	–2.1608
–20	1.0174	–0.1699	2.7034*	0.6667	1.1127	0.1298	–1.7893	–2.7224
–10	–0.1184	0.0396	–0.3857	–0.216	1.5877	2.1301*	–0.3406	1.7163
–5	0.1518	0.6284	0.3534	0.1458	0.4655	0.3176	–0.6689	–0.3863
–4	0.1017	–0.0457	0.0628	–0.605	–1.0979	–0.1466	0.2445	0.9905
–3	0.0761	0.0269	0.6553	–1.1385	0.0287	0.2554	0.5658	0.3242
–2	–0.2571	–0.5012	–0.679	–1.1025	–0.9334	–0.5072	–0.0264	1.1912
–1	0.465	–0.1967	0.5781	1.4143	–0.2744	–0.1371	1.1488	0.9827
0	0.2784	–0.6694	0.8734	–0.0953	0.4266	0.2223	–0.013	–1.9265
+1	–0.801	–0.1034	1.7791	–1.0974	–1.641	–1.0621	–0.764	–2.0524*
+2	–0.2605	–2.6618*	–1.29	–1.2095	–1.9167	–0.7913	–1.3307	–0.8104
+3	–3.4654*	–5.4292*	–2.2604*	–2.1192*	–7.0545*	–4.5352*	–0.4419	–2.363*
+4	0.2806	–0.1587	0.0173	–2.3651*	–0.286	–2.7736*	–0.8914	–0.9232
+5	–0.7089	0.902	1.2842	2.1568*	1.2988	0.7088	0.3423	–2.3079*
+10	0.1439	–0.0794	0.0741	3.8841*	2.8962*	1.8985	–0.2246	0.452
+20	0.4159	–0.4531	–1.3097	–2.2516*	–1.8957	–0.2145	–1.9864*	1.2155
+40	–1.865	0.7344	0.584	–1.4178	–0.473	0.1531	0.5242	–0.88
+60	0.3608	0.7362	0.0482	1.5907	–0.0383	–0.0089	–2.4672*	–1.0128
+90	0.047	1.495	0.8977	2.9298*	1.035	2.5344*	0.4213	–3.0326*
+110	1.0496	0.2128	0.8412	0.7741	0.4641	0.5513	2.483*	–0.5795
+111	–1.6683	–1.3713	–0.8195	–0.0375	–0.6872	0.0802	–2.6228*	–2.3072*
+112	0.1801	–1.2299	–0.7607	0.1416	–1.2573	–0.9956	–0.9056	–0.3298
+113	0.541	0.3479	–1.0633	–2.7179*	0.0452	–0.9577	2.2781*	2.2145*
+114	4.9491*	6.2244*	2.4485*	2.9222*	3.1464*	3.4888*	2.4669*	2.3229*
+115	–0.0278	0.1274	2.1607*	1.1468	–0.5614	0.0852	–2.8425*	3.5855*
+116	0.0068	–1.0864	0.3357	–1.3117	–0.2194	–0.5174	–0.3055	–0.8375

Note: *significant at the 5% or better

Table 8. Standardized Cumulative Abnormal Returns (SCAR) for Each National Equity Market, For Selected Multi-Day Intervals Around the Invasion of Kuwait (Day $t = 0$) and the Initiation of the USA-Iraq War (Day $t = +112$) Market and Risk–Adjusted Return Method

Multi-Day Interval	*SCAR*	*Z-Score*	*SCAR*	*Z-Score*	*SCAR*	*Z-Score*	*SCAR*	*Z-Score*
	USA		*Toronto*		*London*		*Frankfurt*	
(–1,0)	0.5353	0.379	2.0308	1.436	1.4618	1.034	–0.7526	–0.532
(+1,+3)	–3.5692	–2.061*	–0.7025	–0.406	–5.5212	–3.188*	–5.1748	–2.988*
(+1,+5)	–2.8107	–1.257	–2.4055	–1.076	–4.6413	–2.076*	–5.8573	–2.619*
(+111,+112)	–0.2057	–0.145	–0.6323	–0.447	–1.3521	–0.956	–2.5888	–1.831
(+113,+114)	2.0639	1.459	0.6559	0.464	0.4645	0.328	4.1966	2.967*
(+113,+116)	2.8153	1.408	1.1065	0.553	–0.0959	–0.048	2.7214	1.361
	Zurich		*Paris*		*Milan*		*Amsterdam*	
(–1,0)	0.5904	0.417	0.1465	0.104	–0.8359	–0.591	0.7294	0.516
(+1,+3)	–6.4815	–3.742*	–9.1566	–5.287*	–6.644	–3.836*	–3.7843	–2.185*
(+1,+5)	–6.6065	–2.955*	–10.0834	–4.509*	–6.3541	–2.842*	–3.7521	–1.678
(+111,+112)	–2.0915	–1.479	–2.4083	–1.703	–2.1388	–1.512	–1.0361	–0.733
(+113,+114)	3.9725	2.809*	6.2088	4.39*	4.0987	2.898*	1.1955	0.845
(+113,+116)	1.9726	0.986	5.7379	2.869*	2.7151	1.358	0.363	0.182
	Stockholm		*Brussels*		*Australia*		*Tokyo*	
(–1,0)	0.7435	0.526	–0.8661	0.612	1.4516	1.026	1.3189	0.933
(+1,+3)	–4.527	–2.614*	–8.1943	–4.731*	–1.7714	–1.023	–4.4261	–2.555*
(+1,+5)	–4.9553	–2.216*	–7.451	–3.332*	–0.4699	–0.21	–4.6345	–2.073*
(+111,+112)	–1.4883	–1.052	–2.6012	–1.839	–1.5802	–1.117	0.1041	0.074
(+113,+114)	5.4901	3.882*	6.5723	4.647*	1.3852	0.979	0.2043	0.144
(+113,+116)	5.4692	2.735*	5.6132	2.807*	3.8816	1.941	0.0393	0.02
	Hong Kong		*Singapore*		*Seoul*		*Taipei*	
(–1,0)	0.1523	0.108	0.0851	0.06	1.1358	0.803	–0.9439	–0.667
(+1,+3)	–10.6122	–6.127*	–6.3886	–3.688*	–2.5366	–1.465	–5.2257	–3.017*
(+1,+5)	–9.5994	–4.293*	–8.4533	–3.78*	–3.0857	–1.38	–8.4568	–3.782*
(+111,+112)	–1.9445	–1.375	–0.9154	–0.647	–3.5284	2.495*	–2.6371	–1.865
(+113,+114)	3.1916	2.257*	2.531	1.78	4.745	3.355*	4.5375	3.208*
(+113,+116)	2.4107	1.205	2.0988	1.049	1.597	0.799	7.2855	3.643*

Note: *significant at the 5% or better

Kuwait. The results also reinforce those reported for the analysis of portfolios of national markets. Thus our hypotheses about the roles of oil prices and market integration during the Persian Gulf Crisis are not rejected by the data.[3]

Most of the *SCAR*'s for the (+111,+112) interval are negative but insignificant. On the other hand, all the *SCAR*'s for the (+113,+114) interval are positive and most of them are statistically significant. Finally for the (+113,+116) interval, all the *SCAR*'s are positive but most of them are not significant. These results suggest that the Allied Forces-Iraq War of January, 1991, seems to have had much less impact in the national equity markets than the Iraqi invasion of Kuwait on August 2, 1990, probably because of the general consensus that the War was not going to last long.

SUMMARY AND CONCLUSIONS

The paper empirically analyzes the international response of equity prices to the Persian Gulf Crisis. Daily closing price indexes for the time period October 1, 1989 through January 31, 1991 are collected from the *WSJ* and elsewhere for the World Index and 16 national markets: New York S&P 500, Toronto 300 Composite, London FT-100, Frankfurt DAX, Zurich Credit Suisse, Paris CAC 40, Milan Stock Index, Amsterdam ANP-CBS General, Stockholm Affarsvarlden, Brussels Bel-20 Index, Australia All Ordinaries, Hong Kong Hang Seng, Singapore Straits Times, Tokyo Nikkei Average, Seoul-Korea, and Taipei-Taiwan. The data sample is divided into an estimation period containing observations –206 through –44, and an event period containing observations –43 through +119. The event period "0" corresponds to August 2, 1990, the day Iraq invaded Kuwait. Other important dates in the sample are January 16, 1991 (observation $t = +112$), the day the Allied Forces-Iraq War began, and January 24, 1991 (observation $t = +118$), the day the International Coalition launched the ground attack.

Two event-study methodologies are used: Mean-Adjusted Return Method and Market and Risk-adjusted Return Method. Daily and Cumulative abnormal returns for selected intervals and the corresponding *Z*-statistics are computed for each individual national market and for three portfolios of national equity markets: "U.S. and Canada" portfolio, composed of the S&P 500 and Toronto; "Europe" portfolio, composed of the eight European markets: London, Frankfurt, Zurich, Paris, Milan, Amsterdam, Stockholm, and Brussels; and "Asia and Australia" portfolio, composed of Tokyo, Hong Kong, Singapore, Seoul, Taipei, and Australia. Both methodologies produce similar results.

The empirical findings confirm that the Persian Gulf Crisis has had a negative effect on equity market prices. The negative abnormal returns are evidence of the important roles played in the world economies by both oil prices and the integration of national equity markets. The results also suggest that the Gulf War has had a greater negative impact on the European, Asian and Australian markets than on the American and Canadian markets. Thus, national stock markets seemed to have responded to the oil crisis according to the country's dependence on oil. Another important result is that the initiation of the Gulf War had a much lesser impact on equity market prices than the invasion of Kuwait.

The analysis of abnormal returns for individual stock markets indicates that the national markets reacted to both events, the invasion of Kuwait and the beginning of the Gulf War, with lags of two and three days. The statistically significant negative abnormal returns on day $t = +3$ (three days after the invasion of Kuwait), probably reflect investors' fear of a long armed conflict in the Middle East. On the other hand, the statistically significant positive abnormal returns on day $t = +114$ (two days after the beginning of the War) suggest that investors expected a quick end to the Gulf War.

ACKNOWLEDGMENT

We are thankful to Chirag Patel and Wichai Saenghirunwattana for data collection and extensive computational assistance. An earlier version was presented at the *Financial Management Association* meetings in Chicago, the *Eastern Finance Association* meetings in Tampa and the *Southern Finance Association* meetings in Jacksonville. We are grateful to numerous conference participants for their comments. Two anonymous referees of this journal have offered several useful suggestions that improved our analysis.

NOTES

1. We are thankful to Hyun-Mo Sung of Loyola University Chicago and Wen-herng King of the University of British Columbia for obtaining directly from South Korea and Taiwan, respectively, the needed stock market data for these two countries. These two markets were added at the request of an anonymous referee.
2. The results of the tests for shifts in regression coefficients are available from the authors upon request.
3. For a detailed analysis of the role of oil prices during the Gulf Crisis using lead-lag methodology see Malliaris and Urrutia (1994).

REFERENCES

Alexander, G., P. G. Benson, and J. M. Kampmeyer. (1984). "Investigating the Valuation Effects of Announcements of Voluntary Corporate Selloffs." *Journal of Finance*, 39: 503–517.

Brenner, M. (1979). "The Sensitivity of the Efficient Market Hypothesis to Alternative Specifications of the Market Model." *Journal of Finance*, 34: 915–929.

Brown, S. J. and J. B. Warner. (1980). "Measuring Security Price Performance." *Journal of Financial Economics*, 8: 205–258.

———. (1985). "Using Daily Stock Returns: The Case of Event Studies." *Journal of Financial Economics*, 14: 3–32.

Dann, L. (1981). "Common Stock Repurchases: An Analysis of Returns to Bondholders and Stockholders." *Journal of Financial Economics*, 9: 113–138.

Dodd, P. (1980). "Merger Proposals, Management Discretion and Stockholder Wealth." *Journal of Financial Economics*, 8: 105–137.

Dodd, P. and J. B. Warner. (1983). "On Corporate Governance: A Study of Proxy Contests." *Journal of Financial Economics*, 11: 401–438.

Dyckman, T., D. Philbrick, and J. Stephan. (1984). "A Comparison of Event Study Methodologies Using Daily Stock Returns: A Simulation Approach." *Journal of Accounting Research*, 22: 1–33.

Fama, E. F. and J. D. MacBeth. (1973). "Risk, Return and Equilibrium: Empirical Tests." *Journal of Political Economy*, 71: 607–636.
Grubel, H. (1968). "Internationally Diversified Portfolios: Welfare Gains and Capital Flows." *American Economic Review*, 58: 1299–1314.
Gujarati, D. (1970). "Use of Dummy Variables in Testing for Equality Between Sets of Coefficients in Linear Regression." *American Statistician*, 24: 18–21.
Hilliard, J. (1979). "The Relationship Between Equity Indexes on World Exchanges." *Journal of Finance*, 34: 103–114.
Holthausen, R. (1981). "Evidence on the Effect of Bond Covenants and Management Compensation Contracts on the Choice of Accounting Techniques: The Case of the Depreciation Switchback." *Journal of Accounting and Economics*, 7: 73–109.
Klein, A. and J. Rosenfeld. (1987). "The Influence of Market Conditions on Event Study Residuals." *Journal of Financial and Quantitative Analysis*, 22: 345–351.
Leftwich, R. (1981). "Evidence on the Impact of Mandatory Changes in Accounting Principles on Corporate Loan Agreements." *Journal of Accounting and Economics*, 3: 3–36.
Lessard, D. (1976). "World Country, and Industry Relationships in Equity Returns: Implications for Risk Reduction through International Diversification." *Financial Analysts Journal*, 32: 2–8.
Levy, H. and M. Sarnat. (1970). "International Diversification of Investment Portfolio." *American Economics Review*, 60: 668–675.
Malliaris, A. G. and J. Urrutia. (1994). "Oil and World Stock Markets Reaction to the Gulf Crisis." In *International Stock Market Relationships and Linkages*, edited by J. Doukas. Westport, CT: Greenwood Publishing.
Masulis, R. W. (1980). "The Effect of Capital Structure Change on Security Prices: A Study of Exchange Offers." *Journal of Financial Economics*, 8: 139–178.
Patell, J. M. (1976). "Corporate Forecasts of Earnings per Share and Stock Price Behavior: Empirical Tests." *Journal of Accounting Research*, 14: 246–276.
Roll, R. (1988). "The International Crash of October 1987." *Financial Analysts Journal*, 44: 19–35.
———. (1989). "*Price, Volatility, International Market Links and Their Implications for Regulatory Policies.*" Working Paper, University of California, Los Angeles.
Ruback, R. S. (1982). "The Effect of Discriminatory Price Control Decisions on Equity Values." *Journal of Financial Economics*, 10: 83–105.
Solnik, B. (1974a). "An Equilibrium Model of the International Capital Market." *Journal of Economic Theory*, 8: 400–424.
———. (1974b). "The International Pricing of Risk: An Empirical Investigation of the World Capital Market Structure." *Journal of Finance*, 29: 48–54.
Stehle, R. (1977). "An Empirical Test of the Alternative Hypotheses of National and International Pricing of Risky Assets." *Journal of Finance*, 32: 493–502.
Stulz, R. (1981). "A Model of International Asset Pricing." *Journal of Finance*, 9: 383–406.
von Furstenberg, G. and B. N. Jeon. (1989). "International Stock Price Movements: Links and Messages." *Brookings Papers on Economic Activity*, 1: 125–167.
Wheatley, S. (1988). "Some Tests of International Equity Integration." *Journal of Financial Economics*, 21: 177–222.

OIL AND WORLD STOCK MARKETS' REACTION TO THE GULF CRISIS

A.G. Malliaris and Jorge L. Urrutia

ABSTRACT

This paper uses two methodologies to empirically investigate the economic significance of the Gulf Crisis on the oil and world equity markets. The first methodology is an event study based on the market and risk-adjusted return. Daily and cumulative abnormal returns are calculated for selected multi-day intervals for 12 world equity markets. The results indicate that significant negative abnormal returns materialized on the third day after the Iraqi invasion of Kuwait, while significant positive abnormal returns were observed two days after the war began. Furthermore both of these findings are stronger for portfolios of national markets of countries that are oil importing. The second methodology uses Granger causality between oil and world equity markets to confirm the importance of oil. While little causality is detected between oil and world equity markets prior to the invasion of Kuwait, strong contemporaneous causality and an increase in lead-lag and feedback is present between these markets during the Gulf Crisis period.

Research in International Business and Finance, Supplement 1, pages 133–153.

ISBN: 0-7623-0110-4

INTRODUCTION

From early August 1990 to January 1991, the world news was dominated by the Persian Gulf Crisis. The financial press, in particular, attempted to assess the impact of the crisis on world equity and oil markets. Furthermore, because of the significance of the crisis, various assertions were made that this world event had triggered the U.S. macroeconomic recession. It is the purpose of this paper to subject daily data of 12 national stock markets and the oil market to two rigorous methodological analyses which would enable us to obtain specific statistical evidence of what actually the data show. The first methodology is the market and risk-adjusted return event-study approach and the second is the Granger causality approach.

These two methodologies are selected because of the issues we wish to explore. First, motivated by Roll (1988) who suggested that the October 1987 world stock market crash was caused by some "unnamed worldwide triggering variable," we wish to confirm that the Persian Gulf Crisis was an identifiable global event that generated declines in world equity markets. Obviously, declines were both observed and reported in the financial press. However, such casual evidence is not sufficient to confirm the impact of the Gulf Crisis. A rigorous event methodology is needed to evaluate the effect of the Iraqi invasion of Kuwait.

In conducting such an event methodology, one needs to be aware of the joint hypothesis of market efficiency according to which returns of world equity markets continuously adjust to the flow of new information concerning developments in the Persian Gulf during the period of August 1990 to January 1991. In other words, under the grand umbrella of the Persian Gulf Crisis, examination of daily data can be used to reveal the response of aggregate returns to the release of relevant information. For example, while the news of Iraq's invasion of Kuwait was announced early on August 2, 1990, the strong opposition, first, by the United States and almost subsequently by numerous other countries, intensified what was a local conflict between two neighboring Gulf countries into a worldwide major political event. The further escalation, three days after the invasion by the government of Iraq, induced investors worldwide to assess these developments seriously. Similarly, investors daily assessed the eventual resolution of this conflict as the Allied forces prepared to liberate Kuwait and correctly anticipated a quick and successful ground attack by the Allied forces. These issues are discussed in Malliaris and Urrutia (1995).

Embedded in our event methodology is the significance of oil in the world economy. Obviously, Kuwait's invasion disrupted oil production and caused world oil prices to increase dramatically. To investigate the specific impact of oil on world equity markets we use Granger's causality methodology. We hypothesize that the Gulf Crisis with both its actual and potential disruption of world oil output affected world equity returns and, conversely, such equity returns, by the efficiency of world equity markets correctly anticipated the evolution of oil prices.

The next section briefly presents the data used while the third section describes the event study methodology. The Granger causality methodology is the topic of the fourth section. The last two sections are devoted to an analysis of our results and our conclusions, respectively.

DATA DESCRIPTION

Daily closing price indexes for the time period October 1, 1989 through January 31, 1991, are collected from the *WSJ*, for the World Index and 12 national markets: New York S&P 500, Toronto 300 Composite, London FT-100, Frankfurt DAX, Zurich Credit Swisse, Paris CAC40, Milan Stock Index, Amsterdam ANP-CBS General, Australia All Ordinaries, Hong-Kong Hang Seng, Singapore Straits Times, and Tokyo Nikkei Average.

Daily returns are computed as $R_t = 100 * [\ln(P_t/P_{t-1})]$, where P_t and P_{t-1} are daily price indexes for days t and $t-1$, respectively. The data sample is divided into an "Estimation Period" from October 1, 1989 through June 30, 1990 ($t = -206$ to $t = -23$), and an "Event Period," from July 1, 1990 to January 31, 1991 ($t = -22$ to $t = +119$). The event day ($t = 0$) corresponds to August 2, 1990, the day Iraq invaded Kuwait. Other important dates in the data sample are January 16, 1991 ($t = +112$) the day the Allied Forces - Iraq war began, and January 24, 1991 ($t = +118$), the day the International Coalition launched the ground attack.

EVENT-STUDY METHODOLOGY

In order to determine if an asset's returns are abnormal, it is necessary to compare them to a benchmark. This paper uses the market and risk-adjusted return method which takes into account both the market-wide factors and the systematic risks of each security. This method seems to be the favorite procedure of event-study researchers. It presumes that the CAPM generates expected returns and uses a regression model to predict the security's expected returns. This OLS regression procedure, known as the market model, consists of regressing the security's returns on the market's returns. The security's excess return is equal to the difference between the observed return during the event period and the return predicted by the OLS regression.

Let $R_{i,t}$ designate the observed return for national market i at time t. Define $AR_{i,t}$ as the excess or abnormal return for national market i at day t. For every national market, the excess or abnormal return for each day in the event period is estimated using the following formula:

$$AR_{i,t} = R_{i,t} - [\hat{\alpha}_i + \hat{\beta}_i R_{w,t}] \quad (1)$$

where $R_{w,t}$ is the observed return for the World Index at day t of the event period, ($t = -22, +119$), and $\hat{\alpha}_i$, $\hat{\beta}_i$ are the OLS values obtained by running regression (2) for the estimation period ($t = -206,-23$)

$$R_{i,t} = \alpha_i + \beta_i R_{w,t} + \varepsilon_{i,t}\,. \tag{2}$$

The standardized daily abnormal returns for national market i, $SAR_{i,t}$, are given by:

$$SAR_{i,t} = \frac{AR_{i,t}}{S_{i,t}} \tag{3}$$

where $S_{i,t}$ is the square root of national market i's estimated forecast variance, calculated as

$$S_{i,t} = \sqrt{S_i^2 \left[1 + \left(\frac{1}{184} \right) + \frac{(R_{w,t} - \overline{R}_w)^2}{\sum_{k=-206}^{-23} (R_{w,k} - \overline{R}_w)} \right]}\,. \tag{4}$$

In equation (4), $R_{w,t}$, $R_{w,k}$ denote observed returns for the World Index at day t of the event period and day k of the estimation period, respectively and $\overline{R}_w$ is the average return of the World Index for the estimation period, computed by

$$\overline{R}_w = \frac{1}{184} \sum_{k=-206}^{-23} R_{w,k}\,. \tag{5}$$

Finally, S_i^2 is the residual variance for national market i, that corresponds to the mean-squared error of the OLS regression (2) and the number of observations in the estimation period is 184.

The cumulative abnormal returns for national market i, $SCAR_i$, over a multi-day period (t_1, t_2), are computed by

$$SCAR_{i,t_1,t_2} = \sum_{t=t_1}^{t_2} SAR_{i,t}\,. \tag{6}$$

The cross-sectional average standardized daily abnormal return for a portfolio of national markets, at day t of the event period, $ASAR_t$ is given by:

$$ASAR_t = \frac{1}{N} \sum_{i=1}^{N} SAR_{i,t} \tag{7}$$

where N is the number of national markets in the portfolio.

The $ASAR_t$'s can be accumulated over selected multi-day intervals of the event period using

$$ASCAR_{t_1,t_2} = \sum_{t=t_1}^{t_2} ASAR_t . \tag{8}$$

In equation (8), $ASCAR_{t_1,t_2}$ denotes the average standardized cumulative abnormal return for a portfolio of national markets during the (t_1, t_2) interval of the event period.

The null hypotheses to be tested are that the mean excess return for the day t of the event period, and the mean cumulative excess return over a multi-day interval of the event period are equal to zero.

The Z-statistic for the average standardized daily abnormal returns for any event day t is computed as

$$Z_{i,t} = SAR_{i,t} \ , \ Z_t = ASAR_t\sqrt{N} \tag{9}$$

for an individual national market and for a portfolio of national markets, respectively. The Z-statistic for the average standardized cumulative abnormal returns over a multi-day interval (t_1,t_2) of the event period is calculated as:

$$Z_{i,t_1,t_2} = \frac{SCAR_{i,t_1,t_2}}{\sqrt{t_2 - t_1 + 1}}, \quad Z_{t_1,t_2} = \frac{ASCAR_{t_1,t_2}\sqrt{N}}{\sqrt{t_2 - t_1 + 1}} \tag{10}$$

for an individual national market and for a portfolio of national markets, respectively.

These statistics are widely used in event studies, as in Patell (1976), Masulis (1980), Dodd (1980), Dann (1981), Holthausen (1981), Leftwich (1981), Dodd and Warner (1983), and Brown and Warner (1980, 1985).

GRANGER CAUSALITY TESTS

The lead-lag tests used in this paper are based on the Granger tests of causality. The causal test of Granger is essentially a test of the predictive ability of time-series models. A time series $\{Y_t\}$ causes another time series $\{X_t\}$, if present X can be predicted better by using past values of Y than by not doing so, other relevant information, including the past of X, being used in either case. More formally, let $\sigma^2(X/U_t)$ be the variance of X given the information in the universe accumulated since (t-1) and let $\overline{U}(\overline{U} - \overline{Y})$ be the information in the universe with past values of Y included and excluded, respectively. The following definitions of causality are of interest.

1. Unidirectional causality: if $\sigma^2(X/\overline{U}) < \sigma^2(X/\overline{U} - \overline{Y})$ then Y is causing or leading X, denoted by $Y \rightarrow X$.
2. Bidirectional causality or feedback: if $\sigma^2(X/\overline{U}) < \sigma^2(X/\overline{U} - \overline{Y})$, and $\sigma^2(Y/\overline{U}) < \sigma^2(Y/\overline{U} - \overline{X})$ then feedback is occurring, denoted by $Y \leftrightarrow X$.

A description of the several testable forms of Granger causality can be found in Pierce and Haugh (1977), Geweke, Meese, and Dent (1983), and Guilkey and Salemi (1982). In this paper we use the following version of the Granger causal model:

$$\ln Y_t = \alpha_0 + \sum_{i=1}^{m} \alpha_i \ln X_{t-i} + \sum_{j=1}^{m} \beta_j \ln Y_{t-j} + \varepsilon_t \tag{11}$$

$$\ln X_t = a_0 + \sum_{i=1}^{m} a_i \ln Y_{t-i} + \sum_{j=1}^{m} b_j \ln X_{t-j} + \mu_t\,. \tag{12}$$

The definition of causality given above implies that X is causing (leading) Y provided some α_i is not zero in equation (11). Similarly, Y is causing (leading) X if some a_i is not zero in equation (12). If both of these events occur, there is feedback. The statistic is calculated by estimating the above expressions in both unconstrained (full model) and constrained (reduced model) forms, and may be written as:

$$F_1 = \frac{(SSE_r - SSE_f)/m}{SSE_f/(T - 2m - 1)} \tag{13}$$

where SSE_r, SSE_f denote residual sum squares of the reduced and full models, respectively, T is the total number of observations, and m is the number of lags.

Engle and Granger (1987) show that if two nonstationary variables are cointegrated, the Granger causality tests are misspecified and an error correction term model is necessary. If variables X_t and Y_t are both nonstationary in levels but the first differences of the variables are stationary, it is said that X_t and Y_t are both integrated of order one, and denoted as $I(1)$. If variables X_t and Y_t are both $I(1)$, their linear combinations of the form $Z_t = X_t - \alpha Y_t$ are also $I(1)$. However, if there is an α such that Z_t is $I(0)$, the linear combination of X_t and Y_t is stationary and it is said the two variables are cointegrated. If cointegration is present, regressions (11) and (12) are misspecified because they exclude an error correction term that can capture the long-term relationship between the two variables.

Before testing for the presence of cointegration, it is necessary to establish that the two time series are $I(1)$. The tests of stationarity are conducted by means of the Augmented Dickey and Fuller (1981) test, ADF, regression:

$$\ln X_t - \ln X_{t-1} = b_0 + b_1 \ln X_{t-1} + \sum_{i=1}^{m} b_i (\ln X_{t-i} - \ln X_{t-i-1}) + \varepsilon_t\,. \tag{14}$$

The null hypothesis of nonstationarity is H_0: $b_1 = 0$ in equation (14).

Engle and Granger (1987) propose several ways of testing for cointegration. This paper uses the ADF test of cointegration consisting of running first the cointegration regression

$$\ln X_t = \alpha_0 + \alpha_1 \ln Y_t + \varepsilon_t \,. \tag{15}$$

and then running the following ADF regression on the residuals of (15)

$$\varepsilon_t - \varepsilon_{t-1} = b_0 - b_1 \varepsilon_{t-1} + \sum_{i=1}^{m} b_i(\varepsilon_{t-i} - \varepsilon_{t-i-1}) + \mu_t \,. \tag{16}$$

The null hypothesis of no cointegration is $H_0 : b_1 = 0$ in equation (16). If the null is rejected the variables X_t and Y_t are cointegrated and the error correcting models in equations (17) and (18) are needed in testing for causal relationships

$$\ln Y_t = \alpha_0 + \sum_{i=1}^{m} \alpha_i \ln X_{t-i} + \sum_{j=1}^{m} \beta_j \ln Y_{t-i} + \delta\varepsilon_{t-1} + \phi_t \tag{17}$$

$$\ln X_t = a_0 + \sum_{i=1}^{m} a_i \ln Y_{t-i} + \sum_{j=1}^{m} b_j \ln X_{t-j} + c\varepsilon_{t-1} + \mu_t \,. \tag{18}$$

In the above regression equations, the error correction term ε_{t-1} corresponds to the lagged residuals of regression (15).

ANALYSIS OF EMPIRICAL RESULTS

This section of the paper empirically analyzes the response of the equity market prices to the Persian Gulf Crisis by, first, estimating excess returns for each individual national stock market and second, by computing abnormal returns for selected portfolios of national equity markets. Since an event such as the Persian Gulf Crisis could produce changes in the alpha and beta coefficients, we proceed first to test for alpha and beta shifts by means of a procedure suggested by Ruback (1982) and Alexander, Benson, and Kampmeyer (1984). We test for alpha and beta shifts between the pre-event and post-event estimation periods using the following regression model

$$R_{i,t} = \alpha_{i,0} + \alpha_{i,1} D_t + \beta_{i,1} R_{w,t} + \beta_{i,2}(D_t R_{w,t}) + \varepsilon_{i,t}, \tag{19}$$

where $R_{i,t}$ is the observed return for national market i on day t, $R_{w,t}$ is the observed return for World Index i on day t, and D_t is the dummy variable that takes a value of zero for the pre-event estimation period and one for the post-event estimation period.

Table 1. Tests of Alpha and Beta Shifts Between the Pre-Event and Post-Event Periods (*t*-statistic in Parenthesis)

Market	$\alpha_{i,1}$	$\beta_{i,1}$
New York	–0.038 (–0.28)	0.305 (2.63)*
Toronto	–0.004 (–0.05)	0.191 (3.13)*
London	–0.096 (–0.80)	0.230 (2.28)*
Frankfurt	–0.298 (–1.52)	–0.054 (–0.33)
Zurich	–0.261 (–1.81)	0.037 (0.30)
Paris	–0.886 (–1.09)	0.336 (0.49)
Milan	–0.037 (–0.15)	–0.220 (–1.08)
Amsterdam	–0.117 (–0.95)	0.900 (0.86)
Australia	–0.037 (–0.31)	0.046 (0.46)
Tokyo	–0.178 (–0.86)	0.199 (1.13)
Hong-Kong	–0.108 (–0.76)	–0.125 (–1.04)
Singapore	–0.210 (–1.26)	0.080 (0.57)

Note: * Statistically significant at the 5% level.

Generally, the results reported in Table 1 indicate that the shifts in alphas and betas are insignificant and thus are not expected to have an important impact in the computation of abnormal returns. Therefore, the results reported in this paper correspond to those obtained by estimating alphas and betas from the pre-event estimation period containing observations from –206 through –23.

Table 2 reports the abnormal returns, *SAR*s, for the individual national markets. Before the invasion of Kuwait the *SAR*s are more negative than positive but statistically insignificant. For the day $t = +1$ and day $t = 0$ (the day of the invasion of Kuwait) the *SAR*s are negative or positive but insignificant in a statistical sense. All *SAR*s, except Toronto, are negative and statistically significant for day $t = +3$ (three days after the invasion of Kuwait). Most *SAR*s are insignificant on day $t = +112$ that is the day the Allied Forces-Iraq war began. However, on day $t = +114$, (two days after the initiation of the air attack) all national markets, except Toronto, exhibit statistically significant positive excess returns. On day $t = +118$ (the day the Allied Forces launched the ground attack) most *SAR*s are negative but insignificant.

In analyzing the reaction of the world equity markets to the Iraqi invasion of Kuwait, one needs to comment on the synchronization problem discussed in detail in Malliaris and Urrutia (1992). This problem has to do with the wide range of global time zones. For example, when the Iraqi army crossed the borders of Kuwait early in the morning (local Iraqi time) of August 2, 1990, the Tokyo stock market was half-way through its trading session for that day, while the New York stock market had not yet opened. The Tokyo market had negative returns for the day but were statistically insignificant. When stocks began trading in New York on the same day, August 2, 1990, the Iraqi invasion was already near its completion, and the closing S&P Index was down with negative daily returns, which were also statisti-

Table 2. Daily Standardized Abnormal Returns (SAR) for National Stock Markets for the Event Period : July 1, 1990 through January 31, 1991. ($t = -22$ to $t = +119$) Event day $t = 0$, August 2, 1990 : Iraqi invasion of Kuwait; Day $t = +112$, January 16, 1991: war started Day $t = +118$, January 24, 1991: Ground attack began

	New York	*Toronto*	*London*	*Australia*	*Frankfurt*	*Zurich*
−10	−0.6975	−1.2944	−0.6468	−0.4127	1.1011	−0.3720
−9	0.4462	0.1183	−0.4234	−0.3534	−0.3669	−0.1905
−8	−0.5060	0.5882	0.8086	−0.2121	−0.4095	0.2974
−7	−1.3127	−1.1030	−1.6249	−0.0916	−0.3687	−0.9830
−6	0.0886	0.0610	−0.0297	−0.5910	−0.5974	−0.8092
−5	0.4659	0.6314	0.1370	0.3711	−0.1178	0.0826
−4	−0.1124	−0.1874	−0.6297	0.0642	0.3174	−0.3874
−3	−0.6173	−0.0531	−0.5879	−0.6993	−0.4696	−0.4671
−2	0.1402	−0.3526	−0.5379	−0.7343	−0.2755	−0.5844
−1	2.1326*	1.0594	0.4146	0.6019	0.1677	0.5261
0	−1.5434	1.0860	0.9721	0.9317	−0.9588	0.0507
1	−0.5445	−0.4249	−1.9546	1.8771	−0.8696	−0.8947
2	−0.7786	−0.3453	−0.3218	−1.3401	−1.0593	−1.1828
3	−2.3350*	0.1949	−3.5192*	−2.3809*	−3.4958*	−4.8122*
4	−0.0009	−2.0759*	0.8925	0.0068	0.9748	1.6702
5	0.7973	0.3197	−0.0066	1.3414	−1.6965	−1.8079
6	0.5520	0.3800	0.4497	−0.2225	1.0329	0.3998
7	−0.8846	0.2685	−0.4279	0.4814	−0.3026	0.2587
8	0.5917	−0.0335	−0.8096	−0.7882	−1.5710	−2.1509*
9	−0.4114	0.2151	0.0420	0.4902	0.3320	0.0490
10	0.5148	1.0318	0.7019	0.0847	0.8383	1.0585
20	0.6245	−0.6523	0.0354	−1.3869	0.6903	0.1101
40	−0.9570	−0.7496	1.1474	0.6103	−1.3270	0.3142
60	−0.1861	0.9905	−0.9074	0.0596	0.0306	−0.7040
110	0.4296	−0.2130	0.0004	0.8870	−0.1495	−0.5499
111	−0.6745	−0.6674	−1.1219	−0.8686	−2.5290*	−2.2277*
112	0.4790	0.0439	−0.3011	−0.8006	−0.1877	0.0079
113	−0.4848	−1.0986	−1.8528	−1.1707	−0.0358	0.1846
114	2.5903*	1.5816	2.4730*	2.5563*	4.4182*	4.0501*
116	−0.2783	−0.1513	−1.0075	0.3451	−0.7151	−1.0788
117	−0.5425	−0.1653	−0.39	0.0989	−0.7468	0.5522
118	0.0838	−0.6521	−0.5074	−0.4512	−0.7380	0.8078
119	0.9429	1.0109	0.7711	0.4028	0.6898	1.7633

(continued)

cally insignificant. The closing times of the other ten markets fall approximately between Tokyo and New York, with Australia being the first stock market to trade.

On August 3, 1990 when Tokyo, Australia, Hong-Kong, and Singapore started trading, it was known that the invasion had been completed and that the United States had warned Iraq to withdraw. As the hours passed and the markets, first in

Table 2. (Continued)

	Paris	*Milan*	*Amsterdam*	*Tokyo*	*Hong Kong*	*Singapore*
-10	-0.1037	1.0422	-0.3437	-0.2179	1.6269	2.2583*
-9	-0.8662	-0.1863	-0.0011	0.1927	-0.3214	0.0875
-8	-0.2359	-0.1047	0.5802	-1.1659	0.2090	-0.1990
-7	-2.4764*	-0.9020	-0.9308	-1.0964	0.3891	0.1528
-6	-0.3103	-0.9964	-0.2342	-0.4000	-1.7841	-0.6161
-5	-0.4345	-0.3063	0.4732	0.1554	0.4747	0.3374
-4	-1.2461	0.4796	-0.3043	-0.6210	-1.1514	-0.1504
-3	-1.4599	0.0067	-0.6183	-1.1716	0.0023	0.2856
-2	-1.0641	-0.0271	-0.2474	-1.1335	-1.0155	-0.5053
-1	-0.0829	0.4103	0.3957	1.4682	-0.3037	-0.1349
0	-0.8258	-1.2741	0.3683	-0.0960	0.4593	0.2191
1	-2.5759*	-2.3892*	0.1996*	-1.1320	-1.7014	-1.1274
2	-2.9116*	-0.9145	-1.9668*	-1.2518	-1.9668*	-0.8603
3	-5.5254*	-3.6662*	-2.2503*	-2.1868*	-7.3418*	-4.7749*
4	1.4278	-0.2909	1.3896	-2.4402*	-0.3261	-2.9078*
5	-3.4674*	0.5763	-1.3550	2.2365*	1.3247	0.7611
6	0.6362	-0.9412	-0.0573	-2.1320*	-1.8150	0.0058
7	-0.5761	0.0076	-0.0291	-0.6189	-0.5295	-1.7102
8	-0.5708	-1.0897	-1.3832	-3.1688*	-1.1862	-3.0904*
9	-4.1186*	-0.1982	0.3928	1.0227	1.0043	0.1402
10	-0.5716	-0.2230	0.6821	4.0235*	3.0139*	1.9959*
20	0.4357	-0.5809	0.4425	-2.3229*	-1.9955*	-0.2102
40	0.9700	0.9534	-0.1928	-1.4614	-0.5059	0.1683
60	-1.7621	-0.2604	0.0959	1.6498	-0.0308	-0.0201
110	-1.3326	-0.0762	-0.1012	0.8051	0.4790	0.5798
111	-4.0285*	-2.3221*	-1.1149	-0.0332	-0.7351	0.0964
112	0.4705	0.0626	0.0168	0.1511	-1.3152	-1.0472
113	-0.4819	0.5982	-0.7139	-2.8133*	-0.0501	-0.9468
114	5.8185*	3.6398*	1.9894*	3.0303*	3.2259*	3.7073*
116	-0.9798	-1.0850	-0.8667	-1.3511	-0.2501	-0.5333
117	-0.8740	-1.4057	-0.0995	-0.1903	-0.2968	0.2548
118	-2.1601	-0.6337	-0.2443	-0.8043	0.9419	-0.6991
119	1.3499	0.1176	0.5137	0.6483	1.4776	0.4705

Note: * Significant at the 5% confidence level or better.

the Far East, then in Europe and finally in Canada and the United States closed, once again, almost all had negative but statistically insignificant returns. By August 5, 1990, three days after the completion of Kuwait's invasion and the strong warning by the United States and the U.N. Security Council, it became clear to the financial community that such an invasion was no longer a local dispute between two oil-producing Arab neighbors, but rather a global event with the U.S.-Allied Forces taking a strong position against Iraq. When Iraq failed to withdraw from Kuwait on August 5, 1990, early that day Kuwaiti time, first the Far Eastern stock markets followed by the European and finally by New York sold off with negative and statistically significant abnormal returns. Only Toronto did not react on August 5, and instead reacted the following day.

In sum, only five out of twelve national markets exhibit negative abnormal returns in the day of the invasion of Kuwait ($t = 0$) and the day the war started ($t = +112$). However these *SAR*s are statistically insignificant. The significant negative abnormal returns of day $t = +3$ suggest that the national equity markets reacted to the Iraqi invasion of Kuwait with three-days lag. The highly significant negative abnormal returns of day $t = +3$ reflect an increase in uncertainty and an anticipation of a long war. On the other hand, the statistically significant abnormal returns of day $t = +114$ suggest investors' expectations of a quick end to the armed conflict in the Middle East and, therefore, a dramatic reduction in uncertainty about the outcome of the conflict.

The standardized cumulative abnormal returns for individual national markets, *SCAR*s, constructed for several multi-day intervals, are presented in Table 3. Most *SCAR*s for the (–1,0) interval are positive but insignificant. Most *SCAR*s are negative but significant only for Australia, Paris, and Milan for the (0,+1) interval. However , most *SCAR*s are negative and statistically significant for the (0,+3) interval. All *SCAR*s are negative but insignificant for the (+111,+112) and (+117,+118) intervals. The *SCAR*s of Table 3 reinforce the conclusion drawn from the *SAR*s of Table 2, in the sense that national equity markets reacted with several-day lags to the invasion of Kuwait and that the event of August 2, 1990, had a bigger impact on stock prices that the initiation of the war and the ground attack.

In order to get more insights about the impact of the Gulf Crisis on equity prices, countries have been grouped in portfolios according to the degree of their dependence on oil imports as follows:

1. Partial dependence or oil exporters portfolio, composed of New York, Toronto, London, and Australia,[1]
2. European oil importers portfolio, composed of Frankfurt, Zurich, Paris, Milan, and Amsterdam; and,
3. Asian oil importers portfolio, composed of Tokyo, Hong-Kong, and Singapore.

There are other reasons for putting the UK and U.S. markets in the same portfolio. In effect, the major initiative of Operation Desert Shield was taken by these two countries. Therefore, it is expected that defense related companies in the UK and United States benefitted from the Gulf Crisis. Also, big corporations in the United States and UK often hedge against oil price fluctuations through forward and future markets.

Table 3. Standardized Cumulative Abnormal Returns (SCAR) of National Stock Markets for the Event Period : July 1, 1990 through January 31, 1991 ($t = -22$ to $t = +119$). Event Day $t = 0$, August 2, 1990: Iraqi invasion of Kuwait; Day $t = +112$, January 16,1991: war started Day $t = +118$, January 24, 1991: Ground attack began.

	(–1,0)		(0,1)		(0, +3)		(+111,+112)		(+117,+118)	
	SCAR	Z	SCAR	Z	SCAR	Z	SCAR	Z	SCAR	Z
New York	0.5892	0.4166	–2.0878	–1.4763	–5.2021	–2.6011*	–0.1955	–0.1382	–0.4588	–0.3244
Toronto	2.1454	1.5170	0.6612	0.4675	0.5107	0.2554	–0.6234	–0.4408	–0.8174	–0.5780
London	1.3867	0.9805	–0.9825	–0.6947	–4.80235	–2.4118*	–1.4230	–1.0062	–0.8975	–0.6346
Australia	1.5336	1.0844	2.8088	1.9861*	–0.9122	–0.4561	–1.6692	–1.1803	–0.3523	–0.2491
Frankfurt	–0.7910	–0.5593	–1.8283	–1.2928	–6.3835	–3.1918*	–2.7167	–1.9210	–1.4849	–1.0500
Zurich	0.5768	0.4079	–0.8440	–0.5968	–6.8390	–3.4195*	–2.2198	–1.5696	1.3600	0.9617
Paris	–0.9087	–0.6426	–3.4017	–2.4053*	–11.8387	–5.9194*	–3.5580	–2.5159*	–3.0341	–2.1454*
Milan	–0.8639	–0.6109	–3.6633	–2.5904*	–8.2440	–4.1220*	–2.2595	–1.5977	–2.0393	–1.4420
Amsterdam	0.7640	0.5403	0.5679	0.4016	–3.6492	–1.8246	–1.0981	–0.7765	–0.3437	–0.2431
Tokyo	1.3721	0.9702	–1.2281	–0.8684	–4.6666	–2.3333*	–0.1179	–0.0834	–0.9946	–0.7033
Hong Kong	0.1556	0.1100	–1.2422	–0.8783	–10.5507	–5.2754*	–2.0502	–1.4497	0.6452	0.4562
Singapore	0.0842	0.0595	–0.9083	–0.6423	–6.5435	–3.2718*	–0.9509	–0.6724	–0.4443	–0.3142

Note: * Significant at the 5% confidence level or better.

Table 4 shows the daily average standardized abnormal returns, *ASARs*, for the three portfolios. The Iraqi invasion of Kuwait had a global negative effect on all three portfolios of national markets. In effect, the abnormal returns on day $t = +3$ are all negative and significant. However, the *ASARs* are much larger for the oil

Table 4. Daily Average Standardized Abnormal Returns (ASAR) for Portfolios of National Stock Markets for the Event Period: July 1, 1990 through January 31, 1991 ($t = -22$ to $t = +119$). Event Day $t = 0$, August 2, 1990 : Iraqi invasion of Kuwait; Day $t = +112$, January 16, 1991: war started Day $t = +118$, January 24, 1991: Ground attack began.

	Exporters		*European - Imp.*		*Asian - Imp.*	
Event Day	*ASAR*	*z-Score*	*ASAR*	*z-Score*	*ASAR*	*z-Score*
−10	−0.7629	−1.5257	0.2648	0.5920	1.2224	2.1173*
−9	−0.0531	−0.1061	−0.3222	−0.7205	−0.0137	−0.0238
−8	0.1697	0.3394	0.0255	0.0570	−0.3853	−0.6673
−7	−1.0330	−2.0661*	−1.1322	−2.5317*	−0.1849	−0.3202
−6	−0.1178	−0.2356	−0.5895	−1.3181	−0.9334	−1.6167
−5	0.4013	0.8027	−0.0606	−0.1354	0.3225	0.5586
−4	−0.2164	−0.4327	−0.2282	−0.5102	0.6409	−1.1101
−3	−0.4094	−0.9788	−0.6017	−1.3453	−0.2946	−0.5102
−2	−0.3712	−0.7423	−0.4397	−0.9832	−0.8847	−1.5324
−1	1.0521	2.1042*	0.2834	0.6337	0.3432	0.5945
0	0.3616	0.7232	−0.5279	1.1805	0.1941	0.3362
1	−0.2617	−0.5234	−1.3059	−2.9202*	−1.3203	−2.2868*
2	−0.6964	−1.3929	−1.6070	−3.5934*	−1.3596	−2.3549*
3	−2.0101	−4.0201*	−3.9500	−8.8325*	−4.7678	−8.2581*
4	−0.2944	−0.5888	1.0343	2.3128*	−1.8914	−3.2760*
5	0.6129	1.2259	−1.5501	−3.4661*	1.4408	2.4955*
6	0.2898	0.5795	0.2141	0.4787	−1.3137	−2.2755*
7	−0.1407	−0.2813	−0.1283	−0.2869	−0.9529	−1.6504
8	−0.2599	−0.5198	−1.3531	−3.0256*	−2.4818	−4.2986*
9	0.0765	0.1529	−0.7086	−1.5844	0.7224	1.2513
10	0.5833	1.1666	0.3568	0.7979	3.0111	5.2154*
20	−0.3448	−0.6897	0.2195	0.4909	−1.5096	−2.6146*
40	0.0128	0.0256	0.1436	0.3210	−0.5997	−1.0387
60	−0.0109	−0.0217	−0.5200	−1.1627	0.5330	0.9231
110	0.2760	0.5520	−0.4419	−0.9881	0.6213	1.0761
111	−0.8331	−1.6662	−2.4444	−5.4659*	−0.2240	−0.3879
112	−0.1447	−0.2894	0.0740	0.1655	−0.7371	−1.2767
113	−1.1517	−2.3035*	−0.0898	−0.2008	−1.2701	−2.1998*
114	2.3003	4.6006*	3.9832	8.9067*	3.3212	5.7524*
116	−0.2730	−0.5460	−0.9451	−2.1133*	−0.7115	−1.2324
117	−0.2498	−0.4995	−0.5147	−1.1510	−0.0774	−0.1341
118	−0.3817	−0.7635	−0.5936	−1.3274	−0.1872	−0.3242
119	0.7819	1.5638	0.8868	1.9831*	0.8655	1.4991

Note: * Significant at the 5% confidence level or better.

Table 5. Average Standardized Cumulative Abnormal Returns (ASCAR) of Portfolios of National Stock Markets for the Event Period : July 1, 1990 through January 31, 1991 ($t = -22$ to $t = +119$). Event day $t = 0$, August 2, 1990 : Iraqi invasion of Kuwait; Day $t = +112$, January 16, 1991: war started Day $t = +118$, January 24, 1991: Ground attack began.

	(–1,0)		*(0,1)*		*(0,+3)*		*(+111,+112)*		*(+117,+118)*	
	SCAR	*Z*	*SCAR*	*Z*	*SCAR*	*Z*	*SCAR*	*Z*	*SCAR*	*Z*
Exporters Portfolio	1.4137	1.9993*	0.0999	0.1413	–2.6066	–2.6066*	–0.9778	–1.3828	–0.6315	–0.8931
Europe Importers Portfolio	–0.2446	–0.3867	–1.8339	–2.8996*	–7.3098	–8.2629*	–2.3704	–3.7480*	–1.1084	–1.7525
Asian Importers Portfolio	0.5373	0.6581	–1.1262	–1.3793	–7.2536	–6.2816*	–0.9611	–1.1771	–0.2646	–0.3241

Note: * Significant at the 5% confidence level or better.

importer portfolios than for the oil exporter portfolio. The *SAR*s are all negative for day $t = +111$ (one day before the war began), but are statistically significant only for the European importer portfolio. However, for day $t = +114$ (two days after the air attack started), all *SAR*s are positive and significant, but again, larger for the oil importer countries. For day $t = +118$ (the day the ground attack began) all *SAR*s are negative but not statistically significant.

The results of Table 4 indicate that the capital markets of oil importing countries were more affected than those of oil exporting countries by the Gulf Crisis. The abnormal returns for the portfolio of national markets also indicate that the negative impact of the conflict on stock prices was stronger on the days following the invasion of Kuwait than around the actual war.

The portfolios' cumulative abnormal returns (*ASCAR*s), presented in Table 5, indicate that the three portfolios experienced significant negative abnormal returns in the (0,+3) interval. Again, the negative impact is stronger for oil importing countries. The *ASCAR*s are also negative around the initiation of the war, the (+111,+112) interval, but they are significant only for the European oil importing portfolio.

The empirical findings for the portfolios of exporting and importing countries confirm the results reported for the individual national markets. That is, large

Table 6. Augmented Dickey-Fuller Tests of Stationarity for Oil Prices and Selected Equity Prices

Market	b_0	b_1	b_2	b_3	b_4	R^2
New York	0.167	–0.029	–0.068	–0.028	–0.076	0.028
	(0.082)	(0.014)	(0.056)	(0.056)	(0.056)	(2.26)
	(2.043)*	(–2.046)	(–1.211)	(–0.493)	(–1.352)	
Frankfurt	0.055	–0.007	–0.041	0.004	0.056	0.007
	(0.063)	(0.008)	(0.056)	(0.056)	(0.056)	(0.575)
	(0.877)	(–0.885)	(–0.724)	(0.070)	(0.993)	
Tokyo	0.028	–0.0029	0.062	–0.146	–0.005	0.026
	(0.059)	(0.006)	(0.056)	(0.056)	(0.056)	(2.078)
	(0.476)	(–0.500)	(1.095)	(–2.623)	(–0.081)	
Oil	0.029	–0.010	0.099	–0.202	0.023	0.051
	(0.024)	(0.008)	(0.056)	(0.056)	(0.057)	(4.286)*
	(1.196)	(–1.196)	(1.755)	(–3.636)*	(0.410)	

Notes: Model:

$$\ln P_t - \ln P_{t-1} = b_0 + b_1 \ln P_{t-1} + b_2(\ln P_{t-1} - \ln P_{t-2}) + b_3(\ln P_{t-2} - \ln P_{t-3}) + b_4(\ln P_{t-3} - \ln P_{t-4}) + \varepsilon_t$$

The null hypothesis is $b_1 = 0$ (prices are non-stationary).

The critical *t*-statistic for the b_1 coefficient at the 5% confidence level is –2.88 (from Dickey and Fuller 1981).

An asterisk * indicates significant at the 5% level.

Standard errors and *t*-statistics in parentheses.

negative abnormal returns in the days immediately following the invasion of Kuwait, reflecting an increase in market uncertainty and investors' expectations of a long armed conflict. The lesser impact on equity prices of the initiation of the war and the final ground attack suggest a decrease in uncertainty and investors' expectations of a quick end to the war. Finally, the negative impact of the Gulf Crisis was more dramatic in the equity markets of European and Asian importer countries than in those of in oil exporter countries.

Granger causality tests have also been conducted in order to examine the changes produced by the Gulf Crisis in the relationships between the oil market and the equity markets. Daily closing prices for the Arab lite oil spot have been collected from the *Wall Street Journal* for the time period October 1, 1989 through January 31, 1991. Causality tests have been conducted for two time periods, the pre-event period from October 1, 1989 through June 30, 1990; and the event-period from July 1, 1990 through January 31, 1991. Three representative national equity markets have been selected: New York (an oil exporter), Frankfurt (a European oil importer), and Tokyo (an Asian oil importer).

Table 7. Augmented Dickey-Fuller Tests of Stationarity for Oil Returns and Selected Equity Returns

Market	b_0	b_1	b_2	b_3	b_4	R^2
New York	–0.001	–1.242	0.157	0.114	0.024	0.542
	(0.001)	(0.124)	(0.104)	(0.083)	(0.056)	(93.576)*
	(–0.355)	(–10.042)*,a	(1.510)	(1.377)	(0.421)	
Frankfurt	–0.001	(–1.031)	(–0.014)	(–0.016)	(0.034)	0.525
	(0.001)	(0.115)	(0.100)	(0.081)	(0.056)	(87.174)*
	(–0.518)	(–8.976)*,a	(–0.139)	(–0.191)	(0.605)	
Tokyo	–0.001	–1.113	0.172	0.022	0.016	0.485
	(0.001)	(0.116)	(0.098)	(0.077)	(0.056)	(74.481)*
	(–1.398)	(–9.608)*,a	(1.751)	(0.281)	(0.288)	
Oil	0.001	–1.117	0.212	0.001	0.022	0.485
	(0.003)	(0.115)	(0.098)	(0.077)	(0.057)	(74.451)*
	(0.139)	(–9.669)*,a	(2.152)*	(0.007)	(0.395)	

Notes: Model:

$$R_t - R_{t-1} = b_0 + b_1 R_{t-1} + b_2(R_{t-1} - R_{t-2}) + b_3(R_{t-2} - R_{t-3}) + b_4(R_{t-3} - R_{t-4}) + \varepsilon_t$$

where

$$R_t = 100\ln(P_t/P_{t-1})$$

The null hypothesis is $b_1 = 0$ (returns are non-stationary)

The critical *t*-statistic for the b_1 coefficient at the 5% confidence level is –2.88 (from Dickey and Fuller 1981, Table 8.5.2).

An "a" indicates rejection of the null hypothesis at the 5% of significance level.

An asterisk * indicates significance at the 5% level.

Standard errors and *t*-statistics in parentheses.

Prior to the implementation of the Granger causality tests, it is necessary to check first, if prices are integrated of order one, denoted by $I(1)$, and second, if they are cointegrated. The results of the Augmented Dickey and Fuller, (ADF), tests of stationarity for the price levels and the price first differences or returns are presented in Tables 6 and 7, respectively.[2] The null hypothesis of nonstationarity cannot be rejected for price levels but it is rejected for returns. Therefore prices are $I(1)$, and tests of cointegration are appropriate. Table 8 indicates that the null of no-cointegration cannot be rejected in all cases, except for New York stock prices and oil prices. Therefore, Granger causality tests are conducted by running regressions (11) and (12), but for New York-oil we run regressions (17) and (18) which incorporate an error correction term to correct for cointegration. The results presented in Table 9 show[3] contemporaneous causality and strong lead-lag relationships between oil markets and the selected national equity markets. Contemporaneous causality and feedback suggest that oil markets and equity markets reacted simultaneously to the Persian Gulf Crisis and they affected each other during the conflict.

Table 8. Tests Of Cointegration Between Oil Prices And Selected Equity Prices

Independent Variable	*Dependent Variable*	b_1	R^2
New York	Oil	–0.0954	0.073
		(–3.48)[b]	(6.21)*
Oil	New York	–0.072	0.07
		(–2.94)[c]	(5.93)*
Frankfurt	Oil	–0.012	0.032
		(–0.89)	(2.62)*
Oil	Frankfurt	–0.014	0.034
		(–1.12)	(2.79)*
Tokyo	Oil	–0.006	0.02
		(–0.53)	(1.35)
Oil	Tokyo	–0.013	0.023
		(–1.08)	(1.82)

Notes: The model used to test for cointegration is the following:

$$\ln P_{1t} = \alpha_0 + \alpha_1 \ln P_{2t} + \varepsilon_t \qquad \text{(a)}$$

$$\varepsilon_t - \varepsilon_{t-1} = b_0 + b_1\varepsilon_{t-1} + b_2(\varepsilon_{t-1} - \varepsilon_{t-2}) + b_3(\varepsilon_{t-2} - \varepsilon_{t-3}) + b_4(\varepsilon_{t-3} - \varepsilon_{t-4}) + \mu_t \qquad \text{(b)}$$

The null hypothesis of no-cointegration is $H_0 : b_1 = 0$ (in equation *b*).
The *t*-critical at the 5% and 10% of significant levels are 3.17 and 2.84, respectively (from Engle and Granger 1987).
An "b" or a "c" indicate rejection of the null of no-cointegration at the 5% or 10%, respectively.
An asterisk * indicates the individual regression coefficient is different from zero at the 5% level.
t-statistics in parentheses.

Table 9. Granger Causality Test Between Oil Market And Selected National Equity Markets

Independent Variable	*Dependent Variable*	b_0, β_0	b_1, β_1	b_2, β_2	b_3, β_3	F
Oil	Frankfurt	–0.7537	–0.3789	–0.2322	–0.2961	10.26[a]
		(0.1384)	(0.1441)	(0.1454)	(0.1445)	
		(–5.445)*	(–2.629)*	(–1.597)	(2.050)	
Frankfurt	Oil	–0.1145	–0.048	0.017	–0.027	10.14[a]
		(0.0210)	(0.0219)	(0.0222)	(0.0221)	
		(–5.445)*	(–2.186)*	(0.767)	(–1.229)	
Oil	Tokyo	–0.4720	–0.0691	0.1020	0.1070	3.40[a]
		(0.1431)	(0.1440)	(0.1445)	(0.1406)	
		(–3.299)*	(–0.480)	(0.706)	(0.761)	
Tokyo	Oil	–0.0710	–0.0928	0.0239	–0.0617	9.43[a]
		(0.0225)	(0.0220)	(0.0226)	(0.0227)	
		(–3.299)*	(–4.219)*	(1.061)	(–2.723)*	
Oil	New York	–1.1641	–0.6841	–0.3958	0.1934	12.30[a]
		(0.1954)	(0.2062)	(0.2080)	(0.2067)	
		(–5.975)*	(–3.318)*	(–1.903)	(0.935)	
New York	Oil	–0.0840	0.0140	–0.0116	0.0077	11.16[a]
		(0.0147)	(0.0160)	(0.0158)	(0.0156)	
		(–5.724)*	(0.877)	(–0.732)	(0.496)	

Notes:

$$\ln Y_t = \alpha_0 + \sum_{i=1}^{m} \alpha_i \ln X_{t-i} + \sum_{j=1}^{m} \beta_j \ln Y_{t-j} + \delta\varepsilon_{t-1} + \phi_\tau \quad (X_t \to Y_t)^b \qquad \text{(I)}$$

$$\ln X_t = \alpha_0 + \sum_{i=1}^{3} a_i \ln Y_{t-i} + \sum_{j=1}^{3} b_j \ln X_{t-j} + c\varepsilon_{t-1} + \mu_t \quad (Y_t \to X_t)^b \qquad \text{(II)}$$

An asterisk * indicates significant at the 5% confidence level or better.
An "a" indicates rejection of the null hypothesis of no-causality at the 5% level or better.
A "b" means that $c = 0$, $\delta = 0$ if no cointegration (cointegration is present only for oil prices and New York stock prices).
Equation I and II are Granger test of causality. Equation I tests if X is leading Y, and equation II tests if Y is leading X. If both events occur there is a feedback, Coefficients b_0 or β_0 statistically different from zero implies contemporaneous causality. The variable ε_{t-1} corresponds to the error correcting term if cointegration is present. The null hypotheses of no-causality are $\Sigma\beta_j = 0$ or $\Sigma b_j = 0$ for equations I and II, respectively.

SUMMARY AND CONCLUSIONS

The purpose of this paper is to empirically investigate the impact of the Gulf Crisis on national equity markets and the changes in causality relationships between the oil and equity markets during the Iraq-Kuwait conflict. The data consist of daily closing prices for the time period October 1, 1989 through January 31, 1991 for the World Index, Arab light oil and the following national equity markets: New York S&P 500, Toronto 300 Composite, London FT-100, Frankfurt DAX, Zurich Credit

Swisse, Paris CAC40, Milan Stock Index, Amsterdam ANP-CBS General, Australia All Ordinaries, Hong-Kong Hang Seng, Singapore Straits Times, and Tokyo Nikkei Average. The data are divided into an "Estimation period from October 1, 1989 to June 30, 1990 ($t = -206$ to $t = -23$), and an "Event period" from July 1, 1990 to January 31, 1991 ($t = -22$ to $t = +119$). The event day t=0 corresponds to August 2, 1990, the day the Iraqi army invaded Kuwait. Two other important dates in the event period are January 16, 1991 ($t = +112$), the day the war started, and January 24, 1991 ($t = +118$), the day the Allied Forces initiated the ground attack.

Daily and cumulative abnormal returns for selected multi-day intervals are calculated for the individual national markets. Half of the national markets exhibit negative abnormal returns in the day of the invasion of Kuwait ($t = 0$) and the day the war began ($t = +112$). The significant negative abnormal returns on day $t = +3$ indicate that the national markets reacted to the Iraqi invasion of Kuwait after it became clear that the crisis took a global perspective and President Bush committed to use force to liberate Kuwait. The highly negative abnormal returns of day $t = +3$ reflect an increase in uncertainty and anticipation of a long war. On the other hand, the statistically significant positive abnormal return of day $t = +114$ (two days after the war began) suggest that investors correctly anticipated a quick end to the war. Cumulative abnormal returns for individual national indexes reinforce the conclusion that the invasion of Kuwait had a bigger negative impact on stock prices that the initiation of the war and the ground attack.

Daily and cumulative abnormal returns are also computed for the following three portfolios of national markets: oil exporters portfolio composed of New York, Toronto, London, and Australia; European oil importers portfolio composed of Frankfurt, Zurich, Paris, Milan, and Amsterdam; and Asian oil importers portfolio composed of Tokyo, Hong-Kong, and Singapore. It is found that the negative abnormal returns of day $t = +3$ are much larger for the oil importing countries than for the oil exporters. For day $t = +114$ all abnormal returns are positive and significant but larger for the oil importing countries. The empirical findings for the portfolios reinforce the conclusions drawn for individual equity markets. Thus, we confirm large negative abnormal returns in the days following the invasion of Kuwait and a lesser impact caused by the initiation of the war and the ground attack. Finally, the equity markets of European and Asian oil importing countries were more affected than those of oil exporting countries. Our findings suggest a dramatic increase in market uncertainty around the invasion of Kuwait and investors' expectations for a long armed conflict. The lesser effect of the war suggests a reduction of uncertainty after the war started and investors' expectations of a quick end to the armed conflict.

Finally, causality tests are conducted to examine the changes produced by the Persian Gulf Crisis in the lead-lag relationships between the oil market and the equity markets. Little causality is detected for the period before the invasion of Kuwait. However, strong contemporaneous causality and an increase in lead-lag relationships and feedback between oil and equity markets are found for the period during the Persian Gulf Crisis. Thus, oil and stock markets reacted simultaneously to the conflict and they affected each other during the Gulf War.

ACKNOWLEDGMENT

We are thankful to Chirag Patel, Wichai Saenghirunwattana and Henry Wen-Herng King for data collection and extensive computational assistance.

NOTES

1. For brevity of presentation, the tables and analysis describe this as a portfolio of oil exporters.
2. The results of the tests of stationarity and cointegration tests are presented only for the event-period. Prices are also found to be $I(1)$ for the pre-event period. No-cointegration is found for the pre-event period.
3. The results of the Granger causality test are reported only for the event-period. Little lead-lag relationship was detected for the pre-event period.

REFERENCES

Alexander, G., P.G. Benson, and J.M. Kampmeyer. 1984. "Investigating the Valuation Effects of Announcements of Voluntary Corporate Selloffs." *Journal of Finance* 39: 503–517.

Brown, S.J., and J.B. Warner. 1980. "Measuring Security Price Performance." *Journal of Financial Economics* 8: 205–258.

———. 1985. "Using Daily Stock Returns: The Case of Event Studies." *Journal of Financial Economics* 14: 3–32.

Dann, L. 1981. "Common Stock Repurchases: An Analysis of Returns to Bondholders and Shareholders." *Journal of Financial Economics* 9: 113–138.

Dickey, D., and W. Fuller. 1981. "Likelihood Ratio Statistics for Autoregressive Time Series with a Unit Root." *Econometrica* 49: 1057–1072.

Dodd, P. 1980. "Merger Proposals, Management Discretion and Stockholder Wealth." *Journal of Financial Economics* 8: 105–137.

Dodd, P., and J.B. Warner. 1983. "On Corporate Governance: A Study of Proxy Contests." *Journal of Financial Economics* 11: 401–438.

Engle, R.F., and C.W.J. Granger. 1987. "Cointegration and Error correction: Representation, Estimation, and Testing." *Econometrica* 55: 251–276.

Geweke, J., R. Meese, and W. Dent. 1983. "Comparing Alternative Tests of Causality in Temporal Systems." *Journal of Econometrics* 21: 161–194.

Guilkey, D.K., and M.K. Salemi. 1982. "Small Sample Properties of Three Tests for Granger Causal Ordering in a Bivariate Stochastic System." *The Review of Economics and Statistics* 64: 668–680.

Holthausen, R. 1981. "Evidence on the Effect of Bond Covenants and Management Compensation Contracts on the Choice of Accounting Techniques: The Case of the Depreciation Switchback." *Journal of Accounting and Economics* 7: 73–109.

Leftwich, R. 1981. "Evidence on the impact of Mandatory Changes in Accounting Principles on Corporate Loan Agreements." *Journal of Accounting and Economics* 3: 3–36.

Malliaris, A.G., and J. Urrutia. 1992. "The International Crash of October 1987: Causality Tests." *Journal of Financial and Quantitative Analysis* 27: 353–364.

——— 1995. "The Impact of the Persian Gulf Crisis on National Equity Markets." *Advances in International Banking and Finance* 1: 43–65.

Masulis, R.W. 1980. "The Effect of Capital Structure Change on Security Prices: A Study of Exchange Offers." *Journal of Financial Economics* 8: 139–178.
Patell, J.M. 1976. "Corporate Forecasts of Earnings per Share and Stock Price Behavior: Empirical Tests." *Journal of Accounting Research* 14: 246–276.
Pierce, D.A., and L.D. Haugh. 1977. "Causality in Temporal Systems: Characterizations and a Survey." *Journal of Econometrics* 5: 265–293.
Roll, R. 1988. "The International Crash of October 1987." *Financial Analysts Journal* pp: 19–35.
Ruback, R.S. 1982. "The Effect of Discriminatory Price Control Decisions on Equity Values." *Journal of Financial Economics* 10: 83–105.

EQUITY AND OIL MARKETS UNDER EXTERNAL SHOCKS

Jorge Urrutia and A.G. Malliaris

The chapter investigates two hypotheses: first, that the impact of the Persian Gulf Crisis was stronger on the oil market than in the equity market; and, second, that there was an increase in the causal relationship between stock and oil prices during the crisis. Event-study and Granger causality tests confirm both hypotheses. The acceptance of the first hypothesis is consistent with the nature of the conflict which primarily affected the oil market due to the embargo of Iraqi oil. Also, the high degree of diversification of the S&P 500 index lessened the impact of higher oil prices. The confirmation of the second hypothesis agrees with efficient markets in the sense that equity and oil markets reacted quickly and simultaneously to the event.

INTRODUCTION

Global events, such as the market crash of October 1987 and the Persian Gulf Crisis of August 1990, have affected the financial markets around the world. The impact of the market crash on national equity markets has been extensively documented (Roll 1988, Malliaris and Urrutia 1992). However, the Persian Gulf War, even though an important crisis highly publicized by the media, has only been a minor topic of academic research (Malliaris and Urrutia 1994).

It is known that the invasion of Kuwait and the successive events had a negative effect on equity prices and a positive effect on oil prices. The purpose of this chapter is to empirically investigate two hypotheses: first, an event-study methodology is used to investigate the hypothesis that the impact of the Gulf Crisis was stronger on the oil market than in the equity markets; and second, Granger causality tests are employed to investigate the hypothesis of a substantial increase in the causal relationship between stock and oil prices during the Persian Gulf Crisis. The rationale for our first hypothesis is twofold: first, the Gulf Crisis was mainly an oil conflict, and second, the equity indexes contain stocks of companies that benefited from the war, while others were adversely affected. Our second hypothesis is motivated by the efficient market hypothesis. That is, if financial and commodity markets are efficient, then both equity and oil prices change daily responding quickly to fundamental political and war news from the Middle East. This simultaneous reaction to the event increased the short-term linkages between the two markets.

DATA

Daily closing prices for the time period 1 October 1989 through 31 January 1991 are collected from the *Wall Street Journal* for the following instruments: S&P 500 spot, S&P 500 nearby futures, Arab lite oil spot, and crude oil (sweet light) nearby futures.

Daily returns for the spot instruments and daily percentage changes for the futures contracts are computed as $R_t = 100(ln(P_t/P_{t-1}))$ where P_t and P_{t-1} are daily prices for days t and $t-1$, respectively. The data are divided into an "Estimation Period," from 1 October 1989 to 31 May 1990 (observations $t = -206$ to $t = -44$), and an "Event Period," from 1 June 1990 to 31 January 1991 (observations $t = -43$ to $t = +119$). Thus, both the estimation period and the event period contain 163 trading days. The event day, $t = 0$, corresponds to 2 August 1990, the day of the Iraqi invasion of Kuwait. Other important dates on the sample are 16 January 1991, the beginning of the war between the International Coalition and Iraq ($t = +112$), and January 24, 1991 the start of the ground attack ($t = +118$).

METHODOLOGY

This chapter uses event-study and Granger causality methodologies. A brief description of both methods follows.

Event study methodology

The mean-adjusted return method is used to compute abnormal returns. In this method, the security's excess return is equal to the difference between the observed return during the event period and the average return of the security during the estimation period. Given the nature of the data used in this chapter the mean-adjusted return is the appropriate methodology since it does not require the use of the "market" portfolio (Masulis 1980; Brown and Warner 1980, 1985).

Let $R_{i,t}$ designate the observed return for security i at day t. Define $AR_{i,t}$ as the excess or abnormal return for security i at day t of the event period given by:

$$AR_{i,t} = R_{i,t} - \overline{R}_i \tag{1}$$

where $\overline{R}_i$ is the simple average of security i's daily returns in the $(-206, -44)$ estimation period, computed as

$$\overline{R}_i = \frac{1}{163} \sum_{t=-206}^{-44} R_{i,t}. \tag{2}$$

The daily abnormal returns for security i are standardized using

$$SAR_{i,t} = \frac{AR_{i,t}}{S_i} \tag{3}$$

where $SAR_{i,t}$ denotes standardized abnormal return for security i at day t, and S_i is standard deviation of returns for security i, during the estimation period, computed as:

$$S_i = \sqrt{\frac{1}{162} \sum_{i=-206}^{-44} (AR_{i,t} - \overline{AR})^2}. \tag{4}$$

where $\overline{AR}$ is the mean abnormal returns.

The $SAR_{i,t}$'s can be accumulated over selected multi-day intervals of the event period as follows:

$$CAR_{t_1,t_2} = \sum_{t=t_1}^{t_2} SAR_{i,t} \tag{5}$$

where $CAR_{t_1t_2}$ denotes standardized cumulative abnormal returns for security i during the (t_1, t_2) interval of the event period.

The null hypotheses to be tested are that the abnormal return for security i at day t of the event period, $AR_{i,t}$, and the cumulative abnormal return for security i during the (t_1, t_2) interval of the event period, CAR_{t_1,t_2} are equal to zero. The z-statistic for $AR_{i,t}$ is the $SAR_{i,t}$ given by formula (3). The z-statistic for CAR_{t_1,t_2} is calculated as (Patell 1976, Dodd and Warner 1983):

$$z_{t_1t_2} = \frac{CAR_{t_1t_2}}{\sqrt{t_2 - t_1 + 1}}. \tag{6}$$

Granger causality tests

The lead-lag tests used in this chapter are based on the Granger tests of causality. A description of several testable forms of Granger causality can be found in Pierce and Haugh (1977), Guilkey and Salemi (1982), and Geweke, *et al.* (1983). The following version of the Granger causal model is used:

$$\ln Y_t = \alpha_o + \sum_{i=1}^{m} \alpha_i \ln X_{t-i} + \sum_{j=1}^{m} \beta_j \ln Y_{t-j} + \varepsilon_t \tag{7}$$

$$\ln X_t = a_o + \sum_{i=1}^{m} a_i \ln Y_{t-i} + \sum_{j=1}^{m} b_j \ln X_{t-j} + \mu_t. \tag{8}$$

The definition of causality given above implies that X is causing (leading) Y provided some α_i is not zero in equation (7). Similarly, Y is causing (leading) X if some a_i is not zero in equation (8). If both of these events occur, there is feedback. The statistic is calculated by estimating the above expressions in both unconstrained (full model) and constrained (reduced model) forms, and may be written as:

$$F_1 = \frac{(SSE_r - SSE_f)/m}{SSE_f/(T - 2m - 1)} \tag{9}$$

where SSE_r, SSE_f denote the residual sum squares of the reduced and full models, respectively; T is the total number of observations and m is the number of lags.

Test of cointegration

Engle and Granger (1987) show that if two nonstationary variables are cointegrated the Granger causality tests of the forms of equations (7) and (8) are misspecified. Therefore, before testing for causality it is necessary to test for cointegration. This paper uses the Augmented Dickey and Fuller (1981), ADF test of cointegration consisting of running first the cointegration regression

$$\ln X_t = a_0 + a_1 \ln Y_t + \varepsilon_t, \tag{10}$$

and then running the ADF regression on the residuals of (10):

$$\varepsilon_t - \varepsilon_{t-1} = b_0 - b_1 \varepsilon_{t-1} + \sum_{i=1}^{m} b_i(\varepsilon_{t-i} - \varepsilon_{t-i-1}) + \mu_t. \tag{11}$$

The null hypothesis of no cointegration is H_0: $b_1 = 0$ in equation (11). If the null is rejected, variables X_t and Y_t are cointegrated and the Granger regressions (7) and (8) are misspecified and must be corrected with an error correction term, which corresponds to the lagged residuals ε_{t-1} of regression (10).

ANALYSIS OF THE EMPIRICAL RESULTS

This section presents and discusses the results from the event-study and causality tests.

Event-study results

The behavior of spot and futures prices is examined for an event period containing 163 trading days. Thus, the event period extends from day −43 to day +119 relative to the initiation of the Persian Gulf Crisis. The day $t = 0$ corresponds to 2 August 1990: the day Iraq invaded Kuwait.

The standardized cumulative abnormal returns are presented in Table 8.1. As expected the CARs are negative for equity and positive for oil. However, the CARs are negative but insignificant for the spot and futures S&P 500. On the other hand, the spot and futures oil exhibit statistically significant positive CARs from one day after the invasion of Kuwait to one day after the initiation of the war (from $t = +1$ to $t = +113$). Therefore, the cumulative abnormal returns confirm our first hypothesis that the Persian Gulf Crisis had a more significant impact on the oil market than in the stock

Table 8.1 Standardized cumulative abnormal returns (CAR) for the S&P 500 index and oil spot and futures from 43 days before to 119 days after the invasion of Kuwait (day '0' = 2 August 1990)

	S&P 500				*Oil*			
	Spot		*Futures*		*Spot*		*Futures*	
Event day	*CAR*	*z-score*	*CAR*	*z-score*	*CAR*	*z-score*	*CAR*	*z-score*
−40	1.121	0.560	0.921	0.461	−4.085	−2.042*	−3.827	−1.914
−30	−0.706	−0.189	−0.065	−0.017	−4.248	−1.135	−6.632	−1.772
−20	−0.508	0.104	−0.117	−0.024	−1.878	−0.383	−2.824	−0.576
−10	0.174	0.030	0.395	0.068	6.007	1.030	2.367	0.406
−5	−1.371	−0.220	−1.220	−0.195	9.193	1.472	7.102	1.137
−4	−1.632	−0.258	−1.526	−0.241	9.249	1.462	6.989	1.105
−3	−2.165	−0.338	−2.117	−0.331	10.141	1.584	6.389	0.998
−2	−1.738	−0.268	−1.553	−0.240	9.782	1.509	6.836	1.055
−1	0.228	0.035	−1.493	−0.228	10.803	1.647	8.021	1.223
0	−1.774	−0.267	−1.747	−0.263	12.727	1.919	10.031	1.512
1	−2.639	−0.393	−2.509	−0.374	18.073	2.694*	13.518	2.015*
2	−4.067	−0.600	−4.075	−0.601	22.333	3.293*	16.399	2.418*
3	−6.365	−0.928	−6.786	−0.990	27.566	4.021*	23.096	3.369*
4	−6.291	−0.908	−6.174	−0.891	27.997	4.041*	23.581	3.404*
5	−5.529	−0.790	−5.667	−0.810	27.867	3.981*	19.359	2.766*
10	−5.230	−0.712	−5.272	−0.717	29.893	4.068*	20.458	2.784*
20	−8.934	−1.117	−9.419	−1.177	29.551	3.694*	19.771	2.471*
40	−14.761	−1.611	−14.752	−1.610	51.733	5.645*	41.159	4.491*
60	−12.825	−1.258	−12.896	−1.265	43.184	4.235*	34.757	3.408*
90	−9.182	−0.793	−9.349	−0.808	34.425	2.974*	23.285	2.011*
110	−12.379	−0.998	−12.422	−1.001	33.059	2.664*	25.230	2.033*
111	−13.044	−1.048	−12.900	−1.036	26.234	2.107*	31.172	2.504*
112	−12.764	−1.022	−12.889	−1.032	39.133	3.133*	30.059	2.407*
113	−12.204	−0.974	−12.002	−0.958	40.259	3.213*	33.146	2.645*
114	−9.495	−0.755	−8.820	−0.702	21.969	1.748	13.514	1.075
115	−8.551	−0.678	−8.405	−0.667	17.510	1.389	8.255	0.655
116	−8.828	−0.698	−8.632	−0.682	17.837	1.410	13.257	1.048

* Significant at the 5 percent level or better.

market. Intuitively, this is because the primary impact of the Iraqi invasion of Kuwait was on oil prices, due to the oil embargo imposed by the allies to Iraq. While the Iraqi invasion was initially interpreted as a local conflict between two Arab oil producing countries, the strong reaction of the US to the Iraqi aggression, along with the UN condemnation and the Iraqi oil embargo, rapidly gave this crisis a global dimension with a significant increase in oil prices. On the other hand, the US equity market experienced a lesser negative impact probably because the S&P 500 index contains only a small number of companies with oil reserves, the stocks of which appreciated because of anticipated higher profits from higher world oil prices. Also, the overall negative impact of an increase in the price of oil in such a broad index is lesser because of the effect of portfolio diversification.

Plots of the CARs are presented in Figures 8.1 to 8.4. As expected, the graphs show the opposite reactions of the equity and oil markets to the Persian Gulf Crisis. Visual inspections of the graphs also suggest that spot and futures returns were highly correlated during the event. This implies

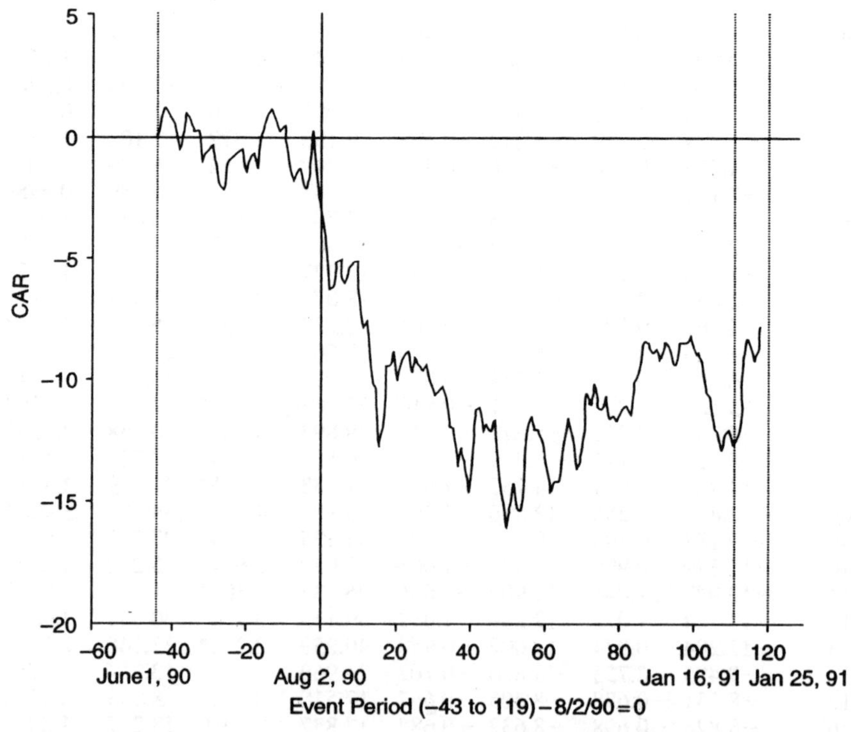

Figure 8.1 Cumulative abnormal returns (S&P 500 spot), mean adjusted returns method

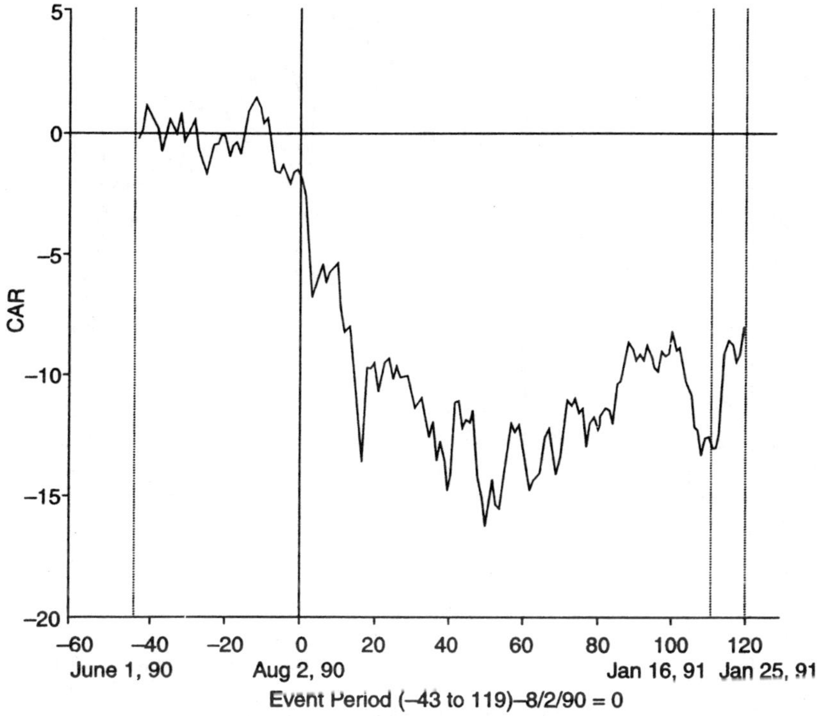

Figure 8.2 Cumulative abnormal returns (S&P 500 futures), mean adjusted returns method

that the price fluctuations were due to news from the Persian Gulf and not the effect of extra trading activities in the futures exchanges. Thus, it does not seem that futures markets contributed to increase price volatility during the Gulf Crisis.

In order to further explore the differential impact of the Persian Gulf Crisis on the oil and markets, mean differences of CARs are computed. In the days immediately following the invasion of Kuwait – that is, in the (+1,+3) and (+1,+5) intervals – the mean differences of CARs between the spot S&P 500 and oil are −19.43 (z = −7.93), and −18.90 (z = −5.98), respectively. For the interval immediate before the start of the war (+111, +112) and the periods immediate after the start of the war (+113, +114) and (+113, +116), the mean differences of CARs are −6.46 (z = −3.23), 20.43 (z = 10.22) and 25.23 (z = 8.92) respectively. Similar results (not reported here) are obtained for the futures contracts. All these differences of means are significant at the 5 percent level or better, and reinforce our finding that the Persian Gulf Crisis had a bigger impact on the oil market than on the stock market.

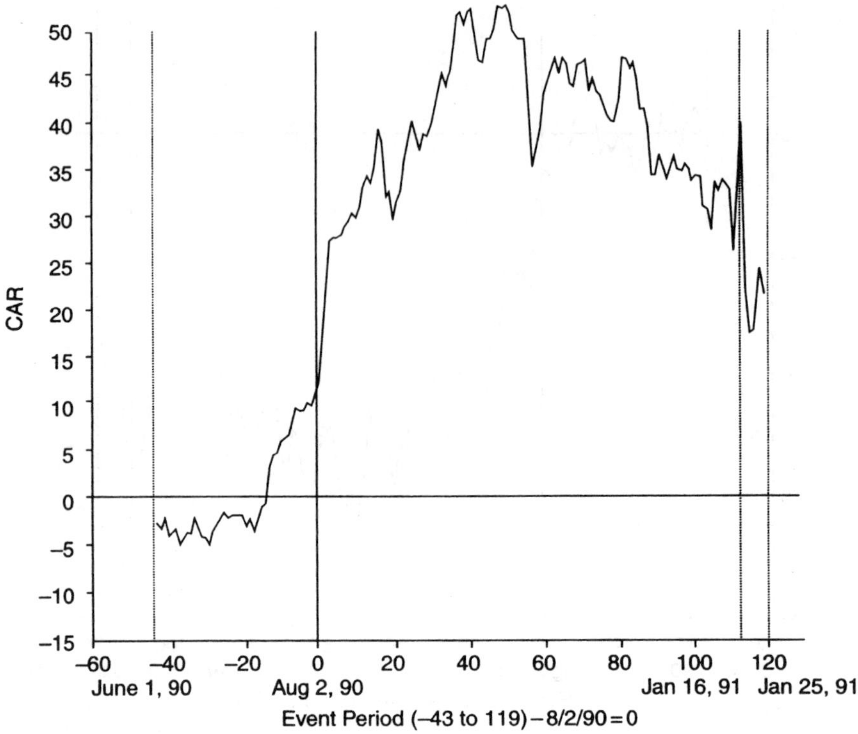

Figure 8.3 Cumulative abnormal returns (oil spot prices), mean adjusted returns method

Causality test results

In order to better capture and contrast the impact of the Gulf Crisis on the relationship between equity and oil markets, the data have been divided in two sets: the pre-Gulf Crisis period, from 1 October 1989 to 31 May 1990; and the Gulf Crisis period from 1 June 1990 to 31 January 1991.

Prior to the implementation of the causality tests we test the time-series for integration and cointegration. The ADF tests of stationarity for the price levels are presented in Table 8.2. The null hypothesis of nonstationarity cannot be rejected for any of the cases; thus, prices are unit roots. The ADF tests of stationarity for returns or percentage price changes, shown in Table 8.3, indicate that the null of nonstationarity is rejected in all cases. Therefore, prices of S&P 500 and oil, spot and futures, are integrated of order one, I(1), and it is necessary to test for cointegration.

Panel A of Table 8.4 shows that cointegration for the pre-Gulf Crisis period is partially rejected. On the other hand, Panel B indicates that all prices are cointegrated during the Gulf Crisis period. Giving that the results of the tests of cointegration are mixed we proceed as follows: when the

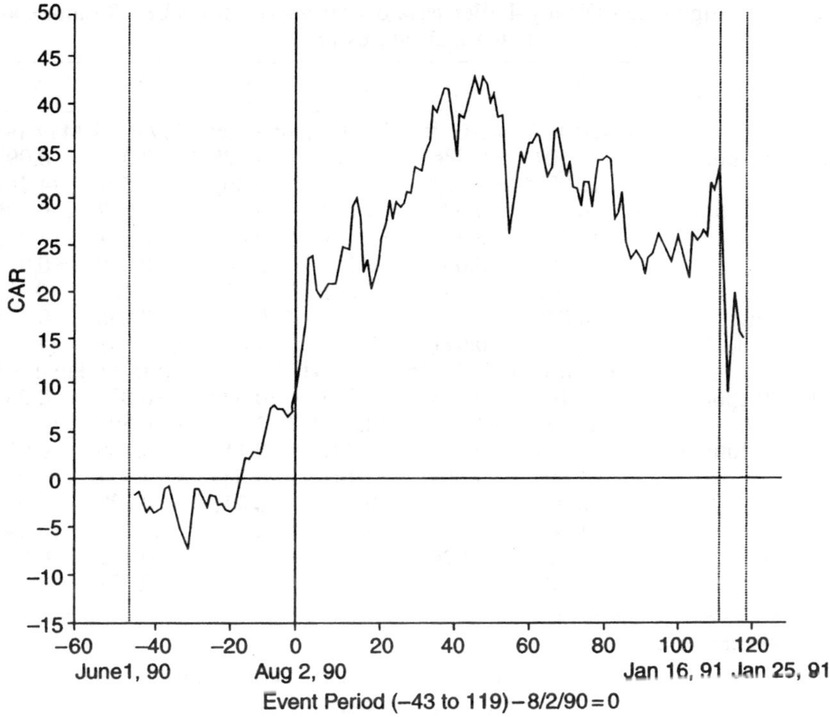

Figure 8.4 Cumulative abnormal returns (oil futures prices), mean adjusted returns method

prices are not cointegrated, the causality tests are conducted by running regressions (7) and (8). When cointegration is present the error correcting terms are incorporated in the regressions.

The results of the Granger causality tests are presented in Table 8.5. Panel A indicates that no lead-lag relationship is detected for the pre-Gulf Crisis period. On the other hand, Panel B shows a dramatic increase in causality during the period of the Persian Gulf Crisis. In effect, strong contemporaneous causality and feedback are found during the period of the conflict. These results confirm our second hypothesis that equity and oil markets are efficient and stock and oil prices changed quickly responding to fundamental news coming from the Gulf. The efficient price reaction increased the linkages of these markets during the crisis. Our result is consistent with those reported by other studies about equity prices behavior during global shocks. In this respect, Malliaris and Urrutia (1992) show that during the October 1987 Stock Market Crash contemporaneous causality increased among national equity markets.

Table 8.2 Augmented Dickey–Fuller tests of stationarity for S&P 500 index and oil spot and futures prices

Contract	b_0	b_1	b_2	b_3	b_4	R^2
	PANEL A: pre-Gulf Crisis Period: 1 Oct 1989 to 31 May 1990					
S&P 500 spot	0.504	−0.086	−0.215	−0.025	−0.047	0.099
	(2.08)*	(−2.08)*	(−2.57)*	(−0.30)	(−0.59)	(4.25)*
S&P 500 futures	0.522	−0.089	−0.197	−0.051	0.057	0.096
	(2.30)*	(2.30)*	(−2.38)*	(−0.49)	(0.71)	(4.09)*
Oil spot	−0.003	0.001	−0.105	−0.001	0.010	0.011
	(−0.05)	(0.01)	(−1.26)	(−0.02)	(0.12)	(0.42)
Oil futures	0.045	−0.015	0.006	−0.056	−0.158	0.035
	(0.65)	(−0.67)	(0.08)	(−0.69)	(−1.95)	(1.39)
	PANEL B: Gulf Crisis Period: 1 June 1990 to 31 Jan 1991					
S&P 500 spot	0.161	−0.028	0.163	−0.090	−0.071	0.060
	(1.78)	(−1.79)	(2.03)*	(−1.11)	(−0.89)	(2.44)*
S&P 500 futures	0.157	−0.027	0.091	−0.113	−0.106	0.055
	(1.69)	(−1.69)	(1.14)	(−1.41)	(−1.33)	(2.22)
Oil spot	0.067	−0.020	0.132	−0.236	0.028	0.081
	(1.60)	(−1.55)	(1.65)	(−2.98)*	(0.34)	(3.35)*
Oil futures	0.089	−0.026	0.026	−0.114	−0.192	0.072
	(1.58)	(−1.55)	(−0.34)	(−1.44)	(−2.37)*	(2.95)*

Notes: The model is

$$\ln P_t - \ln P_{t-1} = b_0 + b_1 \ln P_{t-1} + b_2(\ln P_{t-1} - \ln P_{t-2}) + b_3(\ln P_{t-2} - \ln P_{t-3}) + b_4(\ln P_{t-3} - \ln P_{t-4}) + \varepsilon_t$$

The null hypothesis is $b_1 = 0$ (prices are non-stationary). The *t*-critical at the 5 percent level is −2.88 (from Dickey and Fuller 1981).
An asterisk * indicates that the individual regression coefficient is different from zero at the 5 percent of confidence level.

SUMMARY AND CONCLUSIONS

The chapter has investigated two hypotheses: first, that the impact of the Persian Gulf Crisis was stronger on the oil market than on the equity market; and second, that there was an increase in the causal relationship between stock and oil prices during the Persian Gulf Crisis. We have used data for the spot and futures S&P 500 index and the Arab oil from October 1989 to January 1991. The empirical results have confirmed our hypotheses. In effect, we have found that the impact of the Gulf Crisis was stronger on the oil market than on the equity market. This is consistent with the nature of the conflict, which primarily affected the oil market due to the embargo imposed to Iraqi oil. Also, the lesser impact on the S&P 500 is explained by the high degree of diversification of the index, which includes several stocks that benefited from high oil prices. The Gulf Crisis also produced a dramatic increase in causality between the equity and oil markets. This is consistent with the notion of efficient markets in the sense that both markets reacted quickly and simultaneously to the fundamental

Table 8.3 Augmented Dickey–Fuller tests of stationarity for S&P 500 index and oil spot and futures returns

Contract	b_0	b_1	b_2	b_3	b_4	R^2
PANEL A: pre-Gulf Crisis Period: 1 Oct 1989 to 31 May 1990						
S&P 500 spot	0.012	−1.524	0.246	0.166	0.065	0.633
	(0.11)	(−7.60)[a]	(1.46)	(1.29)	(0.81)	(66.30)*
S&P 500 futures	0.003	−1.442	0.187	0.088	0.088	0.625
	(0.03)	(−7.34)[a]	(1.12)	(0.69)	(1.10)	(64.09)*
Oil spot	−0.163	−1.142	−0.043	0.047	0.063	0.55
	(−0.89)	(−6.67)[a]	(0.29)	(0.40)	(0.76)	(47.40)*
Oil futures	−0.103	−1.227	0.225	0.161	−0.007	0.508
	(−0.63)	(−7.10)[a]	(1.58)	(1.41)	(−0.09)	(39.77)*
PANEL B: Gulf Crisis Period: 1 June 1990 to 31 Jan 1991						
S&P 500 spot	−0.055	0.998	0.157	0.061	−0.023	0.434
	(−0.58)	(−6.48)[a]	(1.21)[a]	(0.57)	(−0.28)	(29.36)*
S&P 500 futures	−0.056	−1.046	0.140	0.030	−0.092	0.475
	(−0.56)	(−6.35)[a]	(1.03)	(0.27)	(−1.14)	(34.54)*
Oil spot	0.247	−1.110	0.239	−0.008	0.019	0.481
	(0.50)	(−6.74)[a]	(1.71)	(−0.07)	(0.23)	(35.37)*
Oil futures	0.197	−1.202	0.235	0.121	−0.081	0.513
	(0.43)	(−6.86)[a]	(1.65)	(1.05)	(−0.97)	(40.25)*

Notes: The model is

$$R_t - R_{t-1} = b_0 + b_1 R_{t-1} + b_2(R_{t-1} - R_{t-2}) + b_3(R_{t-2} - R_{t-3}) + b_4(R_{t-3} - R_{t-4}) + \varepsilon_t$$

where

$$R_t = 100\ln(P_t/P_{t-1})$$

The null hypothesis is $b_1 = 0$ (returns or percentage of price changes are non-stationary). The t-critical at the 5 percent level is −2.88 (from Dickey and Fuller 1981).
An "a" indicates rejection of the null at the 5 percent of confidence level.
An asterisk * indicates that the individual regression coefficient is different from zero at the 5 percent of confidence level.

political and war news coming out of the Middle East. Our results agree with the reported increase in causality among financial markets during global events, such as the market crash of October 1989.

Table 8.4 Tests of cointegration between the S&P 500 index and oil spot and futures prices

Dependent variable	*Independent variable*	b_0	b_1	b_2	b_3	b_4	R^2
		PANEL A: pre-Gulf Crisis Period: 1 Oct 1989 to 31 May 1990					
S&P 500 spot	Oil spot	0.0002	0.1644	−0.3223	−0.1462	−0.1341	0.169
		(0.17)	(4.31)*[a]	(−4.20)*	(−1.84)	(−1.75)	(7.86)*
Oil spot	S&P 500 spot	−0.0020	0.0544	−0.1067	−0.0592	−0.0355	0.053
		(−1.09)	(2.79)*	(−1.32)	(−0.72)	(−0.43)	(2.15)
S&P 500 futures	Oil futures	0.0001	0.1538	−0.2990	−0.1786	−0.0470	0.148
		(0.06)	(3.99)*[a]	(−3.84)*	(−2.26)*	(−0.60)	(6.73)*
Oil futures	S&P 500 futures	−0.0011	0.0703	−0.0535	−0.1744	−0.1463	0.083
		(−0.64)	(2.85)*	(−0.67)	(−2.23)*	(−1.85)	(3.49)*
		PANEL B: Gulf Crisis Period: 1 June 1990 to 31 Jan 1991					
S&P 500 spot	Oil spot	−0.0003	0.1829	−0.1580	−0.3067	−0.0769	0.174
		(−0.38)	(4.49)*[a]	(−1.98)*	(−4.10)*	(−0.99)	(8.07)*
Oil spot	S&P 500 spot	−0.0018	0.1775	−0.1714	−0.3264	−0.0722	0.186
		(−0.36)	(4.50)*[a]	(−2.15)*	(−4.39)*	(−0.93)	(8.75)*
S&P 500 futures	Oil futures	−0.0003	0.2598	−0.2797	−0.3088	−0.2261	0.247
		(−0.41)	(5.83)*[a]	(−3.67)*	(−4.28)*	(−3.05)*	(12.54)*
Oil futures	S&P 500 futures	−0.0014	0.2661	−0.2899	−0.3135	−0.2379	0.257
		(−0.39)	(5.98)*[a]	(−3.82)*	(−4.37)*	(−3.22)*	(13.25)*

Notes: The model used to test for cointegration is the following:

$$\ln P_t = a_0 + a_1 \ln P_{2t} + \varepsilon_t \quad (1)$$

$$\varepsilon_t - \varepsilon_{t-1} = b_0 + b_1\varepsilon_{t-1} + b_2(\varepsilon_{t-1} - \varepsilon_{t-2}) + b_3(\varepsilon_{t-2} - \varepsilon_{t-3}) + b_4(\varepsilon_{t-3} - \varepsilon_{t-4}) + \mu_t \quad (2)$$

The coefficients in the table are from equation (2).
The null hypothesis is H_0: $b_1 = 0$ (no-cointegration).
The t-critical at the 5 percent level in 3.17 (from Engle and Granger 1987).
An "a" indicates rejection of the null hypothesis of no-cointegration at the 5 percent of significance level.
An asterisk * indicates that the individual regression coefficient is different from zero at the 5 percent level.

Table 8.5 Causality tests between S&P 500 index and oil spot and futures prices

Dependent variable	*Independent variable*	b_0, β_0	b_1, β_1	b_2, β_2	b_3, β_3	$H_0: \sum_{i=0}^{3} b_i = 0$ / $H_0: \sum_{i=0}^{3} \beta_i = 0$
PANEL A: Pre-Gulf Crisis Period: 1 Oct 1989 to 31 May 1990						
S&P 500 spot	Oil spot	−0.9487 (−0.98)	−1.6401 (−0.74)	−1.0082 (−0.73)	−0.1379 (0.14)	1.318
Oil spot	S&P 500 spot	−0.0063 (−0.94)	0.0164 (2.04)*	−0.0058 (−0.71)	−0.0026 (−0.38)	1.468
S&P 500 futures	Oil futures	−0.2243 (−0.27)	−1.3758 (−0.43)	−1.5435 (−1.31)	−0.7819 (0.92)	0.589
Oil futures	S&P 500 futures	−0.0023 (−0.29)	0.0084 (0.88)	−0.0141 (−1.48)	0.0092 (1.18)	0.888
PANEL B: Gulf Crisis Period: 1 June 1990 to 31 Jan 1991						
S&P 500 spot	Oil spot	−1.1213 (−5.99)*	1.5224 (4.97)*	−0.4767 (−1.73)	−0.1837 (0.90)	10.258[a]
Oil spot	S&P 500 spot	−0.1721 (−5.79)*	0.0646 (1.18)	0.0211 (0.47)	0.0764 (2.35)*	15.581[a]
S&P 500 futures	Oil futures	−1.3620 (−8.33)*	1.7759 (5.33)*	−0.2790 (−1.10)	0.1661 (0.83)	19.310[a]
Oil futures	S&P 500 futures	−0.2321 (−8.33)*	0.1490 (2.51)*	0.0355 (0.78)	0.0308 (0.92)	20.87[a]

Notes: The causality models are:

$$\ln X_t = a_0 + a_1 \ln X_{t-1} + a_2 \ln X_{t-2} + a_3 \ln X_{t-3} + b_0 \ln Y_t + b_1 \ln Y_{t-1} + b_2 \ln Y_{t-2} + b_3 \ln Y_{t-3} + C_0 \varepsilon_{t-1} + \phi_t \ (Y \rightarrow X)$$

$$\ln Y_t = \alpha_0 + \alpha_1 \ln Y_{t-1} + \alpha_2 \ln Y_{t-2} + \alpha_3 \ln Y_{t-3} + \beta_0 \ln X_t + \beta_1 \ln X_{t-1} + \beta_2 \ln X_{t-2} + \beta_3 \ln X_{t-3} + \delta \varepsilon_{t-1} + \varepsilon_t \ (X \rightarrow Y)$$

The null hypotheses are

$$H_0: \sum_{i=0}^{3} b_i = 0, \ \sum_{i=0}^{3} \beta_i = 0$$

An "a" indicates the null hypothesis is rejected at the 1 percent of confidence level.
The $F_{critical}$ are $F_{152,\,4} = 2.37$ at 5 percent; 3.32 at 1 percent
$F_{153,\,3} = 2.60$ at 5 percent; 3.78 at 1 percent
An asterisk * indicates that the individual regression coefficient is different from zero at the 5 percent confidence level.

REFERENCES

Brown, S.J. and J.B. Warner (1980) "Measuring Security Price Performance," *Journal of Financial Economics*, 8: 205–58.

Brown, S.J. and J.B. Warner (1985) "Using Daily Stock Returns: The Case of Event Studies," *Journal of Financial Economics*, 14: 3–32.

Dickey, D. and W. Fuller (1981) "Likelihood Ratio Statistics for Autoregressive Time Series with a Unit Root," *Econometrica*, 49: 1057–72.

Dodd, P. and J.B. Warner (1983) "On Corporate Governance: A Study of Proxy Contests," *Journal of Financial Economics*, 11: 401–38.

Engle, R.F., and C.W.J. Granger (1987) "Cointegration and Error Correction: Representation, Estimation, and Testing," *Econometrica*, 55: 251– 76.

Geweke, J., R. Meese and W. Dent (1983) "Comparing Alternative Tests of Causality in Temporal Systems," *Journal of Econometrics*, 21: 161–94.

Guilkey, D.K., and M.K. Salemi (1982) "Small Sample Properties of Three Tests for Granger Causal Ordering in a Bivariate Stochastic System," *The Review of Economics and Statistics*, 64: 668–80.

Malliaris, A.G. and J.L. Urrutia (1992) "The International Crash of October 1987: Causality Tests," *Journal of Financial and Quantitative Analysis*, 27: 353–64.

Malliaris, A.G. and J.L. Urrutia (1994) "The Impact of the Persian Gulf Crisis on National Equity Markets," *Advances in International Banking and Finance*, 1: 43–65.

Masulis, R.W. (1980) "The Effect of Capital Structure Change on Security Prices: A Study of Exchange Offers," *Journal of Financial Economics*, 8: 139–78.

Patell, J.M. (1976) "Corporate Forecasts of Earnings per Share and Stock Price Behavior: Empirical Tests," *Journal of Accounting Research*, 14: 246–76.

Pierce, D.A., and L.D. Haugh (1977) "Causality in Temporal Systems: Characterizations and a Survey," *Journal of Econometrics*, 5: 265–93.

Roll, R. (1988) "The International Crash of October 1987," *The Financial Analyst Journal*, 44: 19–35.

NORTH-HOLLAND

North American Journal of
Economics and Finance 13 (2002) 72–92

THE NORTH AMERICAN
JOURNAL OF
ECONOMICS
AND FINANCE

Global monetary instability: The role of the IMF, the EU and NAFTA ☆

A.G. Malliaris*

Department of Economics and Finance, Loyola University Chicago, 820 North Michigan Avenue, Chicago, IL 60611, USA

Received 19 October 2001; received in revised form 21 January 2002; accepted 22 January 2002

I dedicate this paper to my children, Maryanthe and Steven,
who will experience the evolution of our global monetary system

Abstract

This paper argues that the global monetary system has exhibited significant instability since the collapse of the Bretton Woods regime in 1971. The current challenge for economists and policy makers is the creation of a global monetary system that offers greater exchange rate stability without sacrificing international capital mobility. This paper proposes a solution that consists of three components. First, strengthening the international financial architecture to bring stability, primarily to emerging nations. Second, eventually creating a monetary union in NAFTA and extending it to other countries of the Western Hemisphere to bring stability to this region à la the European Monetary Union (EMU). Third, coordinating economic policies among the U.S., EU and Japan to stabilize these three key global currencies. © 2002 Elsevier Science Inc. All rights reserved.

JEL classification: F3; E6

Keywords: Currency fluctuations; Global monetary instability; IFM; EU; NAFTA; Policy coordination

☆ Earlier versions of this paper were presented at the International Conference on Trade, Competitiveness and Social Protection in Antwerpen, Belgium, December 14–15, 2000, at the North American Economics and Finance Association Meetings in New Orleans, LA, January 5–7, 2001 and at the Athens University of Economics and Business in Greece, May 28, 2001. The current version was presented as the Presidential Address to the North American Economics and Finance Association Meetings in Atlanta, GA, January 5, 2002.

* Tel.: +1-312-915-6063; fax: +1-312-915-8580.

E-mail address: tmallia@luc.edu (A.G. Malliaris).

PII: S1062-9408(02)00058-X

1. Introduction

In his Nobel Lecture, Professor Robert Mundell (2000) argues that although the 20th century began with a highly stable global monetary system in the form of the gold standard, it ended with dysfunctional volatility of exchange rates that frequently caused global monetary crises. Mundell concludes that the global monetary system with which the 20th century closed was inferior to that with which it began. Thus, the challenge to economists and policy makers today is to design a system that offers greater exchange rate stability and experiences fewer financial crises.

In this paper, we first review the instabilities of the current global monetary system and, second, argue that the system's stability can be improved. Improvements include reform of the international financial architecture and the role of the International Monetary Fund (IMF), greater cooperation within regions and enhanced policy coordination among regions. In Section 2, we review the relevant features of the current global monetary system and define the meaning of instability. In Section 3, we examine the Asian financial crises as an illustration of the difficulties faced by the global monetary system.

The Asian crises have led academics and policy makers to call for a new architecture for the global monetary system. These ideas are discussed in Section 4. Then, in Section 5, we review the experiences of the European Monetary System (EMS) and European Monetary Union (EMU) with an eye to lessons for monetary cooperation in the Western Hemisphere.

These considerations suggest a three-part reform program anchored by a stronger, more resilient international financial architecture, designed to ensure greater monetary stability generally and among emerging nations in particular. The second component of our proposal seeks to improve regional stability among groups of trading partners. We examine the European experience and argue that it provides a viable model for the U.S. and its trading partners in the Western Hemisphere. The final component addresses the management of monetary and financial relations among the major regional blocs in Europe, the Western Hemisphere, and in Asia, clustered around Japan. These ideas are developed in Sections 6 and 7. Section 8 discusses two possible alternative scenarios focused on Tobin-type taxes or floating exchange rates. Section 9 concludes.

2. The current global monetary system

The current global monetary system was introduced abruptly on August 15, 1971, when the U.S. chose to discontinue the exchange of dollars for gold with foreign central banks. With the breakdown of the Bretton Woods system of fixed exchange rates, national monetary policies in the U.S. and elsewhere became more focused on domestic issues and exchange rates became flexible. The system has evolved to include a variety of exchange rate arrangements.[1] It includes three primary categories of exchange rate regimes.

The first covers hard pegs such as currency boards, dollarization and currency union. Second, come the soft pegs, such as the conventional fixed exchange rate peg, the crawling peg, the exchange rate band, and the crawling band. Third, comes the floating group, ranging from fully flexible exchange rates to various degrees of managed floating. Fischer (2001) reports that in 1991, 16% of the IMF's member countries had hard pegs, 62% had soft pegs and 22% had floating exchange rates. In 1999, Fischer shows that soft pegs had declined to 34% from 62% and that both polar cases had gained, with hard pegs increasing to 24% and floats increasing to 42%. Fig. 1 gives the distribution of exchange rate regimes in 1991 and 1999.

To illustrate the volatility of exchange rates, Mundell (2000) notes that between 1971 and 1980 the German mark doubled against the U.S. dollar; between 1980 and 1985 it halved; between 1985 and 1992 it more than doubled again; since 1992 it has dropped by a third. This is considerable volatility. Similarly, the annualized volatility of the spot exchange rate of the British pound per U.S. dollar fluctuated during the decade 1990–2000 from a low annual rate of 6.6% in 1994 to a high of 13.7% in 1992. The volatility of the Japanese yen per U.S. dollar was at a low of 7.7% in 1996 and a high of 18.1% in 1998. Further illustrations can be found in Table 1 and Fig. 2. Flood and Rose (1999) confirm the high volatility of exchange rates and show that it cannot be explained by increases in the variability of exchange rate fundamentals.

The currencies of the emerging nations also experienced volatility during the last decade. For example, during the Asian crisis, the Korean won and Thai baht both depreciated by over 50%, *vis-à-vis* the dollar. An IMF (1998) study reports that during the 1975–1997 period, prior to the Asian crisis, 158 currency crises occurred in 53 countries, mostly in developing nations.[2]

What are the costs of such high currency volatility? Economic analysis suggests that swings in exchange rates that depart radically from equilibrium values give misleading price signals and add to uncertainty. These factors in turn inhibit real investment and reduce efficiency. Advances in financial engineering have helped large multinational businesses cope with these currency fluctuations through hedging and global distribution of plant facilities. However, these strategies are costly. Why is currency volatility accepted so passively among the key currency countries?

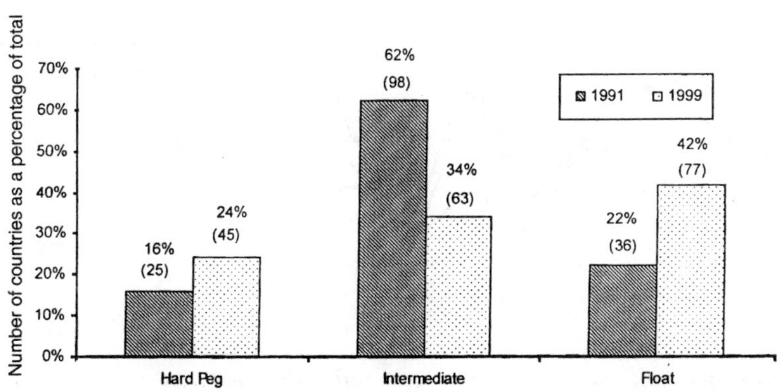

Fig. 1. Exchange rate regimes among IMF countries, 1991 and 1999. Source: Fischer (2001).

Table 1
Volatilities of spot exchange rates expressed in U.S. dollars

Year	British pound (%)	German mark (%)	French franc (%)	Italian lira (%)	Japanese yen (%)	EU euro
1990	9.6	9.3	8.8	8.6	10.5	
1991	12.2	13.6	13.0	12.6	9.7	
1992	13.7	13.9	13.4	16.5	9.0	
1993	11.8	10.5	10.0	11.3	11.0	
1994	6.6	8.6	8.1	8.1	8.9	
1995	8.4	12.3	10.8	10.4	13.7	
1996	6.3	6.5	6.1	5.6	7.7	
1997	8.7	9.6	9.5	8.8	11.4	
1998	7.0	8.6	8.6	8.5	18.1	
1999	6.7	8.9	8.9	8.9	13.3	8.9
2000	7.7	11.8	11.8	11.8	11.0	10.7
Mean	9.0	10.3	9.9	10.1	11.3	9.8

Volcker (1999) asks this question and also proposes three explanations. First, it is well known that in a world of capital mobility, fixing exchange rates implies loss of autonomy in monetary policy. It appears that independence of national monetary policy is valued more than stability of foreign currency rates.

Second, exchange rates involve more than one nation. In the face of undesirable changes among major currencies, the contentious question inevitably arises as to which country assumes the "burden" of initiating appropriate policy changes. The answer is not always clear and its resolution entails sensitive political and difficult economic judgements.

The third difficulty is a narrower political question. Volcker (1999) argues that the traditional constituency favoring stability—the financial community—has effectively reversed its

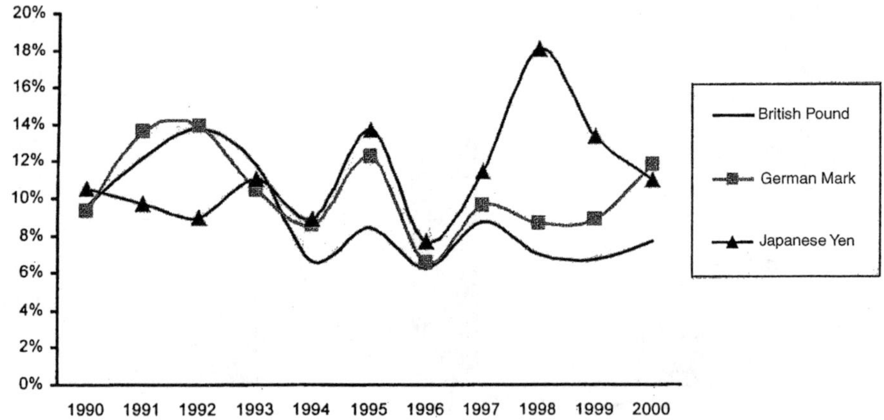

Fig. 2. Volatilities of spot exchange rates expressed in U.S. dollars.

position. That shift, no doubt, is related to the fact that today's financial institutions operating internationally have developed a substantial vested interest in market volatility. Traders are in a strong tactical position to sense market pressure and psychology and to act immediately to take advantage of emerging movements and even to amplify them.[3] The cost of currency fluctuations is borne by importers, exporters, and international investors. But for them, the currency and hedging costs are part of much larger and presumably profitable transactions. The ultimate costs of economic uncertainty and lower productivity are buried among the population at large. Analogous to the politics of protectionism, the gains from volatility are concentrated while the losses are diffused. Discouraging as that may be to stability advocates, there are solid grounds for thinking that the quest for greater stability is not as quixotic as European monetary integration has proved.

Global instability does not manifest itself only in high volatility of exchange rates and currency crises. Capital flows have also been highly volatile, particularly for emerging market economies. When significant capital flow reversals occur, currency crises may lead to banking crises, financial crises, and possibly macroeconomic recessions. The IMF estimates that the cumulative losses in gross domestic product from the potential (trend) growth in the 158 currency crises in 53 countries, mentioned earlier, averaged 4.3% in each country and 7.1% in the 96 crises in which output losses were suffered.[4] Table 2 presents IMF data on currency and financial crises.

According to Mishkin (1999, p. 6), financial instability occurs when shocks to the financial system interfere with information flows so that the system can no longer do its job of channeling funds to countries with productive investment opportunities. Brock and Malliaris (1989) present a comprehensive exposition of the technical concept of stability and its applications. They define stability as the special property of an economic system that allows it to return quickly to its original state after an exogenous shock. Following Mishkin (1999), and Brock and Malliaris (1989), we use the concept of global financial instability to mean exchange-rate and capital-flow shocks that prevent an economy's GDP from recovering quickly.

Hausmann, Panniza, and Stein (1999) show that emerging markets in Latin America that have allowed their exchange rates to float have experienced greater interest-rate volatility than countries that followed fixed exchange rates. Calvo and Reinhart (2000) argue that floating exchange rates can have destabilizing effects on emerging markets. These authors and we understand instability to be the movement of an economy to a lower level of economic activity without an automatic recovery. The shock usually influences the exchange rate, which in turn causes other economic variables to change, such as interest rates, prices, bank loans, real investment, consumption, possibly GDP, and finally, national welfare. Bacchetta and Van Wincoop (2000) develop a general equilibrium framework to study the effect of the exchange rate system on trade and welfare. They show that trade and welfare implications of currency instabilities depend on variables such as preferences and monetary policy rules, and that one cannot a priori assign higher welfare to higher trade.

The international monetary order of the Bretton Woods system was the last systematic attempt to promote financial stability at the world level as a tool for promoting trade and growth. The aim of the agreement was to make the conduct of national economic policies compatible with maintenance of stable international economic conditions. Restricting short-term capital movements was an essential element of the system. Economic historians Bordo and

Table 2
Cost of crises in lost output relative to trend (1975–1997)

	Number of crises	Average recovery time (years)[a]	Cumulative loss of output per crisis (percentage points)[b]	Crises with output losses (%)[c]	Cumulative loss of output per crisis with output loss (percentage points)[d]
Currency crises	158	1.6	4.3	61	7.1
Industrial	42	1.9	3.1	55	5.6
Emerging markets	116	1.5	4.8	64	7.6
Currency crashes[e]	55	2	7.1	71	10.1
Industrial	13	2.1	5.0	62	8
Emerging markets	42	1.9	7.9	74	10.7
Banking crises	54	3.1	11.6	82	14.2
Industrial	12	4.1	10.2	67	15
Emerging markets	42	2.8	12.1	86	14
Currency and banking crises[f]	32	3.2	14.4	78	18.5
Industrial	6	5.8	17.6	100	17.6
Emerging markets	26	2.6	13.6	73	18.8

Source: IMF World Economic Outlook (May 1998, p. 79).

[a] Average amount of time until GDP growth returned to trend. Because GDP growth data are available for all countries only on an annual basis, by construction the minimum recovery time was 1 year.

[b] Calculated by summing the differences between trend growth and output growth after the crisis began until the time when annual output growth returned to its trend and by averaging over all crises.

[c] Percent of crises in which output was lower than trend after the crisis began.

[d] Calculated by summing the differences between trend growth and output growth after the crisis began until the time when annual output growth returned to its trend and by averaging over all crises that had output losses.

[e] Currency "crashes" are identified by crises where the currency component of the exchange market pressure index accounts for 75% or more of the index when the index signals a crisis.

[f] Identified when a banking crisis occurred within a year of a currency crisis.

Eichengreen (1993) document that the system worked remarkably well during the decade of the 1950s and contributed to the restoration of both the European and Japanese economies. However, the system collapsed at the beginning of the 1970s, when the two conditions that had ensured its success in the preceding three decades ceased to hold. These conditions were stable macroeconomic policies in the country issuing the reserve currency, and capital mobility that was effectively controlled.

The oil crisis and the accommodating monetary policies of the U.S. Federal Reserve contributed to high and persistent inflation during most of the 1970s. Exchange rate flexibility restored the effectiveness of subsequent tight monetary policies introduced by Fed Chairman Volcker in controlling inflation, but did not prevent the emergence of severe unemployment, economic stagnation, and losses in economic welfare in the late 1970s and early 1980s. The restrictive monetary policies pursued during the early 1980s have produced a lasting reduction in inflation and a curbing of wage pressures. The conviction has grown that the internal and external value of each currency depends on the confidence of investors in the economy's potential to grow with price stability.

It would nonetheless be simplistic to imagine that each country's effort to stabilize its economy is sufficient to ensure stable economic and monetary conditions at the international level. An important part of the international banking system, and more generally of financial markets, operates outside national borders. The quantity of money and credit created and exchanged is beyond the direct control of any international authority. Furthermore, it is hard for uncoordinated national policies to prevent fluctuations in the prices of financial assets from imparting destabilizing impulses to the real economy. The high degree of financial and trade integration means that every country can be hit by the shock waves emanating from other regions.

In addition to Mundell and Mishkin, Summers (2000) gives further insights into recent international monetary instabilities and global financial crises, which include those of Mexico in 1994; Thailand, Korea, Indonesia, Malaysia, Philippines, Hong Kong and Taiwan in 1997; and Russia in 1998. During 2001, both Turkey and Argentina experienced serious financial instabilities. We start with a review of one of these crises in order to draw representative lessons about the performance of the global system in times of crisis. We choose the Asian crisis because it began with a currency crisis that grew into a banking and financial crisis, and ultimately led to recession in some countries.

3. The Asian crisis

It is argued by Radelet and Sachs (1998) and also by Moskow (1999), that most market participants and analysts did not anticipate the Asian crisis. Data on capital flows, credit ratings, IMF annual reports, and other indicators support this observation. The biggest warnings came from Thailand, Korea, Malaysia and Indonesia, whose stock markets declined by more than 50% during 1997 and continued to decline further in 1998, while their economic fundamentals did not show signs of deterioration. Certainly, traditional warning indicators, such as current account deficits, overvalued exchange rates, diminished export growth, net foreign direct investment and industrial excess capacity gave some reasons for concern, but the signals were muted and generally ignored. While East Asian currencies had appreciated in real terms in the 1990s, the real appreciation was considerably less than in most of Latin America. Current account deficits were very high in Thailand and Malaysia in 1996, but considerably lower in Indonesia and Korea.

The biggest indicators of risk were financial, such as short-term debts to international banks. Asian banks lent these short-term borrowed funds in foreign currencies to long-term borrowers domestically to finance both plant and equipment investments and also real estate. After the onset of the currency crisis, the default of such loans was one of the factors that contributed to the banking crisis. However, neither the growth of short-term borrowing nor other financial indicators, such as declining equity prices, growing current account deficits, declining credit quality of domestic loans, or slowing export growth, among others, guaranteed the onset of the crisis. They merely warned of potential economic problems. In other words, all the factors commonly cited, such as over-investment, heavy indebtedness to foreign banks, low foreign currency reserves, high degree of non-performing commercial loans, moral hazard, and excess supply of real estate construction, seemed to be necessary but not sufficient conditions for a major financial crisis. Put differently, one could not predict the actual onset of capital flight by international investors and speculators that caused the currency crisis and subsequently the financial and banking crisis.

There are at least two theories attempting to explain the Asian crisis. One theory is based on economic fundamentals and the other on financial panic. The theory based on economic fundamentals argues that weak domestic macroeconomic factors precipitate a balance-of-payments crisis. A country under a fixed exchange rate regime with weak macroeconomic fundamentals becomes vulnerable to a speculative currency attack. The model of Burnside, Eichenbaum, and Rebelo (1998) implies that the collapse of a fixed exchange rate happens after agents learn that future deficits will rise, but before the government implements its new monetary policy. Under this scenario, standard macroeconomic aggregates, such as past inflation, interest rates and fiscal deficits, are not useful in predicting currency crises. Such crises are often triggered by expectations of deteriorating fundamentals that induce currency speculation and capital outflows. Defense against speculation drains the troubled country's foreign reserves, and financial and economic crises follow.

In contrast, theories based on financial panic attribute the crisis to an exogenous change in investor confidence, leading to liquidity problems. This loss of confidence among investors leads to a sudden withdrawal of short-term capital from the troubled country. In East Asia, this difficult situation was aggravated by the highly leveraged state of these economies, whose liabilities included large amounts of short-term debt denominated in foreign currencies. As capital flight led to severe currency devaluation, it became more difficult for these countries to cover their external liabilities, and they plunged into a banking and financial crisis.

Economists have not decided which theory best explains the onset of the financial crisis in Asia, because it is difficult to reconcile a number of discrepancies between theory and reality. For example, many economic fundamentals in Asia were incompatible with an impending crisis. Many Asian economies were characterized by low inflation, above-average GDP growth, fiscal budgets that appeared to be in balance or surplus, and high rates of real investment. However, asset bubbles and insolvent banks provided early evidence of potential economic difficulties.

Problems also hamper the applicability of financial panic theories. The dramatic shift in investor confidence required by such theories is unlikely to have been completely exogenous. Economic fundamentals must have played a role in investors' minds. Furthermore, why did investors suddenly experience a loss of confidence? After all, investors knew the economic status of these countries well before the onset of the crisis. Though it may be difficult to determine the exact causes of the Asian debacle, authors such as Lachman (1999), Guitian (1999), and Portes (1999), ultimately link the Asian financial crisis to the inherent instabilities of the global monetary system.[5]

4. The IMF and the new financial architecture

If the current global monetary system is characterized by instabilities, what is the role of multilateral institutions in managing or averting them? Most observers agree that the Asian crisis was a crucial test for the IMF. Many complain that the IMF did not anticipate the crisis. In the years prior to the crisis, the phenomenal economic growth of the Asian tigers was widely praised. Stable currencies and the abundant flow of foreign capital almost assured continued growth. As capital flows began to slow down, the currencies became over-valued and stock markets started to decline, but neither the IMF nor many others understood the implications. There were signs of overheating, of stock market and real estate bubbles, of excessive short-term borrowing from foreign banks to finance long-term domestic investments, and other indicators, but the IMF did not see them as harbingers of impending crisis.

The IMF has also been criticized for the way it handled the Asian crisis once it occurred. The main elements of the initial response were tight fiscal and monetary policies, backed by "bailout funds" mobilized by the IMF. Such policies were aimed at limiting the magnitude of currency depreciation, rebuilding foreign currency reserves, preventing an outright default on foreign obligations, and restoring economic confidence. The IMF also responded by enforcing capital adequacy standards that led to bank closures in certain countries. For example, 58 out of 91 finance companies in Thailand were suspended, and 56 were eventually liquidated. In Indonesia, 16 commercial banks were physically closed, while in Korea, 14 out of 30 merchant banks were suspended. These steps were taken to limit losses that had been accumulated by these institutions and to restore confidence in the banking system. Furthermore, additional initiatives were introduced to restructure and reform the banking sector, to curb monopolies and promote free competitive market structures, to restore price stability, and to avoid recession.

Those who defend the IMF claim that the Asian economies have recovered rather rapidly. Against the complaint that the IMF did not anticipate the crisis, they argue that economists have difficulty predicting turning points in any economy. They also note that the governments of some of the countries involved appear to have withheld information from the IMF. The IMF was unaware, for example, of costly attempts to defend exchange rates and by the time the IMF was asked for assistance, these economies had reached a critical stage of vulnerability. The degree of currency risk hedging was also hidden from the IMF. Strategies to offset risk, including volatile derivatives and other instruments, are very difficult to monitor because they are off-balance-sheet transactions. Prior to the crisis, there was little hedging of currency risk by Asian financial institutions. The collapse of unhedged institutions during the crisis contributed to financial contagion. Finally, the IMF's recommendation of tight fiscal policy was based on fears that economies were "overheated". When the IMF realized that such fears were unwarranted, it shifted in favor of looser fiscal policies.

Some critics claim that the IMF prematurely rushed to extend funds to crisis countries and that such actions worsened the situation by sending signals that the IMF would always come to the rescue. They argue further that the IMF released funds without obtaining guarantees that countries would comply with suggested reforms, and that its enforcement of such reform agreements was weak. Others complain that rather than maintaining its traditional role of lending, the IMF became involved in mandating structural reforms for borrowing countries.[6] Some in the international community have questioned the IMF's monetary policy recommendations. Several observers have argued that the IMF's recommendations worsened the crisis. Others have highlighted the time-inconsistency of IMF recommendations. What may have been correct to contain and resolve the immediate crisis may not be appropriate for the long-run stability and growth of the Asian economies. In this camp, the belief is widespread that the

IMF must redefine its purpose and policies in order to remain effective in the contemporary global economy.[7]

All these criticisms of the IMF approach to the Asian crisis have stimulated the search for a new financial architecture.[8] Currently, there is limited consensus among economists on what the new global architecture should be. Some, like Schwartz (1999), believe the IMF has no role in the new global architecture. Schwartz reviews the record of the IMF as a manager of currency crises and concludes that it has had limited success. Kroszner (1999) recommends that the IMF's role needs to be reduced. Fewer bailouts will reduce moral hazard and enhance market discipline. Others, including Litan (1999, p. 425), acknowledge that both currency fluctuations and rapid reversals in capital movements demand an IMF that can act as a "crisis and prevention manager". Eichengreen (1999) suggests that the IMF should carefully monitor short-term borrowing by domestic banks and discourage excessive borrowing. Fischer (1999) argues that the stability of the global monetary system requires a lender of last resort and offers recommendations for improving the functioning of such a lender.

The IMF itself has proposed a list of four initiatives to strengthen the architecture of the global financial system. First, the IMF plans to encourage member country policies to be more transparent, to introduce new policy guidelines and to incorporate vulnerability assessment into bilateral and multilateral surveillance. Second, the IMF plans to undertake concerted action to strengthen the global financial system by developing and disseminating international standards to guide financial practices and by supporting structural reforms in financial sectors. Third, the IMF proposes to limit moral hazard and reinforce market discipline by involving the private sector more actively in crisis prevention. Finally, the IMF remains committed to contributing to the study of exchange rate regimes and of the sequencing of capital account liberalization and to adapting the Fund's financial facilities, resources and organization to the evolving global monetary system.[9]

The debate on global financial architecture has not produced agreement on its key features. Regardless of new roles for the IMF or the World Bank, leadership by the U.S., the EU and Japan will continue to be critical in ensuring global monetary stability. Strengthening the financial architecture is a key component in our proposal to reduce instabilities in the global monetary system. An improved architecture and better response adjustment mechanisms are of particular importance in dealing with financial crises in countries which are not members of trading blocs or currency unions.

Improvements in global architecture and multilateral response mechanisms will not be enough on their own, however. They must be supplemented by regional cooperation and by policy coordination among the "big three," the U.S., the EU and Japan. We turn to these issues below.

5. The evolution of regional monetary arrangements

The primary example of regional monetary cooperation is found in Europe. There, international finance specialists have wrestled with the challenge of the "impossible trinity," according to which no economy can simultaneously experience a fixed exchange rate, free capital mobility and a monetary policy dedicated to domestic economic goals. The choices available to policy makers are: (i) fixed exchange rates, free capital mobility and the loss of monetary policy autonomy; (ii) fixed exchange rates, controlled capital mobility and an independent monetary policy; or (iii) flexible exchange rates, free capital mobility and an independent monetary policy.

Each of these three choices has both advantages and disadvantages. The first option was in place for a long period in the European Union, as it sought to stabilize exchange rates among members. Padoa-Schioppa (1994) chronicles the road to monetary union in Europe, with its numerous initiatives, successes and temporary setbacks. These efforts were at times questioned and the experiment had its share of crises, but the quest culminated in establishment of EMU.

An important milestone in Europe's pursuit of monetary stability came with the launch of the EMS in 1979. Its three basic purposes were (i) to provide a zone of monetary stability, (ii) to support closer monetary cooperation, and (iii) to foster economic and monetary integration in Europe. A key feature was the Exchange Rate Mechanism (ERM), which required members to anchor their currencies to the Deutsche mark, the dominant currency within the region. Thus, the monetary policy of the Bundesbank effectively set the pace of inflation in the EU. While the other countries in the ERM focused their monetary policies on exchange rate targeting, the Bundesbank pursued price stability. The EMS limited exchange-rate fluctuations and helped accelerate the process of monetary integration.

In the early 1990s, the EU took three important steps in light of decisions adopted at the Maastricht summit. First, application of convergence criteria for inflation, interest rates, budget deficits, and budget levels and elimination of currency devaluations. Second, formation of the European Monetary Institute, as predecessor of the European Central Bank. Third, selection of the first group of 12 members of the EMU and adoption of irrevocably fixed exchange rates of their currencies against the euro.[10]

How successful were European efforts to reduce currency instability, first via the EMS and recently via the EMU? While the EMS functioned very well between 1979 and 1992, not least by facilitating reduction and convergence of national inflation rates, it came under significant

Table 3
Volatilities of spot exchange rates expressed in German mark

Year	British pound (%)	French franc (%)	Italian lira (%)
1990	17.4	1.6	2.4
1991	25.5	1.6	2.1
1992	26.0	2.4	10.7
1993	21.0	4.4	8.7
1994	14.1	1.8	5.9
1995	19.1	5.0	12.9
1996	11.0	2.2	6.1
1997	15.1	1.6	4.2
1998	13.8	1.4	1.7
1999	7.1	0.0	0.0
2000	10.1	0.0	0.0
Mean	16.4	2.0	5.0

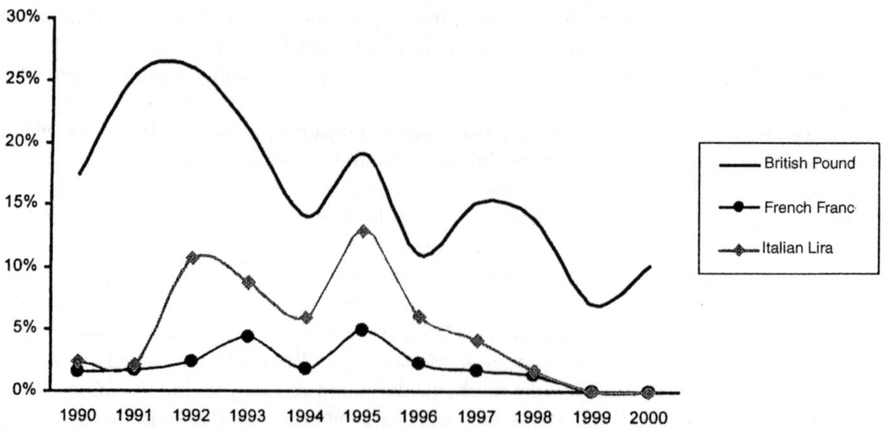

Fig. 3. Volatilities of spot exchange rates expressed in German marks.

pressure as speculators attacked exchange rates in 1992 and again in 1993.[11] Table 3 and Fig. 3 illustrate volatilities among a sample of EU member currencies in terms of German marks.

The first speculative attack was generated by uncertainties created by the failure of the first referendum on the Maastricht Treaty in Denmark on June 2, 1992 and led ultimately to devaluation of the British pound, Italian lira, Spanish peseta, and Portuguese escudo. The crisis of 1993 resulted from the severe recession in most of the EU member states and the unexpectedly high costs of German unification.

The EU's experience suggests that the road towards monetary union may initially require the reduction of currency fluctuations through a mechanism like the EMS. During the process, national monetary and fiscal policies need to be coordinated to allow important fundamentals to converge in member countries. In Europe, the Maastricht Treaty set the tone by providing a well-formulated scheme for convergence of fundamental economic variables such as interest rates, inflation, national budget deficits and government indebtedness. These were the preconditions for implementation of monetary union.

6. NAFTA: the road ahead

It is argued in this section that NAFTA could benefit from the EMU's experiences. While NAFTA started as a free trade agreement among the U.S., Canada and Mexico, a number of proposals have been made to widen and deepen the arrangement. Widening would involve the admission of additional members from Central and South America, while deepening includes monetary integration and policy coordination of various forms.

Widening of NAFTA is currently under discussion in negotiations on the Free Trade Area of the Americas (FTAA). Deepening in terms of closer monetary cooperation has received some academic attention in Canada and other countries, but is of little interest to policy makers in

Washington. However, implementation of the EMU may yet stimulate interest in Washington as the role of the dollar as a world currency comes to be challenged by the euro. The extensive use of the dollar in international transactions offers benefits to the U.S. economy in terms of seigniorage gains and the flexibility to finance trade deficits. Grubel (2000) argues that the establishment of the euro will threaten these benefits. Expanding the dollar area throughout the Western Hemisphere may help the U.S. defend the preeminence of its currency.

The literature offers three possible alternatives for regional monetary cooperation. These are dollarization, currency boards, and monetary union. Under full dollarization, the dollar becomes the legal tender in the particular country. The costs and benefits of dollarization to small countries are reviewed by Antinolfli and Keister (2001), Velde and Veracierto (1999) and others. For its part, the U.S. would come under pressure to share seigniorage and monetary policy decision-making and to provide lender-of-last resort services. Eichengreen (2000) discusses dollarization and emphasizes that it requires reforms in both the labor market and the fiscal policies of the dollarized country. Labor markets must be flexible to accommodate asymmetric shocks and the government sector must adhere to a long-term, permanent and credible budget constraint. Alexander and von Furstenberg (2000) claim that a weakness of dollarization is that when a superior alternative emerges that yields comparable stability benefits at lower costs, countries will have strong incentives to opt out of dollarization. In particular, von Furstenberg (2000) argues that dollarization is a second-best approach to monetary union.

According to Berg and Borensztein (2000), a currency board is essentially full dollarization with an exit option. The currency board can be removed when the local currency gains enough credibility in international markets. A currency board is essentially a monetary institution that fixes a country's exchange rate. According to Wagner (2000), it is characterized by (i) an exchange rate that is fixed not just by policy, but by law, (ii) a reserve requirement ensuring that each dollar's worth of domestic currency is backed by a dollar's worth of foreign reserves, and (iii) a self-correcting balance of payments mechanism in which a payments deficit automatically contracts the money supply and spending.

Unlike the preceding options which can be undertaken unilaterally, monetary union requires agreement between two or more countries to adopt a common currency. Alexander and von Furstenberg (2000) argue that one of the differences between dollarization and monetary union is that in dollarization, reforms of the economic system of the dollarized country may be initiated during or after the adoption of the dollar. In the monetary union, on the other hand, countries are forced to implement reforms in order to meet entrance requirements into monetary union, as in the aforementioned Maastricht criteria.

We do not know today how NAFTA will evolve and, in particular, how it will resolve currency fluctuations as a potential obstacle to regional trade integration in the Americas. McKinnon (2000), Arndt (2000), Courchene and Harris (2000) and Grubel (2000) offer numerous useful suggestions and potential scenarios. The whole question of instability and the optimal exchange rate system comes down to whether benefits from financial stability exceed the costs associated with losing policy sovereignty. The nations of NAFTA will eventually face the same question.

The Western Hemisphere is today subject to considerable exchange-rate instability. As the case of Argentina shows, financial and exchange-rate crises can undermine political stability. In the long run, the need for political stability may induce the U.S. and its hemispheric neighbors to undertake greater policy coordination. Monetary integration and financial stability in the region could significantly contribute towards global monetary stability.

7. The three major currency blocs

We have discussed two of the three building blocks toward a more stable global monetary and financial system. The first involved improvements in the international financial architecture designed to help countries and regions around the globe to avoid and cope with financial crises. The second proposes monetary cooperation and eventual monetary union among some or all of the nations of the Western Hemisphere in order to stabilize financial markets and facilitate growth and development in that region. The model here is Europe and EMU. That leaves the third and last block, which is to ensure stability in the relationship among the world's three major currencies—the dollar, the euro and the yen. While the basic regime among the three is likely to be a floating rate system, we argue in this section that coordination of economic policies among the U.S., EU and Japan is the necessary third component of our proposed scheme to ensure global monetary stability.

The role of the U.S. dollar as the world's central currency remains much as it was before the collapse of the Bretton Woods agreement. The U.S. currency functions as the invoice currency for world commodity trade, as the dominant vehicle currency in the world's spot and forward foreign exchange markets, and as the official exchange reserve asset of choice. The arrival of the euro is likely to change all that.

Pollard (2001) considers the various factors which will affect the role of the euro *vis-à-vis* the dollar as world currencies. One is the size of the market spanned by the EMU. The EU countries constitute an economic mass slightly larger than that of the U.S., and European exports to the rest of the world will be similar in magnitude to American exports. Countries in Europe's periphery, including many eastern European countries, will choose the euro because they are so open to EU trade. The euro should also play an important role in wealth portfolios around the globe, although there is disagreement among experts about the share of portfolios that will be allocated to euro-denominated assets, the speed with which that conversion will take place, and the extent to which it will come at the expense of the dollar.

There is little doubt, however, that the euro will play an important role in the evolving global monetary system. Hence, the stability of its relationship *vis-à-vis* the other major currencies will be of concern to more than just the inhabitants of the three economies. One way to promote stability in this relationship is through coordination of monetary, fiscal and economic policies among the U.S./expanded NAFTA, the EU and Japan to achieve Maastricht-type convergence of fundamentals. This is the third component of our scheme to achieve global monetary stability. Bofinger (2000) presents a detailed framework for stabilizing exchange rate relationships among global currencies.

Our proposed system thus consists of an improved international financial architecture, regional monetary cooperation in Europe and the Western Hemisphere (and wherever else it is possible and constructive) and coordination of macro policies among the dollar-, euro-, and yen-blocs.

8. The alternatives: controlling capital mobility or flexibility of exchange rates

Two key assumptions at the basis of our model are that international capital mobility will remain high and that countries will be willing to sacrifice policy sovereignty to varying degrees in order to achieve exchange-rate stability. That is why policy coordination plays such a central role in our system.

But suppose that we underestimate the demand for policy autonomy, so that policy coordination at regional and "big-three" levels will be difficult to achieve. Suppose, to take the worst-case scenario, that EMU fails as predicted by Feldstein (2000). Then there are two alternatives: fixed rates, inward-looking macro policies and capital controls or inward-looking macro policies, mobile capital and floating rates.

8.1. The Tobin tax

Tobin (1974) has argued that global capital mobility is less important than either the independence of national monetary policy or currency stability. However, there is by now a considerable body of experience which suggests that, outside of authoritarian political systems, the openness of capital accounts is inevitable because of an unwillingness by electorates in most countries to accept regulatory constraints on their search for optimal global investments.

Tobin (1974, 1978) proposed an international tax on foreign exchange transactions to improve the macroeconomic performance of economies subject to external financial shocks. This tax has two objectives. The first is to make exchange rates reflect long-run fundamentals relative to short-range expectations and risks. The second is to preserve and promote autonomy of national macroeconomic and monetary policies.

There are three justifications for a Tobin tax. The first claims that such a tax could reduce exchange rate volatility under certain conditions. The second justification is offered by Kaul and Langmore (1996), who emphasize revenue potential. Proceeds from such a Tobin tax could be shared between national governments and multilateral institutions in a way that renders the tax attractive to all. The third, and most important justification for our purposes, is that a Tobin tax enhances the independence of monetary and fiscal policy.

Tobin's (1978) original rationale for a foreign exchange transactions tax was to enhance policy autonomy in a world of high capital mobility. Tobin argued that currency fluctuations often have very significant economic and political costs, contrary to the views of the early proponents of floating rates. Although it is theoretically possible for the government of a financially open country to pursue autonomous monetary and fiscal policies, assuming it is prepared to accept exchange rate fluctuations, in practice such fluctuations often disrupt the allocation of resources and disproportionately burden producers and consumers of traded goods. Governments are thus reluctant to exercise their macroeconomic independence. A Tobin tax, by breaking the interest rate parity condition, will allow authorities to pursue policies which differ from those prevailing abroad, without exposing them to large exchange rate movements.

There are three reservations about implementing a Tobin tax. The first is political feasibility. It is not clear that a government and its numerous constituencies can agree on such a tax. Financial interests have considerable political influence and will lobby in opposition.

Financial interests will also emphasize the economic inefficiency of such a tax. Determining the international distribution of tax receipts is also not straightforward.

The second obstacle to effective implementation is capital migration. It can be argued that the geographical coverage of the tax must be complete. If the Cayman Islands, for example, fail to impose it, then the world's foreign exchange business will move there, and both the volatility of exchange rates and the autonomy of national macroeconomic policies will be affected.

A third obstacle is asset substitution. A tax limited to spot transactions would encourage the substitution of short-dated forwards and futures. Kenen (1996) therefore recommends applying the tax to spots, forwards and futures alike. Peter Garber (1996) suggests that the tendency to substitute tax-exempt for taxable instruments could eliminate all the effects of the tax. To be effective, the foreign exchange transactions tax will have to be generalized to other financial instruments.[12]

Several countries have applied taxes and restrictions on capital inflows and outflows that serve some of the functions of a Tobin tax. From the standpoint of currency stability, autonomy of macroeconomic policy and defensibility of the exchange rate regime, there is little evidence that such controls have discernible effects. For example, the Korean government used such measures in an attempt to limit the movement of the won in order to insulate Korean exporters from volatile exchange rates and to prevent the build-up of an excessively heavy external debt burden. Chilean policy-makers implemented limits on capital inflows to insulate the economy from destabilizing speculative attacks. Neither of these actions yielded significant results.

In summary, at this stage, the feasibility and effectiveness of a foreign exchange transactions tax remain under debate. Neely (1999) gives a comprehensive survey on capital controls and discusses important questions that remain unanswered, including questions about the operation of foreign exchange markets, the scope for asset substitution, and the composition of foreign exchange transactions.[13] For these reasons, we view this option as inferior.

8.2. Floating rates

The option of freely fluctuating exchange rates in a world of free capital mobility has been defended by proponents of free markets originating in the seminal paper of Friedman (1953) and surveyed in Gylfason (2000) and LeBaron and McCulloch (2000). The efficiency and optimality properties of free markets, and by implication of freely fluctuating exchange rates, are not the issue of debate. Also, the advantage of freely fluctuating exchange rates to allow monetary policy to pursue domestic goals is well-recognized. Both the efficiency considerations and the independence of monetary policy are significant benefits.

Opponents of floating typically point to transactions costs and uncertainty considerations. They fear the negative effects of exchange-rate volatility and sustained misalignments on economic growth. Calvo and Reinhart (2000) have underscored this argument against freely fluctuating exchange rates. They argue that countries often experience "fear of floating" because they are not prepared to accept the extent of exchange rate volatility generated by such a regime. Most policymakers are concerned with the consequences of freely fluctuating exchange rates on domestic inflation, on the allocation of resources, volume of exports and imports and on financial portfolios. Depending on the degree of such "fear of floating", domestic monetary policy loses its independence by responding to movements of the exchange rate.[14]

Some critics of floating have raised the issue of national versus global welfare. It is clear that maximizing national welfare in a world of free capital mobility may be pursued with an independent monetary policy and flexible exchange rates. This does not automatically suggest, however, that maximizing the joint welfare of two countries with two currencies is achieved when each country independently maximizes its own welfare by following its own independent monetary policy under free capital mobility and floating rates.

9. Conclusions: toward a more stable global monetary system

This paper represents an attempt to improve the performance of global monetary arrangements. The objective is to reduce financial instability and enhance the system's ability to prevent exchange-rate crises altogether or to deal with them more effectively when they occur. It begins by examining recent exchange-rate crises in Asia and monetary cooperation in the EMU. Both experiences provide important insights and lessons for improving the global system.

Any attempt to improve the system's performance must take account of the constraints imposed by the "impossible trinity," according to which economies can at most achieve two of the following three objectives: stable exchange rates, capital mobility and autonomous macro policies.

The approach proposed here gives priority to the first two objectives and develops ways of accommodating the constraint on policy autonomy. The proposal has three building blocks, each designed to make domestic policies conform with the systemic constraint.

The first block focuses on the international financial infrastructure, seeking to improve the multilateral guidelines for fiscal, monetary, and financial policies and tightening standards of performance as well as surveillance. This block is important because it helps set the framework conditions. As the world's financial and capital markets become more integrated, the need for common standards asserts itself.

Although improvements in systemic architecture play a crucial role, they cannot solve all problems. Regional cooperation designed to enhance monetary stability among groups of trading partners can make an important contribution. Our model here is the EMU: it provides a tested example for greater monetary and financial cooperation in the Western Hemisphere.

Improvements in global architecture and greater regional cooperation will go a long way toward reducing uncertainty and enhancing financial stability. That leaves relations among the three major economies—the EU, Japan (with possible linkages to other Asian economies) and the monetary bloc in the Western Hemisphere. In order to ensure stability of exchange rates within the group—among the euro, yen, and dollar—we propose intra-group policy coordination in a process that would mimic the Maastricht Treaty's convergence criteria.

Notes

1. Eichengreen (1999), Alexander and von Furstenberg (2000), and Fischer (2001) describe the current global monetary system.

2. Kaminsky and Reinhart (1999) review 71 currency crises in 20 countries during the period 1970–1995.
3. Sweeney (1997, 2000) validates Volcker's claims by describing the foreign currency markets, currency speculation and the role of Central Banks in foreign currency interventions.
4. Kaufman (2000a, 2000b) reviews currency and banking crises and Mishkin (1999) presents further dimensions of global financial instability beyond currency fluctuations and capital inflows followed by sudden outflows. Williamson (2000) and Chang and Velasco (2000) offer detailed analyses of exchange rate policies for emerging markets.
5. For detailed reviews of the Asian crisis, see Aghevli (1999), Corsetti, Pesenti, and Roubini (1999), Delano (1999), Elizondo (1999), Goldstein (1999) and Villanueva (1999).
6. See Guitian (1999), Meltzer (1999), Kashyap (1999), Litan (1999) and Schwartz (1999) for representative discussions of the role of the IMF in global crises.
7. Stiglitz (1999) offers guidelines for such a reform.
8. Key references to this topic are Calomiris (1998), Meltzer (1998), Rogoff (1999), Fischer (1999), Kroszner (1999), Eichengreen (1999), Schwartz (1999) and Krueger (2000), among others.
9. A detailed description of these initiatives is available at the IMF's web site (www.imf.org).
10. Eichengreen (1993) and Kondonassis and Malliaris (1994, 1996, 1998)) review the Maastricht Treaty and Eichengreen (1997) evaluates the overall experiment of the European Monetary Union. A post-Maastricht perspective on European monetary integration is given by Welfens (1996).
11. Buiter, Corsetti and Pesenti (2001) provide a comprehensive assessment of the 1992–1993 ERM crisis.
12. Eichengreen (1996) offers further evaluations of the Tobin tax.
13. Quirk (1999), Hochreiter (2000), Gylfason (2000) and Wagner (2000) give a comprehensive analysis of exchange rate regimes and capital mobility.
14. For further references evaluating fixed versus floating exchange rates, see Tornell and Velasco (2000) and Leduc (2001).

Acknowledgments

The paper has benefited significantly from comments and remarks by numerous conference participants. I am thankful to Marc Hayford for several corrections and to Alex Kondonassis and Chris Paraskevopoulos for productive collaborations on similar topics. George Kaufman and Sven Arndt provided insightful comments on an earlier version. I am grateful to both for challenging my ideas and the way they were expressed. Finally, I am also thankful to Mary Malliaris and Carolyn Tang for extensive editorial assistance and to Ben-Dor Hagit, Gozde Yazar and Fotis Giannakoulis for research assistance.

References

Aghevli, B. B. (1999). Asian crisis: Causes and remedies. In W. C. Hunter, G. G. Kaufman, & T. H. Krueger (Eds.), *The Asian financial crisis: Origins, implications and solutions* (pp. 157–166). Boston: Kluwer Academic Publishers.

Alexander, V., & von Furstenberg, G. M. (2000). Monetary unions—a superior alternative to full dollarization in the long run. *North American Journal of Economics and Finance, 11*, 205–225.

Antinolfli, G., & Keister, T. (2001). Dollarization as a monetary arrangement for emerging market economies. *Review of the Federal Reserve Bank of St. Louis, 83*, 29–39.

Arndt, S. W. (2000). Mini symposium: A common currency for Canada and the US? *North American Journal of Economics and Finance, 11*, 1.

Bacchetta, P., & Van Wincoop, E. (2000). Does exchange rate stability increase trade and welfare? *The American Economic Review, 90*, 1093–1109.

Berg, A., & Borensztein, E. (2000). The pros and cons of full dollarization. IMF Working Paper.

Bofinger, P. A. (2000). A framework for stabilizing the Euro/Yen/Dollar triplet. *North American Journal of Economics and Finance, 11*, 137–151.

Bordo, M., & Eichengreen, B. (1993). A retrospective on the Bretton Woods system. In M. Bordo & B. Eichengreen (Eds.), *A collection of essays reevaluating the Bretton Woods experience*. Chicago: University of Chicago Press.

Brock, W. A., & Malliaris, A. G. (1989). *Differential equations, stability and chaos in dynamic economics*. Amsterdam: Elsevier.

Buiter, W. H., Corsetti, G., & Pesenti, P. A. (2001). *Financial markets and European monetary cooperation: The lessons of the 1992–1993 Exchange Rate Mechanism crisis*. Cambridge: Cambridge University Press.

Burnside, C., Eichenbaum, M., & Rebelo, S. (1999). What caused the recent Asian currency crisis. In W. C. Hunter, G. G. Kaufman, & T. H. Krueger (Eds.), *The Asian financial crisis: Origins, implications, and solutions* (pp. 17–26). Boston: Kluwer Academic Publishers.

Calomiris, C. W. (1998). *Blueprints for a new global financial architecture*. Mimeo, Columbia Business School.

Calvo, G. A., & Reinhart, C. M. (2000). Fear of floating. Working Paper 7993, National Bureau of Economic Research.

Chang, R., & Velasco, A. (2000). Exchange rate policy for developing countries. *The American Economic Review: Papers and Proceedings, 90*, 71–75

Corsetti, G., Pesenti, P., & Roubini, N. (1999). What caused the Asian currency and financial crisis? *Japan and the World Economy, 11*, 305–373.

Courchene, T. J., & Harris, R. G. (2000). North American monetary union: Analytical principles and operational guidelines. *North American Journal of Economics and Finance, 11*, 3–16.

Delano, V. (1999). An analysis of financial crisis. In W. C. Hunter, G. G. Kaufman, & T. H. Krueger (Eds.), *The Asian financial crisis: Origins, implications and solutions* (pp. 485–489). Boston: Kluwer Academic Publishers.

Eichengreen, B. (1993). European monetary unification. *Journal of Economic Literature, 31*, 1321–1357.

Eichengreen, B. (1996). The Tobin tax: What have we learned? In Ul H. Mahbub, K. Inge, & I. Grunberg (Eds.), *The Tobin tax* (pp. 273–287). New York: Oxford University Press.

Eichengreen, B. (1997). *European monetary unification, theory, practice and analysis*. Cambridge: MIT Press.

Eichengreen, B. (1999). *Toward a new international financial architecture: A practical post-Asia agenda*. Washington, DC: Institute for International Economics.

Eichengreen, B. (2000). When to dollarize. Working Paper, UC Berkeley.

Elizondo, E. (1999). Lessons from the crisis. In W. C. Hunter, G. G. Kaufman, & T. H. Krueger (Eds.), *The Asian financial crisis: Origins, implications and solutions* (pp. 467–470). Boston: Kluwer Academic Publishers.

Feldstein, M. (2000). Europe can't handle the Euro. *Wall Street Journal*, February 8, 2000, A26.

Fischer, S. (1999). On the need for an international lender of last resort. *Journal of Economic Perspectives, 13*, 85–104.

Fischer, S. (2001). Is the bipolar view correct? *Journal of Economic Perspectives, 15*, 3–24.

Flood, R. P., & Rose, A. K. (1999). Understanding exchange rate volatility with the contrivance of macroeconomics. *Economic Journal, 109*, 660–672.

Friedman, M. (1953). The case for flexible exchange rates. In *Essays in positive economics*. Chicago: University of Chicago Press.

Garber, M. P. (1996). Issues of enforcement and evasion in a tax on foreign exchange transactions. In Ul H. Mahbub, K. Inge, & I. Grunberg (Eds.), *The Tobin tax* (pp. 129–142). New York: Oxford University Press.

Goldstein, M. (1999). Early warning indicators of financial crises. In W. C. Hunter, G. G. Kaufman, & T. H. Krueger (Eds.), *The Asian financial crisis: Origins, implications and solutions* (pp. 321–330). Boston: Kluwer Academic Publishers.

Grubel, H. G. (2000). The merit of a Canada–US monetary union. *North American Journal of Economics and Finance, 11*, 19–22.

Guitian, M. (1999). Lessons for the international financial system. In W. C. Hunter, G. G. Kaufman, & T. H. Krueger (Eds.), *The Asian financial crisis: Origins, implications, and solutions* (pp. 461–466). Boston: Kluwer Academic Publishers.

Gylfason, T. (2000). Fix or flex? Alternative exchange rate regimes in an era of global capital mobility. *North American Journal of Economics and Finance, 11*, 173–189.

Hausmann, R., Panizza, U., & Stein, E. (1999). Why do countries float the way they float? Working Paper 418, Inter-American Development Bank.

Hochreiter, E. (2000). Exchange rate regimes and capital mobility: Issues and some lessons from central and eastern European applicant countries. *North American Journal of Economics and Finance, 11*, 155–171.

IMF (May 1998). *World Economic Outlook*. Washington, DC: The Fund.

Kaminsky, G. L., & Reinhart, M. C. (1999). The twin crises: The causes of banking and balance of payments problems. *The American Economic Review, 89*, 423–500.

Kashyap, K. A. (1999). Comments on "What's wrong with the IMF" and "Containing the risks". In W. C. Hunter, G. G. Kaufman, & T. H. Krueger (Eds.), *The Asian financial crisis: Origins, implications and solutions* (pp. 291–302). Boston: Kluwer Academic Publishers.

Kaufman, G. G. (2000). Banking and currency crises and systemic risk: A taxonomy and review. *Financial Markets Institutions and Instruments, 9*, 69–131.

Kaufman, G. G. (2000b). Banking and currency crises and systemic risk: Lessons from recent events. *Economic Perspectives (Federal Reserve Bank of Chicago), 24*, 9–28.

Kaul, I., & Langmore, J. (1996). Potential uses of the revenue from a Tobin tax. In Ul H. Mahbub, K. Inge, & I. Grunberg (Eds.), *The Tobin tax* (pp. 255–271). New York: Oxford University Press.

Kenen B. P. (1996). The feasibility of taxing foreign exchange transactions. In Ul H. Mahbub, K. Inge, & I. Grunberg (Eds.), *The Tobin tax* (pp. 109–128). New York: Oxford University Press.

Kondonassis, A., & Malliaris, A. G. (1994). Towards monetary union of the European community: History and experiences of the EMS. *American Journal of Economics and Sociology, 53*, 291–301.

Kondonassis, A., & Malliaris A. G. (1996). European monetary integration: Lessons for other trading agreements. In C. Paraskevopoulos et al. (Eds.), *Economic integration in the Americas* (pp. 129–136). Cheltenham: Edward Elgar Publishing Limited.

Kondonassis, A., & Malliaris A. G. (1998). The European Monetary Union in transition. In C. Paraskevopoulos (Ed.), *European Union at the crossroads* (pp. 7–15). Cheltenham: Edward Elgar Publishing Limited.

Kroszner, S. R. (1999). Less is more in the new international financial architecture. In W. C. Hunter, G. G. Kaufman, & T. H. Krueger (Eds.), *The Asian financial crisis: Origins, implications and solutions* (pp. 447–457). Boston: Kluwer Academic Publishers.

Krueger, A. O. (2000). Conflicting demands on the International Monetary Fund. *The American Economic Review: Papers and Proceedings, 90*, 38–42.

Lachman, D. (1999). Asian currency crisis. In W. C. Hunter, G. G. Kaufman, & T. H. Krueger (Eds.), *The Asian financial crisis: Origins, implications and solutions* (pp. 135–138). Boston: Kluwer Academic Publishers.

LeBaron, B., & McCulloch, R. (2000). Floating, fixed, or super fixed? Dollarization joins the menu of exchange rate options. *The American Economic Review, 90*, 32–37.

Leduc, S. (2001). Who cares about volatility? A tale of two exchange-rate systems. *Federal Reserve Bank of Philadelphia Business Review*, (1st Quarter), 16–25.

Litan, E. R. (1999). Does the IMF have a future? What should it be? In W. C. Hunter, G. G. Kaufman, & T. H. Krueger (Eds.), *The Asian financial crisis: Origins, implications and solutions* (pp. 425–441). Boston: Kluwer Academic Publishers.

McKinnon, R. (2000). On the periphery of the international dollar standard: Canada, Latin America, and East Asia. *North American Journal of Economics and Finance*, *11*, 105–121.

Meltzer, A. (1998). Asian problems and the IMF. Testimony prepared for the Joint Economic Committee, U.S. Congress.

Meltzer, A. (1999). What's wrong with the IMF? What would be better? In W. C. Hunter, G. G. Kaufman, & T. H. Krueger (Eds.), *The Asian financial crisis: Origins, implications and solutions* (pp. 241–260). Boston: Kluwer Academic Publishers.

Mishkin, S. F. (1999). Global financial instability: Framework, events issues. *Journal of Economic Perspectives*, *13*, 3–20.

Moskow, H. M. (1999). The Asian financial crisis. In W. C. Hunter, G. G. Kaufman, & T. H. Krueger (Eds.), *The Asian financial crisis: Origins, implications and solutions* (pp. 11–14). Boston: Kluwer Academic Publishers.

Mundell, R. (2000). A reconsideration of the twentieth century. *The American Economic Review*, *90*, 327–340.

Neely, C. J. (1999). An introduction to capital controls. *Review of the Federal Reserve Bank of St. Louis*, *81*, 13–30.

Padoa-Schioppa, T. (1994). *The road to monetary union in Europe*. Oxford: Clarendon Press.

Pollard, S. P. (2001). The creation of the Euro and the role of the dollar in international markets. *Review of the Federal Reserve Bank of St. Louis*, *83*, 17–36.

Portes, R. (1999). An analysis of financial crisis: Lessons for the international financial system. In W. C. Hunter, G. G. Kaufman, & T. H. Krueger (Eds.), *The Asian financial crisis: Origins, implications and solutions* (pp. 471–478). Boston: Kluwer Academic Publishers.

Quirk, P. (1999). Performance of exchange rate systems in the face of capital mobility. In P. Gray & S. R. Scheherazade (Eds.), *The quest for exchange rate stability in the next millennium*. Stamford: JAI Press.

Radelet, S., & Sachs, J. (1998). The onset of the East Asian financial crisis. National Bureau of Economic Research Working Paper #6680.

Rogoff, K. (1999). International institutions for reducing global financial instability. *Journal of Economic Perspectives*, *13*, 21–42.

Schwartz, A. (1999). Assessing the IMF's crisis prevention and management record. In W. C. Hunter, G. G. Kaufman, & T. H. Krueger (Eds.), *The Asian financial crisis: Origins, implications and solutions* (pp. 453–457). Boston: Kluwer Academic Publishers.

Stiglitz, J. (1999). Reforming the global economic architecture: Lessons from recent crises. *The Journal of Finance*, *54*, 1508–1521.

Summers, L. (2000). International financial crises: Causes, prevention and cures. *The American Economic Review: Papers and Proceedings*, *90*, 1–16.

Sweeney, R. J. (1997). Do central banks lose on foreign exchange intervention? A review article. *Journal of Banking and Finance*, *21*, 1667–1684.

Sweeney, R. J. (2000). Does the Fed beat the foreign exchange market? *Journal of Banking and Finance*, *24*, 665–694.

Tobin, J. (1974). *The new economics one decade older. The Eliot Janeway lectures on historical economics in honor of Joseph Schumpeter*. Princeton, NJ: Princeton University Press.

Tobin, J. (1978). A proposal for international monetary reform. *Eastern Economic Journal*, *4*, 153–159.

Tornell, A., & Velasco, A. (2000). Fixed versus flexible exchange rates: Which provides more fiscal discipline? *Journal of Monetary Economics*, *2*, 399–436.

Velde, F., & Veracierto, M. (1999). Dollarization in Argentina. *Chicago Fed Letter*, *142*.

Villanueva, D. (1999). An analysis of financial crisis. In W. C. Hunter, G. G. Kaufman, & T. H. Krueger (Eds.), *The Asian financial crisis: Origins, implications and solutions* (pp. 485–489). Boston: Kluwer Academic Publishers.

Volcker, P. (1999). The quest for exchange rate stability: Realistic or quixotic? In P. Gray & S. R. Scheherazade (Eds.), *The quest for exchange rate stability in the next millennium*. Stamford: JAI Press.

von Furstenberg, G. M. (2000). US—dollarization in Latin America: A second best monetary union for overcoming regional currency risk. Working Paper, Fordham University.

Wagner, H. (2000). Which exchange rate regimes in an era of high capital mobility? *North American Journal of Economics and Finance*, *11*, 191–203.

Welfens, P. (1996). *European Monetary Union: Post-Maastricht perspectives on monetary and real integration in Europe*. New York: Springer.

Williamson, J. (2000). *Exchange rate regimes for emerging markets: Reviving the intermediate option*. Washington, DC: Institute for International Economics.